P9-CRQ-839

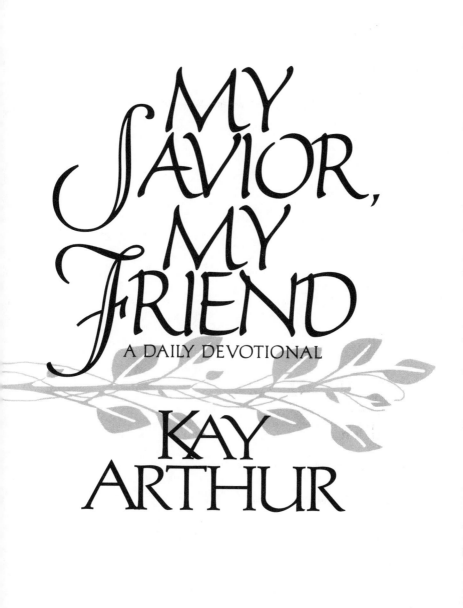

My Savior, My Friend

A DAILY DEVOTIONAL

KAY ARTHUR

HARVEST HOUSE PUBLISHERS
Eugene, Oregon 97402

Except where noted, all Scripture quotations in this book are taken from the New American Standard Bible, © 1960, 1962, 1963, 1968, 1971, 1972, 1973, 1975, 1977 by The Lockman Foundation. Used by permission.

References marked KJV are taken from the King James Version of the Bible.

MY SAVIOR, MY FRIEND

Published by Harvest House Publishers
Eugene, Oregon 97402

Library of Congress Cataloging-in-Publication Data

Arthur, Kay, 1933-
My Savior, my friend / Kay Arthur.
p. cm.
ISBN 1-56507-351-7
1. Bible. N.T. John Meditations. 2. Devotional calendars. I. Title.
BS2615.4.A78 1995 95-14442
242'.2—dc20 CIP

Printed in the United States of America.

95 96 97 98 99 00 01 02 — 10 9 8 7 6 5 4 3 2 1

January

Jesus, Sent to Explain the Father

1 "Tom is dead, Kay. He has hung himself."

The words pierced my heart. Somehow, I could not grasp the fact that the man I once thought I would spend all the days of my life with, the father of my two precious sons, was gone. The reality that I could not reconcile my marriage raced through my mind. I was filled with questions. I felt numb. I needed understanding.

I ran to the telephone to call my pastor. He wasn't home. Over the years I have thanked my God that my call went unanswered. There was One who was home, and as He has countless times since that day, He comforted my heart as He spoke to me from the Scriptures I was learning. I had known Jesus only a short time when my husband committed suicide, but I was saturating myself in the Word and getting to know my God. In my moment of need, what I had hidden in my heart was used by my God to give definition and understanding.

As I cried out in my pain and horror to God, He spoke to me in the silence of my heart. Oh, I did not hear an audible voice, but I did hear that still, small voice in the chambers of my heart that I have now come to recognize quickly over the years. He said three things to me and they were all from the Word I was hiding in my heart. Yet I don't think I even realized that at the time. He said, "Kay, in everything give thanks, for this is the will of God in Christ Jesus concerning you. All things work together for good to those who are called according to His purpose. I will not give you anything you cannot bear."

In my moment of darkest need as a baby Christian, I saw the way God used His Word to lead, to direct, to comfort, to speak, to give understanding about what to do. As the years have passed, I have continued to saturate myself in it. It is in His Word that I find all I need for life and godliness, and that I continue to discover my God—who He is, how He acts and reacts, what He desires of me and for me. It is in my time alone in the Word that I have developed an intimate, personal, vital relationship with the living God of the universe.

I am convinced beyond a shadow of any doubt that the most valuable pursuit we can embark upon is to know God.

Daniel 11:32 says that those who know their God will be strong and do exploits. I echo a hearty "Amen and amen" in the chambers of my innermost being each time I read the verse or hear it quoted. Knowing the Word of God and the God of the Word has radically changed me from the inside out, and has established my life on an immovable and sure foundation.

I'll share more over the next few days that will help you understand why I am so convinced. Just know today that God wants to establish you on the same foundation, and He longs to be known by you!

2 Before I met the Lord Jesus Christ, I pursued many things in my search for happiness. I longed for one thing: a happy marriage like the one I had seen in my parents' home. I longed for the comfort of knowing I was loved, regardless of whether I was pretty or ugly, rich or poor, happy or sad.

My dream seemed to be taking form and substance when I met Frank Thomas Goetz, Jr.—a man who looked great in a white dinner jacket, a man who shot golf in the low 70s, a man who was offered contracts to pitch baseball for the Pirates, the Yankees, the Phillies, and the Indians.

Tom was a man whose family was prominent in the social community, and who, of all things, loved me!

On our honeymoon I began to realize that dreams don't always come true—even though you have hoped for them, even though you have worked for them, and even though you have saved yourself for them. Tom sat me down and said, "Kay, you are now Mrs. Frank Thomas Goetz, Jr., and these are the things I don't like about you. I want them changed."

My horror knew no boundary. My pain no limit. I thought surely I would awaken from this nightmare and find Tom curled up by my side! But this was no dream. Tom went into depression, and we spent days on end in our suite while I watched other couples outside on the beach walking hand in hand, sitting on their beach blankets with picnics and talking for hours on end.

My dream was shattered. Try as I did to put all the pieces together, after six years and two sons, a night came when Tom, inflamed by the angry words of my tongue which had been set on fire by hell, backhanded me. My husband was a gentleman, and I knew I had pushed him to the brink, but I was so miserable I did not care.

By this time I had money, mink, modeling, and I was about to walk away from my husband, take my two young sons from their father, and fall into the snare of the enemy. I would continue my pursuit of happiness in the arms of man after man. Yet my longing would remain unfulfilled.

Over the next few years I pursued happiness in many forms, but reality slapped me in the face one day when a friend said, "Kay, why don't you stop telling God what you want and tell Him that Jesus Christ is all you need."

You can imagine that I thought him awfully rude to tell me what I should tell God. I also thought that talking about God at a party was most inappropriate!

Beloved, are you pursuing possessions in your search for happiness? Are you adding titles to your name? Are you moving into bigger homes in more prestigious neighborhoods? Are you finding happiness? I understand. Tomorrow I'll share how I came to the end of my pursuit.

3 I went home from that party so angry I could burst. I couldn't fathom the arrogance of a man who thought he knew what I needed! But I also could not silence the reverberation of his words, "Tell God that Jesus Christ is all you need."

Yet I remained confident that I knew what I needed: someone to love me unconditionally, and to love and father my boys who, by now, were really missing their dad whom they loved with all their hearts.

The next day I awoke early. I was sick and did not think I could go to work. The frightening part of my sickness was that I was convinced it had no cure. I did not feel ill. I felt sick of life, sick of being unhappy, sick of trying and never getting there, sick of not being loved, sick of always wanting more.

I called the research lab where I worked and said I could not come in. I knew my sons needed my attention, and I wanted them to have it. I went downstairs to bake a cake and to pull gear together to take the boys camping.

Mark, my younger son, was hanging around underfoot, hungry for a mom's love. All of a sudden I looked at Mark, cupped his little face in my hands, and through trembling lips with shaky voice said, "Mark, Mommy has to be alone for a moment. Can you let Mommy be alone?"

I hurtled up the steps, threw myself facedown on my bed, and cried, "God, I don't care what You do to me. I don't care if You paralyze me from the neck down. I don't care what You do to my two sons. I don't care if I never see another man . . . if You will just give me peace."

God was immediate in His response to my plea, which encompassed the three worst things I could think of! He gave me the Prince of Peace. Everything changed. I did not know what had happened. I did not know the term "salvation," but I knew I had peace!

Not long after my salvation, I told God I would go back to Tom. I knew if He had changed me He could change anyone, and I was praying for Tom!

Then the call came that Tom had committed suicide. I knew I had been the instigator. Many times he had told me that he could not forget the terrible things I said to him. His therapist had been unable to help Tom resolve the cutting words that had lodged in his soul and festered like a cancer.

It may sound callous to you, but I knew that the Kay Lee Goetz who had inflicted those wounds was dead. She had been buried at the cross of Calvary when she accepted the redeeming work of Jesus Christ on her behalf. She was a new creature in Christ Jesus. Old things had passed away. All things had become new.

I had to walk in the newness of life provided for me by His death and resurrection. I did not know what the future held, but I knew He held it. I knew too that the pursuit of Him was vital to my well-being and wholeness.

I had found happiness; and beyond that I had found something I'm not sure I could have conceived of—contentment! I came to understand that God was my all in all. That He loved me whether I was rich or poor, sick or well, happy or sad. He had demonstrated His love in the ultimate of ways—He had sent His Son, and He died for me!

You, Beloved, can pursue many things, but only one pursuit will end in contentment and joy—the pursuit of knowing your God by knowing His Word. It is this pursuit that I want to encourage you to embark on in these days as we look at the Gospel of John and see the "so great salvation" He has provided for you.

If you are well into this pursuit, you know what I am saying. I am glad for the opportunity to join you as we look at the Gospel of John together for these next months.

4 John is a book that will draw you into a deeper intimacy with the Lord Jesus Christ. While our first few days together may seem technical, please be patient as we

lay a foundation. Our study will become intensely practical as we move into next week, but this week I want to give you some skills that will prove invaluable to you as you spend time in the Gospel of John. These skills are totally transferable—you will be able to use them in all of your studies.

I know that our Father is going to do something very special in your relationship with Him as a result of studying John devotionally on a daily basis. And I believe He will do something very special in our relationship, as I have the privilege of ministering His Word to you in obedience to His call upon my life.

Now then, in the light of all this, let's begin. Whenever you study any book of the Bible, it is essential that you thoroughly familiarize yourself with three fundamental things: the author's *purpose* in writing, the *theme* of the book, and its *structure.* Understanding the purpose, theme, and structure of a book will help you interpret it correctly.

Therefore, as we begin our study of John, I want us to look at the apostle John's purpose, which is clearly stated in John 20:30,31: "Many other signs therefore Jesus also performed in the presence of the disciples, which are not written in this book; but these have been written that you may believe that Jesus is the Christ, the Son of God; and that believing you may have life in His name."

We gain a number of key insights from observing these two verses. First, we see that John is going to record for us a select number of signs that Jesus performed in the presence of His disciples. And while John is not going to record all the signs that Jesus did, still the account he gives will be comprehensive enough to demonstrate to his readers that Jesus is the Christ, the Son of God. And the reason John wants us to believe this is that, in believing, we might have life in His name. We cannot save ourselves, but He can save us if we will but believe.

To derive the maximum benefit from this devotional study, read through John as often as possible. As you read each chapter, train yourself to ask the "5 W's and an H": Who? What? When? Where? Why? How? Asking such questions will help you see exactly what the Word of God is saying. When you interrogate the text with the 5 W's and an H, you ask questions like these:

a. *What* is the chapter about?
b. *Who* are the main characters?
c. *When* does this event or teaching take place?
d. *Where* does this happen?
e. *Why* is this being done or said?
f. *How* did it happen?

The "when" of events or teachings is very important and should be marked in your Bible in an easily recognizable way. I mark these in the margin of my Bible beside the verse when the time phrase occurs with a clock like the one shown here: ⏰.

Well, that's enough information for today. Please don't be discouraged and wonder why in the world you bought this book when all you wanted was a nice devotional. You'll soon see that this devotional study—if you hang in there with me—will be a treasured book, for as you and I walk together through the Gospel of John, you'll become Jesus' friend, or you'll develop a more intimate friendship with Him and all the time you invest will be well worth that!

5 Remember, yesterday I told you that it was important when studying a book of the Bible to discover the structure of a book—the way the author lays out his material to achieve his purpose. Well, today we will look at the structure of the Gospel of John. It may be a tedious day for you, but remember that the practical is coming! We need to lay the foundation on which to build the practical truths of this Gospel.

If you are naturally curious like me, you have looked ahead to the chart called "JOHN AT A GLANCE." Don't be put off by this chart! Its content will become remarkably practical in the coming days.

On the top of the chart, you will see a section of vertical lines numbered 1 to 21 where chapter themes are recorded. Read through the themes, noting that the major subject of each chapter is condensed down into a title of a few words. These themes will give you an idea of the content of the Gospel of John.

The section of the chart called "Segment Divisions" groups together chapters that have a common theme. Notice that there are different ways to group the chapters.

Remember, the theme of John is the life that comes from believing in Jesus Christ. You will see that each segment of John is structured to achieve his purpose by recording a group of signs performed by Jesus in the presence of His disciples, so that we might believe that Jesus is the Christ, the Son of God, and, in believing, might have life in His name.

In John 1, John introduces Jesus as the Christ, the Son of God. In John 2 through 11, John records various signs which prove the fact that Jesus is God. In John 12, we come to the pivotal point of the Gospel as we see that finally Jesus' hour has come to prove that He is the Christ, the Son of God. I call this chapter the "Climax of Purpose." It is decision time! Up to this point in the Gospel, Jesus has said that His hour has not yet come; however, in John 12:23,27, Jesus says, "The hour has come for the Son of Man to be glorified. . . . Now My soul has become troubled; and what shall I say, 'Father, save Me from this hour'? But for this purpose I came to this hour." In John 12, our Lord is anointed for burial and proclaimed as King. The Son of Man will be glorified in His supreme obedience. Judgment has come; there will be a clash of light with darkness, of belief with unbelief!

In John 13 through 17, Jesus teaches His disciples about the life that belongs to those who believe. In John 18 through 20, we behold Jesus as He obtains that life for us through His death, burial, and resurrection. In John 21, as Jesus meets His disciples on the shore of the Sea of Galilee and talks with Peter, we see the true purpose of life—to love Jesus, feed and tend His sheep and lambs, and follow Him.

Thus, we can see a couple of ways to look at the Gospel of John:

Chapters 1–11: that you may believe that Jesus is the Christ, the Son of God

Chapter 12: His hour has come

Chapters 13–21: that you might have life

or

Chapter 1: introduces Jesus

Chapters 2–11: gives signs that prove Jesus is the Christ

Chapter 12: decision time

Chapters 13–17: life that belongs to those who believe Christ

Chapters 18-20: obtaining that life by death and resurrection

Chapter 21: purpose of life

I know this has been a heavy day, and I have prayed as I've written it asking God to use it to ignite a spark of excitement in you as you begin to see all the treasures laid up for us in this Gospel.

Beloved, keep reading through John as you are able to! Familiarity with the book will certainly impact your life.

6 The more time you spend pursuing the one thing that matters, the deeper your intimacy with the Father and His Son will be. We are building a foundation for the truths we will discover in the Gospel, and the foundation must be a sure one. Before we get into the first chapter, I want to share a few more insights on the book as a whole, as a help in understanding this Gospel.

As we have seen, there is one central theme in John: the life that comes as a result of believing that Jesus is the

Christ, the Son of God. Merrill Tenney calls John "The Gospel of Belief."

There are a number of key words in John. These are important words often used by the author in order to convey his message. Certain key words will show up throughout the book, while others will be concentrated in specific chapters or segments. When you mark a key word, you will also want to mark its synonyms (words that mean the same thing in the context) and any relative pronouns *(he, his, she, her, it, we, they, us, our, you, their, them)* in the same way you mark the key word.

Marking words for easy identification can be done by colors and symbols or a combination of the two. However, colors are easier to distinguish than symbols. If I use symbols, I keep them very simple. For example, I color the word repent yellow but put a red diagram over it. The symbol conveys the meaning of the word. Mark key words in a way that is easy for you to remember.

You should devise a color-coding system for marking key words throughout your Bible, so that when you look at the pages of your Bible, you see instantly where a key word is used.

It is easy to forget how you are marking particular words. Therefore, I recommend cutting a three-by-five card in half lengthwise and writing the key words on that. Color code the words and then use the card as a bookmark. You may want to make one bookmark for words you are marking throughout your Bible and a different one for any specific book of the Bible you are studying.

Now, let me give you some of the key words for the Gospel of John. Then as you read through the book, you can assign each word and its synonym a special color or symbol and mark the word as you see it repeated in the text. Some of the words are *believe, world, light, signs, life, glory* or *glorify, Son of God, Son of Man, Christ, witness.*

As you read John, you will see that it is laid out chronologically. You will also want to watch for time phrases such as "after these things" and "on the third day," etc. Don't forget to use the clock symbol or a symbol of your own to note time.

Also, watch the sequence of the feasts which are mentioned throughout the Gospel. The references to the various annual feasts show you that the signs Jesus did were spread out over a period of approximately three-and-a-half years.

John is also careful to give attention to geographical locations. Because places are important in a historical or biographical book of the Bible (and John is a historical book), you will also find it helpful to mark them in a distinguishable way. I simply underline every reference to location in green (grass and trees are green!) using my four-color ballpoint pen. In showing us the location of Jesus' signs, John allows us to see that Jesus did not perform His signs in a corner, but where others could see and testify of them. This gave Jews, religious leaders, Samaritans, and Gentiles the opportunity to believe He was who He said He was—the Son of God, the Son of Man.

As you study John, you will read detailed explanations of Jesus' encounters with various kinds of people. You will come to understand better how to approach people with the gospel. You also will learn much of the conflict of belief with unbelief and light with darkness, as people plot to ensnare Jesus and even to kill Him. You will watch as Jesus is told He has a demon and watch as He is accused of being a breaker of the Law and a Samaritan.

Although the way people respond to Him brings pain, there is a sweet side—His relationship to His disciples. Although some walk away because of Jesus' hard sayings—for He never diminishes or compromises His message for the purpose of luring them in—still others stay, for they know He has the words of life. As you draw near and behold the intimacy Jesus develops with His disciples, you will see how they became the people they were meant to be. And I pray that you, too, Beloved, will long to follow Him even more closely.

7 Among the Gospels, John holds a unique place. The Synoptic Gospels—Matthew, Mark, and Luke—focus on the humanity of Jesus Christ and were written basically within the same time period of A.D. 55 to 68. The Gospel of John, however, was not written until between A.D. 85 and 90. And as we have seen, John's writing was to prove without a shadow of doubt that Jesus was truly and fully God while being truly and fully man.

In Matthew, written between A.D. 58 and 68, we behold Jesus the King. In Mark, written between A.D. 55 and 65, we behold Jesus the servant. In Luke, written between A.D. 60 and 68, we see Jesus as the perfect man, with emphasis on the virgin birth of our Lord and, of course, on a detailed genealogy that takes us all the way back to Adam.

In John, we behold Jesus as God, one with the Father, the One whose name is I AM. And since God has no genealogy, John simply takes us back to the beginning when "the Word was with God, and the Word was God" (John 1:1). And in his majestic introduction, John sweeps us from the beginning to the fullness of time when "the Word became flesh, and dwelt among us, and we beheld His glory, glory as of the only begotten from the Father, full of grace and truth" (John 1:14). In John, we see Jesus, the divine Son, "the only begotten God, who is in the bosom of the Father" (John 1:18) and who comes to earth to explain the Father.

O Beloved, as we devotionally examine this divine Gospel, may the eyes of your heart eagerly drink in the beauty of the relationship of the Son to His Father. Keep your eyes on Jesus, the One who will explain to you the Father heart of God, who loved you so much "that He gave His only begotten Son" so that you would not perish but have everlasting life (John 3:16). In John 1, you will see Jesus proclaimed as "the Lamb of God" who will take away your sins (1:36). In John 2, you will hear Him say that He is the temple of God, destroyed by men, but raised by the Father (2:19). In John 3, Jesus shows us how He is like the serpent in the wilderness—raised up so that those who look to Him shall not die though bitten by the serpent (3:14). In John 4, He is the Christ who satisfies your deepest needs so that you never thirst again (4:14). In John 5, we see Him as the Son of God, doing nothing on His own initiative but always and only doing those things which please the Father (5:30).

As we move into the study of this Gospel, how I pray that you will know an insatiable longing to abide in Him and to have His words abide in you.

8 Lamb of God. Temple of God. Like the serpent in the wilderness, the Christ, the Son of God. What other proclamation does John make of Him so that we might believe that Jesus is the Christ, the Son of God?

In John 6, we see that Jesus is the True Bread that has come down from God out of heaven so that we might eat and live forever (6:35).

In John 7, Jesus cries that those who thirst should come to Him, for He is the Fountain of Living Water. He assures us that those who believe in Him shall have rivers of living water flowing from their innermost beings (7:37,38).

In John 8, having forgiven the woman taken in adultery, He turns to those walking in darkness and proclaims that those who follow Him shall not walk in the darkness but shall have the light of life, because He is the Light of Life (8:12). And so you cannot miss it, in this chapter Jesus explains that if you do not believe that He is God, the I AM, you shall die in your sins (8:24).

In John 9, Jesus is seen as the Son of Man who gives sight to the blind (9:39).

Then in John 10, we hear the voice of the Good Shepherd calling His sheep by name, and then laying down His life for them so they will never perish but will have eternal life (10:3,11).

In John 11, we hear Him promise Martha that He is the resurrection and the life, and that anyone who believes in Him shall live even if he dies (11:25).

In John 12, His hour has finally come. It is time for the Son of Man to be glorified, for the grain of wheat to fall into the ground and die so that it can bear much fruit (12:23,24).

In John 13, we find our Teacher and Lord girding Himself with a towel and washing His disciples' feet—leaving us an example of love's servanthood (13:14-17).

In John 14, we hear Jesus, the express image of the Father, telling us that through the gift of the Holy Spirit we shall do the works that He did because He is going to the Father (14:12).

In John 15, we see how life in Him is possible. We discover that He is the Vine and that we are the branches, and we come to understand that through abiding in Him, we bear much fruit (15:5).

In John 16, Jesus explains that He must go away so that He can send the Holy Spirit as our Helper who shall guide us into all truth (16:7,13).

In John 17, our hearts burn as we hear our High Priest interceding on our behalf with the Father, asking that we might be one even as They are one (17:22).

In John 18, Jesus stands before Pilate as the King of the Jews, and the crowd shouts, "Not this Man, but Barabbas" (18:37,40).

And in John 19, we look upon the Crucified One, the Son who cries, "*Tetélestai*—It is finished!" (19:30).

In John 20, death is conquered! The tomb is empty! Jesus becomes the Giver of Life (20:21-23).

In John 21, as Lord He says, "Tend My lambs. . . . Shepherd My sheep. . . . Follow Me!" (21:15,16,19).

Considering who Jesus is and who sent Him, wouldn't you be foolish not to believe and obey Him?

9 From the very beginning, John makes his purpose clear: to establish that Jesus is God. This fact is critical and essential. To miss His deity is to miss salvation! Thus, John takes us back to the beginning when there was no one but the Father, the Spirit, and the Logos, the Word: "In the

beginning was the Word, and the Word was with God, and the Word was God. He was in the beginning with God. All things came into being by Him, and apart from Him nothing came into being that has come into being. In Him was life, and the life was the light of men" (John 1:1-4).

John wants to make sure we know that life is found only in one place—in God's Son. At a later date, John will write another epistle in which he says, "He that hath the Son hath life; and he that hath not the Son of God hath not life" (1 John 5:12 KJV). It is that simple, Beloved. Apart from Jesus, you are dead in your trespasses and sins. You are among the living dead who will never pass from death to life unless they receive Jesus Christ for who He is—God and the only Savior of the world.

"But as many as received Him, to them He gave the right to become children of God, even to those who believe in His name" (John 1:12). And how would God make it possible for sinful men, women, and children to become children of God?

The Word, the Logos, would become flesh and dwell among us so that we could behold His glory, "glory as of the only begotten from the Father, full of grace and truth" (John 1:14). Jesus, "the only begotten God, who is in the bosom of the Father" (John 1:18), would explain the Father to us. Then through His death, burial, and resurrection, Jesus would become "the way, and the truth, and the life" (John 14:6) by whom we might come to the Father. And grace and truth would be realized through Jesus Christ (John 1:17).

O Beloved, have you ever really laid hold of the truth of all that Jesus is: the eternal Logos, the Creator of the world, the Son of God, the Light of life, God in the flesh? Has His grace—His pleasure, His delight, His favorable regard, His graciousness, His lovingkindness, His goodwill, His unmerited favor—ever overwhelmed you so as to save you from death and hell and give you life, eternal and abundant?

The Law given through Moses condemns; grace pardons. The Law exposes our sin; grace covers it. The Law diagnoses our illness; grace cures it. The Law shuts us up and plays the demanding schoolmaster; grace provides us with an indwelling Teacher, the Holy Spirit, and liberates us! "For the Law was given through Moses; grace and truth were realized through Jesus Christ" (John 1:17).

Read John 1:1-18 and think upon these things.

10 Do you have a hard time relating to God the Father? Maybe it is because your earthly father fell so drastically short of what a father should be! Maybe your father divorced your mother and left you fatherless. Maybe you could never please your father and always fell short of his expectations. Perhaps your father was too busy to spend time with you. He merely gave orders and dished out punishment when you didn't do what you were supposed to. Maybe you were molested, abused, or beaten by your father. You picture God as someone to fear because you wonder if He, too, will wrong you if you ever give Him an opportunity.

O Beloved, I understand how hard it may be to entrust yourself to another Father when your experience has been horrendous or void of anything meaningful. And yet, there is a bridge that will span all of that! The Lord Jesus Christ is the bridge which enables you to experience the fullness of all that a child should know and have in a father.

John tells us that it is Jesus who explains to us the Father (1:18). Jesus says, "He who beholds Me beholds the One who sent Me" (12:45). "If you had known Me, you would have known My Father also" (14:7). "He who has seen Me has seen the Father" (14:9). He could say this because He was one with the Father (10:30); the Father was abiding in Him (14:10).

Jesus came that you might have God for your Father—a perfect Father who loves you unconditionally, a Father who will never leave you nor forsake you. A Father who will always come to your aid, a Father who loves you so much that He gave up His only begotten Son that you might have life—and have it abundantly!

Just before Jesus died, He prayed to the Father on our behalf: "Holy Father, keep them in Thy name, the name which Thou hast given Me, that they may be one, even as We are" (John 17:11). Oneness with the Father—eternal oneness—enveloped in His love forever and ever. It is this relationship that God wants you to understand and embrace. He sent His Son to explain Himself to you! He longs to be your Father God.

O Beloved, why don't you read through the Gospel of John beginning with chapter 1 and reading a chapter each day. As you read, list all that you learn about Jesus Christ as He explains the Father. You should get a notebook and have it with your Bible and this book, so that as you spend time with the Father in the Gospel of John you can note what He is teaching you. I'll ask you to make some notes on things we do together. It will be exciting to look back later at all you learn! In the meantime, day by day, as you weave each truth into a blanket of security, you can snuggle warm and secure in its truth. It will set you free from misconceptions of the fatherhood of God, which would keep you from trusting Him.

11 Wouldn't it be wonderful to know and understand why God created you? Don't you long to realize His purpose for your life and to live within the context of that purpose? John the Baptist knew and lived accordingly. "There came a man, sent from God, whose name was John. He came for a witness, that he might bear witness of the light, that all might believe through him. He was not the light, but came that he might bear witness of the light" (John 1:6-8).

Witness is a key word in the Gospel of John. The noun form is used 14 times in the book, the verb form 33 times. How well it fits with John's purpose! The Greek word[1] for *witness* is *martus* or *martur:* "one who can or does affirm what he knows, has seen, or heard." From this word we get our English word *martyr:* "one who bears witness by his death." How well this word describes John the Baptist, who was beheaded by Herod because he stood without compromise for righteousness.

Imagine what it was like when John the Baptist appeared in the wilderness, breaking God's 400 years of silence with the words, "Behold, the Lamb of God who takes away the sin of the world! This is He on behalf of whom I said, 'After me comes a Man who has a higher rank than I, for He existed before me' " (John 1:29,30).

Finally, the fullness of time had come, bringing the long-awaited Messiah. Once John the Baptist bore witness, others, upon seeing Jesus, knew that John's witness was true. Andrew introduced his brother Simon Peter to Jesus saying, " 'We have found the Messiah' (which translated means Christ)" (John 1:41). And when Philip met Jesus, he found Nathanael and said to him, "We have found Him of whom Moses in the Law and also the Prophets wrote, Jesus of Nazareth, the son of Joseph" (John 1:45). When Nathanael met Jesus, he said, "Rabbi, You are the Son of God; You are the King of Israel" (John 1:49). What was happening? As each one met and recognized Jesus, they bore witness to others of Christ!

O Beloved, I can tell you one sure purpose for your life, and that is to bear witness of what you know about your Lord and your God. Are you affirming to others what you have seen and known about Jesus Christ? That's a witness! Don't be afraid of it—just tell others what you know. God will do the rest!

12 Is God concerned about the little things in your life that seemingly have nothing to do with the spiritual realm? Yes, He is! I pray for parking places! When I can't find something, I keep asking, "Father, show me where it is." Whether I find the item or not doesn't affect a single soul's salvation, nor does it affect the course of the church. Yet, I constantly talk to my Father about the everyday things of life.

Jesus, Sent to Explain the Father

Some people might say, "God is too busy running the universe to be troubled with parking places and lost articles!" But is He? Let's look together at John 2 and see what we can find in that chapter that might give us some insight.

Here we have an account of the first sign ever performed by our Lord. The very recording of this event gives it great significance. On the surface, it does not seem to be an earthshaking miracle, especially if you compare it to miracles which result in the lame walking, the blind seeing, and the dead rising. In John 2, Jesus turns water into wine. Now granted, it was an enormous amount of wine (120 to 180 gallons), and it was the best wine they had ever tasted—far better than the host had served!

This sign clearly demonstrated Jesus' power over the elements. Yet there is another significant reason for this miracle. Jesus turned water into wine to save a family embarrassment and shame. In those days, weddings were very important events. A host was obligated to have ample wine. After all, hadn't he drunk amply at the weddings of his friends? To run out of wine would not only embarrass him greatly, but would put him in their debt. Jesus changed water into wine because He cared about the plight of His host.

Jesus cares! He cares about everything that has to do with you! And because He cares, you know that your Father God cares. Remember, Jesus is explaining the Father to you. That is why He tells us in 1 Peter 5:7 to cast "all your anxiety upon Him, because He cares for you."

Jesus didn't turn water into wine to astound a crowd or simply to prove His power over the elements. He had just told His mother, "My hour has not yet come" (John 2:4), so we know that He did not perform the miracle to demonstrate His deity. No, Jesus performed this sign because of a need, to save the host from great embarrassment.

Tuck that thought into your heart today. Treasure it. Your Father God cares about your daily everythings that concern you. Run to Him with everything. He loves it!

13 Twice in His ministry Jesus cleansed the Temple, throwing out the moneychangers. His first encounter with these men was at the beginning of His public ministry. The second was at the end. In fact, the final cleansing was the crushing blow that brought Him to the house of Annas, then to Caiaphas, both of whom profited from the sales in the Temple area. Zeal for His Father's house consumed our Lord. They were making His "Father's house a house of merchandise" (John 2:16).

I wonder what would happen if Jesus visited many of the ministries around the world today. What would He find? What would He do? He always sees beyond the apparent, beyond what we say to the very heart attitude that motivates us. Christian leaders need to walk in great integrity!

The first cleansing of the Temple in Jerusalem caused the Jews to ask, "'What sign do You show to us, seeing that You do these things?' Jesus answered and said to them, 'Destroy this temple, and in three days I will raise it up.' The Jews therefore said, 'It took forty-six years to build this temple, and will You raise it up in three days?' But He was speaking of the temple of His body. When therefore He was raised from the dead, His disciples remembered that He said this" (John 2:18-22).

The resurrection of Jesus Christ from the dead would be the ultimate of signs! Yet it is this sign that most people stumble over, coming up with all sorts of lame explanations to rationalize what happened to the body of Jesus Christ during and after His crucifixion.

Some say that Jesus never died on the cross: "He merely swooned, and the coolness of the tomb revived Him." But to that we would have to ask, "What about the blood and water that poured forth from His side when the soldier thrust in his spear?" (John 19:34). Blood and water are a sign of a ruptured heart.

Others say that His body was stolen. If so, the disciples pulled off quite a feat with that many soldiers guarding the tomb! If the disciples took the body, were they foolish enough to die martyrs' deaths for Someone who did not rise from the dead?

Others say, "But where are the witnesses of His resurrection, other than the deluded apostles?" Is 500 enough—"at one time," no less? First Corinthians 15:6 tells us of this sighting by 500 to which the skeptics say, "But that is in the Bible!" As a book of historical evidence and authenticity, there is more manuscript evidence of the Bible—both Old and New Testaments—than there is for other works we accept as genuine.

O Beloved, when you deal with skeptics and the Word of God, never forget you're in spiritual warfare against the god of this world who has blinded their eyes—even of religious people! It was the same in Jesus' day.

14 The Jews asked for a sign, and Jesus gave them sign after sign. Even after the ultimate of signs, His resurrection, they still refused to believe. Beginning in chapter 2 of his Gospel, the apostle John records for us a select number of signs which will prove beyond a shadow of a doubt that Jesus is the Christ, the Messiah, the Promised One foretold by the prophets. Then John writes, "Many other signs therefore Jesus also performed in the presence of the disciples, which are not written in this book; but these have been written that you may believe . . ." (John 20:30,31).

Three different Greek words are used to describe the supernatural works which Jesus performed during His public ministry. John, however, uses only one of these: *sign(s)*. The Greek word for *sign(s)* is *sēmeion*, and is used in John 2:11,18,23; 3:2; 4:48,54; 6:2,14,26,30; 7:31; 9:16; 10:41; 11:47; 12:18,37; and 20:30. Except for the resurrection, which is referred to as a sign in John 2:18,19, all the signs are recorded in the first segment of his Gospel. It is interesting that John preferred to use *sēmeion* over the other two Greek words translated "miracles"—*dunamis*, a supernatural power; and "wonders"—*teras*, something strange that causes awe.

Yet *sēmeion* is John's choice—the Holy Spirit's, really. This word carries with it a sense of going beyond the miracle, the wonder, the awe of it all, to note the significance of the sign itself. A sign *(sēmeion)* was an indication, an attesting. Signs appeal to the understanding, while wonders appeal to the eyes and imagination. Through the signs, John wants us to believe that Jesus is the Christ, not just another good man. As we will see in John 3, Jesus' signs did capture attention and attest to His deity! Nicodemus came to Jesus at night and said, "Rabbi, we know that You have come from God as a teacher; for no one can do these signs that You do unless God is with him" (John 3:2).

John records signs which show that Jesus is Lord, Master over all. He records five signs that no other Gospel mentions: water into wine, healing the royal official's son, the man lame for 38 years, the blind man, and raising of Lazarus from the dead.

Take some time now, Beloved, to look up each use of the word *sign(s)* in the Gospel of John. Remember, I gave these to you earlier as we began today. In your notebook, list each sign and note what Jesus is Master over. I know that you will be blessed and encouraged, for your Lord is still Master over all—and that includes you!

15 Why must we be born again in order to enter the kingdom of God? Why can't God accept us the way we are? Why is a new birth necessary? And how does one go about being born again?

We want to answer these valid questions as we move on to John 3. So, before you go further, stop and read this chapter. The Word of God is alive and powerful. It discerns the thoughts and intentions of your heart. It sets you free from that which isn't truth. There is a supernatural, life-giving power to the Word of God. Jesus says, "The words that I have spoken to you are spirit and are life" (John 6:63). Never, never, never neglect the Word of God, my dear friend.

We must be born again, or born from above, because we are born into sin and our hearts are deceitful and desperately wicked. We are spiritually dead and doomed to an eternal death unless we are born again.

Romans 5:12 explains our state: "Therefore, just as through one man sin entered into the world, and death through sin, and so death spread to all men, because all sinned." Jeremiah 17:9 says, "The heart is deceitful above all things, and desperately wicked; who can know it?" (KJV).

Is it any wonder then that we read in 1 Corinthians 15:50: "Flesh and blood cannot inherit the kingdom of God . . ."? We cannot enter the kingdom of God in our natural state. Something supernatural must change us. That supernatural event is the second birth! We must be born again.[2]

How is it possible to be born again? That's the question Nicodemus, a ruler of the Jews, had. He questioned Jesus: "How can a man be born when he is old? He cannot enter a second time into his mother's womb and be born, can he?" (John 3:4).

No! That is not the way a second birth is accomplished. Thus, Jesus answers, "Truly, truly, I say to you, unless one is born of water and the Spirit, he cannot enter into the kingdom of God. That which is born of the flesh is flesh; and that which is born of the Spirit is spirit" (John 3:5,6).

Think on it, Beloved. Talk to your Father about it. Tomorrow we'll continue where we left off. I love you and appreciate your willingness to spend time in the Word of God so that you can know truth . . . and so that you can walk in a new level of intimacy with your Savior. May He become your dearest friend, too!

16

How can we be born again? If we have deceitful and desperately wicked hearts, how can we ever hope to enter the kingdom of heaven?

Let's listen again to Jesus' answer to Nicodemus: "Do not marvel that I said to you, 'You must be born again.' The wind blows where it wishes and you hear the sound of it, but do not know where it comes from and where it is going; so is everyone who is born of the Spirit" (John 3:7,8).

Being born again is a supernatural happening—like the wind. You don't see the wind; you only see its effects. You see the tree sway or the paper flutter.

What does Jesus mean when He says you must be "born of water and the Spirit" (John 3:5)? The Spirit of God brings us into the family of God by convicting us of sin, righteousness, and judgment (John 16:8). Then by His indwelling, He makes us new creatures in Christ Jesus, becoming our Helper, Guide, Instructor, and the Guarantee of our redemption (2 Corinthians 5:17; John 14:16, 17,26; 16:13; Ephesians 1:13,14). Romans 8:9 spells it out clearly: "If anyone does not have the Spirit of Christ, he does not belong to Him."

But what does Jesus mean when He says we must be "born of water" (John 3:5)? This is a question scholars have debated over the years. Let me briefly share several interpretations so that you will be aware of differences of opinion. Then I will share my interpretation and why I hold to that position. You can then take the interpretations to the Scriptures and to the Holy Spirit as your Teacher. The correct interpretation must agree with the whole teaching of God's Word.

Let's wait until tomorrow to look at these views. Today, thank the heavenly Father that He Himself has made a way for you to be born again.

17

Today we will consider what it means to be born of water. As we look at the different opinions, I will number each for you so you can follow me easily.

1. Some believe that *water* refers to literal water and, therefore, is a reference to water baptism. They believe the reference signifies the water of repentance, which is connected with baptism. This view doesn't allow for salvation apart from water baptism. Some would use Titus 3:5,6 to

support this belief: "He saved us, not on the basis of deeds which we have done in righteousness, but according to His mercy, by the washing of regeneration and renewing by the Holy Spirit, whom He poured out upon us richly through Jesus Christ our Savior."

2. A second view is that *water* symbolizes the cleansing work of the Holy Spirit; thus, the water refers to the Holy Spirit Himself. Proponents of this view translate John 3:5 in this way: "born of water, even the Spirit." Those who hold this view also use John 4:14 and 7:37,38 to support their belief that the Holy Spirit is synonymous with water. In both of these passages, the Holy Spirit is likened to "water springing up to eternal life" and to "rivers of living water."

3. Others believe that the use of *water* in this context is a reference to our physical birth. They stand on the fact that in order to be born spiritually, we must first be born physically. This third interpretation of John 3:5 holds to the view that the reference to water refers to the sack of water which is broken in the process of our physical birth. Therefore, the reference to water is nothing more than this! Those who hold this belief propose that John 3:5 is a parallel to the statement which follows: "That which is born of the flesh is flesh, and that which is born of the Spirit is spirit" (3:6).

4. The fourth view of John 3:5 is that *water* is a reference to the Word of God. This is the view I hold, which, of course, does not make it the correct view. However, I would like to explain why I hold this particular interpretation. Whether you agree or not, Beloved, as I explain my interpretation, you will learn a vital truth that will help you to share the gospel with others, and also to interpret difficult passages.

Whenever you come to a passage that is hard to interpret, you need to remember three things: 1) You must consider the whole counsel of God. Scripture will not contradict Scripture. 2) You must go from the known to the unknown. There are certain truths that are obvious. Begin with what you know to be true because it is clearly taught in the Word. 3) You should go from the clear to the obscure. Don't strain at gnats and swallow camels. Don't get caught up in the controversy of interpretation and miss what God wants to say. Remember, the Scriptures were written for common people. God chose the foolish so that "no man should boast before God"; "Christ Jesus . . . became to us wisdom from God" (1 Corinthians 1:27-30). Also, as helpful as a knowledge of Greek and Hebrew can be, I still believe that a thorough knowledge of the whole counsel of God is the best means of interpreting the Word of God. Scripture interprets Scripture, and it never contradicts itself.

In John 3, there is much about salvation that is obvious, much that is sufficient to bringing a man to salvation, whether or not he has the correct interpretation of "born of water." Why bother then with the meaning of this part of the passage? Because God tells us to study to show ourselves approved unto Him, workmen that need not be ashamed, "handling accurately the word of truth" (2 Timothy 2:15).

Tomorrow we are going to look at what the whole counsel of God teaches regarding being born again and why Jesus uses the term "born of water." However, today you need to simply remember what you learned about handling the Word of God.

18 What do we learn from the whole counsel of God regarding being born again? And why do I believe that "born of water" is a reference to the Word of God? Let me explain what the Bible teaches about being born into God's family, and I think you will see why I believe that "the water" in John 3:5 is synonymous with the Word. If we go back to John 1:12,13, we see that being born again is supernatural—not of man. John 1:12,13 says, "But as many as received Him, to them He gave the right to become children of God, even to those who believe in His name, who were born not of blood, nor of the will of the flesh, nor of the will of man, but of God."

When any person is born again, it is because God is the instigator of salvation. The new birth doesn't occur because man wills it so. Nor is it a result of man's bloodline or because his flesh desired it. Man is born again by the will of God.

Let's look at some of the Greek words used in John 1:12,13. The word for *children* is *teknon,* denoting prominence in relation to birth. The Greek word for *son (huios)* refers more to our adoption as sons, to our heirship.

In John 1:12, the word *received* seems to be synonymous with "believe in His name." The verb *believe* is a present participle which indicates a present and continuous activity of faith. In other words, once you genuinely believe, you will keep on believing. The preposition *in* of "in His name" (1:12) is *eis* in the Greek and indicates more than acceptance of a statement. It implies resting in, trusting in, availing oneself of all that Jesus is.

Receiving and believing in Jesus, then, is not merely acknowledging the facts regarding who He is and what He has accomplished. It is rather accepting and trusting Him as Savior, the Lord God who is the only means of obtaining forgiveness of sins and life eternal.

The word for *born* in John 1:13 is *gennaō,* which means "to beget children." This begetting is of God, who is the Author of salvation.

Now that we have seen who initiates our birth, let me show you why I believe that *water* in John 3:5 is a reference to the Word of God. We'll look at the whole counsel of God by doing some cross-referencing.

In John 5:24, Jesus says, "Truly, truly, I say to you, he who hears My word, and believes Him who sent Me, has eternal life, and does not come into judgment, but has passed out of death into life." According to this passage, belief is preceded by hearing God's Word.

In James 1:18, we read, "In the exercise of His will He brought us forth by the word of truth." Watch the terminology used by God. "Brought us forth" is *apokueō,* which means "to give birth to." It comes from *kueō*, which means "to be pregnant." According to James, what does God use in order to effect our spiritual birth? The Word of God! Think about it, dear friend.

19 If it is the Word of God that God uses to cause a person to be born again, truly it is a supernatural Word! "You have been born again not of seed *[spora]* which is perishable but imperishable, that is, through the living and abiding word of God. For, 'ALL FLESH IS LIKE GRASS, AND ALL ITS GLORY LIKE THE FLOWER OF GRASS. THE GRASS WITHERS, AND THE FLOWER FALLS OFF, BUT THE WORD OF THE LORD ABIDES FOREVER' " (1 Peter 1:23-25).

God is telling His children that it takes the Word of God for a person to be born again. Like the parable of the sower, the seed sown in our hearts is the Word of God (Mark 4:14). If we receive God's Word, believe it, put our trust and confidence in it, it results in our being born again. Why? Because it is an imperishable seed that abides forever and brings a man to belief. " 'WHOEVER WILL CALL UPON THE NAME OF THE LORD WILL BE SAVED.' How then shall they call upon Him in whom they have not believed? And how shall they believe in Him whom they have not heard? And how shall they hear without a preacher? And how shall they preach unless they are sent? Just as it is written, 'HOW BEAUTIFUL ARE THE FEET OF THOSE WHO BRING GLAD TIDINGS OF GOOD THINGS!' However, they did not all heed the glad tidings; for Isaiah says, 'LORD, WHO HAS BELIEVED OUR REPORT?' So faith comes from hearing, and hearing by the word of Christ" (Romans 10:13-17).

As you can see from this passage, calling upon the Lord brings salvation, but a person cannot call on Someone they do not know anything about! That is why God calls you and me to go forth as His witnesses, testifying to that which we have heard, seen, and learned about Jesus Christ and about the whole counsel of God's Word.

You don't need to be anxious about bringing about a decision for Jesus Christ—that is not your responsibility. As you have seen, salvation does not come by the will of man, by human power or persuasiveness. It comes by the will of God! Therefore, you simply sow the imperishable seed of God's Word and God gives the increase. Doesn't that take the pressure off? You are not responsible for another's salvation.

Elizabeth Neubold, a friend of mine, once said, "Witnessing is simply one beggar telling another beggar where to get bread!" If you have found the Bread of Life and are satisfied, how can you keep that Source to yourself?

I think it is obvious that the Word plays an integral part in being born again. So you now understand my reason for believing that "born of water" refers to the Word of God. I also have one more reason for holding this point of view. Look up John 15:3 and Ephesians 5:26, and you'll see that the Word of God is symbolized by water.

Let me ask you one question as we end our time today: Are your feet beautiful in God's eyes? They are if you are sharing His Word and what He has done in you by it with others.

20 Being born again is a supernatural act of God that changes a person. Like the wind, you don't see it happen. But again like the wind, you know it has happened because you can see its effect. It is often gradual. Its timing is different—slower in some, faster in others—but it is there. Children grow! If there is no effect, then there has been no genuine birth. Don't be deceived! "No one who is born of God practices sin[3] because His seed *[sperma]* abides in him; and he cannot sin, because he is born of God. By this the children of God and the children of the devil are obvious: anyone who does not practice righteousness is not of God, nor the one who does not love his brother" (1 John 3:9,10).

It is possible to enter the kingdom of heaven only by being born again. For it is our new birth that changes us, making us new creatures with the indwelling Holy Spirit, who causes us to walk in God's statutes and keep His commandments (Romans 8:1-4; Ezekiel 36:27).

In new birth God removes our deceitful heart of stone and gives us a heart of flesh. "Moreover, I will give you a new heart and put a new spirit within you; and I will remove the heart of stone from your flesh and give you a heart of flesh. And I will put My Spirit within you and cause you to walk in My statutes, and you will be careful to observe My ordinances" (Ezekiel 36:26,27).

Thus, Paul writes to the Corinthians: "You are our letter, written in our hearts, known and read by all men; being manifested that you are a letter of Christ, cared for by us, written not with ink, but with the Spirit of the living God, not on tablets of stone, but on tablets of human hearts" (2 Corinthians 3:2,3).

Being born again makes a person an overcomer, as far as sin and the world is concerned.

First John was written "to you who believe in the name of the Son of God, in order that you may know that you have eternal life" (1 John 5:13). It is a book that lays before its reader the evidences of being born again, of being a genuine child of God. As in his Gospel, John uses the metaphor "born again" to describe true salvation. "Whoever believes that Jesus is the Christ is born of God; and whoever loves the Father loves the child born of Him. By this we know that we love the children of God, when we love God and observe His commandments. For this is the love of God, that we keep His commandments; and His commandments are not burdensome. For whatever is born of God overcomes the world; and this is the victory that has overcome the world—our faith. And who is the one who overcomes the world, but he who believes that Jesus is the Son of God?" (1 John 5:1-5).

O Beloved, according to God's Word, are you born again?

21 When Jesus told Nicodemus that he must be born of water and of the Spirit if he ever wanted to enter the kingdom of heaven, Nicodemus asked, "How can these

things be?" (John 3:9). In other words, "How can this new birth come to pass?"

As we look at the remainder of John 3, we are going to see two ways that the new birth "can be." It can come to pass because of what God did out of love and mercy in lifting up the Son of Man—even as Moses lifted up the serpent in the wilderness. Second, it can come to pass because of what we do in response to what God did. Beloved, before we look at this, please take a few minutes and prayerfully read through John 3:7-36.

Man can be born again and enter the kingdom of heaven because of what God did to the Son of Man, the Lord Jesus Christ. "And as Moses lifted up the serpent in the wilderness, even so must the Son of Man be lifted up; that whoever believes may in Him have eternal life" (John 3:14,15).

Do you remember when Moses lifted up the serpent in the wilderness? The account is in Numbers 21. God had brought the children of Israel out of their bondage in Egypt through His mighty power, leading all the way by a pillar of cloud during the day and a pillar of fire at night. As they went, God delivered them from the hands of their enemies, except when they would not fully obey Him.

Yet, for all God's provisions on their journey, they were still discontented. "And the people spoke against God and Moses, 'Why have you brought us up out of Egypt to die in the wilderness? For there is no food and no water, and we loathe this miserable food' " (Numbers 21:5).

God gave them manna every morning and provided meat in the form of quail, but nothing could satisfy them. They had cried out in their bondage, and God had delivered them. Now, in even the simpler things, they would not trust God but continually murmured that they were going to die. Finally, God had enough: "The LORD sent fiery serpents among the people and they bit the people, so that many people of Israel died. So the people came to Moses and said, 'We have sinned, because we have spoken against the LORD and you; intercede with the LORD, that He may remove the serpents from us.' And Moses interceded for the people. Then the LORD said to Moses, 'Make a fiery serpent, and set it on a standard; and it shall come about, that everyone who is bitten, when he looks at it, he shall live.' And Moses made a bronze serpent and set it on the standard; and it came about, that if a serpent bit any man, when he looked to the bronze serpent, he lived" (Numbers 21:6-9).

It was a look of faith that saved them from death. And for us, it is looking on the One who was made sin for us, and believing that this is the only act of obedient faith which will keep us from perishing. Have you looked to Him in faith's obedience?

22 Bitten and doomed to die because of their sin, the only hope for the children of Israel was to believe God and look at the serpent lifted up in the wilderness. Otherwise, death's certain judgment awaited them. Little did they realize that this serpent on the pole would become a type of the Messiah, the Savior of the world. The Savior who, although He knew no sin, would be made sin for us that we "might become the righteousness of God in Him" (2 Corinthians 5:21).

The serpent on the pole was representative of God's love, for He gave His only begotten Son so that who ever believes in Him, though bitten because of sin, would not perish but have eternal life (John 3:16; see also vv. 17-21). Instead of perishing, they would receive everlasting life because they heard and heeded God's Word and were born again, not of corruptible seed, but of the Word of God which lives and abides forever. Hallelujah! Believe! Do what God says!

Those who love evil, who practice it habitually, who hate the Light because it exposes their sin, are not candidates for the kingdom of heaven. However, those who sin but genuinely hate it and long to be set free will look to the Savior hanging on God's tree. As they look with faith's obedience, they will be saved, just as those who looked to the serpent in the wilderness were healed.

In the wilderness, it was trust and obey—or die! There is no middle of the road, no safety lane. "He who believes in the Son has eternal life; but he who does not obey the Son shall not see life, but the wrath of God abides on him" (John 3:36). The word for *obey* is *peithō* and is a present active verb, thereby showing habitual, though not perfect, obedience that comes from persuasion, as a result of genuine faith.

Never let anyone convince you otherwise, Beloved. Genuine faith is seen in its obedience to the Word of God.

23 Exalting Jesus Christ was John the Baptist's reason for living. He did not follow Jesus Christ to bask in His glory or be noticed as part of Jesus' "intimate circle." John's desire was not to increase his own popularity by his association with Jesus Christ. How rare he was! Even his own disciples could not understand him.

John had been baptizing in Aenon near Salim. When his disciples knew that Jesus "was spending time with them and baptizing . . . they came to John and said to him, 'Rabbi, He who was with you beyond the Jordan, to whom you have borne witness, behold, He is baptizing, and all are coming to Him' " (John 3:22,26). It seems, doesn't it, that they were jealous that Jesus was drawing more followers than their teacher, John the Baptist?

This is not a new problem. We begin to measure our success by the number of followers we can draw into our church, our ministry, our group. We want them to be *ours*. We want to build our little kingdom and put a fence around it, so no one can entice away our followers. We get caught up in our own little worlds and miss His world where the harvesters are too few. We don't want our followers to go out into the world as harvesters unless they go out under our flag, so that our ministry gets the glory.

How avaricious our flesh is for glory! How vain! No wonder Jesus warned us to watch and pray, for "the spirit is willing, but the flesh is weak" (Matthew 26:41).

We can learn tremendously valuable lessons from John's response, especially in our time when there is so much promotion of Christian "superstars."

As our ministry has become increasingly well-known, it has been a battle to resist those who want to promote "me." I have also been on guard in my own heart so that I would encourage other ministries similar to ours when possible. I never want to come to a place where I think we have a corner on the truth.

How well I need to remember John's words of wisdom: "A man can receive nothing, unless it has been given him from heaven" (John 3:27). Whatever measure of ministry the Lord has so graciously allowed you or me to perform in His vineyard, it truly is a privilege from Him, something for which He has gifted us. As 1 Corinthians 12:4-6 teaches, the gifts, the ministries, and the effects all come from the Godhead. "For from Him and through Him and to Him are all things. To Him be the glory forever. Amen" (Romans 11:36).

May John's sober assessment of life be ours: "He must increase, but I must decrease" (John 3:30). Will you pray for me in this respect, my beloved friend, as I have just prayed for you?

24 "He had to pass through Samaria" as surely as He had to leave His Father's ivory palaces and come to earth as a Man. Love drove Him from His heavenly home to earth because man would perish—eternally chained to his sin—unless the Son of Man came and died in his stead. It was that same love that caused Jesus to pass through Samaria rather than go around it.

The Jews despised the Samaritans. Because they considered them nothing more than dogs, no respectable Jew would sully the sandals on his feet with Samaritan soil. The walk from Jerusalem to Galilee might be shorter if one were to go through Samaria, but it wasn't worth it since the Jews had no dealings with the Samaritans.

Jesus had to pass through Samaria because "she" was there—a woman whose craving for happiness and satisfaction had caused her to drink at many polluted wells, each one leaving her still unsatisfied. As usual, our Lord's timing was perfect. In the heat of the day at high noon, the woman of Samaria put her water pot on her head and journeyed down the road that led to Jacob's well. I'm sure she chose that time to go for water, for she knew that the women of her city with their forked tongues would not be there. It was painful to hear them chattering as she approached, and then go to whispers as she neared, and then go as silent as the stones once she was in earshot. It was easier to bear the heat of the day than the fire of their condemning eyes.

I imagine the Samaritan woman, like me on the day I met Jesus the Christ, thought it was just another ordinary day. I wonder if she, too, found it hard to get out of bed, to face another day? I wonder if her dreams were sweeter than her life, for in dreams you can be loved by the perfect man; life is as you always hoped and prayed it would be. You can be wildly in love, deliriously happy, ecstatically romantic. My dreams came from the Hollywood productions of the 1940s and 1950s. Hers probably came from the stories passed down from one generation to another, as young and old gathered at wells to chat or as they sat beside fires burning brightly in the night.

My life, like the Samaritan woman's, was a tragedy. It played like a movie you wish you had never seen and read like a novel you don't want to read. It was so sad, so empty, so seemingly pointless. "Why couldn't it have been written with a happy ending?" Life with one lover after another, but never with the one who played the role according to my script.

If the expression was as old as Samaria, I'm sure she too felt, "I've made my bed; now I've got to sleep in it." Little did she know when she rolled out of bed that morning that she wouldn't have to sleep in it any longer. That day Jesus "had to pass through Samaria" (John 4:4).

25 From the day the Samaritan woman met Jesus, she would never be the same. If you have truly met Him, if you have drunk freely of the water that springs up to eternal life, I know you understand what I mean.

Before we go back to this wonderful story in John 4, I hope you will stop and read John 4.

I'll never forget the first time I visited Jacob's well. I went crazy buying every article the Greek Orthodox priest sold! I so related to "the woman at the well," this sinful woman of Samaria, that I bought the crudely shaped wooden plaque bearing the clay form of the Samaritan woman and her water pot sitting on the edge of the well. I also bought the little, brightly painted ceramic replicas of water pots and filled them with the water from Jacob's well.

My treasures were carefully wrapped and brought home, where the plaque was tucked away because it did not fit in my decor. The bottles were given away, but they weren't filled with the water, since it evaporated in the Jerusalem heat.

Although my souvenirs lost their original excitement, never again will I read John 4 without seeing the whole setting in my mind. Never will I forget where I sat in the garden outside the little grotto-like structure erected around Jacob's well, looking at Mount Gerizim and Mount Ebal and thinking what it must have been like for my Samaritan friend to walk to that well every day, passing between these two mountains.

Mount Gerizim was the mount of blessing; Ebal was the mount of cursing. These were the mountains where Joshua had the priests stand and read the blessings and the cursings of the Old Covenant: blessings if they obeyed God and cursings if they did not! (Joshua 8:33,34).

Surely those cursings resounded off Mount Ebal as my Samaritan friend passed under its shadow day in and day out. Surely the barrenness of that mountain, in comparison to Gerizim, reminded her of the barrenness of her own life because she had not heeded the words given earlier by

Moses: "I call heaven and earth to witness against you today, that I have set before you life and death, the blessing and the curse. So choose life in order that you may live, you and your descendants, by loving the LORD your God, by obeying His voice, and by holding fast to Him; for this is your life and the length of your days, that you may live in the land which the LORD swore to your fathers, to Abraham, Isaac, and Jacob, to give them" (Deuteronomy 30:19,20).

O Beloved, do you live in the shadow of a mountain of curses because you have failed to obey God? Or have you drunk of Him and never been the same?

26 Do you know someone like the Samaritan woman—who has obviously messed up his or her life? Have you ever approached that one with the good news of the gospel of Jesus Christ? Probably many of you would say, "No!" Probably it's "no" because you just wouldn't know how to approach such a person. As a matter of fact, if you are a typical Christian, witnessing to anyone is not the easiest thing in the world to do, unless God has given you the spiritual gift of evangelism.

Well, Beloved, not having the gift of evangelism does not let you or me off the hook when it comes to sharing the gospel of Jesus Christ! This is the duty of every child of God. Paul wrote, "I am under obligation both to Greeks and to barbarians, both to the wise and to the foolish. Thus, for my part, I am eager to preach the gospel" (Romans 1:14,15). We are to "preach the word," to "be ready in season and out of season" (2 Timothy 4:2), for "faith comes from hearing, and hearing by the word of Christ" (Romans 10:17), and "how shall they hear without a preacher?" (Romans 10:14).

In the light of our obligation and of the desperate plight of those enslaved to sin, as even once we were, let's see what we can learn from John 4 and the way our Lord presented the gospel to this needy woman.

I believe the most common method of evangelism, and probably one of the most effective and biblical means of evangelism, is what Dr. Joe Aldrich, president of Multnomah School of the Bible, terms "lifestyle evangelism." The premise of lifestyle evangelism, as I understand it, is that sharing the gospel is a natural outflow of your life as you are in contact with those who do not know Jesus Christ. It does not mean that you "buttonhole" everyone that you meet and share the gospel with them. Rather, it means that your sharing of Jesus Christ is a natural outflow of your life. You share as you go with any you come into contact with, in a daily walk ordered under the lordship of Jesus Christ.

Stop and pray about this concept. Are you sharing the gospel at all, Beloved? We'll discuss it some more tomorrow.

27

"Going from door to door, passing out tracts, and asking people if they are saved just isn't for me!" Are those your sentiments? I understand. Don't feel guilty. There are many who feel this way. While this is an effective means of evangelism for some, I do not believe it is for everyone. Nor do I believe you will see it taught in the Scriptures as "the way" to evangelize.

That ought to enable many of you to breathe a sigh of relief. However, it does not let you off the proverbial hook when it comes to your responsibility to the lost. As I understand the Scriptures, lifestyle evangelism is the responsibility of every Christian. And I don't think one of us can escape our responsibility. Jesus said, "You are the salt of the earth" (Matthew 5:13).

Salt does three things. It brings out the flavor of food. Your life ought to bring forth the flavor of Christ. Second, salt stops the spread of corruption. Your life of righteousness ought to have that effect among your associates and associations. Third, salt causes a person to thirst. Does your life make others thirsty for the One you have and the changes Jesus brings?

Matthew not only tells you that you are salt, he also points out that "you are the light of the world." So "let your light shine before men in such a way that they may see your good works, and glorify your Father who is in heaven" (Matthew 5:14,16). Living "in the midst of a crooked and perverse generation, among whom you appear as lights in the world, holding fast the word of life" (Philippians 2:15,16) puts you in the position for lifestyle evangelism. Thus, you are able to fulfill Matthew 28:19,20: "Go therefore and make disciples of all the nations [in other words, don't exclude anyone because of their nationality or religious persuasion] . . . teaching them to observe all that I commanded you; and lo, I am with you always, even to the end of the age." The main command is, "Make disciples"; the other verbs are all participles. Therefore, it could be translated, "Make disciples . . . baptizing . . . teaching."

This is a natural evangelism, a lifestyle evangelism which takes the pressure and guilt off of sharing the gospel. This lifestyle enables you to make witnessing a natural outflow of sharing the One who lives within with those He brings into your path. You speak to those the Spirit of God says to speak to!

Isn't this what we see in John 4? Jesus had to go through Samaria—the Spirit of God was leading Him. As He went, He shared.

You see the same type of incident in John 3. Jesus was in Jerusalem, led by the Spirit. Nicodemus, who saw the lifestyle of Jesus and was attracted to Him, came to Him at night because he knew Jesus was from God. And Jesus gave Nicodemus what he had been searching for— the way to be sure you have eternal life.

Do people come to you? Do you share by your life and as the Spirit leads with those who are in your days? If not, why not?

28 Is there a formula for sharing the gospel? Is there a particular way you can share so that you'll see results most of the time? As you look at Jesus' lifestyle evangelism, and as you compare John 3 and John 4, you find that our

Lord dealt with Nicodemus and the Samaritan woman differently!

Although there is no pat way to share the gospel when you witness, you must make sure that it is the gospel you share and not just your "sweet" story or your "exciting" conversion.

Our goal for today is to see how Jesus ministered the gospel to those with whom the Father brought Him into contact. There are some precious and valuable insights which will help you, Beloved. Why don't you stop and ask God to really minister to you? He loves to have you seek His face!

If you are going to witness, then you need to be in contact with those who are lost! Exposure is of primary importance in witnessing. There is a mentality among some Christians that we ought to stay as far away from "the world" as possible. As a result, some find themselves so involved in Christian activities—living in Christian communes, taking Christian vacations, and working in Christian organizations—that the world never has a chance to see their lifestyle.

Do you have any exposure to lost people at all? One of the things you find Jesus doing, although He was criticized for it, was spending time with lost people.

The Pharisees were horrified when Jesus went to Matthew's home and ate with many tax-gatherers and sinners. When they asked Jesus' disciples, "Why is your Teacher eating with the tax-gatherers and sinners?" Jesus said, "It is not those who are healthy who need a physician, but those who are sick. But go and learn what this means, 'I DESIRE COMPASSION, AND NOT SACRIFICE,' for I did not come to call the righteous, but sinners" (Matthew 9:11-13).

Sinners had access to our Lord. Do they have access to you? Do they even know you exist? Do they have a chance to see your good works, to watch your lifestyle enough so that they ask you to give a reason "for the hope that is in you" (1 Peter 3:15)?

Jesus went through Samaria purposefully. He stayed at the well when His disciples went to get something to eat. Jesus knew she would be there! Ours, Beloved, is a "go" gospel—go into the world because there we will find those who are lost and need to be found.

Have you thought of beginning each day by making yourself available to the Father so that your life might be a witness to those He wants to touch through you? Try it—see what happens.

29 When you witness, it is best to meet people where they are, rather than with a tract or an immediate presentation of the gospel. Of course, the way you meet an individual will depend on circumstances and the time you have. As far as we know, Jesus had only one opportunity to talk with both Nicodemus and the Samaritan woman. Yet, His approach with each was different.

With Nicodemus, Jesus moved into the subject of salvation immediately. Of course, Nicodemus was interested, and Jesus knew that by his question; and since Nicodemus was a Pharisee, his life was invested in spiritual matters. Jesus knew why Nicodemus had come.

However, with the woman at the well, it was another story. Her interest was water. So Jesus met her there. Let's watch how Jesus dealt with her and see what He did so that we might use the same principles in our witnessing.

Take a few minutes and read through John 4 from the perspective of witnessing, and then list your insights in your notebook. It will make a difference for you if you dig these truths out on your own before you learn them from someone else. As you read John 4, list what you learn from the way Jesus dealt with this lost woman. And if you have extra time, try the same thing for Nicodemus in John 3:1-21. We'll talk more tomorrow!

30 As I have studied the Word, I have learned much that has helped me in sharing the gospel. Because of the lifestyle to which God has called me, I really do not have time for long-term, intimate friendships with people who are lost. Jack and I live right on the conference grounds of Precept Ministries; therefore, we do not have any close associations with neighbors. Plus, as heads of a ministry, our lives are extremely busy in dealing with a staff of 120-plus, with those who come to our various programs and conferences, and also with those we meet as we travel. Therefore, most of our witnessing is done when we are "on the road."

However, what I have learned from studying John 3 and 4 and other segments of the Word has helped me greatly. So let me share from John 3 and 4, and see how it compares with what you saw. If you are going to share the gospel, you need contact with those who are lost.

Sometimes people will come to you as Nicodemus did to Jesus. Or, if you are dealing with a long-term associate or friend, then you may find your friend coming to you for help with a problem or simply asking you about the difference in your life. In this case, your walk with Christ has opened the door, and you are ready to move in. How? This is what Joe Aldrich shares in a fascinating and inspiring book, *Life-Style Evangelism,* which I mentioned earlier. You will have to read it. It is absolutely super!

At other times, you will find yourself in the path of someone you don't even know. What do you do then? Well, the first thing I do is to ask God if He wants me to share, and if He does, to open the door or to show me how to open it.

Jesus opens the conversation with the Samaritan woman by asking her for a drink. He focuses on a subject that is appropriate to the occasion and center on her immediate interests. From there, Jesus will turn the conversation to salvation, to show her how it will benefit her.

He does the same thing with Nicodemus, explaining that if Nicodemus is born again, he will see the kingdom of heaven. This was what every Pharisee wanted!

What do you see Jesus doing as He presents the gospel? First, there is contact. Then He relates the truth of the Word of God to where the person is.

O Beloved, learn the Word so you can relate it to any need or question of man. Begin by scratching people where they itch! Thus they'll be more eager to listen.

31 When you share the gospel, it is vital that you do not get sidetracked on controversial issues which would keep the lost from even hearing what they need to hear. Avoid arguments. Don't get tied up in the nonessentials. Remember, a lost person cannot even begin to comprehend the things of God apart from the Spirit of God.

Jesus totally avoided the woman's retort that Jews had no dealings with Samaritans. Also, He did not debate with her about which mountain was the true mountain from which to worship. Instead of getting caught up in controversy, Jesus engaged her attention by talking about things she was interested in. He related what He said to spiritual matters: "Whoever drinks of the water that I shall give him shall never thirst; but the water that I shall give him shall become in him a well of water springing up to eternal life" (John 4:14). When she asked for the water, Jesus confronted her with her sin. You see the same thing in Jesus' dealing with Nicodemus when He confronted him with his unbelief (John 3:11,12).

When you share the gospel, you must confront the lost with their sin. Christ came to save sinners. The issue of sin must be dealt with because only salvation can deliver them from sin. This, Beloved, is where repentance enters. People see their sin, then repent, then believe.

Jesus confronted the Samaritan woman with her sin by asking her to call her husband. There has been many a time, as I have prayerfully shared the gospel, when God has caused me to ask a specific question in order to bring a person face-to-face with his or her sin. At this point, the conversation can become very touchy. However, if I confront in love, if I share how I was a slave to sin before I came to know Jesus Christ, then the person sees my genuine concern and is not offended as his or her sin is exposed.

There are three more points I want to share to help you in sharing the gospel. First, make sure people see that salvation is by faith, not by works. Jesus brings this out in John 4:21-24 and 3:13-15. Second, when you share, remember in salvation the issue is, "What will you do with Jesus?" Do not get sidetracked! And finally, don't push salvation. Give the Holy Spirit time to convict. Only God can give the increase. So don't pick green fruit! He is the Lord of the harvest. You just make sure your meat is to do the will of Him who sent you. Then get out into those fields which are white (overripe) unto harvest. You won't be sorry (unless, of course, you don't go)!

John at a Glance

Theme of John: *Eternal life through Jesus Christ, Son of God*

Segment Divisions

Structure of Book	*Written*	*Signs and miracles*	Ministry	Chapter Themes
introduces Jesus as	*that you may believe Jesus is the Christ, Son of God*		To Israel	1 *prologue—the Word / John the Baptist / calling disciples*
gives signs that prove Jesus is Christ, Son of God		*water to wine*		2 *wedding Cana / cleansing temple*
				3 *born again*
		heals noble-man's son		4 *woman at well / royal official*
		heals lame man		5 *father / son*
		feeds 5,000 walks on water		6 *bread / feeding 5,000*
				7 *feast of tabernacles / thirst—drink*
				8 *adulterous woman / truth sets free*
		heals blind man		9 *blind man*
				10 *sheep / shepherd*
		raises Lazarus from dead		11 *raising Lazarus*
decision time	*hour has come*		To Disciples	12 *dinner at Bethany / king on donkey*
life that belongs to those who believe God	*that you may have life*			13 *last supper / washing—disciples*
				14 *Father's house / hearts be troubled*
				15 *abide / vine and branches*
				16 *Holy Spirit / another Helper*
				17 *Lord's prayer / high-priestly prayer*
obtaining of that life—by death and resurrection			To All Mankind	18 *arrest and trial*
				19 *crucifixion*
		resurrection appearances		20 *resurrection*
purpose of life: love and follow			To Disciples	21 *Do you love me?*

Author:
John

Date:
about A.D. 85

Purpose:
that his readers would believe that Jesus is the Christ, God's Son, and thus have eternal life

Key Words:
signs / miracles
believe
life
judge
judgment
witness
true, truth
king
kingdom
love
works
commandments
fruit
abide
ask
world
light
glory (glorify)
Son of God
Son of Man
Christ
witness

February

Walking with Jesus— Life in a Different Dimension

1 If you could see signs and wonders and miracles, would it make a difference in the way you respond to God and to His Word? The Jews kept asking to see signs. Yet many who saw Jesus perform them still did not believe that He was the Christ, the Son of God. It is no wonder that Jesus became weary with them and said, "Unless you people see signs and wonders, you simply will not believe" (John 4:48).

For many, one sign is seldom good enough. How deceitful and desperately wicked is the heart of a man or woman who does not know Jesus! To recognize Him for who He is would be to acknowledge that He is God, and man wants to be his own god. He doesn't want to submit to anyone or anything but his own desires, his own ambitions.

Jesus was born to die for your sins and mine. Yet before He died, He performed many signs so that men might know beyond a shadow of a doubt that He truly was the Christ—sent to be "the Lamb of God who takes away the sin of the world!" (John 1:29).

As we continue our devotional study of the Gospel of John, we will look at a select number of signs recorded by the apostle John which "have been written that you may believe that Jesus is the Christ, the Son of God; and that believing you may have life in His name" (John 20:31). O Beloved, my prayer for you is that your mind and heart may be so taken captive by the truths recorded in the Gospel of John that you will not need to see signs but may be able to walk in faith, taking God at His word. I pray you will walk by faith and not by sight "having been firmly rooted and now being built up in Him and established in your faith" (Colossians 2:7).

As we move through the first 12 chapters of John, we behold various signs which prove beyond a shadow of a doubt who Jesus is. And as we carefully scrutinize His life, we come to know our heavenly Father in a new dimension. We see Jesus as "the only begotten God, who is in the bosom of the Father" who came to explain Him (John 1:18), for those who have seen Jesus have seen the Father (John 14:9).

Then in John 13, as Jesus draws aside to be alone with His disciples for the last few hours of His earthly life, we are drawn into a deep intimacy with Him. This deep knowing is the legacy of those who belong to the Father through the Son. As you spend time in this Gospel each day, it is my prayer that your Savior will become your dear, dear Friend.

2 "Do you wish to get well?" It seems like a rather foolish question on the surface! At first you think, "Who wouldn't wish to get well?"

I ask these questions, and my mind races to a man sitting at one of the gates surrounding the Old City of Jerusalem. As I recently came out of the Old City into the noise of lumbering buses jammed to the doors with Arabs and to the honking of irate, impassioned cab drivers, as I felt the bright sunshine which had been shielded by the walled, crowded, narrow streets of the Old City, a man sitting on the ground caught my attention. He was happily conversing with other beggars until a foreign tourist came by. At that point, all conversation ceased, and a hand was lifted as dark eyes silently pled for alms. The other hand pulled up a pant leg to make sure the already exposed ulcer—bright pink, glazed over with white purulent patches glistening in the sun—was not missed.

My nurse's heart brought my feet to a halt. I wanted to bend down and shield the open wound from the dust sent flying by the traffic scurrying through the gate. His leg needed tending. It should be washed, medicated, and dressed by someone who cared. Why, unattended it would only eat away until it reached his bone, and then he could lose his leg!

Arrested by his plight, I stopped to gaze at his leg and look into the darkness of his eyes, until my friend gently took me by my elbow and propelled me toward our destination. I was a tourist and did not know about these things. She then proceeded to tell me that this man did not wish to be made well. He made his living from his wound. No need to confront the complexities of responsibility as a citizen of Israel when one could merely sit down in the dust and dirt of Jerusalem and receive pity along with a few shekels.

My wounded beggar could have been healed. The hospital doors were open to him and medicine was available, but he did not wish to get well. As I looked back in curious fascination, I caught one last glimpse of someone less than what he could have been.

The man in John 5 had been sick for 38 years. We do not know how long he had been lying beside the pool of Bethesda. All we know is that when Jesus passed by and asked him if he wished to be made well, he had to make a choice. Either he could continue in his normal habit of life, or he could relinquish it for healing.

Suppose, Beloved, Jesus asked you if you wanted to be made well—emotionally, physically, spiritually? What would you answer? Think about it, read John 5, and we'll talk about it more tomorrow.

3 Have you ever blamed your condition on what others have not done for you? Maybe you have been greatly hurt or disappointed, and you feel crippled, as if you can't

live the way you want to. You think of what you might have been, if only you hadn't suffered so.

Do you understand, Beloved, what I am saying? It could mean wholeness to you and a new lease on life. If you relate to what I just said, then you can relate to the certain man of John 5 who had been crippled for 38 years. "But," you may say, "I am not physically crippled." Granted. But physically crippled or emotionally handicapped because of what has happened to you, the underlying precept is still the same.

The infirm man had a problem similar to that of many people today: He was resigned to his infirmity. That is why Jesus asked him if he wished to get well. Jesus knew his heart and looked beneath the outward circumstances to the inward condition. The man's answer gives us insight into his real condition: "Sir, I have no man to put me into the pool when the water is stirred up, but while I am coming, another steps down before me" (John 5:7).

I think of people who are sick in the sense that they are not whole, people with wounds that have come from relationships with others, wounds that have never been tended and healed. Wounds that could be healed if the person stopped blaming another for the condition and acted in faith; wounds that could be healed if he had stopped his self-pity and dull acceptance of the infirmity and moved to the obedience of faith.

The infirm man of John 5 had to take action. Jesus told him to rise, take up his pallet, and walk. If he really wanted to be made whole, he had to stop blaming others. No more lying around—apathetic, resigned to his state, saying, "I am what I am; I am where I am; and I will always be here because others have failed me." He needed to believe Jesus and get up and go on with life.

Beloved, there is a balm in Gilead. It is the Word of God (Psalm 107:20). There is a Great Physician there. It is God our Healer, our Jehovah-Rapha (Exodus 15:26). Cry out, "Heal me, O LORD, and I will be healed; save me and I will be saved, for Thou art my praise" (Jeremiah 17:14).

4 Sin has an awful price. It can affect every aspect of our being—physically, emotionally, spiritually. It is interesting that Jesus said to the man who had been in his sickness 38 years, "Behold, you have become well; do not sin anymore, so that nothing worse may befall you" (John 5:14). So many times we think of sin as gross acts. Yet according to the Scriptures, the root of all sin is independence from God. In the Garden of Eden Adam and Eve chose to disobey God's Word and to seek their own good.

In Romans 14:23, we read: "Whatever is not from faith is sin." Therefore, not to believe God's Word and to live independently of what He says is sin. Often the people who ask me for counseling fall into two categories: Some say, "I know God's Word says that, *but,* you see, in my case it is different." Then there are those who say, "If that is what God's Word says, then I am going to live accordingly, no matter how I feel."

It is the latter group, Beloved, who are healed, made whole, and are useful to the kingdom of heaven. They take action and begin to walk in the victory of faith. Not to be made whole or well, emotionally or spiritually, is sin. It is to refuse to believe God. And when we do this, even greater woes may befall us.

You may feel that I am avoiding the issue of physical healing. Therefore, let me explain. I believe that God can and does heal physical illnesses today. However, I do not believe that the Scriptures teach that physical healing is for everyone in every situation.

It is interesting to me that in John 5 there was "a multitude of . . . sick, blind, lame, and withered" people lying around the pool called Bethesda (5:3). Yet we see Jesus healed only one of them. There was no mass healing service. Why? Obviously, mass healing did not serve the purpose of our sovereign God.

I believe that sometimes God heals people to bring Himself glory and sometimes allows a child of God to endure physical illness for His glory.

However, for a child of God to be emotionally or spiritually crippled because of the past is not scriptural. The Word promises us that "God causes all things to work together for good to those who love God, to those who are called according to His purpose. For whom He foreknew, He also predestined to become conformed to the image of His Son" (Romans 8:28,29). Be healed, Beloved.

5 Have you ever known people who boxed God into the confines of their own legalism? Who defined holiness and Christianity according to a set of rules or traditions or commandments which they themselves ordained? The Pharisees did this. They took the clear teachings of the Word of God and added to them dos and don'ts that would keep the Jews from even coming close to breaking the commandments of the Old Testament.

The Jews added rules to what God said about the Sabbath. In Exodus 20, God said: "Remember the sabbath day, to keep it holy. Six days you shall labor and do all your work, but the seventh day is a sabbath of the LORD your God; in it you shall not do any work, you or your son or your daughter, your male or your female servant or your cattle or your sojourner who stays with you. For in six days the LORD made the heavens and the earth, the sea and all that is in them, and rested on the seventh day; therefore the LORD blessed the sabbath day and made it holy" (20:8-11).

On the seventh day, "even during plowing time and harvest you shall rest" (Exodus 34:21). To break the Sabbath meant death. God's word through Moses was clear: It was to be "a sabbath of complete rest to the LORD; whoever does any work on it shall be put to death. You shall not kindle a fire in any of your dwellings on the sabbath day" (Exodus 35:2,3).

Death for breaking the Sabbath was not merely an ordinance written in the book of the Law and never executed. Numbers 15 records an incident of a man gathering wood on the Sabbath day: "And those who found him gathering wood brought him to Moses and Aaron, and to all the congregation; and they put him in custody because it had not been declared what should be done to him. Then the LORD said to Moses, 'The man shall surely be put to death; all the congregation shall stone him with stones outside the camp.' So all the congregation brought him outside the camp, and stoned him to death with stones, just as the LORD had commanded Moses" (15:33-36).

It was because of the gravity of breaking the Law that the Jews built a hedge of protection around it with their codification of the Law. Their reasoning was that if their people kept these traditions, then there was no way they could come close to transgressing God's Law.

Though their intentions may have been good, these Jews came to consider man-made traditions equal with the Law. Therefore, they considered disobedience of these punishable with the same punishment meted out for disobeying the Law. In their good intentions, they added to the Word of God. How dangerous and how crippling! Their legalism so blinded them that they missed who Jesus was. Have you missed Him or His grace because of your legalism?

6 Resisting another's legalistic interpretation of Scripture often brings persecution. How hard it is when this comes from those who profess to have the same heavenly Father. Until He healed the man at the pool of Bethesda, things had gone fairly smoothly in the ministry of our Lord. Merrill Tenney calls the time preceding John 5 "the period of consideration."[1]

However, when He healed this man, Jesus entered into a period of controversy which began in Judea but exacerbated in Galilee. The controversy came from His own people, the Jews.

The primary source of contention was the Pharisees' claim that Abraham was their father, allowing them also to claim God as their Father (John 8:39-41). They saw themselves as the protectors and interpreters of the Law. The

Pharisees occupied the majority of the seats in the Sanhedrin which, under Rome, was the ruling body over the Jews.

This period of controversy in Jesus' public ministry was inaugurated because Jesus healed the man on the Sabbath. The Jews said to the man, " 'It is the Sabbath, and it is not permissible for you to carry your pallet.' But he answered them, 'He who made me well was the one who said to me, "Take up your pallet and walk." ' . . . And for this reason the Jews were persecuting Jesus, because He was doing these things on the Sabbath" (John 5:10-16).

Over and over, we see Jesus healing on the Sabbath. That interests me! He could have healed on another day of the week, but He didn't choose to. When our Lord healed on the Sabbath, He exposed the degree to which their legalism had become twisted.

Sometimes people today get so caught up in their legalistic understanding of Christianity that they miss what God is doing, or they seek to stifle it.

O Beloved, don't let it happen to you! Watch that you don't persecute or demean other children of God just because they don't fit your religious mold. You may be resisting the work of God.

7

As we move into adulthood, we want to be free to make our own decisions, to answer to ourselves rather than to others. This desire is part of the maturing process. And yet, independence must not spill over into our walk with our Lord.

The secret of spirituality, of being used of God, is dependence, not independence. Never is this truth more beautifully or powerfully illustrated for us than in the relationship of our Lord Jesus Christ to His heavenly Father. I want us to look at this relationship in detail, for in it we learn invaluable insights that need to be incorporated into our own lives.

It was the very relationship Christ claimed with the Father which heightened the controversy between the Jews and Jesus. When they questioned Jesus' healing of the man on the Sabbath, He answered them, " 'My Father is working until now, and I Myself am working.' For this cause therefore the Jews were seeking all the more to kill Him, because He not only was breaking the Sabbath, but also was calling God His own Father, making Himself equal with God" (John 5:17,18). To make oneself equal to God or claim to be God falsely was considered blasphemy, and the Word of God said that blasphemy was punishable by death.

To explain why He healed the man on the Sabbath, Jesus answered, "Truly, truly, I say to you, the Son can do nothing of Himself, unless it is something He sees the Father doing; for whatever the Father does, these things the Son also does in like manner" (John 5:19). Jesus healed the man on the Sabbath because that was the pleasure of His Father. In total dependence upon the Father, Jesus executed God's desire.

And in doing so, He modeled for us how we are to live as children of God. As we live more and more in total dependence upon the Father, we will become more and more like Jesus.

And to be like Jesus, dear child of God, is the whole reason for our existence and life upon this earth!

To be like Jesus, we must learn to walk as Christ walked with His Father, doing nothing on our own initiative. May it be our habit of life to "always do the things that are pleasing to Him" (John 8:29), and to be mature enough to not live independently of Him—but in total dependence.

8 Is it possible to live in total dependence upon the Father? Yes! Our Lord Jesus Christ lived that way because He lived by the Spirit. We too are to be controlled or filled by the Spirit.

You may say to me, "But, Kay, Jesus was God!" Yes, Beloved, Jesus is God. However, when He lived here on earth as the Son of Man, He lived as God always intended man to live—in complete dependence upon Him and His

Word. To live in dependence is to walk in the Spirit. Dependence upon the Father dictates that we live by faith, taking God at His Word.

In Genesis 3, man sinned when he "turned to his own way" (Isaiah 53:6), when he ceased to believe and submit to God, when he chose not to do what God commanded. It was at this point that the Spirit of God left man, and man passed from life into death (Romans 5:12). And it is not until man passes from death to life that he is saved.

And how does salvation affect man's relationship to the Spirit of God? "He saved us, not on the basis of deeds . . . but according to His mercy, by the washing of regeneration and renewing by the Holy Spirit, whom He poured out upon us richly through Jesus Christ our Savior" (Titus 3:5,6).

Jesus lived and walked by the same Spirit who indwells every believer. Jesus modeled for us what God intended for man when He created him. Thus, we see Jesus beginning His ministry with "the Spirit descending and remaining upon Him" (John 1:33), the same Spirit with whom He shall baptize every believer at salvation (1 Corinthians 12:13). This is the same Holy Spirit who indwells us, who leads us, who guides us into all truth. We will see who He is clearly when we study John 14–16. It is the Spirit of God who "searches all things, even the depths of God" and then makes them known unto us so that we have the mind of Christ (1 Corinthians 2:10-16).

Now then, Beloved, let us return to John 5 where Jesus defined His dependence upon the Father. "The Son can do nothing of Himself, unless it is something He sees the Father doing; for whatever the Father does, these things the Son also does in like manner. For the Father loves the Son, and shows Him all things that He Himself is doing" (John 5:19,20).

A life of dependence upon the Father begins when we become "children of God" (John 1:12), for then the Spirit of God indwells us and reveals to us the mind of God, so that we know what pleases Him. We learn His heart. Then we must choose to do what God has shown us. Jesus said, "I do nothing on My own initiative, but I speak these things as the

Father taught Me" (John 8:28). We too are to speak the things the Father teaches us—and do the things He has taught us, the things which please Him.

Now then, Beloved, "the one who says he abides in Him ought himself to walk in the same manner as He walked" (1 John 2:6).

9

"Jesus claimed nothing less for Himself than deity. He demanded nothing less from His followers than obedient faith."[2] In today's portion of John 5, Jesus addresses both of these issues.

In John 5:18, we find the Jews seeking to kill Jesus "because He not only was breaking the Sabbath, but also was calling God His own Father, making Himself equal with God." As Jesus answered them, He showed them that He, like the Father, possessed the sovereign rights of deity.

The first sovereign right of deity is authority over life and death. Deuteronomy 32:39 says, "See now that I, I am He, and there is no god besides Me; it is I who put to death and give life." In John 5:25-27, Jesus points out to the Jews that "an hour is coming and now is, when the dead shall hear the voice of the Son of God; and those who hear shall live. For just as the Father has life in Himself, even so He gave to the Son also to have life in Himself; and He gave Him authority to execute judgment, because He is the Son of Man."

Jesus' statements lay clear claim to His equality with the Father. Then He speaks of those He will call forth on that day. Jesus now spells out what life in the Spirit produces.

Those who are truly saved follow Him (John 10). It is a life that follows Jesus Christ that produces good deeds. Good works follow salvation and show our faith to be genuine (James 2:14-26). As Jesus says in the Sermon on the Mount, "So then, you will know them by their fruits" (Matthew 7:20).

Genuine salvation will produce good works. Listen to Jesus' words: "Do not marvel at this; for an hour is coming, in which all who are in the tombs shall hear His voice, and shall come forth; those who did the good deeds to a resurrection of life, those who committed the evil deeds to a resurrection of judgment" (John 5:28,29).

Jesus is not teaching that good works save us. Rather, He is saying that those who possess salvation, eternal life, do good deeds. Our works illustrate our character. Men made righteous produce righteous deeds. Think on these things, Beloved.

10 Not only does a sovereign God have power over death and life so that He can raise the dead, but He also has the authority to judge. Judgment is another sovereign right of God. God is "the Judge of all the earth" (Genesis 18:25). Thus, in John 5, Jesus also substantiates His deity by telling the Jews that the Father "gave Him authority to execute judgment, because He is the Son of Man" (5:27). God the Father "has given all judgment to the Son" (John 5:22).

Not only is judgment the sovereign right of God, God is the Creator, the Sustainer. Thus, Jesus states, "For just as the Father has life in Himself, even so He gave to the Son also to have life in Himself" (John 5:26). "For just as the Father raises the dead and gives them life, even so the Son also gives life to whom He wishes" (John 5:21).

Finally, the last sovereign right of God in this chapter is the right to receive honor. All are to "honor the Son, even as they honor the Father" (John 5:23). If Jesus were not God, then God would not give His glory to Him (Isaiah 42:8).

With all these statements, Jesus is claiming nothing less than deity for Himself. But is Jesus' witness true? Would His testimony of His deity stand alone in the Jews' court of justice? No, and Jesus knows it, for He says, "If I alone bear witness of Myself, My testimony is not true" (John 5:31) or admissible as legal evidence.

Therefore, in John 5, Jesus lays before the Jews other witnesses who will testify that His witness to His deity is true. What are these witnesses? Well, I want you to find out for yourself by reading John 5:31-47. When you dig out truth on your own, it stays with you. As you read, mark every use of the word *witness* in a distinctive way or a distinctive color. Then list in your notebook those things or people which bear witness to Jesus' deity.

There are many who claim to belong to God and seek to have you join their churches; yet when you get down to the issue of the deity of Jesus Christ, you find that they believe Jesus was a good man, a god, but not God incarnate (in the flesh).

Now then, Beloved, should someone question you, would you be able to share that which bears witness to the fact that Jesus Christ is God?

11

Isn't it amazing how a person can be confronted with truth after truth, one truth substantiating and confirming the other, and still refuse to believe? Yet the same person is so quick to buy a lie! To be deceived! Have you ever wondered why? It is because men's hearts are deceitful and desperately wicked. Therefore, they love darkness rather than light, and will not come to the light lest their deeds be exposed (John 3:19,20). "The god of this world has blinded the minds of the unbelieving, that they might not see the light of the gospel of the glory of Christ, who is the image of God" (2 Corinthians 4:4). Thus, as it says in John 5:40, "You are unwilling to come to Me, that you may have life."

The Jews had ample witnesses. The Father bore witness of His Son through His word to John the Baptist, through the works which He accomplished through His Son, and sometimes when He spoke audibly from heaven about Jesus.

Finally, the Word of God itself bore witness to Jesus Christ. How I love Jesus' words: " 'O foolish men and slow of heart to believe in all that the prophets have spoken!' . . . And beginning with Moses and with all the prophets, He explained to them the things concerning Himself in all the Scriptures" (Luke 24:25,27). These were the Scriptures the Jews searched because they thought that in them they had eternal life, and it was these that bore witness of Jesus (John 5:39).

If they searched the Scriptures looking for eternal life, then why did they miss it? They thought for sure that heaven was their destination. However, as you read through John 5:37-47, you see the "negatives" in their lives that would send them to hell. They were men who had never heard the voice of God at any time nor seen His form (John 5:37); yet they would not listen to Jesus, the One who had heard and seen God.

They would not accept His witness. Second, they did not have God's Word abiding in them (John 5:38). They knew the Word backward and forward, but it wasn't at home in them. Third, they were unwilling to come to Jesus that they might have life (John 5:40). And, as Jesus would say later, "No one comes to the Father, but through Me" (John 14:6). Fourth, they did not have the love of God in themselves (John 5:42). Fifth, they were quick to receive others, but they did not receive Jesus. Isn't that the same with so many people today? They are quick to believe other books, other opinions, but not the Bible. Sixth, they sought glory from one another, but not from God. Men love the praise of men more than the praise of God. And finally, they wouldn't believe Moses. If they had, they would have believed Jesus, for Moses wrote about Him. It is the same today in the "school of higher criticism," which denies the literal veracity of God's Word. O Beloved, may you not identify with these "negatives" in any way!

12 Have you ever walked out of the door of your private, secure world and taken a good look at the outside world around you? Has your heart ever been moved to compassion? Have you ever wondered what you could do to meet the needs of the multitude? We live in a time of great apathy. For the most part, we are a self-centered generation. When a person turns his or her focus on self, apathy follows.

However, I don't believe I am writing to the typical Christian. I don't believe that you would have such an interest in the Word of God if you were, shall I say, ordinary. Typical. Run-of-the-mill. Someone who reads and uses a devotional like this is hungering to know God better. Such a one has a desire to understand the Word of God, and a passion for godliness, holiness, for greater intimacy with God.

Therefore, when I ask if you have ever taken a good look at the world around you and been moved to compassion, I believe you probably have. I don't think you are simply wrapped up in your own private world.

Yet when you look at the world, are you ever overwhelmed? When you look at the state of affairs in your country, when you look at morality, at what is going on in the schools, at what is happening in the homes of your friends, in their marriages, in their children, are you overwhelmed? Do you feel like someone needs to do something? Do you wonder where that someone is?

Well, let me ask you a question, Beloved. Have you ever thought that maybe you were that someone? *Me!* Did I hear you say, "*Me!*" with an incredulous gasp? I understand.

You think, "I have so little to offer." Or, "The need is so overwhelming. Who could ever begin to make a difference?" Or, "I am not prepared for this. I have so little in the way of talents, gifts, capabilities, or time. There's no way I could ever . . . Why, it would take . . ."

Hang on, Beloved. A change could be coming if you listen carefully to what God is about to show you through His Word, if you have a soft and tender heart of flesh and not of stone. Keeping in mind what you have just read, now turn to the infallible Word of God and read John 6:1-14; Matthew 14:13-21; Mark 6:30-44; and Luke 9:10-17.

Since all four Gospels record the same event, there has to be great significance to it. And there are surely some principles which are applicable to your life. Ask God to speak to you. Then write down your insights in your notebook.

13 They were an excited multitude, for they were seeing things they had never seen. Many had come from great distances, walking the dusty roads of Galilee. The news had spread like a brush fire. More than 5000 men, along with women and children, had converged on Jesus. When they looked out on that small Sea of Galilee and saw where He was headed, they took off, literally running on foot from their towns. Jesus went by boat to a desolate place to be alone with His disciples; but when He saw the multitude, like sheep without a shepherd, He had compassion on them.

Jesus spent the day teaching them about the kingdom of God and healing their sick. And although the hour grew late and they had made no prior provision for food or lodging, I am sure they thought, "Why go home?" They might miss something! Besides, it was a lovely time of year. It was Nisan, the beginning of months. Spring had arrived! It was time once again to celebrate the Passover.

The multitude didn't seem concerned, but the disciples were. They came to Jesus saying, "The place is desolate, and the time is already past; so send the multitudes away, that they may go into the villages and buy food for themselves" (Matthew 14:15). Can you imagine their shock when Jesus replied, "They do not need to go away; you give them something to eat!" (Matthew 14:16)?

Can you relate to how the disciples must have felt? Here were 5000 hungry men, not counting the women and children. Feed them?

Philip analyzed the situation immediately. It was impossible! Why, it would take two-thirds of a year's wages to feed this mob! That's 200 denarii! It wouldn't be sufficient "for everyone to receive a little" (John 6:7). Of course, we know that Jesus was testing Philip to see if he would look beyond the impossibility of the situation to the God of the Impossible, the One who had just asked him, "Where are we to buy bread, that these may eat?" (John 6:5).

Isn't that our problem so often, Beloved? We find ourselves overwhelmed by a seemingly impossible need, and we forget to look to God. We forget His word to His people: "Behold, I am the LORD, the God of all flesh; is anything too difficult for Me?" (Jeremiah 32:27). "Call to Me, and I will answer you, and I will tell you great and mighty things, which you do not know" (Jeremiah 33:3).

To which we ought to reply: "Ah Lord GOD! Behold, Thou hast made the heavens and the earth by Thy great power and by Thine outstretched arm! Nothing is too difficult for Thee" (Jeremiah 32:17). But sometimes we, like Philip, forget to look beyond natural resources to the supernatural. Talk to your God about your feelings.

14 Do you ever feel that you have a little faith, but not enough? You see a need, you look at what you have or at what you are and it seems inadequate, so you don't do anything. I understand. As far as natural talents, ability, education, personality, I am just not a winner. You may respond, "But you write books, have a radio program, a television program, you write inductive Bible study courses, and travel all over the world teaching the Bible. I disagree with you." I don't think I am being modest. I just don't feel talented—naturally.

All of my 29 years as a lost person, I tried to be a winner. I worked hard, but I never really made it. I studied like mad and could not get above a 92 average. I wanted to be part of the "in crowd," but I was always on the outside looking in! I would like to have been "the queen" of something, but no one ever thought of nominating me. I once heard of a "Possum Queen," and probably would have settled for that! I have no musical talent. I brought home a clarinet and a baritone saxophone, but I didn't get beyond wetting my reed and getting a sore lip. Although I took piano lessons—I wanted to play "Twelfth Street Rag" for Daddy—I never got through Book One. I tried piano lessons even after I was saved and still didn't pass Book One! I thought about taking singing lessons. I could see myself on stage belting out songs as I did my soft-shoe routine. I loved to dance. I would turn on the record player in my bedroom and work up my routines, but they were never seen on stage. My stuffed animals were my only audience. I tried out for the leads in plays. I got parts, but never the lead!

I share all of this, Beloved, to let you see that I tried, but the little I had wasn't enough, until I met Jesus. Then one day as a year-old Christian, I heard Stuart Briscoe say, "God doesn't need your ability. All He needs is your availability!" Availability I had! So I began to make myself available to Him, and in His grace, He took my little bit of faith, which was surrendered to Him, and began to use it.

In John 6, you see quite a contrast between Philip and Andrew, Simon Peter's brother. Philip looked at the hungry multitude from a pragmatic point of view: "There is no way because our natural resources are not adequate enough to pull it off." Andrew, bless his heart, looked to see if there might be a way. He scouted out the situation and came up with a little boy's lunch. "There is a lad here who has five barley loaves, and two fish, but what are these for so many people?" (John 6:9).

The loaves were about the size of pancakes, and the fish were fish—not salmon! This lunch wasn't much, in light of the 5000-plus around, and yet, it was more than adequate because God was in it.

O Beloved, give Him your small faith, and watch it become more than adequate.

15 Jesus could have been crowned instead of crucified, if He had fulfilled the desire of the people rather than meeting their deeper need. After He fed the multitude they wanted to make Him king because He took care of their temporal needs (John 6:14,15).

But Jesus had a higher purpose. The physical part would die, but the spiritual part of man would live forever. Thus, our Lord needed to go beyond the temporal to the eternal. The sign of the loaves and fish was a springboard for giving the multitude the very precepts of life. Jesus knew the opportunity to teach them would come the next day. And many returned: "When the multitude therefore saw that Jesus was not there, nor His disciples, they themselves got into the small boats, and came to Capernaum, seeking Jesus. . . . [Jesus said,] 'Truly, truly, I say to you, you seek Me, not because you saw signs, but because you ate of the loaves, and were filled. Do not work for the food which perishes, but for the food which endures to eternal life, which the Son of Man shall give to you, for on Him the Father, even God, has set His seal' " (John 6:24-27).

Let me ask you a question, Beloved. Why do you follow Jesus? Do you seek Him for the benefits that are yours as a child of God? Because of promises that seem to cover your material needs? Because of some health-wealth doctrine? Because He has healed you? Or because He has taken care of a problem for you?

And what if He didn't meet your temporal needs in a way that you thought He would? What if He allowed you to suffer? What if you asked and didn't receive what you asked for? Would you still embrace Him as your Lord and Savior? Would you still want Him as King of your life? Would you let Him rule if what He was going to ask or expect of you was costly or painful? Have you ever been guilty of seeking Him merely for benefits?

O Beloved, He desires your spiritual good, your eternal good, and that rarely comes in the school of plenty. Rather, it happens usually in the school of discipline or affliction. First the cross and then the crown, for Him—and for you.

16 If you seek for signs, then one is not enough to satisfy. You constantly want the reassurance of a miracle. Otherwise, you have to walk in total faith. Miracles and signs are easier, more exciting, concrete "now" evidence. When the multitude asked Jesus, " 'What shall we do, that we may work the works of God?' Jesus answered and said to them, 'This is the work of God, that you believe in Him whom He has sent.' They said therefore to Him, 'What then do You do for a sign, that we may see, and believe You? What work do You perform? Our fathers ate the manna in the wilderness; as it is written, "HE GAVE THEM BREAD OUT OF HEAVEN TO EAT" ' " (John 6:28-31).

When the multitude reminded Jesus that Moses provided them with daily bread, they weren't considering the fact that there was a day when that bread ceased, a day when God said to Joshua, "Only be strong and very courageous; be careful to do according to all the law which Moses My servant commanded you; do not turn from it to the right or to the left, so that you may have success wherever you go. This book of the law shall not depart from your mouth, but you shall meditate on it day and night, so that you may be careful to do according to all that is written in it . . ." (Joshua 1:7,8).

In Joshua's day, for the most part, the signs were over. They had seen the power of God; now they were to walk in faith. Now also, with the multitude, it was a matter of believing in the One God had sent down from heaven: Jesus, the true Bread of Life. He was the Bread of God, but they had a hard time understanding that! Jesus reminded them that Moses hadn't given them manna; God had.

The multitudes were missing what God now was giving them " 'the true bread out of heaven. For the bread of God is that which comes down out of heaven, and gives life to the world.' They said therefore to Him, 'Lord, evermore give us this bread.' Jesus said to them, 'I am the bread of life; he who comes to Me shall not hunger, and he who believes in Me shall never thirst. But I said to you, that you have seen Me, and yet do not believe' " (John 6:32-36).

It is chilling, isn't it? To think that a person could see Jesus perform His signs, could hear all that He said in His teaching, could talk with Him face-to-face and still not believe in Him. It is heartbreaking to think that people could walk away from the only One who could satisfy a hunger and thirst that came from the very depths of their beings. They walked away because they wanted signs, or a salvation that came by working the works of God. Yet only one thing would do, and that was to believe, to rely on, to trust in Jesus Christ.

O Beloved, we have His Word! We have enough. Read it and believe. "An evil and adulterous generation craves for a sign" (Matthew 12:39). Walk by faith and not by sight. You will be satisfied!

17 Before we begin our day together, read John 6:31-71.

Much of what Jesus said was not easy to take! As a matter of fact, after His discourse in the synagogue in Capernaum, many of His disciples said, "This is a difficult statement; who can listen to it?" (John 6:60). What had Jesus said that was difficult to listen to? "As a result of this many of His disciples withdrew, and were not walking with Him anymore" (John 6:66). What was it?

Well, Beloved, if you carefully read John 6:31-71, you probably know. This is a passage of Scripture that sometimes brings much controversy and schism in the body of Jesus Christ. How I pray that you will simply let the Word of God say what it says, without trying to take it to extremes that are not warranted in the Word of God.

Many times we become the product of a denomination's particular brand of theology, so that we can't let the Word of God speak for itself. When we view the Word in this way, we often miss what God is saying, because we can't reach a logical conclusion or because we cannot reason it all out in our minds.

We forget that there is a mystery to the gospel. We also forget that we have finite brains compared to the infinite wisdom of God, who says in His Word: "Oh, the depth of the riches both of the wisdom and knowledge of God! How unsearchable are His judgments and unfathomable His ways! For WHO HAS KNOWN THE MIND OF THE LORD, OR WHO BECAME HIS COUNSELOR? Or WHO HAS FIRST GIVEN TO HIM THAT IT MIGHT BE PAID BACK TO HIM AGAIN? For from Him and through Him and to Him are all things. To Him be the glory forever. Amen" (Romans 11:33-36).

O Beloved, may we never be guilty of putting reason above revelation. When we read difficult sayings, may we not walk away or grumble, as some of Jesus' disciples did, but may we bow the knee in humility and submission and say, "Lord, if it pleases You, it pleases me." "We have believed and have come to know that You are the Holy One of God" (John 6:69).

The statement Jesus made in the synagogue in Capernaum was difficult because He brought those in Galilee face-to-face with the same truth He had given the Jews of Judea: His incarnation. Jesus was the Bread of God who had come down from heaven (John 6:33,58). He was sent by God to do God's will (John 6:38). Therefore, if they did not like what He was doing, they were going against God. Jesus did not act independently from the Father. Thus, when Jesus healed on the Sabbath, it was because God the Father wanted to heal on the Sabbath. The Jews were being confronted with God in the flesh, with One who was telling them that heaven was gained by faith, not works. To the Jew, that was a difficult statement.

18 There was more to Jesus' difficult statement than the fact of His incarnation. Jesus also told them, "The bread . . . which I shall give for the life of the world is My flesh" (John 6:51). This statement totally destroyed the illusion that man's works or self-righteousness could ever win eternal life. Whether they believed it or not, they understood His words when He said, "I say to you, unless you eat the flesh of the Son of Man and drink His blood, you have no life in yourselves. He who eats My flesh and drinks My blood has eternal life, and I will raise him up on the last day" (John 6:53,54).

There is only one way to have eternal life, and that is by Jesus abiding in us and we in Him. When Jesus said, "He who eats My flesh and drinks My blood abides in Me, and I in Him" (John 6:56), He was showing them the total identification that alone could bring eternal life. There was no other way to heaven. Being a Jew, being circumcised, and keeping the Law wouldn't do it. They had to be united with Him.

All of these things combined to make a difficult statement. But then Jesus made it even harder to take when He put His finger on what kept the Jews from believing. It is interesting that in the period of controversy in Jesus' ministry (John 5 and 6), He did not "tone down" His doctrine. He couldn't because, as He would say later, "My teaching is not Mine, but His who sent Me" (John 7:16).

What was this controversial teaching? It was that God is the initiator of salvation. Listen to what Jesus says:

> All that the Father gives Me shall come to Me, and the one who comes to Me I will certainly not cast out (John 6:37).
>
> And this is the will of Him who sent Me, that of all that He has given Me I lose nothing, but raise it up on the last day (John 6:39).
>
> No one can come to Me, unless the Father who sent Me draws him; and I will raise him up on the last day (John 6:44).
>
> Everyone who has heard and learned from the Father, comes to Me (John 6:45).
>
> For this reason I have said to you, that no one can come to Me, unless it has been granted him from the Father (John 6:65).

What does this show us, Beloved? I believe it shows us our total impotence to save our own souls, and it shows our Father's total sovereignty over life and death! God is God. We do not necessarily know these truths before we are saved. All we may understand is the inscription on the other side of the coin of salvation: "WHOEVER WILL CALL UPON THE NAME OF THE LORD WILL BE SAVED" (Romans 10:13).

We come to Jesus Christ because we see our sin and His salvation. However, as we get into the Word of God and pore over the Scriptures in childlike faith, we cannot help but see that we came because the Father gave us to the Son. This "difficult saying" prostrates me in wondrous awe and eternal gratitude. How do you feel in light of this incredible truth?

19 The fact that God had mercy on you, the fact that He chose you, ought to bring you great comfort and assurance. According to John 6, you came to Jesus because the Father gave you to Him. You came because it was granted to you by the Father. You came because you were drawn by the Father. You came because you heard and learned from the Father (John 6:37,39,44,45,65).

Because the Father is the Author of your salvation, He also will be the Completer of it. Jesus will not cast out those who are given to Him (John 6:37). He does not lose anyone (John 6:39), but raises them up on the last day (John 6:39,40,44,54). "He who began a good work in you [the work of salvation] will perfect it until the day of Christ Jesus" (Philippians 1:6).

This, Beloved, is your blessed assurance. It is not license to sin, to walk your own way, to deny Jesus and live your own life. Those who are true children of God will manifest the reality of their salvation by their continuance in the faith (Hebrews 3:6,14; 1 John 2:19; Colossians 1:23; 1 Corinthians 15:2). Judas is an example of those who look like believers but aren't.

When some of the disciples walked away because of Jesus' teaching, "Jesus said therefore to the twelve, 'You do not want to go away also, do you?' Simon Peter answered Him, 'Lord, to whom shall we go? You have words of eternal life. And we have believed and have come to know that You are the Holy One of God' " (John 6:67-69).

After Jesus talked about those who were His being given by the Father to the Son and after He explained they would not be cast out but would be raised up on the last day, He also let the twelve know that Judas' actions would not negate these truths. Thus, when Peter, as the spokesman of the group, avowed the fact that they had truly believed in Jesus, "Jesus answered them, 'Did I Myself not choose you, the twelve, and yet one of you is a devil?' Now He meant Judas the son of Simon Iscariot, for he, one of the twelve, was going to betray Him" (John 6:70,71).

It is interesting, isn't it, that right up until they celebrated the last Passover together, just before Jesus' arrest, none of the disciples could tell that Judas was the one ("a devil," Jesus called him)? It wasn't that Judas lost his salvation; it was that he never was saved. The Father never gave Judas to the Son. But at the same time, let me assure you that Judas made his choice. It isn't that he wanted to be saved but couldn't be. Judas had every opportunity that the other apostles had, but he never, so to speak, ate Jesus' flesh and drank His blood. He never had eternal life.

But you may say to me, "It doesn't fit. How could both statements be true? If God didn't give Judas to Jesus, doesn't that leave Judas with no choice?" No, Beloved. Leave it alone. This is a revelation you don't try to reason out. You simply bow the knee and believe what God says. Judas betrayed Jesus. He acted by choice and regretted it, but he never repented.

Thank God today for His mercy. Thank Him that He is giving you opportunities to respond.

20 "Many other signs therefore Jesus also performed in the presence of the disciples, which are not written in this book; but these have been written that you may believe that Jesus is the Christ, the Son of God; and that believing you may have life in His name" (John 20:30,31). Three other Gospels had been written, and yet a fourth was necessary. A Gospel was needed that would show, without a shadow of a doubt, that Jesus was the Christ, the Messiah, the One promised in the Old Testament. A Gospel was needed to focus on the central fact that Jesus is God.

Let us never forget to keep the purpose of the Gospel of John before us, for it is the key to proper understanding and interpretation. The first 11 chapters of John lay before us a selected number of signs performed by Jesus which conclusively prove that Jesus was the Son of God, God in the flesh. The whole thrust of this Gospel is the deity of Jesus Christ. You know that when one refers to the deity of Christ it is another way of saying that Jesus is God. It calls us to understand that He possesses the same character, the same attributes as God the Father, although they are two separate Persons.

The relationship of Jesus Christ to God is that of Sonship. Jesus is the only begotten Son of God. As the Son of God, He holds a unique position. We become sons of God by virtue of the new birth. We are "born not of blood, nor of the will of the flesh, nor of the will of man, but of God" (John 1:13). Jesus was not born; He was not created. He has always existed: "In the beginning was the Word, and the Word was with God, and the Word was God. He was in the beginning with God. . . . And the Word became flesh, and dwelt among us, and we beheld His glory, glory as of the only begotten from the Father, full of grace and truth" (John 1:1,2,14).

Jesus became man, God in the flesh, through the virgin birth. God placed Jesus in the womb of the virgin Mary so that He might take upon Himself flesh and blood. "Since then the children share in flesh and blood, He Himself likewise also partook of the same, that through death He might render powerless him who had the power of death, that is, the devil" (Hebrews 2:14).

Man's sin gave Satan the power of death over man, for sin puts man under the power of Satan (Ephesians 2:1-3). Therefore, when "God so loved the world, that He gave His only begotten Son, that whoever believes in Him should not perish, but have eternal life" (John 3:16), God enabled us to be set free from sin. Therefore, the very minute we believe in the Lord Jesus Christ, God removes us from Satan's power of death by making us His children.

When we believe in the Lord Jesus Christ, we pass "out of death into life" (John 5:24). We are turned from darkness into light, from the power of Satan into the kingdom of God, where we receive forgiveness of sins and an inheritance among those who are sanctified (Acts 26:18).

Thank God today that Jesus is the Son of God! Thank Him that Jesus became the Son of Man to render powerless him who had the power of death, so that you might have life!

21 As you read through the Gospel of John, you see that Jesus constantly demonstrated the life that would belong to those who believe. In John 3, we see that life which comes in His name begins with the new birth (3:3-5). In John 4, we see that it is a life that quenches our thirst, satisfying that unexplained craving within the soul of every person for eternal life (4:10,14). In John 5, we see that it is a life that is to be lived in total dependence upon the Father as shown to us in the relationship of the Son to the Father (5:19,30). In John 6, we see that it is a life of total identity with the Son as we abide in Him and He in us (6:56).

Now as we turn to John 7, we are going to see that it is a life which will be lived on a different timetable, a different dimension than that of the world. This life in a different dimension will put us into conflict with the world. And yet, as Jesus says, "If the world hates you, you know that it has hated Me before it hated you. If you were of the world, the world would love its own; but because you are not of the world, but I chose you out of the world, therefore the world hates you. Remember the word that I said to you, 'A slave is not greater than his master.' If they persecuted Me, they will also persecute you; if they kept My word, they will keep yours also. But all these things they will do to you for My name's sake, because they do not know the One who sent Me" (John 15:18-21).

As John 7 opens, we find Jesus in conflict with His half brothers because they are "of the world." They do not understand that Jesus is not of this world, that He has a different Father. They can't comprehend that He doesn't operate on the same level of worldly reasoning. He lives life on a different timetable, from an eternal perspective.

It was the Feast of Tabernacles, the fall of the year, the month of Tishri when every Jew was to go to Jerusalem to celebrate the feast and live in booths made from branches of trees. "His brothers therefore said to Him, 'Depart from here, and go into Judea, that Your disciples also may behold Your works which You are doing. For no one does anything in secret, when he himself seeks to be known publicly. If You do these things, show Yourself to the world.' For not even His brothers were believing in Him. Jesus therefore said to them, 'My time is not yet at hand, but your time is always opportune. The world cannot hate you; but it hates Me, because I testify of it, that its deeds are evil' " (John 7:3-7).

O Beloved, are there members of your family who do not understand you because, like Jesus' brothers, they have not believed on Him? Is there a conflict because they do not understand your lifestyle? Because they want to tell you how you should spend your time and what you should give yourself to? Jesus understands. Talk to Him about it.

22 We are so conscious of time. To some, time drags. To others, time is fleeting. To the Christian, time is precious. Yet, we are never to live under its pressure. Like our Lord, we are to live on God's timetable, for it is to God that we shall be accountable for how we spend our time.

How I have had to learn this! There are so many demands on my time because of the type of ministry to which the Lord has called me. I have had to learn to say no. Sometimes that is very difficult because I feel people may not understand. Then I go back to Scriptures like John 7 and am comforted and reassured by the life of my Lord.

In the body of Christ, it seems that many have so little time for the Word of God and the work of ministry because they have entangled themselves "in the affairs of everyday life" (2 Timothy 2:4). In Ephesians 5:15,16 we read: "Therefore be careful [literally, look carefully] how you walk, not as unwise men, but as wise, making the most of your time, because the days are evil."

We are to redeem the time, as the King James Version says, to make the most of our time. There are two other principles we need to remember also. *Our times are in His hand.* Psalm 31:13-15 says, "For I have heard the slander of many, terror is on every side; while they took counsel together against me, they schemed to take away my life. But as for me, I trust in Thee, O LORD, I say, 'Thou are my God.' My times are in Thy hand; deliver me from the hand of my enemies, and from those who persecute me."

This is a principle our Lord certainly had to live by, because the Jews were constantly trying to take His life. John 7 opens with this statement: "And after these things Jesus was walking in Galilee; for He was unwilling to walk in Judea, because the Jews were seeking to kill Him." Yet later, we find Jesus going to Judea during the Feast of Tabernacles. Although His life is being threatened, He can go in confidence because He knows that His times are also in God's hand. Thus, we read: "They were seeking therefore to seize Him; and no man laid his hand on Him, because His hour had not yet come" (John 7:30). "His hour had not yet come" is a reference to the time of His crucifixion, a time set by the Father.

The second principle is that *our days are numbered by God.* Psalm 139:16 says, "Thine eyes have seen my unformed substance; and in Thy book they were all written, the days that were ordained for me, when as yet there was not one of them." No need to be ruled by the fear of death or the pressure of man, Beloved. We move on a different timetable—God's.

23 There are two truths I want to share so you can live in such a way so as not to be ashamed when you see your heavenly Father face-to-face.

The first truth, which I mentioned yesterday, is that you are to *daily redeem the time*, to make the most of it. God has numbered your days. Although you do not know your length of days, you are still to live in the light of the fact that they could end at any time. When your days end, there will be no more time to live for God, to walk in the good works He has foreordained for you to walk in (Ephesians 2:10). When you redeem the time, you commit each day to the lordship of Jesus Christ and walk in faith's obedience. Then whenever your days come to an end, you will not be ashamed.

I believe that is how it was with Sallie Irby, one of our Precept coordinators and trainers. Single and 37, Sallie was a dynamic woman of God whose life packed a spiritual wallop, impacting the lives of so many. She had just told her friend and co-laborer, Julie, that she felt God was getting ready to do something special in her life. It *was* special! She got to see her Father God in person. About a week later, Sallie was killed in an accident. Days before her death, Sallie sat with Julie and me in the lobby of our Administration Building, talking of the future of Precept Bible studies in her area. Sallie was redeeming the time!

The second truth you need to remember is that *God is sovereign*. He is in control of all of time, all of history. He "does according to His will in the host of heaven and among the inhabitants of earth; and no one can ward off His hand or say to Him, 'What hast Thou done?' " (Daniel 4:35). Therefore, God is never caught off guard. God does not make snap decisions, nor is He suddenly confronted with a problem He has not foreseen. "For the LORD of hosts has planned, and who can frustrate it?" (Isaiah 14:27). Your sovereign God is in control of all your problems, as well as your solutions. "Besides Me there is no God. . . . I am the LORD, and there is no other, the One forming light and creating darkness, causing well-being and creating calamity; I am the LORD who does all these" (Isaiah 45:5-7).

Sallie's death was under God's sovereignty. God's purpose *will not* be thwarted. Therefore, Beloved, you can move according to His timetable. Be in tune to God. Redeem your days, being careful how you spend your time. Then in His sovereignty, when He calls you home, you like Sallie will be able to say, "I glorified Thee on the earth, having accomplished the work which Thou hast given Me to do" (John 17:4).

24 As you read through the Gospel of John, you are acutely aware that our Lord was in the world but not of it. He was on earth, but He lived life on a higher plane. You see His life, and you long to live like He did. And you know what, Beloved? It is possible, for Jesus lived as God intends us to live, as God has provided for us to live. As the Son of Man, Jesus lived His life in total dependence upon the Father. And, Beloved, you and I can live that way too—by the Spirit.

I would like you to read through John 7 from the perspective of living life in a different dimension. If you are going to live in this other dimension, then there will be no self-promotion. As you read John 7:1-9, you see Jesus' brothers urging Him to promote Himself, to make the most of the world's opportunities. They felt the Feast of Tabernacles would be a good time for Him to work His miracles in Jerusalem. If Jesus wanted to be known publicly, then He needed to show Himself to the world!

If you are going to live in God's dimension and not the world's, you must live on the basis of His teaching, His Word, not your own pet theories, philosophy, psychology, traditions, or prejudiced interpretations. In John 7:14-18, Jesus tells us that His teaching was not His. Rather it was "His who sent Me" (v. 16). "He who speaks from himself seeks his own glory" (v. 18).

How careful we must be in handling the precepts of God, that we do not read or interpret the Word through our prejudices. This is a matter of the will. Jesus says, "If any man is willing to do His will, he shall know of the teaching, whether it is of God, or whether I speak from Myself" (John 7:17). If we are willing to do God's will, then we should have discernment in evaluating what we hear that is supposedly from the Word of God. In his *Word Studies,* Marvin Vincent says, "Sympathy with the will of God is a condition of understanding it."[3] The Pharisees lived on tradition, placing it above the Word. Life in a different dimension is based on everything that proceeds out of the mouth of God (Deuteronomy 8:3).

What place does the Word of God have in your life? How willing are you to do His will as revealed in His Word?

25 Things are not always as they seem. Therefore, if we are going to live in a different dimension, we must not judge according to appearance. In John 7:19-24, we find the Jews bent on killing Jesus. Obviously, their plot was not known by the multitude. However, it is obvious that most of the people were not sympathetic toward our Lord.

Like the Jews, the multitudes were not judging with righteous judgment but according to appearance. They were running on emotion, caught up in the heat of the moment. They were running on a "mob mentality." They were blindly following their leaders without responsibly evaluating the situation. They were going strictly by the way things seemed. They had not stopped to think things through, to seek the wisdom of God

Thus, while Jesus was teaching in the Temple, He exposed the treachery of the Jews' hearts: "Did not Moses give you the Law, and yet none of you carries out the Law? Why do you seek to kill Me?" (John 7:19). The Jews had missed the reality that the Law went deeper than external obedience. This is so well explained in the Sermon on the Mount when Jesus told His disciples, "For I say to you, that unless your righteousness surpasses that of the scribes and Pharisees, you shall not enter the kingdom of heaven" (Matthew 5:20). The scribes and Pharisees had an external righteousness, but that was all. They held to the letter of the Law, but they missed the heart of the Law. Thus, in the Sermon on the Mount, our Lord explains an inward righteousness, which would see its outworking in obedience to the Law of God.

Although the Jews would justify their plot to put Jesus to death by accusing Him of breaking some aspect of the Law which was punishable by death, still what they intentionally planned to do was kill Him. This plan was nothing short of murder!

Have you ever had anger in your heart toward another because you judged according to appearance rather than with righteous judgment?

26 "Do not judge according to appearance, but judge with righteous judgment" (John 7:24) was Jesus' statement to the multitude. He exposed the Jews' plot to kill Him when He said, "Did not Moses give you the Law, and yet none of you carries out the Law? Why do you seek to kill Me?" (John 7:19). Here was the only One who would ever perfectly fulfill the Law, and yet they were accusing Him of breaking the Law because He had healed a man on the Sabbath. Yet the whole time they had murder in their hearts! Then when Jesus exposed their desire to kill Him, "the multitude answered, 'You have a demon! Who seeks to kill You?' " (John 7:20).

Beloved, can you see the blindness of those who judge by appearance and not by righteous judgment, who get hot over an issue and spiel off before they evaluate the situation? Do you suppose there were those in this crowd who would later join the mob shouting, "Not this Man, but Barabbas," when they could have chosen Jesus? Men who would shout, "Crucify Him!" as they became ploys in the Jews' desire to exterminate Jesus? Here He was, God incarnate, and they were accusing Him of having a demon!

Have you ever had anyone judge you unjustly? Has anyone ever accused you of being on the side of Satan when you were standing for God?

I have received letters from people who have judged me because of my clothing or because I wore earrings, a wedding band, a ring, and a necklace. Their questions have made me careful to examine what I wear. But what hurt me was their accusations against my heart, all because they did not approve of my appearance. I constantly seek to be pure before God. They judged me according to appearance.

But do you know the result of such instances in my own life? I have realized that I have been guilty of the same thing toward others. I have been brought up short! I need to give others what I want for myself—judgment that is not according to appearance but according to righteous judgment.

How can we do this? First, never judge according to the letter of the Law. Always look at the heart of the Law. For instance, the Sabbath was for man's benefit. Therefore, if one could circumcise on the Sabbath, why couldn't a man be healed on the Sabbath (John 7:22,23)?

Second, don't accuse; find out the facts. Get the "victim's" side of the story. Third, let him explain his heart. What happened may have been a distortion of what was in his heart. If he says it was, then give him the benefit of the doubt. Fourth, walk in love. Love hopes, believes, and endures all things.

Determine before the Father to judge as you'd like to be judged.

27 Are you a people-pleaser? Because I've always wanted to be liked, I need to be very careful in this area. I have not always won the war! But since God knows my heart, since He knows I want to live in a different dimension, He is always faithful to show me when I have failed.

If we are going to live life on a higher plane, we must not be pleasers of men, but of God. I teach teenagers as well as adults, and this has been a joy to my heart. Each year we have Teen Conferences and an annual Summer Boot Camp for teens at Precept Ministries headquarters. These times are designed to equip the teens as soldiers for the Lord.

I often ask the teens questions to keep me in touch and current with where they are coming from. I ask them to answer anonymously. To the question, "What is the greatest pressure you face?" the number-one answer is "peer pressure." They feel pressured to conform to the crowd!

You can see why a strong family bond is so important. When a child receives security and acceptance at home, he doesn't feel driven to seek it someplace else.

Teens aren't the only ones who have to deal with pressures to conform. Adults are constantly confronted with the pressures of a world that says you have to conform if you are going to make it. This is why our relationship with our heavenly Parent is so important. The stronger the relationship, the greater our resistance to conform to the world, to please men rather than God. And like the teens I mentioned, the more we are sure of the Father's total acceptance, the freer we are from needing acceptance from the world.

As you read John 7, you can see that the crowds were being greatly influenced by the Jews. The fear of men was bringing a snare. In fact, it was keeping some from believing on the only One who could ever satisfy their deepest needs. In John 7:13 we read: "Yet no one was speaking openly of Him for fear of the Jews." What a contrast this is with our Lord who said, "And He who sent Me is with Me; He has not left Me alone, for I always do the things that are pleasing to Him" (John 8:29).

If you are going to live in a different dimension, you should constantly ask yourself, "Am I now seeking the favor of men, or of God? Or am I striving to please men? If I were still trying to please men, I would not be a bond-servant of Christ" (Galatians 1:10).

28 The key to living life in a different dimension is life in the Spirit. Jesus knew He was teaching a mixed multitude, people who were following Him for all sorts of reasons. As they sought Him at the feast, they asked, " 'Where is He?' And there was much grumbling among the multitudes concerning Him; some were saying, 'He is a good man'; others were saying, 'No, on the contrary, He leads the multitude astray' " (John 7:11,12).

Yet among them were those who had a genuine thirst for life on a different dimension. So, "On the last day, the great day of the feast, Jesus stood and cried out, saying, 'If any man is thirsty, let him come to Me and drink. He who believes in Me, as the Scripture said, "From his innermost being shall flow rivers of living water." ' But this He spoke of the Spirit, whom those who believed in Him were to receive; for the Spirit was not yet given, because Jesus was not yet glorified" (John 7:37-39).

What a proclamation that was! The Spirit of God indwelling any who thirsted? Under the Old Covenant, the Spirit of God came intermittently upon priests, prophets, and kings. Here was the New Covenant promise of the Spirit being given to anyone who thirsted, who believed in Jesus. And it would be such an indwelling that rivers of living water would flow from a person's innermost being continuously!

From the days of Moses and Leviticus, the Jews had added a great deal of ceremony to the Feast of Booths. Every day except the last day, the priests would go to the pool of Siloam and fill their pitchers with water. Then they would return to the Temple area and with the blast of trumpets would march seven times around the altar and then pour water from the pitchers, while they sang Isaiah 12:3: "Therefore with joy shall ye draw water out of the wells of salvation" (KJV). They would sing the Hallel, Psalms 113 through 118, ending with: "The stone which the builders rejected has become the chief corner stone. This is the LORD'S doing; it is marvelous in our eyes. This is the day which the LORD has made; let us rejoice and be glad in it. O LORD, do save, we beseech Thee; O LORD, we beseech Thee, do send prosperity! Blessed is the one who comes in the name of the LORD; we have blessed you from the house of the LORD. The

LORD is God, and He has given us light; bind the festival sacrifice with cords to the horns of the altar. Thou art my God, and I give thanks to Thee; Thou art my God, I extol Thee. Give thanks to the LORD, for He is good; for His lovingkindness is everlasting" (Psalm 118:22-29).

The One about whom they sang was in their presence! He was the stone the builders would reject. But to others, He became the foundation stone for life in a different dimension, life in the Spirit.

29 You can't live in a different dimension—above the pull of the flesh, the pressures of people, the philosophies of the world—unless you live and walk by the indwelling Spirit of God. Life in this dimension is one of continuous dependence, continuous abiding. To put it in the words of John 7, this life is a continual coming and drinking. In John 7:37 Jesus says, "If any man is thirsty, let him come to Me and drink." The literal meaning of the words is, "Let him keep coming to Me, and let him keep drinking."

O what a Hallel they sang when Jesus stood and cried out this promise on that last day of the Feast! Day by day they had poured out water from their golden pitchers on the altar, and now the Water of Life was among them. It was from God's altar, the cross, that the indwelling of the Spirit would be made possible. For not until Christ was glorified in His death, burial, resurrection, and ascension could the blessed Holy Spirit come to indwell man and be the pledge of our inheritance of eternal life (Ephesians 1:14).

The priests had sung, "Blessed is the one who comes in the name of the LORD" (Psalm 118:26), and there He was! But were they blessing Him? No! For the most part, the religious leaders were seeking to get rid of Him.

They recited, "Bind the festival sacrifice with cords to the horns of the altar." But they missed the fact that the Lamb of God who would take away the sin of the world was standing in their midst.

During the Feast of Tabernacles, the Jews would light four huge candelabra called *menorahs*. Jesus, the Light of the World, stood before them as they sang, "The LORD is God, and He has given us light" (Psalm 118:27). Remember how John opens his Gospel? "In Him was life, and the life was the light of men. And the light shines in the darkness; and the darkness did not comprehend it. . . . There was the true light which, coming into the world, enlightens every man" (1:4,5,9).

Again and again Jesus referred to Himself as "the light of the world," and promised that those who follow Him will not walk in darkness (John 8:12). Again, Beloved, you have it—life on a different timetable because it is life in the Spirit.

O Beloved, have you drunk of the Fountain of living waters? If you have, the Spirit within has witnessed with your spirit that you are a child of God. Then, "Walk by the Spirit, and you will not carry out the desire of the flesh" (Galatians 5:16). You will live life on the highest plane.

March

And What If You Don't Believe Jesus Is God?

1 To be born in sin is something we cannot help, for "in sin my mother conceived me" (Psalm 51:5). We are all sinners at birth, bearing the consequence of Adam and Eve's sin in the Garden of Eden, for "through one man sin entered into the world, and death through sin" (Romans 5:12).

However, no human being has to die in his sin. Remember, the Gospel of John was written that "you may believe that Jesus is the Christ, the Son of God; and that believing you may have life in His name" (John 20:31). Believing that Jesus is God causes us to pass from death to life, from the kingdom of Satan to the kingdom of heaven.

What does it truly mean to "believe that Jesus is the Christ, the Son of God"? It means believing that Jesus Christ is God in the flesh, one with the Father in nature. Or to put it another way, it is to believe in the deity of Jesus Christ.

When we speak of the deity of Jesus, we mean Jesus is God. According to the Word of God, if you do not believe in the deity of Jesus Christ, you will "die in your sins" (John 8:24).

To "die in your sins" means that you will spend eternity in the lake of fire where the worm dies not and the fire is not quenched (Mark 9:43-48). To "die in your sins" is to miss heaven! To miss life!

For the next several days, I want us to look at the deity of Jesus Christ. Because this doctrine distinguishes true Christianity from the cults, it is crucial that we understand it. I want you to be able to "contend earnestly for the faith which was once for all delivered to the saints" (Jude 3). Therefore, let me give you an outline which we will follow. Day by day, we will cover these points: Jesus Christ is God because: 1) He is eternal; 2) He is the Word, explaining the Father—a) as the radiance of His glory, b) as the exact representation of His nature, c) as the "I AM," d) as being one with the Father, e) as possessor of the sovereign rights of God; 3) He is Creator; 4) in Him is life; and 5) He is Lord.

Study well and mark your Bible. Ask God the Father to reveal truth upon truth to you as we turn to behold the deity of the Lord Jesus Christ.

2 *Jesus Christ is God because He is eternal.* He has always been; He will always be. In the very first words of his Gospel, John sets out to establish unequivocally that Jesus is the promised Messiah, the Son of God. John accomplishes this by showing that Jesus, like the Father, is eternal: "In the beginning was the Word, and the Word was with God, and the Word was God. He was in the beginning with God" (John 1:1,2). Then so there is no doubt as to who "the Word" is, John says further, "And the Word became flesh, and dwelt among us, and we beheld His glory, glory as of the only begotten from the Father, full of grace and truth" (1:14).

When John tells us under the inspiration of the Holy Spirit that the Word is "the only begotten from the Father," it does not mean that Jesus was created by God or had a beginning in time. No, Beloved, when it says that Jesus is "the only begotten from the Father," it is referring to His incarnation when mankind would behold His glory as of the *only* begotten *from* the Father. We must never forget that there is only one Man in all of time who was uniquely God and Man—the Lord Jesus Christ.

It is vital that you understand this truth, Beloved, for there are some who teach that we are God. Yes, God *indwells* the person who believes on the Lord Jesus Christ, but that person will never *become* God. That is heresy!

O Beloved, beware of anyone who teaches this damnable doctrine, for it is straight from the devil who wanted to be as God and who persuaded Eve that she could be as God through disobedience to the clear command of God. How I pray that God will use this devotional study to establish you in His Word, so you won't be carried about by every wind of doctrine and cunning craftiness of men by which they lie in wait to deceive you (Ephesians 4:13,14).

Remember that Jesus alone is God. He is the Eternal One. Micah 5:2 prophesied His birth and, at the same time, showed us His eternity: "But as for you, Bethlehem Ephrathah, too little to be among the clans of Judah, from you One will go forth for Me to be ruler in Israel. His goings forth are from long ago, from the days of eternity." Jesus has always been and will always be uniquely the Son of God who became the Son of Man.

3 *Jesus Christ is God because He is the Word, and as the Lord, He explains the Father.* Many have said to me that they can relate to Jesus Christ, but they have a hard time relating to God the Father. This is either because they have a distorted image of a father, or because they cannot understand the actions of God in the Old Testament. Usually, it is because of earthly fathers who were distant, harsh, uncaring, absent, unreasonably demanding, cruel, or perverted. Therefore, it is easy to understand why they have a hard time in developing an intimate relationship with God.

However, Jesus came to remove that distance. "No man has seen God at any time; the only begotten God, who is in the bosom of the Father, He has explained Him" (John

1:18). Your image of God the Father may have been distorted by an earthly father. However, this distortion can be corrected if you will get to know Jesus Christ. You must believe and embrace the truth of the Word of God above your feelings.

Jesus has explained your heavenly Father. As you embrace truth and walk in it, and as you continue to spend time in the Word, you will come to know the true character of your heavenly Father, and will become more secure and comfortable in His unconditional love. Jesus is the Word become flesh, so that you might know God, and that God might become your Father through His Son. And who is the Son? He is God.

Let's go back to John 1:18 for a moment. Remember our subject is the deity of Jesus Christ, understanding and embracing the truth of it so that you do not die in your sins. In John 1:18, we see Jesus as "the only begotten God, who is in the bosom of the Father." Once again, John uses the phrase, "the only begotten" as he did in John 1:14. Remember, *begotten* does not refer to the creation of Jesus, for He has always been. Jesus is eternal. He has no beginning; He has no end. He has always existed; He will always exist. He is God—one with the Father and yet separate as a Person.

If you ever say the Nicene Creed, you remember the phrase referring to Jesus which says "begotten, not made." The fathers of the faith wanted to make sure that Christians understand that Jesus is not a created being. Rather He is God, equal with the Father in His eternal existence.

He was begotten as the Son of Man: "Since . . . the children share in flesh and blood, He Himself likewise also partook of the same, that through death He might render powerless him who had the power of death, that is, the devil" (Hebrews 2:14). Therefore, it was planned in the eternal counsels of God that "by the grace of God He might taste death for everyone" (Hebrews 2:9).

Who was it who hung upon Calvary's cross? It was the only begotten God, God the Son, explaining the unconditional love of God the Father.

4 Jesus can explain the Father to us because He has always been with God. *He can also explain the Father to us because He is the radiance of His glory.*

The basis, or should I say the "seedbed" of doctrinal truth regarding the deity of Jesus Christ as taught in the Gospel of John, is found in the first verses of his Gospel: "In the beginning was the Word, and the Word was with God, and the Word was God. He was in the beginning with God. All things came into being by Him, and apart from Him nothing came into being that has come into being. In Him was life, and the life was the light of men" (1:1-4).

Before you go any further, Beloved, I want you to stop and list in your notebook everything that you learn about the Word from John 1:1-4. John tells us, without a shadow of doubt, that the Word is Jesus who became flesh and dwelt among us, showing us His glory, the glory of the Father.

Hebrews 1 is another key chapter of the Bible that stresses the deity of Jesus Christ. As we look at the first three verses of this chapter, you will understand why I have *"the radiance of His glory"* in our outline for this month. "God . . . in these last days has spoken to us in His Son. . . . And He is the radiance of His glory" (Hebrews 1:1-3).

The Greek word for *glory* is *doxa,* which comes from *dokeō,* meaning "to seem." Therefore, *glory* refers to the nature and the acts of God in His self-manifestation. To glorify someone means to give a high estimate of who they are to others. If you see Jesus, you see the Father, for Jesus is the radiance of His glory. Ponder this truth today in your heart.

5 Have you beheld the glory of Jesus, Beloved? Have you seen that He truly is the radiance of God's glory? Throughout the Gospel of John, you will find the words *glory* and *glorify* used repeatedly, for John's purpose in writing is that you might believe that Jesus is the Christ, the Son of God, and one with the Father. To see Jesus is to see the Father, for Jesus is the radiant light of God's glory. Hallelujah!

Don't miss the awesome statement John makes in 12:41. Having quoted Isaiah 53:1 and Isaiah 6:10, John says, "These things Isaiah said, because he saw His glory, and he spoke of Him." The words *His glory* and *Him* are references to Jesus Christ. Note in the following verses how the pronouns refer back to Jesus: "These things Jesus spoke, and He departed and hid Himself from them. But though He had performed so many signs before them, yet they were not believing in Him; that the word of Isaiah the prophet might be fulfilled, which he spoke, 'LORD, WHO HAS BELIEVED OUR REPORT? AND TO WHOM HAS THE ARM OF THE LORD BEEN REVEALED?' For this cause they could not believe, for Isaiah said again, 'HE HAS BLINDED THEIR EYES, AND HE HARDENED THEIR HEART; LEST THEY SEE WITH THEIR EYES, AND PERCEIVE WITH THEIR HEART, AND BE CONVERTED, AND I HEAL THEM.' These things Isaiah said, because he saw His glory, and he spoke of Him" (John 12:36-41).

Isaiah 6 and 53 are prophecies of Jesus in His preincarnate state. Isaiah shows us the deity of Jesus Christ as the radiance of God's glory. No other Old Testament prophet gives us a greater description of our Lord Jesus Christ.

In Isaiah 6:1-3, he tells us of seeing the Lord on His throne, "lofty and exalted," with the seraphim calling out, "Holy, Holy, Holy, is the LORD of hosts, the whole earth is full of His glory." Then we read of Isaiah's conviction of his sin and the purging of that sin so that his iniquity is taken away and his sin is forgiven. After this, Isaiah writes, "Then I heard the voice of the Lord, saying, 'Whom shall I send, and who will go for Us?' " (6:8).

Whoa! Did you note "Who will go for *Us?*" The "Us" implies more than one. The "Us," beloved reader, shows that more than God the Father is there. The Son is there and we are seeing His glory, for He is one with the Father—one in nature, one in attributes, one in glory.

6 The glory emanating from the Son is the radiant light of God's glory. To see Jesus is to see the Father, for They

are one in nature. As John 1:1 says, "The Word was with God." From the very beginning, Jesus was completely identified with the Father. Throughout his Gospel, John confirms this truth, for he knows that if we do not believe that Jesus is God, we will surely perish.

In Jesus' high priestly prayer, He makes this statement: "And now, glorify Thou Me together with Thyself, Father, with the glory which I had with Thee before the world was" (John 17:5). Glory belongs to God alone. "I am the LORD, that is My name; I will not give My glory to another" (Isaiah 42:8). God will not share His glory with man.

Jesus is the One of whom Isaiah wrote: "For a child will be born to us, a son will be given to us; and the government will rest on His shoulders; and His name will be called Wonderful Counselor, Mighty God, Eternal Father, Prince of Peace" (9:6). Jesus was born as a child, but given as a son! Because Jesus has always been the Son of God, when He came to earth as God's Son, He was given to us. However, He was born as the incarnate Son of Man.

Jesus became a man, taking on, as Philippians 2:7 says, "the likeness of men." In all the Word of God, there is no greater passage on the incarnation than Philippians 2. Yet in the same passage, we once again have confirmed to us the deity of Jesus Christ: "Have this attitude in yourselves which was also in Christ Jesus, who, although He existed in the form of God, did not regard equality with God a thing to be grasped, but emptied Himself, taking the form of a bond-servant, and being made in the likeness of men. And being found in appearance as a man, He humbled Himself by becoming obedient to the point of death, even death on a cross" (Philippians 2:5-8).

Jesus became the Son of Man, and for the rest of eternity He will bear man's likeness, having regained for man what was lost by Adam. Because the Son of God was born a man, because He paid sin's penalty as a man, because He was raised from the dead as a man, you and I who believe these truths so as to submit to Him as God will sit with Him, ruling and reigning forever (Revelation 1:6; 2:26,27; 5:9,10).

7 O Beloved, where do you run when you are confused? Where do you run when you are without strength? Where do you run when you still need the arms and security of a father? Where do you run when turmoil rages within or without?

You can run to Jesus! His name is "Wonderful Counselor." He will instruct you in the way you should go (Psalm 32:8). His name is "Mighty God." You can exchange your strength for His. His name is "Eternal Father." He has loved you with an everlasting love (Jeremiah 31:3). He has engraved you on the palms of His hands (Isaiah 49:16). He will never leave you nor forsake you (Hebrews 13:5). As a father pities his children, so He pities you (Psalm 103:13). He is "Prince of Peace," so "let not your heart be troubled" (John 14:1). In the world, you shall have tribulation. But take courage, Jesus has overcome the world (John 16:33). And this is the victory that has overcome the world—your faith (1 John 5:4).

"Cursed is the man who trusts in mankind and makes flesh his strength, and whose heart turns away from the LORD." But, "Blessed is the man who trusts in the LORD and whose trust is the LORD" (Jeremiah 17:5,7). You can run to Him because He is God.

Not only is Jesus the radiance of God's glory, but *He is also the Word, explaining the Father as the exact representation of God's nature* (Hebrews 1:3). When we speak of the nature of God, we are referring to the very essence of God, those attributes which make God uniquely God. The word *representation* in Hebrews 1:3 is from the Greek *charaktēr*. A *charaktēr* was the impress made by a die or seal. It gave the idea of exact correspondence to the object whose image it bore.

When I was in my early teens, it became the fad to use sealing wax on our letters. We would buy a stick of wax in our favorite color and then melt it over the flap of the envelope. Then while the wax was still warm and soft, we would make an impression of the letters of our name or of a signet ring. This left the impress of our "symbol."

You may think that the phrases "radiance of His glory" and "exact representation of His nature" mean the same thing. However, there is a difference that is beautiful in its contrast. In the phrase "radiance of His glory," we see Jesus' total identity with the Father. In the phrase "exact representation of His nature," we see that Jesus and the Father are two distinct Beings possessing the same character, the same attributes.

Jesus is all that God is. He does not just have what God has. There is a difference!

8 Jesus does not merely possess some of what God has. He *is* all that God is! He is equal with the Father, possessing every attribute of God. He is not merely One in whom the Father dwells, in the way that He indwells every born-again child of God through the Holy Spirit. Jesus is the very essence of God—"the exact representation of His nature" (Hebrews 1:3). The same truth is seen in the Gospel of John in the statement that "the Word was with God" (1:1).

In the phrase "the Word *was* God," we see a parallel to the phrase "He is the radiance of His glory" from Hebrews 1:3. In the phrase "the Word was *with* God," we see the parallel in Hebrews 1:3 to "the exact representation of His nature." The latter shows Jesus as a distinct Person apart from the Father and yet possessing the same nature as God.

In John 14:6, Jesus has just told the 11 apostles that He is the way to the Father when Philip says, "Lord, show us the Father, and it is enough for us." To which Jesus replies, "Have I been so long with you, and yet you have not come to know Me, Philip? He who has seen Me has seen the Father; how do you say, 'Show us the Father'? Do you not believe that I am in the Father, and the Father is in Me?" (14:8-10).

To see Jesus was to see God because Jesus is the exact representation of His nature. Paul brings this out so powerfully in Colossians 1:15-17 when, speaking of Jesus, he writes: "And He is the image of the invisible God, the first-born of all creation. For by Him all things were created, both in the heavens and on earth, visible and invisible, whether thrones or dominions or rulers or authorities—all things have been created by Him and for Him. And He is before all things, and in Him all things hold together."

Some who do not believe in the deity and incarnation of Jesus Christ—such as the Mormons, Jehovah's Witnesses, or those involved in Christian Science or the Way International—like to point you to Colossians 1:15: "the first-born of all creation." They use this phrase to say that Jesus was created by God, that He is not eternal but had a beginning.

However, to make it say this goes against the context of this passage and also against the context of all of Scripture, for as we have seen, Jesus is eternal. "First-born of all creation" refers to priority of position. Paul's point in this passage is to show that Jesus rightfully has "first place" or preeminence "in everything" because He is God (Colossians 1:18). All was created through Him and for Him—even you, Beloved!

9 He is also head of the body, the church; and He is the beginning, the first-born from the dead; so that He Himself might come to have first place in everything. For it was the Father's good pleasure for all the fulness to dwell in Him, and through Him to reconcile all things to Himself (Colossians 1:18-20).

There was no one born of Adam's race who could reconcile man to God, because everyone bears the image of Adam, and is a partaker of Adam's sin. "For all have sinned and fall short of the glory of God" (Romans 3:23).

As God said, "Let *Us* make man in *Our* image, according to *Our* likeness" (Genesis 1:26). But that image was destroyed when Adam and Eve chose to believe the devil, that serpent of old, rather than God. With a bite of the forbidden fruit, man was separated from God. Intimacy was exchanged for enmity because man wanted to be as God. And "through one man sin entered into the world" (Romans 5:12), leaving mankind without hope apart from the mercy and grace of God. But "God so loved the world, that He gave His only begotten Son" (John 3:16).

There it is, God's remedy for sin! A whole new race in which we can see the image of God! And how did this "race" come into being? Jesus was begotten of the Father in order to take upon Himself flesh and blood so that He could pay the wages of man's sin, which was death (Romans 6:23).

God gave a prophetic promise in Isaiah 7:14: "The Lord Himself will give you a sign: Behold, a virgin will be with child and bear a son, and she will call His name Immanuel." A virgin was to conceive? But that is impossible! It takes a sperm and an egg to make a child. Yes, Beloved, it does!

When the angel of the Lord told Mary she was going to "conceive in [her] womb, and bear a son" who "will be great, and will be called the Son of the Most High," she asked, "How can this be, since I am a virgin?" (Luke 1:31,32,34). The angel had the answer: "The Holy Spirit will come upon you, and the power of the Most High will overshadow you; and for that reason the holy offspring shall be called the Son of God. . . . For nothing will be impossible with God" (Luke 1:35,37).

There it was—a promise of God, a provision of another Adam, the last Adam, who would become "a life-giving spirit" (1 Corinthians 15:45). The first Adam brought death, but the last Adam provided life. And who was this last Adam? He was " 'Immanuel,' which translated means, 'GOD WITH US' " (Matthew 1:23). He was "the only begotten from the Father, full of grace and truth" (John 1:14). He was the exact representation of God's nature, the Son of God and Man who would pay for our sins and reconcile us to God. O worship Him!

10 *Jesus is God because He is the Word, explaining the Father as the I AM.* I want to make sure you have a very clear understanding of the great significance of this point over the next several days.

Dr. Walter Martin, author of the outstanding book *The Kingdom of the Cults*, used John 8:24 time and time again to bring Jehovah's Witnesses to the realization of the deity of our Lord Jesus Christ. I cannot recommend this book enough for Christians who are serious about sharing their faith.

I want us to look at John 8:24 and other related passages that will help us understand the full implication of this statement from the mouth of our Lord: "I said therefore to you, that you shall die in your sins; for unless you believe that I am *He;* you shall die in your sins." You will notice that "He" is in italics because it was added by the translators. The text actually reads, "If you do not believe that I am, you shall die in your sins." The "I am" in this verse is called the *egō eimi* because those are the Greek words which were translated "I am."

Let's look at the two other uses of the *egō eimi* in this chapter. The first is in John 8:28: "When you lift up the Son of Man, then you will know that I am *He,* and I do nothing on My own initiative, but I speak these things as the Father taught Me." The second is in John 8:58: "Jesus said to them, 'Truly, truly, I say to you, before Abraham was born, I am.' " After this last statement, the Jews "picked up stones to throw at Him; but Jesus hid Himself, and went out of the temple" (John 8:59). Why did the Jews want to stone Him? Understand that and you will see the significance of Jesus' claim of being I AM.

11 When Moses met God at the burning bush and received his commission to be God's spokesman before Pharaoh, he asked God a question: " 'Behold, I am going to the sons of Israel, and I shall say to them, "The God of your fathers has sent me to you." Now they may say to me, "What is His name?" What shall I say to them?' And God said to Moses, 'I AM WHO I AM'; and He said, 'Thus you shall say to the sons of Israel, "I AM has sent me to you." '

And God, furthermore, said to Moses, 'Thus you shall say to the sons of Israel, "The LORD, the God of your fathers, the God of Abraham, the God of Isaac, and the God of Jacob, has sent me to you." This is My name forever, and this is My memorial-name to all generations' " (Exodus 3:13-15).

The Jews wanted to stone Jesus when He said, "Before Abraham was born, I am" (John 8:58). They understood clearly that Jesus was claiming to be God. They knew that I AM was the memorial-name of God to all generations, and they believed Jesus was blaspheming the name of God. They did not believe He was God.

On another occasion, when Jesus said, "I and the Father are one," the Jews again wanted to stone Him. Jesus answered, "I showed you many good works from the Father; for which of them are you stoning Me?" The Jews answered Him, "For a good work we do not stone You, but for blasphemy; and because You, being a man, make Yourself out to be God" (John 10:30-33).

Because the Jews were blind to the fact that Jesus truly was God, that He was equal with the Father and the exact representation of the Father, they viewed His claim to be I AM as blasphemy. Their beliefs gave them every right to stone Him. They knew the Law said, "Moreover, the one who blasphemes the name of the LORD shall surely be put to death; all the congregation shall certainly stone him. The alien as well as the native, when he blasphemes the Name, shall be put to death" (Leviticus 24:16).

Jesus had laid hold of "the Name." That they understood without doubt. O Beloved, the question is, "Do you know that Jesus claimed to be God?" Jehovah's Witnesses claim that in John 10:33 the Jews were not saying that Jesus was making Himself out to be God but *a* god. Don't believe that diluted reasoning! The Jews wouldn't have tried to stone a man for that. They understood that Jesus was taking for Himself the memorial-name of God—I AM. But because they refused to believe in the deity of Jesus Christ, they would die in their sins. They would never know life.

What about you, Beloved? Will you die in your sins, or do you believe that Jesus is I AM, God Himself?

12 Of all the names of God, none is reverenced more than "Jehovah." This name is a substitute for *Yahweh,* the proper name for God. *Yahweh,* or the Tetragrammaton *YHWH,* has been referred to as the great and terrible name of God. Because of Exodus 20:7 which says, "You shall not take the name of the LORD your God in vain, for the LORD will not leave him unpunished who takes His name in vain," and because of Leviticus 24:16 which pronounced the death sentence on anyone who blasphemed the name of the LORD, the Jews were even afraid to pronounce or use the name *Yahweh.* Therefore, they substituted *Jehovah* for *Yahweh* or *YHWH.*

As you read through the Old Testament, you will find LORD all in capital letters in most versions. This translation represents some 6400 occurrences of *YHWH.* Where *YHWH* is linked with *Adon* or *Adhōnāy, YHWH* will be translated "God." There are about 315 of these combinations which are usually translated "Lord GOD."[1] You can see an example of this usage in Genesis 15:2. *Adon* or *Adhōnāy* is the name of God meaning "Lord" and is written with lowercase letters except for the *L.*

Now, Beloved, I have shared all this for a purpose. First, I want you to learn more and more about our Father's infallible Word. But I also want these insights to impact the way you live. Knowledge is not to be gained just for the sake of knowledge, but for the sake of holiness. Once you really understand what God is revealing through His name—I AM or Jehovah—you should be liberated from any fear that you will ever find yourself in a situation where you feel you cannot cope. That's enough to keep one reading, isn't it?

Now then, let me review what I have just said before I give you more encouraging news, truths that will bless you immensely. So, as I tell my Precept students, "Hangeth thou in there."

1. *YHWH* or *Yahweh* is translated "LORD" in the Old Testament and written in uppercase letters, although the *L* is larger. However, when this word is combined with *Adon* or *Adhōnāy*, it will be translated "Lord GOD."

2. From about the twelfth century on, the Jews referred to *YHWH* as *Jehovah*. They used the word *Jehovah* instead of *Yahweh* because they felt it too holy to pronounce. Or they were afraid that they might in some way use this name in vain and thus blaspheme the name of the LORD.[2]

Tomorrow we will see the relationship of *Jehovah (YHWH)* to God's memorial-name—I AM.

13 God's memorial-name, I AM, is closely related to God's personal name, *YHWH*. In Exodus 3:14, "AM" is the Hebrew[3] word *havah*, which means "to be." *Jah*, one of the names of God, is the present tense of the verb "to be." Therefore, it corresponds to "I AM." *Jehovah* then would correspond to "I AM WHO I AM," which is how God responded to Moses when he asked God's name (Exodus 3:14).[4]

When God says that His name is "I AM," He is showing Himself as Jehovah, the Self-existent One. For us He is, "I AM, I am everything you will ever need." To which we ought to say, "Hallelujah," which means "Praise be to *Jah* [God]." The name I AM, *Jehovah*, reveals God as the One who is able to supply all your needs through Christ Jesus your Lord. As the Self-existent One, He can never be confronted by a claim He cannot meet—as long, of course, as it is according to His will and not in violation of His character. This, Beloved, is why David could write: "The LORD is my shepherd, I shall not want" (Psalm 23:1).

Now then, reason with me for a moment. We have also seen that Jesus is I AM, the *egō eimi*. *Eimi* in the Greek means "to be, to exist, or to have existence or being." Therefore, Jesus is the Self-existent One. And if that is true, then life can be found only in Him.

Think back with me for a moment to John 1:4, where, referring to Jesus as the Word, John states, "In Him was life." Jesus has always been. He is eternal. He was in the beginning with God. He is God. Therefore, since Jesus is God, since He is the Self-existent One, life cannot be any place else but in Him. Now then, you can better understand Jesus' statement in John 8:24: "I said therefore to you, that you shall die in your sins; for unless you believe that I am *He,* you shall die in your sins."

We are born sinners, Beloved, and "the wages of sin is death" (Romans 6:23). "And you were dead in your trespasses and sins. . . . But God, being rich in mercy, because of His great love with which He loved us, even when we were dead in our transgressions, made us alive together with Christ (by grace you have been saved)" (Ephesians 2:1,4,5).

Thus, we see that the only way we can have life is to believe that Jesus is the Christ, the Son of God, the I AM. And when in faith—apart from any works on our part—we believe in the Lord Jesus Christ, then the wonderful mystery of the gospel takes place, "which is Christ in you, the hope of glory" (Colossians 1:27). "And the witness is this, that God has given us eternal life, and this life is in His Son. He who has the Son has the life; he who does not have the Son of God does not have the life" (1 John 5:11,12).

O praise be to Jehovah who has given us everything we need in Christ Jesus. May you run to Him—your I AM—for your every need, asking in His name.

14 Often when all is calm and peaceful, the wind of adversity can begin to blow, and we find ourselves caught in a raging storm. Fear strikes our hearts. O Beloved, when times like this are upon you, may you hear Jesus say, "It is I; do not be afraid" (John 6:20).

If you were to read John 6:20 in the Greek, you would find the *egō eimi* again in this passage. A literal translation would read: "I AM; do not be afraid." In the light of what we have seen these past two days, you can appreciate this passage even more, and understand why they didn't have to be afraid. Jesus, the Self-existent One, was there with them. In the sudden storm that caught them in the midst of the sea, Jesus was there. He was adequate for every need that would arise. Oh, how our Lord longed to have His disciples learn this truth! Oh, how He longs to have us absorb this reality! It will not remove us from the storms, but it will enable us to weather them in a great peace that passes all understanding. This same story is recorded in Mark 6:47-52: "And when it was evening, the boat was in the midst of the sea, and He was alone on the land. And seeing them straining at the oars, for the wind was against them, at about the fourth watch of the night, He came to them, walking on the sea. . . . They supposed that it was a ghost, and cried out; for they all saw Him and were frightened. But immediately He spoke with them and said to them, 'Take courage; it is I [I AM—*egō eimi*], do not be afraid.' And He got into the boat with them, and the wind stopped; and they were greatly astonished, for they had not gained any insight from the incident of the loaves, but their heart was hardened."

What was the insight they should have gained from the loaves of bread and the fish that Jesus had just multiplied in order to feed the multitude? They should have recognized that Jesus was the Christ, the Son of God, that He was the all-sufficient, self-existent God. They should have noted that He was the One who could—and would—meet all their needs.

Yet what happened? In the midst of the storm, they forgot what they had seen their God do in a previous situation. O Beloved, have you ever gone through a trial experiencing His all-sufficient grace, only to hit the next storm and totally forget how you made it through the first storm with Jesus "in your boat"? Always remember, dear friend, who is in the boat with you!

15 Trials do not come into your life by happenstance, Beloved. Your Sovereign Father, who has you in His hands, filters trials first through His fingers of love. No storm could arise if you were not able to weather it. Can you hear what I am saying, or is your mind closed? Have you become insensitive to who God is and what your Lord Jesus has wrought for you?

After the feeding of the 5000, the disciples set out to cross the Sea of Galilee, "and the sea began to be stirred up because a strong wind was blowing" (John 6:18). They "had not gained any insight from the incident of the loaves, but their heart was hardened" (Mark 6:52) or "their mind was closed."[5]

In Mark 8, we find the disciples once again in a boat on the Sea of Galilee. This time, however, the trial takes a different form. Now they have no bread. They forgot it. Yet look who is in the boat with them! Jesus—the One who is the Bread of Life, who fed a multitude, who calmed a storm, and who said, "I AM; be not afraid." The Scripture continues: "And they had forgotten to take bread; and did not have more than one loaf in the boat with them. And He was giving orders to them, saying, 'Watch out! Beware of the leaven of the Pharisees and the leaven of Herod.' And they began to discuss with one another the fact that they had no bread" (8:14-16).

Can you imagine, Beloved? Here is their Lord trying to teach them valuable truths, and they are missing it because they are occupied with the need of the moment. Have you ever missed what God was trying to teach you because you were so occupied with the need rather than with the One who supplies all your needs? "And Jesus aware of this, said to them, 'Why do you discuss the fact that you have no bread? Do you not yet see or understand? Do you have a hardened heart? HAVING EYES, DO YOU NOT SEE? AND HAVING EARS, DO YOU NOT HEAR? And do you not remember, when I broke the five loaves for the five thousand, how many baskets full of broken pieces you picked up?' They said to Him, 'Twelve.' 'And when I broke the seven for the four thousand, how many large baskets full of broken pieces did you pick up?' And they said to Him, 'Seven.' And He was saying to them, 'Do you not yet understand?' " (8:17-21).

What did our Lord want them to understand? He wanted them to remember He was everything they would ever need—and much more. There was no situation of life or circumstance that would arise but what He, Jehovah, was there—in the boat with them. He was able not only to meet their needs abundantly but also to calm the storm and bring them safely to shore.

O give glory to I AM—"to Him who is able to do exceeding abundantly beyond all that we ask or think" (Ephesians 3:20). And in your next storm, don't forget who He is!

16 Not only do we know that Jesus is God because He is eternal and because He, as the Word, explained the Father as the radiance of His glory, as the exact representation of His nature, and as the "I AM." We also know that Jesus is God because He is one with the Father. This truth brings us to the next point of our outline: He is the Word, explaining the Father, as being one with the Father.

When Jesus said, "I and the Father are one" (John 10:30), He used the neuter form of *one—hen* in the Greek, meaning "one in essence." Had Jesus used the root word *heis* instead of *hen,* He would have been referring to Himself and the Father as numerically one, or one person. "Sabellius, a second-century heretic and the forerunner of the Unitarians, taught that Jesus was only a radiation, a manifestation of God."[6] Yet John's use of *hen* clearly dispels this.

Jesus was showing us that while He and the Father were two separate personalities, they were one in essence—in their nature, in their attributes. And the Jews understood exactly what Jesus was saying. There was no question on their part that He was proclaiming Himself as God. They felt Jesus was guilty of blasphemy and they wanted to stone Him.

O Beloved, I cannot tell you how vital it is that you know these things. Study well. Make notes of these points in your Bible. Then when you encounter someone who does not believe in the deity of Jesus Christ and who is trying to persuade you to join his or her sect, you can be used by God to show this person the truth. You may become God's instrument to turn someone from darkness to light, from the power of Satan to the kingdom of God! Have you ever had the joy of being used of God in this way? O Beloved, it is so awesome! Get prepared and watch God use you.

In his book *The Legacy of Jesus,* John MacArthur makes this statement: "The single, central, most important issue about Jesus is the question of His deity. Everyone who studies about Jesus must confront the issue, because of His claims to be God. C.S. Lewis has observed that 'the one thing we must not say' about Jesus is that He is a 'great moral teacher' but not God: 'A man who was merely a man and said the sort of things Jesus said would not be a great moral teacher. He would either be a lunatic—on a level with the man who says he is a poached egg—or else he would be the Devil of Hell. You must make your choice. Either this man was, and is, the Son of God; or else a madman or something worse.' "[7]

Think on these things, Beloved.

17 Have you ever desired a greater intimacy with the Father, yet felt that God was too awesome and too far removed for you to enjoy that type of relationship? Has your vision of God been of a Person who seemed so holy that you felt you could not endure His presence? Or have you ever felt a paralyzing fear in respect to God?

O Beloved, if you will get to know Jesus Christ in an intimate way through studying and meditating upon the Word, you will find this intimacy dispelling your misconceptions of God. Because Jesus was one in essence with the Father, He could say, "And he who beholds Me beholds the One who sent Me" (John 12:45). As you behold "as in a mirror the glory of the Lord" (2 Corinthians 3:18), you will find yourself more and more enraptured with the Father heart of

God. You will become more and more secure in your knowledge of Him.

Remember, Jesus came to explain the Father. In John 14 we find our Lord preparing the disciples for His departure. They are about to go through the trauma of seeing the One for whom they have left all die an ignominious death on a cross. And until His resurrection, their grief will be almost unbearable. For although He told them of His death and resurrection, it was almost as if they were deaf. They could not comprehend the horror of what He was communicating.

Thus, we hear our Lord in the Upper Room assuring them that He is going to His Father's house to prepare a place for them. He tells them that if He goes away, He will surely return for them. It is at this point that Thomas asks, " 'Lord, we do not know where You are going, how do we know the way?' Jesus said to him, 'I am [*egō eimi*] the way, and the truth, and the life; no one comes to the Father, but through Me. If you had known Me, you would have known My Father also; from now on you know Him, and have seen Him' " (John 14:5-7).

There it is once again. *When you get to know Jesus, you will get to know the Father, for They are one in essence.*

Philip said to Him, " 'Lord, show us the Father, and it is enough for us.' Jesus said to him, 'Have I been so long with you, and yet you have not come to know Me, Philip? He who has seen Me has seen the Father; how do you say, "Show us the Father?" Do you not believe that I am in the Father, and the Father is in Me?' " (John 14:8-10).

I leave you, Beloved, with Jesus' question to Philip. Consider it His question to you: Do you believe Jesus is one with the Father and, therefore, that He is God? And what are you doing in order to get to know your Father God intimately as your Friend?

18 What is the ultimate goal, the supreme purpose, of your life? This is a very crucial question, because those without goals usually live purposeless lives that are wasted and often regretted. Don't ever forget that you will be held accountable before your God for how you spend your life. It is He who brought you into existence.

Fulfillment comes from knowing that you have achieved your purpose. What is the ultimate goal, the supreme purpose, of your life? Write out your answer in your notebook.

As the day of our Lord's crucifixion hovered as a dark cloud over the disciples, in their presence Jesus lifted up His eyes to heaven and said, "Father, the hour has come; glorify Thy Son, that the Son may glorify Thee" (John 17:1). To the very end of His life, Jesus' desire was to glorify the Father, to give an exact estimate of who the Father was. As the curtain of death was about to go down, ending the drama of a life lived with one ultimate goal, Jesus could say, "I glorified Thee on the earth, having accomplished the work which Thou hast given Me to do" (John 17:4). And because He achieved this goal, there was an encore: the resurrection!

And what was Jesus' desire for those He would leave behind? It was that they too would achieve oneness: "And the glory which Thou hast given Me I have given to them; that they may be one, just as We are one; I in them, and Thou in Me, that they may be perfected in unity, that the world may know that Thou didst send Me, and didst love them, even as Thou didst love Me" (John 17:22,23).

Again we see Jesus' deity confirmed, as He refers over and over to His oneness with the Father. Don't miss the fact that this oneness gave Him His purpose in life, and then held Him to this purpose. Even in the agony of Gethsemane He prayed, "My Father, if it is possible, let this cup pass from Me; yet not as I will, but as Thou wilt" (Matthew 26:39).

O dear child of God, may you so make oneness with the Father your goal that you will realize daily that your ultimate goal too is to glorify Him on earth by accomplishing the work He has given you to do. "For we are His workmanship, created in Christ Jesus for good works, which God prepared beforehand, that we should walk in them" (Ephesians 2:10).

19 If you are going to allow the Word of God to speak for itself, without twisting it or distorting it, you must believe that Jesus is one with the Father, God in the flesh. In Colossians 2:9 we read: "For in Him all the fulness of Deity dwells in bodily form." God said it again and again as men moved by the Spirit of God wrote for us the Word of God. It is there in the Old Testament, in the Gospels, in Acts, in the Epistles, and in Revelation: Jesus is God.

Philippians gives us one of the clearest descriptions of the deity and humanity of Jesus Christ in the form of a word of exhortation to those in Philippi. Let's look at it verse by verse, and I will explain it as we go along. Don't miss the exhortation: "Have this attitude in yourselves which was also in Christ Jesus, who, although He existed in the form of God, did not regard equality with God a thing to be grasped" (Philippians 2:5,6). There it is again: Jesus is equal with God, the same as God in essence.

The Greek word for *form* is *morphē*, and I don't want you to miss its wonderful depth of meaning. Therefore, I want to share what W.E. Vine has to say in his *Expository Dictionary of Old and New Testament Words: "Morphē* denotes "the special or characteristic form or feature" of a person or thing. . . . An excellent definition of the word is that of Gifford: '*morphē* is therefore properly the nature or essence, not in the abstract, but as actually subsisting in the individual, and retained as long as the individual itself exists.' . . . Thus in the passage before us [Philippians 2:6] *morphē Theou* is the Divine nature actually and inseparably subsisting in the Person of Christ. . . . The true meaning of *morphē* in the expression 'form of God' is confirmed by its recurrence in the corresponding phrase, 'form of a servant.' It is universally admitted that the two phrases are directly antithetical, and that 'form' must therefore have the same sense in both" (From Gifford, *The Incarnation*, 16,19,39).[8]

Because Jesus was God, He continued to be God even when He took the form of a servant.

20 Although Jesus was God, He "did not regard equality with God a thing to be grasped" (Philippians 2:6). He did not hang on His right to be God in a way that kept Him from taking upon Himself the form of a bond-servant. Here is the exhortation to us as children of God. We are to be willing to humble ourselves, even as Jesus our Lord did. Although He retained His deity at all times, Jesus was willing to lay aside His rights as God in order that He might be "made in the likeness of men. And being found in appearance as a man, He humbled Himself by becoming obedient to the point of death, even death on a cross" (Philippians 2:7,8).

There was no more shameful or painful death than that of crucifixion. And yet God the Son was willing to obey God and serve us in this way, so that we might not have to die in our sins but could have eternal life.

As you read the Gospel of John, you will see two titles used of Jesus repeatedly. He is called "Son of God," which shows His deity, and "Son of Man," which shows His humanity. As we see Jesus as the Son of God and the Son of Man in Philippians, we are convicted in our hearts that we must have the attitude of our Lord.

After all, if He who is God was willing to become a bond-servant that He might lay down His life for us, then shouldn't we be willing to lay down our lives, our personal rights, for the sake of others? How can we cling to our puny rights when Jesus, the Son of God, was willing to empty Himself of His just rights as God?

O Beloved, in a time when there is so much emphasis on self, on being number one, how vital it is that you be "firmly rooted" in Him, "built up in Him and established in your faith, just as you were instructed, and overflowing with gratitude. See to it that no one takes you captive through philosophy and empty deception, according to the tradition of men, according to the elementary principles of the world, rather than according to Christ. For in Him all the fulness of Deity dwells in bodily form, and in Him you have been made complete" (Colossians 2:7-10).

In the light of what we have learned, why don't you examine your relationship with other people? Is there anything you are doing from selfishness or empty conceit? Are you regarding yourself as more important than others? Do you care only about your own interests, or are you seeking ways that you might please your mate, your children, family members, and fellow Christians? Who is number one in your life—you or God? If God, then others will come before you.

21 Anyone who possesses the sovereign rights to raise the dead, to judge mankind, and to receive honor that belongs to God must certainly be God. In John 5 we see a magnificent portrait of the Son in His relationship to the Father. It is the same truth laid out in last month's devotional: Jesus Christ is God because He is the possessor of the sovereign rights of God.

Let's look at how the Son explains to a group of angry Jews one of His sovereign rights as the Son of God: "For this cause therefore the Jews were seeking all the more to kill Him, because He not only was breaking the Sabbath, but also was calling God His own Father, making Himself equal with God" (John 5:18). It is at this point that Jesus refers to Himself over and over as "the Son," showing what the Son can do because He is the Son. He explains to them that a day is coming when all the dead shall be raised and that He has the right to act as the Son of God to call them forth: "Truly, truly, I say to you, an hour is coming and now is, when the dead shall hear the voice of the Son of God; and those who hear shall live. . . . Do not marvel at this; for an hour is coming, in which all who are in the tombs shall hear His voice, and shall come forth; those who did the good deeds to a resurrection of life, those who committed the evil deeds to a resurrection of judgment" (John 5:25,28,29).

Jesus makes His statement regarding the resurrection of the dead in John 5, and then in John 11 gives them a foretaste of His authority over death, as He "cried out with a loud voice, 'Lazarus, come forth' " (11:43). Lazarus, who had been dead four days, came forth suddenly. He must have been propelled, because he certainly was unable to walk in his grave clothes! Those who witnessed the event knew that Jesus was the Son of God. If Jesus had not specifically said, "Lazarus," I am sure that all the dead would have come forth in obedience to the voice of God!

Not only will Jesus raise the dead, but as God He will also judge them (John 5:22). The Father "gave Him authority to execute judgment, because He is the Son of Man" (John 5:27). And this is only right, for Jesus demonstrated that man could live in obedience to God. And finally, all will "honor the Son, even as they honor the Father. He who does not honor the Son does not honor the Father who sent Him" (John 5:23).

22 Have you ever wondered why people are so eager to embrace evolution and so adamantly opposed to the biblical account of creation? I think the root of this paradox is pride, and the root of pride is sin. It is turning to our "own way" (Isaiah 53:6) and refusing to submit to the ownership of God. After all, didn't that "serpent of old who is called the devil and Satan" (Revelation 12:9) offer Eve a way to be her own god if she would eat of the forbidden fruit of the tree of the knowledge of good and evil? Didn't Satan tell Eve that in the day she ate of the fruit from that tree she would be like God, knowing good and evil? Of course! It is all recorded for us in Genesis 3. Man did not want God to rule over him. He wanted to be his own god.

It is this attitude that causes people to reject the Bible's idea of creation. For if we are created, if there is a cause behind this universe, if we did not evolve from a lower form of life but are a unique and special creation, then there has to be a Creator. And you have to spell *Creator* with a capital

C, for He has to be other than we are. And if we have a Creator, then we are accountable to live in obedience to Him, because we owe our existence to Him. The Word of God states: "In the beginning God created the heavens and the earth. . . . Then God said, "Let Us make man in Our image. . . ." And God created man in His own image, in the image of God He created him; male and female He created them. . . . The LORD God formed man of dust from the ground, and breathed into his nostrils the breath of life; and man became a living being. . . . And the LORD God commanded the man . . ." (Genesis 1:1,26,27; 2:7,16).

From Genesis, it is clear that the Creator is the LORD God, YHWH Elohim. And who is this YHWH Elohim? Well, a careful reading of Genesis 1:26 indicates that YHWH is more than one: "Then God said, 'Let *Us* make man in *Our* image.' " This fact, of course, brings us to the third major point of our outline on the deity of Jesus Christ: *Jesus Christ is God because He is Creator.*

O Beloved, do not grow weary of our subject. In all probability you know without a shadow of a doubt that Jesus is God. However, there are so many who do not know, and their tactics are subtle in their attempts to deceive.

May we never need Paul's word of admonition: "For if one comes and preaches another Jesus whom we have not preached, or you receive a different spirit which you have not received, or a different gospel which you have not accepted, you bear this beautifully" (2 Corinthians 11:4).

23 When God said, "Let Us make man in Our image," Jesus Christ was right there with Him. In John 1:3 we read: "All things came into being by Him; and apart from Him nothing came into being that has come into being."

In Paul's epistle to the Colossians, he establishes the fact that Jesus "is the image of the invisible God, the first-born of all creation" (1:15). Therefore, Jesus is not part of creation; He is Creator. Thus, Paul goes on to say, "For by Him all things were created, both in the heavens and on earth, visible and invisible, whether thrones or dominions or rulers or authorities—all things have been created by Him and for Him" (1:16).

Yet another epistle leaves us with no doubt that Jesus is Creator, and that is Hebrews. This is a difficult but magnificent book which Christians desperately need to understand if they are going to endure trials without throwing away their confidence in Jesus Christ. It was written to believers who were suffering for their faith and who needed to understand the importance of holding fast, not drifting away but going on to maturity by coming boldly to the throne of grace and finding help in the time of need (4:14-16) from their great high priest, the Lord Jesus Christ, who ever lives to make intercession for them and who is able to save them forever (7:25).

In Hebrews 1, Jesus is established as being "much better than the angels" and the One of whom the Father said: "LET ALL THE ANGELS OF GOD WORSHIP HIM." The angels were ministers of God, "but of the Son He says, 'THY THRONE, O GOD, IS FOREVER AND EVER.'. . .and 'THOU, LORD, IN THE BEGINNING DIDST LAY THE FOUNDATION OF THE EARTH, AND THE HEAVENS ARE THE WORKS OF THY HANDS; THEY WILL PERISH, BUT THOU REMAINEST . . . THY YEARS WILL NOT COME TO AN END'" (Hebrews 1:4,6,8,10-12, quoting from Psalm 45:6,7; 102:25-27).

Dear one, Jesus is your Creator—worthy of your obedience, your submission. If you fight this, you will be fighting God. And no man fights God and wins—you only die in your sins.

24 "And I saw the dead, the great and the small, standing before the throne" (Revelation 20:12). The rich and poor, powerful and weak, great and small, educated and ignorant, red, yellow, black, white, all have one thing in common: They are dead. Not just physically dead, but spiritually dead. Men, women, and teenagers who are twice dead, "for whom the black darkness has been reserved forever" (Jude

13). Men, women, and teenagers who do not possess the Lord Jesus Christ.

And because they do not, they stand before God's throne to be forever condemned to the lake of fire. This lake of fire is "the second death" (Revelation 20:14). God prepared the lake of fire "for the devil and his angels," not for man (Matthew 25:41). Yet it shall become the eternal abode of all those whose names are "not found written in the book of life" (Revelation 20:15).

It is not God's will that any should perish. He wants you to come to repentance, to have a change of mind about who Jesus Christ is. He wants all to believe that He is God, Jehovah, so they will not have to die in their sins. But multitudes do not come to Him that they might have life. *In Jesus is life,* and in Him alone. So now we come to the fourth major point of our outline on the deity of Jesus Christ: Jesus Christ is God because in Him is life.

In John 1:4 we read: "In Him was life, and the life was the light of men." In Genesis 2:7 it says man was mere dust until "the LORD God . . . breathed into his nostrils the breath of life; and man became a living being [soul]."

There is no life apart from Jesus Christ, for life abides in Him alone. Jesus is "the bread of God . . . which comes down out of heaven, and gives life to the world" (John 6:33). "Everyone who beholds the Son and believes in Him" will "have eternal life," and Jesus Himself "will raise him up on the last day" (John 6:40).

Believers will not stand at the Great White Throne Judgment of God. Because they have believed that Jesus is God and have accepted Him as Lord and Savior, they have also accepted His finished work at Calvary where the Lamb of God, the Son of Man, died in their stead and covered their sins. He has breathed into them the breath of life, and sealed them "in Him with the Holy Spirit of promise, who is given as a pledge of our inheritance, with a view to the redemption of God's own possession, to the praise of His glory" (Ephesians 1:13,14). They will never see the second death, for God has given them eternal life, "and this life is in His Son" (1 John 5:11).

Jesus stood before Martha, the grieving sister of Lazarus who had been dead four days, and said, "I am the resurrection and the life; he who believes in Me shall live even if he dies, and everyone who lives and believes in Me shall never die" (John 11:25,26). The second death has no power over those who have believed Jesus is God.

25 The news came! The tomb was empty! His body had not been stolen. Jesus was alive! He had appeared to some of the disciples, and they said to Thomas, one of the twelve, " 'We have seen the Lord!' But he said to them, 'Unless I shall see in His hands the imprint of the nails, and put my finger into the place of the nails, and put my hand into His side, I will not believe' " (John 20:25). It was hard for Thomas to believe. Jesus had been so dead! He had seen those spikes suspending his Hope by the hands. He had watched the spear being thrust into the breast upon which John had leaned. He had seen blood and water pouring forth from His broken heart through the gaping hole. Jesus had bled like an ordinary man and had died as all men do. He had been buried like everyone else. Jesus couldn't be alive, could He?

It had been a special three years. A time filled with hope and purpose that had come to an end. Faith was gone, buried in a tomb. Thomas could not resurrect it unless he could put his fingers in the nail holes of a living Jesus and unless He could put his hand in Jesus' side. Only then would Thomas believe: "And after eight days again His disciples were inside, and Thomas with them. Jesus came, the doors having been shut, and stood in their midst, and said, 'Peace be with you.' Then He said to Thomas, 'Reach here your finger, and see My hands; and reach here your hand, and put it into My side; and be not unbelieving, but believing.' Thomas answered and said to Him, 'My Lord and my God!' " (John 20:26-28).

Thomas believed. He saw Jesus for who He was—his Lord and his God. It is this confession that brings us to the fifth and last major point of our outline on the deity of Jesus Christ: Jesus Christ is God because *He is Lord.*

Once again we need to turn to that classic passage on the deity and humanity of Jesus Christ, Philippians 2. This time I want to take you beyond the humiliation of Jesus Christ at Calvary to that which is yet to come, His exaltation by the Father: "And being found in appearance as a man, He humbled Himself by becoming obedient to the point of death, even death on a cross. Therefore also God highly exalted Him, and bestowed on Him the name which is above every name, that at the name of Jesus EVERY KNEE SHOULD BOW, of those who are in heaven, and on earth, and under the earth, and that every tongue should confess that Jesus Christ is Lord, to the glory of God the Father" (Philippians 2:8-11).

O Beloved, if God the Father will cause every knee to bow and every tongue to confess that Jesus is Lord, who are we to contradict God? Know this: If you refuse to bow now and confess Jesus as your Lord and your God, you will someday confess who He is. But if your physical death comes first, it will be too late for you.

26

There is a superficial faith, and there is a real faith. Real faith is seen over the proverbial long haul. Real faith endures. It shows in the trials of life, in the times of testing. Faith can be *proclaimed* as real, but it isn't *seen* as genuine until it is tested. Real faith is proven faith that stands the test.

As you read through the Gospel of John, you see two different types of believing which result in either a superficial faith or the genuine thing. Let me give you an example of what I mean, and then let me share with you what I believe makes the difference between the superficial and the real. In John 2:23-25 we read: "Now when He was in Jerusalem at the Passover, during the feast, many believed in His name, beholding His signs which He was doing. But Jesus, on His part, was not entrusting Himself to them, for He knew all men, and because He did not need anyone to bear witness concerning man for He Himself knew what was in man."

Jesus knew that many people were convinced by the signs He performed, but were not genuinely convinced about Jesus Himself, for He would not entrust Himself to them.

In John 6, we see the same thing happening. Jesus gathered quite a group of followers because of the signs He performed. Some were even considered disciples, until they heard His hard sayings. "As a result of this many of His disciples withdrew, and were not walking with Him anymore" (John 6:66).

When Jesus asked the twelve if they wanted to go away also, "Simon Peter answered Him, 'Lord, to whom shall we go? You have words of eternal life. And we have believed and have come to know that You are the Holy One of God' " (John 6:68,69). As the spokesman, Peter was telling Jesus that it was more than the signs they had believed. It was His words. It was His Person. They were convinced that Jesus was God and that He had given them the truth of God. Peter was saying, in essence, that their faith was the real thing. It wasn't based on signs. Their faith rested in a true knowledge and commitment to the words and Person of Jesus Christ.

Yet while Peter was speaking, Jesus pointed out that one of the twelve did not have genuine faith. He knew that in the time of testing, Judas' faith would fail.

27 Some people believe in signs and in the Jesus who performs them. Others believe in Jesus for who He is, not just for what He performs.

Some will follow Him as long as He performs the way they want Him to. Others will follow Him, no matter what happens.

Some possess Jesus. Others Jesus possesses. Therein lies the difference between superficial and real faith. It is all wrapped up in believing in who He is.

Genuine, saving faith accepts that Jesus is the Christ—the promised Messiah of whom the Old Testament prophesied. Genuine, saving faith accepts the fact that Jesus is the Son of God and, thereby, all that God is. If I am going to acknowledge Jesus as God, then I must be willing to live accordingly. If Jesus is God, then He has a right to rule over me.

Paul calls real faith "the obedience of faith" (Romans 1:5). If Jesus is God, then I am not my own. There is to be a total commitment of myself to God so that He possesses me. "Do you not know that your body is a temple of the Holy Spirit who is in you, whom you have from God, and that you are not your own? For you have been bought with a price: therefore glorify God in your body" (1 Corinthians 6:19,20). It is recognizing Jesus for who He is and accepting and submitting to who He is—my Lord and my God—that brings genuine faith.

Real faith is not mere intellectual assent. Genuine faith is comprised of a firm conviction based on knowledge, a personal surrender, and conduct inspired by such a surrender. Salvation is surrendering yourself to God and to what He has revealed about His Son.

It is all pure grace. There is absolutely nothing that you as a destitute sinner can do to save yourself. In genuine faith, you simply put your trust in all that Jesus Christ is and in all that He has accomplished in His death, burial, and resurrection.

As you read Paul's words, notice that Jesus is Lord because He is God: " 'THE WORD IS NEAR YOU, IN YOUR MOUTH AND IN YOUR HEART'—that is, the word of faith which we are preaching, that if you confess with your mouth Jesus as Lord, and believe in your heart that God raised Him from the dead, you shall be saved; for with the heart man believes, resulting in righteousness, and with the mouth he confesses, resulting in salvation. For the Scripture says, 'WHOEVER BELIEVES IN HIM WILL NOT BE DISAPPOINTED.' For there is no distinction between Jew and Greek; for the same Lord is Lord of all, abounding in riches for all who call upon

Him; for 'WHOEVER WILL CALL UPON THE NAME OF THE LORD WILL BE SAVED' " (Romans 10:8-13).

Genuine faith does not rest on signs or benefits, but on the Savior who is the Lord Jesus Christ, God incarnate.

28 Jesus once turned to a group of Jews "who had believed Him" and told them what constituted genuine discipleship, genuine salvation: "If you abide in My word, then you are truly disciples of Mine; and you shall know the truth, and the truth shall make you free" (John 8:31,32). Just before this He had said to them, "Unless you believe that I am He, you shall die in your sins" (8:24).

True faith produces a changed life because it produces obedience. Obedience and belief go hand in hand, just as disobedience and unbelief go hand in hand. Many Scriptures teach this truth, but I will simply give you Hebrews 3:18,19 to show you the parallel between disobedience and unbelief.

Now when I say real faith produces obedience, I do not mean that a true child of God will not sin. However, the true child of God will change in respect to sin. "How shall we who died to sin still live in it?" (Romans 6:2).

A true believer's life changes in respect to sin because he has believed in Him! (See 1 John 3:7-10.) A person must believe that Jesus is God if he wants to be saved. And if I acknowledge Jesus as God, along with all this implies, I am turning from sin, or running my own life, to Jesus, who as God has the right to run my life. If I acknowledge Jesus as God, then I am going to believe what He says. I am going to know the truth, and the truth will make me free (John 8:32).

Also, although I was a slave to sin, for "everyone who commits sin is the slave of sin" (John 8:34), I will now be free from slavery to sin, for "if therefore the Son shall make you free, you shall be free indeed" (John 8:36). This freedom comes—as we read in 1 John 3—because His seed abides in me, and I cannot practice habitual sin (as a way of life) because I am born of God. Here again is the difference between genuine and superficial faith.

29 If you read John 8:31-59, we found our Lord making very strong statements to some Jews who had believed in Him. From the context of this passage, it seems that theirs was a superficial belief, for Jesus said to them: "If God were your Father, you would love Me; for I proceeded forth and have come from God, for I have not even come on My own initiative, but He sent Me. Why do you not understand what I am saying? It is because you cannot hear My word. You are of your father the devil, and you want to do the desires of your father. He was a murderer from the beginning, and does not stand in the truth, because there is no truth in him. Whenever he speaks a lie, he speaks from his own nature; for he is a liar, and the father of lies. But because I speak the truth, you do not believe Me. Which one of you convicts Me of sin? If I speak truth, why do you not believe Me? He who is of God hears the words of God; for this reason you do not hear them, because you are not of God" (John 8:42-47).

All mankind has one of two fathers—either God or the devil. It is easy to spot some who have the devil as their father, but not all. The religious, those who have a superficial faith, are sometimes hard to discern, for even they are deceived, believing heaven is their home and God is their Father. Let me quote what Lawrence O. Richards says in his *Expository Dictionary of Bible Words:*

> There is counterfeit belief, which exists as a limited trust in Jesus. Counterfeit belief acknowledges that there is something special about Jesus but refuses to accept Scripture's full testimony about him. Saving faith goes beyond limited belief. It recognizes Jesus as Son of God and trusts completely in him as he is unveiled in God's Word. Saving faith demonstrates belief by acting on the words Jesus has spoken (John 8:31-32).
>
> In making a faith commitment, a person considers the evidence and accepts God's testimony about who

Jesus is. The one who does not believe may be impressed with the evidence but will hold back from entrusting himself or herself to Jesus.

Yet it is only by believing, as a total commitment of oneself to the Lord, that life can be found. How vital then that we consider the testimony of Scripture, accept it, and believe on the one who speaks words of promise there.

John sees believing as an active, continuing trust in Jesus. The act of believing draws an individual across the dividing line between death and eternal life. That act of faith is described by John as receiving Jesus (Jn 1:12) and as coming to him (Jn 6:35), as well as loving him (1 Jn 4:19).[9]

O Beloved, does this help you to tell real faith from the counterfeit?

30 "Your father is the devil. You are doing the deeds of your father." When you hear statements like these, do you imagine someone involved in witchcraft—contacting the dead, offering animal or human sacrifices in a black mass? Or, when you hear of the deeds of the devil, do you think of drug abuse, immorality, pornography, stealing, murder? All of these seem to be obvious deeds of the devil, don't they? They are easy to spot and to define as not being of God.

And yet in the context of Jesus' statements that the Jews' father was the devil and the deeds they were doing were of the devil himself, the devil's deeds are not always blatant. They are not as easily discerned in this passage as those I have just mentioned. And yet, the deeds of the devil have one root source from which every deed springs: "the lie."

"The lie" is that which contradicts truth—*anything* which goes against what the Word of God teaches. It is the nature of the devil to go against the Word of God. Listen again to John 8:44: "You are of your father the devil, and you want to do the desires of your father. He was a murderer from the beginning."

In other words, the devil wanted to destroy Adam and

Eve. He wanted them to believe his lie that assured them: "You surely shall not die!" (Genesis 3:4). All the time the devil knew that they would die! And die they did—spiritually and later physically. Death entered the world because Adam and Eve believed the devil's lie. The devil was a murderer. He "does not stand in the truth, because there is no truth in him. Whenever he speaks a lie [literally, "the lie"], he speaks from his own nature; for he is a liar, and the father of lies" (John 8:44). It is the very nature of the devil to lie, to contradict the truth, to deceive men so that they turn from truth. Therefore, every lie that has ever been perpetrated—every contradiction of the truth of God's Word—has its root in the devil, for he is the father of lies, the one who conceives them.

O Beloved, do you realize what God is saying? Everything that contradicts the Word of God has its root in the devil. And the fruit of the root is death, for the devil is a murderer. The Word of God is truth!

Jesus prayed, "Sanctify them in the truth; Thy word is truth" (John 17:17). And what is the truth about Jesus Christ? "Unless you believe that I am *He,* you shall die in your sins" (John 8:24). If you do not believe that Jesus is God, the devil has murdered you, because you believed his lie, and you will spend eternity in the lake of fire. Do you believe?

31 Well, beloved friend, it has been quite a month, hasn't it? It is my prayer that you now have a clear understanding of the deity of Jesus Christ and that you feel confident that you could share the truth of it with another.

Take today and pray through what you've learned. Then write out in your notebook a simple explanation of the deity of Jesus Christ. It will be an exercise to cement in your mind all that you've learned so that you are prepared to "contend earnestly for the faith which was once for all delivered to the saints" (Jude 3). Remember, that was our goal for this month together.

Take time too to thank God for His incredible plan of salvation!

April

Truths That Will Loose Death's Grave Clothes

1 For the first time he saw the light of day, and all because of the One who was the Light of the world. According to John 9, the man had been blind from birth. Then Jesus came, spat on the ground, made clay of the spittle, applied it to his eyes, and told him to wash in the pool of Siloam. The man went to the pool blind and came back seeing!

No more would he sit as a beggar. No longer would his life be an object of pity. No longer would he be condemned to darkness. Light had come, and with that light came life! The man believed on the One who removed the veil of blindness from his eyes.

Whenever I read this account, I cannot help but think of how it parallels my life—and the life of every child of God. As I note the amount of space devoted to this incident, I believe that God wanted John to show us a picture of what takes place when a person comes to know the Lord Jesus Christ in a personal way.

The parallels between John 9 and our salvation are many, for we were also once in spiritual darkness. We were each born blind to the glorious light of the gospel of Jesus Christ. Did we not also sit as beggars, poverty-stricken when it came to any righteousness which might cover our spiritual nakedness? And in our blindness, did we not grope through life, unable to see where we were going?

Yet, once we were healed of sin's awful disease, did everyone rejoice with us over the change in our lives? Weren't there some who didn't want to admit that our transformation was a sheer miracle? Didn't many deny that only Jesus Christ could make such a transformation? Didn't people who once accepted us now reject us and want to kick us out of their "fellowship"? Reality was that they, too, were in darkness, but they did not recognize their blindness.

This month as we continue our devotional study together, I want you to see what it means to belong to the family of God, to be turned from darkness to light, from the power of Satan to the kingdom of God. I want you to know what happens when you hear the voice of your Shepherd and come into His fold, where no one can snatch you from His hand. I want you to behold truths which will loosen death's grave clothes so that you will walk in peace, trusting the One who is the Resurrection and the Life. Finish today's time by reading John 9.

2 It is the work of God to do the supernatural! When we recognize our own state of impotence, then God is ready to take over in His all-powerful way. It is not until we come to an awareness of our total poverty of spirit in regard to saving ourselves that we can ever be saved. Jesus said, "Blessed are the poor in spirit, for theirs is the kingdom of heaven" (Matthew 5:3).

There was one thing the blind man of John 9 knew for certain: He was blind and there was no human cure for his blindness. If sight depended on him or any person, he would remain blind. When the disciples passed the blind man sitting outside the Temple, they asked Jesus, " 'Rabbi, who sinned, this man or his parents, that he should be born blind?' Jesus answered, 'It was neither that this man sinned, nor his parents; but it was in order that the works of God might be displayed in him. We must work the works of Him who sent Me, as long as it is day; night is coming, when no man can work' " (John 9:2-4).

God was going to do what He alone could do: the supernatural. When the supernatural is done, God is glorified.

O Beloved, are the works of God being displayed in you because you have been saved and are different than you used to be? His supernatural transformation begins: 1) when you see your own impotence; 2) when you realize you cannot change yourself; 3) when you know you cannot commend yourself to God; 4) when you simply take God at His Word and believe Him.

Only then is God able to open your eyes so that you might turn from darkness to light, and from the dominion of Satan to God, and might receive forgiveness of sins and an inheritance among those who have been sanctified by faith in Him (Acts 26:18). As God allowed the blindness of the man so that "the works of God might be displayed in him" (John 9:3), so I believe God allows us to get into the messes we do so we will look to Him in our poverty of spirit and be saved.

Do you know people who think they can straighten up their lives and make it to heaven? O Beloved, they are still blind! Maybe God will use you to introduce them to the Light of the world before the night comes and there is no more opportunity. Pray that they will not be like the Pharisees who thought they could see, but who were blind and whose sin remained.

3 The work of Jesus Christ will always bring division. That is hard for some to accept; they think that when a person comes to know Jesus Christ, he is automatically put at peace with everyone. They misunderstand the announcement of the angels at the birth of Jesus, and hear only, "Peace on earth, good will toward men." In reality, the angels declared, "Glory to God in the highest, and on earth peace among men with whom He is pleased" (Luke 2:14).

Or, "On earth peace among men of [His] good pleasure or [His] good will."

Peace on earth is not an automatic by-product of Jesus Christ's first coming to the earth. When Jesus was received as God and Savior, it often resulted in division.

In John 9, you probably noted that Jesus' healing of the blind man brought a division among the people. When the blind man—or anyone—confessed Jesus to be the Christ, they would be "put out of the synagogue" (9:22). To put a Jew out of the synagogue was to cut him off from learning the Word of God and from worshiping with other believers.

Jesus was eager for those who would consider following Him to understand this reality. Thus, He said, "Do not think that I came to bring peace on the earth; I did not come to bring peace, but a sword. For I came to SET A MAN AGAINST HIS FATHER, AND A DAUGHTER AGAINST HER MOTHER, AND A DAUGHTER-IN-LAW AGAINST HER MOTHER-IN-LAW; and A MAN'S ENEMIES WILL BE THE MEMBERS OF HIS HOUSEHOLD. He who loves father or mother more than Me is not worthy of Me; and he who loves son or daughter more than Me is not worthy of Me" (Matthew 10:34-37).

Jesus is God. As God, He must have the preeminence in our lives. Not to give Him this is to be guilty of idolatry. We cannot put anyone or anything in His rightful place in our lives. Thus, following Jesus brings division with anyone who would resent or object to Jesus having first place in your life.

But you may say, "I love my mother, my father, my husband, my child, my in-laws. It grieves me to be at odds with them because I cannot accept their beliefs or follow some of their ways." I understand. The grief of rejection and separation is difficult, but it must not deter you from fully following your Lord and walking in His light.

4 When you embrace the Lord Jesus Christ, you embrace the cross. You cannot separate Jesus from Calvary because He was born to die. He was "the Lamb of God who

takes away the sin of the world!" (John 1:29). And since "the wages of sin is death" (Romans 6:23), the sin of the world could be taken away only through His death. At His death He became our substitute. Jesus, who knew no sin, was made sin for us "that we might become the righteousness of God in Him" (2 Corinthians 5:21).

It is the cross that brings division. The cross of Calvary separates us from death unto life, from sin unto righteousness, from hell unto heaven, from being under Satan's dominion to being under God's. The cross also separates us from the world and from all who are of the world, whether they are religious or rank sinners. Any who have not believed on the Lord Jesus Christ belong to the world and its system.

What was true of Paul should also be true of us: "But may it never be that I should boast, except in the cross of our Lord Jesus Christ, through which the world has been crucified to me, and I to the world" (Galatians 6:14). Embracing Jesus brings division because the cross is the place where life begins and is to be lived.

In Galatians 2:20, we read: "I have been crucified with Christ; and it is no longer I who live, but Christ lives in me; and the life which I now live in the flesh I live by faith in the Son of God, who loved me, and delivered Himself up for me." The cross is the place where self-life ends. The life in which you were once god is over. Your love of self or of others can no longer have preeminence over your love of God. Jesus told those who would follow Him, "If anyone comes to Me, and does not hate his own father and mother and wife and children and brothers and sisters, yes, and even his own life, he cannot be My disciple. Whoever does not carry his own cross and come after Me cannot be My disciple" (Luke 14:26,27).

How prophetically right the Jews were when they said to the man blind from birth, "You are His disciple" (John 9:28), for that was exactly what he was going to become. Although they tried to persuade the blind man that Jesus was a sinner and not the Christ, he knew that Jesus was sent from God. And because the blind man took hold of this truth, "they put him out" of the synagogue (John 9:34). But even that separation could not force him to change his mind about Jesus. "He worshiped Him" (John 9:38).

O Beloved, have you experienced the separation that taking up your cross and following Him brings? Don't despair! You have seen the Light. You are blind no more!

5 Not only did the Jews kick the blind man out of the synagogue, but they also wanted Jesus out of both the synagogue and the Temple. As a matter of fact, the Jews wanted Jesus Christ dead! The Jewish leaders were to be the shepherds of Israel, taking care of the flock of God. Yet they were more concerned about themselves and their own welfare than the welfare of the sheep.

Instead of rejoicing over the healing of this blind son of Israel, they became angry with him because he said that he had been healed by Jesus. Too many were following Jesus and listening to His teachings, and it threatened their power. Jesus violated their interpretation of the Law and broke their traditions. Why, soon the Jewish leaders might lose their hold over the people, and eventually their place of rulership under the Romans! Now here before them stood a witness who insisted that Jesus had healed him. They could not have it!

The rejection of the blind man by the Jewish leaders prompted Jesus to use the metaphor of the Shepherd and His sheep. Jesus wanted to point out that He, the very One they were rejecting, is the only way into God's true sheepfold. And so He said that everyone else is a thief and a robber.

Let me urge you to read John 9:35 through John 10, marking each use of the words *sheep* and *shepherd*. You might mark each *shepherd* with a crook, like this: shepherd and each *sheep* with another mark or color.

After you finish, list in your notebook everything you learn from John 10 about the Shepherd and the sheep. You will be blessed by what you see, and will be better able to understand our future lessons.

6 Jesus said, "I am the good shepherd; and I know My own, and My own know Me" (John 10:14). Others may not recognize Jesus. They may say, as the Jews did, "You are a Samaritan and have a demon" (John 8:48). Or they may accuse Jesus of being "insane" (John 10:20); but that does not change who He is any more than it changes who you are when men reject and revile you and say all manner of evil against you falsely (Matthew 5:11).

Read the Word, Beloved, and you will know what God says about you. Then believe that, rather than the angry accusations of sinful men. Read the whole counsel of God—the Word in its entirety—and you will know the truth about Jesus Christ. Remember, John 8:32 says, "You shall know the truth, and the truth shall make you free."

It is Satan who is the father of lies. Many times Satan uses religious men as his tools in his effort to destroy the flock of God. The Jews were the ones who had the demon, so to speak. Because they were of their father, the devil, it followed that they would want to do the desires of their father.

No wonder they wanted to kill Jesus and rid themselves of those who followed Him! Yet in their very plot to kill Jesus, they would be part of the sovereign plan of God to sacrifice the Shepherd for the sake of His sheep. In this incredible metaphor in John 10, Jesus points out the Jews as mere hirelings who flee when the wolf comes because they are "not concerned about the sheep" (10:13). Their concern is their own profit! No, these Jews would not take Jesus' life until He, as the Good Shepherd, was ready to lay down His life for the sheep. And no matter what they said about Jesus, they were wrong. In John 10, we see Jesus as: a) the True Shepherd: the Door of God's sheep (10:1-9); b) the Good Shepherd: the One who lays down His life for the sheep (10:10-21); and c) the Father's Shepherd: the One to whom the Father gave the sheep (10:22-42).

John 10 begins with the words "truly, truly." The King James Version renders it "verily, verily." One of my black sisters told me they translate it "sho' nuff, sho' nuff," and that is exactly what "truly, truly" or "verily, verily" means. It means that what Jesus is saying is absolutely true, absolutely sure. You can stake your life on it.

According to John 10, there is only one way to get into the fold of the sheep, and that is through the Door. Jesus said, "Truly, truly, I say to you, I am the door of the sheep" (10:7). There is absolutely no other way to enter into eternal life for Jew or Gentile, Muslim, Catholic, or Protestant. Each may enter only through Jesus, the Shepherd of the sheep, the One who is one with the Father.

7 The Old Testament is filled with references to God as the Shepherd of His people Israel. Therefore, since Jesus is God incarnate, it is only logical that He would explain to the Jews that He is the true Shepherd of Israel and not only of Israel but of "other sheep, which are not of [Israel's] fold" (John 10:16). When a Jew heard Jesus say that He was "the good shepherd," immediately his mind would run to key Old Testament passages where the metaphor of the *shepherd* or *sheep* played a major role.

One of these passages is in Isaiah—that awesome book which speaks repeatedly of the coming of Messiah, of His titles and His kingdom. In Isaiah 53—a chapter now seldom read in many synagogues because it so accurately describes the redemptive ministry of Jesus Christ—we meet our proneness to wander: "All of us like sheep have gone astray, each of us has turned to his own way; but the LORD has caused the iniquity of us all to fall on Him" (53:6). Wouldn't the remembrance of this verse correlate with the fact that Jesus had just said He would lay down His life for the sheep?

Surely Jesus' reference to *shepherd* and *sheep* would cause them to recall the comforting words of Psalm 23:1: "The LORD is my shepherd, I shall not want." The Hebrew word for *LORD* was the most holy and awesome name of

God, *YHWH*, first called *Yahweh* and then later called *Jehovah*. With the use of this name, they should have understood that if Jesus was their Shepherd, then Jesus is Jehovah—one with God! And if Jesus is our Shepherd, then He is the One who will provide all our needs, who will guide us all the days of our lives, and who will cause us to "dwell in the house of the LORD forever" (23:6).

Where the shepherds of Israel had failed to properly care for the flock of God, Jesus would not fail. Surely this would bring to the Jewish mind Ezekiel 34, where God tells of His distress with the shepherds of Israel, hirelings who cared more for themselves than for the flock of God. Thus, God said to Ezekiel, "Son of man, prophesy against the shepherds of Israel. Prophesy and say to those shepherds, 'Thus says the Lord GOD, "Woe, shepherds of Israel who have been feeding themselves! Should not the shepherds feed the flock? . . . My flock was scattered over all the surface of the earth; and there was no one to search or seek for them" ' . . . 'Behold, I Myself will search for My sheep and seek them out' " (34:2,6,11).

Ezekiel prophesied for God, and there God was in the Person of His Son, the true Shepherd, the Good Shepherd, the Father's Shepherd who came that His sheep might have life and have it more abundantly. What did it matter that they had cast out the blind man? Jesus gave him sight and took him into God's fold!

8 If any animal ever needed a shepherd to care for it, it is a sheep. I believe God made sheep helpless to give us a picture of our desperate need of Him as the Shepherd of our life.

The book that has been most helpful to me in this study is Phillip Keller's *A Shepherd Looks at Psalm 23*. It would be excellent to use in your family devotions. I want to share with you some wonderful insights on sheep. As you read, keep reminding yourself that you are His sheep.

Sheep need constant care and guidance. Their welfare depends solely upon the care they receive from their shepherd. So the more attentive the shepherd, the better cared for are the sheep. When you see sheep that are weak, sickly, and infested with pests, you can be sure their shepherd does not tend them well. It is possible too that they have been left to the care of hirelings who do not feel personally responsible.

Psalm 23:1 says "The LORD is my shepherd, I shall not want." Obviously, if the sheep doesn't want, his shepherd is attending him well. The remainder of Psalm 23 recounts the ways in which the Shepherd meets the needs of His sheep. You will find the information I am about to give you far more exciting if you read Psalm 23 before you go any further.

We know the Christian's life is to be one of rest—the rest of faith. If we are weary and heavy-laden, Jesus bids us come to Him that He might give us rest (Matthew 11:28). Sheep need rest, but they cannot lie down in green pastures unless they are free from four things. We will consider these tomorrow. Today, thank your Shepherd for His constant attention to your every concern.

9 If the sheep are going to rest, they must be free from flies, parasites, and other pests that would affect their health and make them restless.

They must also be free from hunger. If not fed properly, sheep will be moving about constantly, foraging for food. And in their foraging, they are apt to wander and fall prey to wolves. This is why God constantly reminds His undershepherds to feed His flock. And this is why, my beloved friend, I write books and other study material.

Another factor that will hinder sheep from lying down in green pastures is fear. They must sense no danger from without. Because sheep are helpless, timid, and feeble, they easily fall prey to other animals. When they encounter another animal, they will often stop dead in their tracks and freeze, rather than running for safety or crying out. Without their shepherd, they are totally defenseless.

If sheep are going to rest, they must also be free from tension. If other sheep are tormenting them, they do not lie down in peace, but stay on their feet continuously.

Have you ever been or are you being tormented by those in the body who are not tender and caring, who do not love you unconditionally? When you are sick and hurting, lean and weak, does it seem they come to your destruction rather than your aid? Have you ever been shoved about by the strong and been wounded as they pushed you aside in your weakened state?

O Beloved, if you understand what I am saying, then I urge you not to do the same to another! In 1 Thessalonians, Paul urges the brethren, "Admonish the unruly, encourage the fainthearted, help the weak, be patient with all men. See that no one repays another with evil for evil, but always seek after that which is good for one another and for all men" (5:14,15).

When there is sin in the camp, it must be dealt with so that the sinning one is brought to repentance. However, this process should always be entered into as the Shepherd of sheep would do it—in love governed by a desire for the highest good of another.

In Ezekiel 34, God was upset not only with the shepherds of Israel, but also the fat and strong sheep who did not care for the lean and weak. For when they are not cared for, in their restlessness they scatter. Thus, God Himself searches for His scattered sheep, seeks them out, and leads them to rest: "I will seek the lost, bring back the scattered, bind up the broken, and strengthen the sick; but the fat and the strong I will destroy. I will feed them with judgment. . . . I will judge between one sheep and another, between the rams and the male goats...between the fat sheep and the lean sheep. Because you push with side and with shoulder, and thrust at all the weak with your horns, until you have scattered them abroad, therefore, I will deliver My flock" (34:16-22).

What lessons our Shepherd has for us as His sheep! May we learn them well so we don't have to be judged by Him.

10 Sheep are creatures of habit. If they are left to themselves, they will graze the same ground over and over again, walking the same trails until the land becomes wasteland, eroded with gullies from the path worn by the sheep. Ground overgrazed by sheep often becomes polluted with parasites and disease. Thus, God writes through Ezekiel: "Is it too slight a thing for you that you should feed in the good pasture, that you must tread down with your feet the rest of your pastures? Or that you should drink of the clear waters, that you must foul the rest with your feet? And as for My flock, they must eat what you tread down with your feet, and they must drink what you foul with your feet!" (34:18,19).

I believe God was irate with the fat and strong sheep, because they were fouling up and polluting the Word of God with their false prophecies, their visions and dreams. They had the Word of God, but they were not giving it to the people. Jeremiah, a contemporary of Ezekiel, said to the prophets, "For you will no longer remember the oracle of the LORD, because every man's own word will become the oracle, and you have perverted the words of the living God, the LORD of hosts, our God" (Jeremiah 23:36).

If sheep are not led to proper pastures, they will eat or drink things that are harmful to them. Therefore, many times the shepherd goes before them and prepares a table for their grazing. The "table" will be carefully searched for any plants that could poison the sheep. Thus in Psalm 23:5, we read of the Lord, our Shepherd, preparing a table for us in the presence of our enemies. The Shepherd's concern is that His sheep be properly nourished.

Sheep cannot live without water, and yet they can go for months without actually drinking water, if the weather is not too hot. Sheep get their water from three sources: streams or springs, deep wells, or the dew on the grass. The morning dew can carry them until their grazing takes them to streams, springs, or wells. The secret is for the sheep to eat the grass while it is still wet with dew. It is that day-by-day grazing on grass laden with morning dew that sustains them during the heat of the day.

O what a lesson for us as the sheep of His pasture! Grazing in the morning, so we can withstand the heat of the day! Remember what Jesus said: "If any man is thirsty, let him keep coming to Me and let him keep drinking." Are you drinking the dew, dear one?

11 The condition of the sheep reflects the love and the care of the shepherd—or the lack of it. God has always been the true Shepherd of His sheep, and yet He has appointed under Him earthly shepherds to watch over His flock. He is the Chief Shepherd; they are undershepherds.

We see this both in the Old and New Testaments. In 1 Peter 5:2-4, we find an admonition to the elders: "Shepherd the flock of God among you, exercising oversight not under compulsion, but voluntarily, according to the will of God; and not for sordid gain, but with eagerness; nor yet as lording it over those allotted to your charge, but proving to be examples to the flock. And when the Chief Shepherd appears, you will receive the unfading crown of glory."

In this passage, you see the concern of the Father that the shepherd lay down his life for the sheep, rather than shepherding them for personal gain. As you read John 10, you can't miss Jesus' repeated statement that He was going to lay down His life for the sheep. Over and over again, God stresses the fact that the primary concern of the shepherd is to be the welfare of his sheep. O what a difference it would make in Christendom if each leader, each undershepherd, understood that the condition of his flock was a reflection of his love and care for his sheep!

In the verses from 1 Peter, you saw that the shepherd is not to lord it over his sheep. There is to be only one lord in Christendom, and that is the Lord Jesus Christ. No person is to have preeminence. And any man or woman who is a true follower of Jesus will follow His example: "For even the Son of Man did not come to be served, but to serve, and to give His life a ransom for many" (Mark 10:45).

In John 10, as in Ezekiel 34, you see the vivid contrast between the Jews' and Jesus' shepherding of God's flock. The Jewish leaders used the sheep for their benefit rather than seeing that they existed for the benefit of the sheep.

O Beloved, I do not know what responsibilities the Lord has given you in His kingdom; even if He has given you only one little sheep to tend, remember that the condition of that sheep reflects on your shepherding.

Why don't you take a few minutes to meditate upon your lifestyle. How does it compare to the high calling of your Shepherd? How are you living as His sheep? Are you sure that you are in His fold, that you have entered in by Him, the only Door to the Father?

12

When a shepherd would bring his flocks from the fields into a nearby village, he would often leave them in a sheepfold for the night. There they would file into a lean-to erected against the wall of a building, and join sheep from other flocks.

You might wonder how the shepherd would sort his sheep from the others, since they all look so much alike. You might think they needed a distinctive mark.

However, sorting out sheep by identifying their marks is not necessary for a true shepherd. His sheep know his voice. When he calls them, they respond.

When Jesus spoke of the sheep and the Shepherd to the Pharisees, He was telling them why the blind man had seen and believed, and also why they had become blind. They were blind because they were not His sheep. If they belonged to Him, they would hear His voice and follow Him. He wanted to show them there was only one way into God's fold—through the door. He did not want them to miss the fact that He was the Door.

Sheep recognize the voice of their shepherd. Another may try to imitate the shepherd's call, and may even use the same names for the sheep the shepherd uses, but it won't entice them. The sheep know the voice of their shepherd! Therefore, when the shepherd comes to the sheepfold to claim his sheep, "To him the doorkeeper opens, and the sheep hear his voice, and he calls his own sheep by name, and leads them out. When he puts forth all his own, he goes before them, and the sheep follow him because they know his voice. And a stranger they simply will not follow, but will flee from him, because they do not know the voice of strangers" (John 10:3-5).

O little sheep, doesn't it absolutely thrill your heart to know that you were His before the foundation of the world? When you heard His Word, His voice, you knew at last you had found your Shepherd. Hallelujah!

13 Those who came before Jesus, claiming to be Messiah and to know the way to life eternal, were thieves and robbers. They wanted to use the sheep for their own selfish purposes. They were coming "to steal, and kill, and destroy" (John 10:10), just like the one they represented, their father, the devil. But "the sheep did not hear them." They fled, knowing that their voice was not the voice of the true Shepherd (John 10:5).

God has given me the great joy of hearing testimonies of many people who in their search to know God went from one religion to another but were never satisfied, until finally they met Jesus. They discovered that He was the Door! Once they entered in through Him, they were saved and went "in and out" and found pasture (John 10:9).

When people are truly born again because they hear the voice of the Shepherd and in faith believe the truth of the Word of God, then they enter through the Door and find perfect security. They are home at last, a part of God's flock, His forever family. Now they walk in perfect liberty, for they "shall go in and out," and finding pasture, they have perfect sustenance (John 10:9). Finding the truth and feasting on the truth, God's Word, they are now able to rest.

And what shall be the end of these sheep? The beginning! The beginning of life eternal. Jesus said, "My sheep hear My voice, and I know them, and they follow Me; and I give eternal life to them, and they shall never perish; and no one shall snatch them out of My hand. My Father, who has given them to Me, is greater than all; and no one is able to snatch them out of the Father's hand" (John 10:27-29).

Once again, Jesus is reminding those who do not believe that the reason for their unbelief is because they were not given by the Father to the Son. He said, "You do not believe, because you are not of My sheep" (John 10:26).

Throughout the Gospel of John we have seen man's responsibility to believe and be born again. But we have also seen that our birth into His family is by the will of God. This is the Godward aspect of salvation which doesn't contradict or make void the human aspect. The Word teaches both. Accept both in faith.

14 Do you struggle with seemingly contradictory Scriptures? Some show, on the one hand, the responsibility of man in believing on the Lord Jesus Christ; and others, on the other hand, say that we are given to the Son by the Father, chosen by Him before the foundation of the world. Don't try to rationalize them so that you distort their meaning. Instead allow the Scriptures to speak for themselves.

Faith doesn't need to reason and say, "But if God chooses and gives, then man is not responsible; he is a mere robot!" Faith merely bows the knee and says, "Father, whether I can reconcile the sovereignty of God and the free will of man in relation to salvation is not important. I recognize that Your ways are not my ways and that Your thoughts are not my thoughts. Yours are so much higher than mine. Therefore, I will simply take You at Your Word. I will not carry any doctrine to any extreme to which You do not carry it. I will simply believe what You say and allow You to speak for Yourself."

Now then, Beloved, having said all that, let's return to John 10. You must understand this passage in its context. Remember that John wrote so his readers might know of the signs which Jesus performed which showed Him to be the Christ, the Son of God. These were written that we might believe and in believing might have life in His name (John 20:30,31).

But what about those who saw the signs and did not believe? Why did some believe and others did not? Why did the religious leaders for the most part not believe? And why did they try to take away Jesus' life?

Let's take these questions one by one, for the answers are all in John 10. The Jewish leaders for the most part did not believe because they were not of God's sheep. "The Jews therefore gathered around Him, and were saying to Him, 'How long will You keep us in suspense? If You are the Christ, tell us plainly.' Jesus answered them, 'I told you, and you do not believe; the works that I do in My Father's name, these bear witness of Me. But you do not believe, because you are not of My sheep' " (10:24-26).

God is the Author, the Initiator of our salvation: They saw the signs but did not believe. Let me remind you again of what Jesus said to the multitude who followed Him because of the loaves and fish. He told them that we are given by the Father to the Son, drawn to Him by the Father; and as we hear and learn from the Father, we come to Jesus (John 6:37,39,44,45).

O Sheep, this is for your comfort. Accept it and rest in the character of your God.

15

If you can accept the sovereignty of God in your salvation as taught in the Word of God, it will bring you great peace in dealing with the death of your loved ones. So often I have watched people agonize over the death of another because they were not sure whether the person really knew the Lord Jesus Christ. And in their agony, they would begin to torment themselves with "if onlys": "If only I had been a better witness." "If only I had gone to see her and had shared the gospel one more time." "If only he hadn't died so suddenly. Maybe if he had lived longer, he would have been saved." To live with these "if onlys" is not only agony, it is needless. No "if only" would have saved them if they had not already been saved.

This reality is the blessed comfort of understanding the teaching our Lord gives to us in John 6 and 10. Those who are truly His sheep cannot die without hearing the voice of the Shepherd. His sheep *will* hear His voice.

When speaking to the Jews, Jesus said, "I have other sheep, which are not of this fold; I *must* bring them also, and they *shall* hear My voice; and they *shall become* one flock with one shepherd" (John 10:16). Of all that the Father has given Jesus, He will "lose nothing, but raise it up on the last day" (John 6:39). A person who has been given to the Son by the Father cannot die until he believes on the Lord Jesus Christ. And if a person dies without receiving the Lord Jesus Christ, then he never would have believed even if he had lived for hundreds of years.

God does not lose His sheep. They hear His voice, He gives them eternal life, and they shall never perish. This, Beloved, is the comfort of understanding the Godward aspect of salvation. God is in control of life and death.

Deuteronomy 32:39 says, "See now that I, I am He, and there is no god besides Me; it is I who put to death and give life. . . . There is no one who can deliver from My hand." Jesus has "the keys of death and of Hades" (Revelation 1:18).

Jesus confronted the religious leaders who were plotting to put Him to death with this truth. They had no power to take His life from Him. In one mighty breath Jesus addressed the disregard these leaders showed for their sheep and also confronted their impotence to take His life: "For this reason the Father loves Me, because I lay down My life that I may take it again. No one has taken it away from Me, but I lay it down on My own initiative. I have authority to lay it down, and I have authority to take it up again" (John 10:17,18). These leaders were not willing to lay down their lives for the sheep. They had just put one out, because he believed on Jesus when He touched his physical blindness. But Jesus had taken him in. He was one of God's sheep.

Do you wonder if you are? O Beloved, the very desire to be His sheep is because you are—or because you are in the process of becoming one.

16 Remember I said that if you were going to be saved, you couldn't die before salvation? Let me share the content of two letters, one from a Precept student, Joyce, and the other from her Precept leader. I shed tears of joy when I read these as I thought, "Father, this is what life and ministry are all about . . . people coming to know You and Your Word! O thank You for these women who are reaching out to others."

Both letters centered around the same person: a 74-year-old woman.

Dear Kay,

I must share my experience with you. I am taking the Genesis II course. Several Fridays ago in early January, my friend Susie visited our Precept study with me. We were nearing the end of the Genesis course. Susie became so excited that she ordered the In & Out for Genesis II.

Susie is a registered nurse. She is now 74, so she doesn't nurse but she is active. She is married to a physician who was stricken with a massive stroke and is confined to a nursing home with only the use of his right arm and hand. Susie was a constant visitor to her husband at the nursing home.

I had worked for her husband for 29 years, and during those years, Susie and I had become close friends. But during the last several years, we had drifted apart. I was so thrilled with this new Precept Bible study I had to share this with her, but at first, Susie found many excuses why she could not attend. After her first visit, that changed.

At this point, let me share the Precept leader's insight:

As Joyce mentioned, she and Susie have been close friends for many years, but lately they had seen less of each other. Joyce was so overjoyed when Susie finally decided to attend our Bible study. As Susie heard us share what we had learned, and listened as you taught on tape, I could see the knowledge and joy of the Lord bring a glow to her face.

I think one of the outstanding benefits of being a Precept leader is being able to watch the expressions change as people grasp a new truth of God's Word and how it relates to them. Susie was very enthusiastic about getting into the Genesis II study.

The story will be continued tomorrow, but let me give you something to think about. Are you reaching out to others? Sharing your faith? Don't forget—you may want to get Joe Aldrich's book, *Life-Style Evangelism*. It will show you how you can in a very natural way.

17

Back to Joyce's letter:

On Friday, January 23, Susie and I attended class. After class, one of the ladies asked Susie if she had ever given her life to Christ. She said excitedly, "Yes, I went forward when I was only 11 years old, and I remember that day."

The Precept leader then shared this: "As another member of the class and I talked with Joyce and Susie after class about being born again and how Susie could be sure if she was, I suggested Susie read 1 John and especially note the phrases such as: 'We know that we have come to know Him if . . .' "

Back now to the student's letter:

I drove Susie home, and she asked me about the Trinity. Then she said she loved the calm directness of our leader. As we talked, she shared that she wondered if she would be able to have enough strength for the things that would be facing her in days to come. I told her she would have strength given to her beyond human understanding. Little did I know!

Then Friday evening, I phoned her and asked her if she had listened to your testimony tape. She was so excited and exclaimed she was just going to phone me. She said she had listened to the first side, and then she said, "I must be born again. Next Friday I want to stay after class and talk with our leader, and I want to again verbally give my life to Christ before people. I want to have you come up with me and hold my hand."

On Sunday afternoon, January 25, 1987, Susie was visiting her husband at the nursing home when she had a massive coronary and dropped dead.

Before the next Friday class, Susie was buried. When we met the following Friday, we all felt God had personally touched our lives.

Our friend and classmate had left this world. Buried Thursday, January 29.

In the casket, by her head, was a card placed there by her family. They found the note on the wall of her kitchen, near her opened Bible. The note read:

God is my Father; Jesus is my personal Savior; the Holy Spirit lives within me. If God is for us, who can be against us?

Her daughters said she called each of them that Friday night and was so happy. His sheep had heard His voice, and He had given her eternal life.

18 Our Lord's words bring division. This often makes delivering the gospel a difficult assignment, because we want to be accepted, approved. We don't like to be laughed at, ridiculed, rejected. Yet many times living for Jesus Christ results in this treatment. A popular gospel which can be accepted by all is not the true gospel. The way to heaven is narrow, "the gate is small," and few there are who enter in (Matthew 7:13,14).

How well our Lord reminded us: "Woe to you when all men speak well of you" (Luke 6:26). If they did not speak well of our Lord, should they speak well of us? Of course not! "A slave is not greater than his master" (John 13:16).

As I say all this, I am not excusing people who are rude and ungracious in their delivery of the gospel. It is His words that are to convict and, thus, sometimes bring offense. Our behavior or manner in delivering His gospel should never offend.

Although He hated the sin, Jesus always loved the sinner. Thus, you find Him eating with publicans and sinners, coming not to condemn those who were already condemned but offering them life. However, life was not offered on their terms but on His. It is at this point that the gospel brings offense. It can never be compromised.

Salvation is always on God's terms. When the gospel is presented on those terms, we can be sure His sheep will hear His voice. However, those who are not His often will turn and revile not only the gospel but also those who deliver it.

We see this in John 10:19: "There arose a division again among the Jews because of these words." This is not the first mention of a division in the Gospel of John. In John 7:43, we read: "So there arose a division in the multitude because of Him." And again in John 9:16, we read of how the words of Jesus divide: "Therefore some of the Pharisees were saying, 'This man is not from God, because He does not keep the Sabbath.' But others were saying, 'How can a man who is a sinner perform such signs?' And there was a division among them."

In each of these incidents, the division existed among religious people. Of course, there will be a division with the world because men prefer darkness rather than light. But you expect that response of the world.

When Jesus' words cause division among those who profess to be His followers, it is hard. A division is usually created by those who call Him "Lord, Lord" but who do not do the things He commands them. The division may result too from those who have a form of godliness but know nothing of the power of God. They know about God, but have never entered into a relationship with Him. They have a "self-righteousness" that has not submitted to His righteousness. Therefore, His words bring division.

19 Standing on the Washington shoreline of the Pacific Ocean, he lifted his head toward heaven, gazed at the billows of clouds, and addressed the God who dwelt far beyond them. He was confident that if God was there He could hear his challenge: "God, if You really exist, if Jesus is really Your Son, then let me walk on water like Jesus let Peter do." Frank wanted to know if God existed, but he wanted to know on his terms. So with gauntlet thrown to the ground, he stepped into the water, not onto the water! He waded up to his knees and then turned back. He was adamantly convinced there was no God. He lived with his conviction until, as an old man in his seventies, unable to speak and dying of cancer, he finally took God at His Word and gave in to Jesus. A day later Frank entered into the presence of the God who had not enabled him to walk on water just to prove Himself God.

People have not changed. Like the Jews, Frank pressured Jesus for more evidence of who He was. At the time of the Feast of Dedication, "Jesus was walking in the temple in the portico of Solomon. The Jews therefore gathered around Him, and were saying to Him, 'How long will You keep us in suspense? If You are the Christ, tell us plainly.' Jesus answered them, 'I told you, and you do not believe; the works that I do in My Father's name, these bear witness of Me' " (John 10:23-25).

Frank wanted a new work, a repeat of a miracle God had performed when Peter walked on water. The Jews had seen many signs. They had heard from Jesus' own lips that He was the Son of God, the I AM, one with the Father. But they would not believe. They understood very clearly that

Jesus claimed to be God (John 10:33), but still they would not believe.

How plain does Jesus have to be? How plain does God have to be? God has supernaturally superintended the writing of His Word. He has watched over it and kept it from error in the original manuscripts and preserved it down through the centuries. He has given us evidence after evidence in history and archaeology of the veracity of His Word. Yet we want Him to let us walk on water!

Enough, Beloved! You have enough evidence. You have a record of His works done in the presence of many witnesses—miracles which no man could do apart from God. And you have a record of His words—words which are spirit and life. Now you must take God at His word. Faith comes just as it did to Frank, through the hearing of God's Word. Your part is to believe.

20 Sometime after the winter of the Feast of Dedication and before the Passover, Jesus went to stay beyond the Jordan, where John the Baptist had done his baptizing. It was during this time that Lazarus, Jesus' friend, became ill. His sisters Mary and Martha sent a message from Bethany to inform Jesus of Lazarus' illness. Whether they suspected that Lazarus would have died or not, we do not know.

However, there is one thing we know for sure. Mary and Martha were well aware of the Lord's healing ministry. And there is no record in the Scriptures of anyone ever dying in the presence of our Lord. From what they both said to Jesus after Lazarus' death, I am sure they believed that should death have come lurking in the shadows of their brother's room, it could not have dared touch him in the presence of the Son of God!

Yet, Jesus did not go to Bethany when He received the message of Lazarus' illness. Lazarus died and Jesus came later. When He arrived, both Mary and Martha were convinced that if only Jesus had come, Lazarus "would not have died" (John 11:21,32).

For the remainder of this month, I want us to study and meditate on some invaluable truths from John 11 that will enable you to handle death better when you meet it face-to-face—either in your own life or in the life of a loved one. Often even Christians are ill-prepared to confront and deal with death. It seems to be an enemy, an unwelcome intruder. We may feel that if we don't consider it, then it cannot happen.

How wrong we are! Unless Jesus returns, we will all see death. When death grasped Caesar Brogia by the hand, he cried, "When I lived, I provided for everything but death; now I must die, and I am unprovided to die!"

When Dr. Charles Weigle, the composer of the song, "No One Ever Cared for Me Like Jesus," died, he was in a hospital room in Chattanooga, Tennessee. A nurse, walking by his room, saw him sitting up in bed with his arms stretched toward the ceiling. Stepping into his room, she said cheerfully, "Are you all right, Dr. Weigle?" "O Nurse, I'm going home. I'm going home." Touched by the sweetness of her frail patient, she went to his bed, patted his arm, and replied tenderly, "No, Dr. Weigle, you can't go home. You're too sick." But he looked at her, arms still raised: "No, I am going home." And he went home—straight into the arms of the One who had cared for him.

Read John 11, asking God to remove any fears or misconceptions of death that would bind you.

21 Have you ever wondered how love could allow suffering and death? Have you ever thought that if you were God, you certainly would put an end to evil, to war, to suffering, to death? If you have, you are not alone. Those thoughts are common to man.

Evil, war, suffering, death are hard to experience, but God permits them because they serve His purposes. Remember that His purposes are far beyond our comprehension because our understanding is finite. So God bids us "walk by faith, not by sight" (2 Corinthians 5:7). He calls us to "look not at the things which are seen, but at the things which are not seen" (2 Corinthians 4:18). He instructs us to give thanks in all things (1 Thessalonians 5:18). He comforts us with the knowledge that all things will "work together for good to those who love God, to those who are called according to His purpose" (Romans 8:28).

As we look at John 11, I want to share eight truths which will loosen death's grave clothes. In the loosening you will be set free from the fear of death and from the sorrow which has no hope.

The first truth is: *Love allows suffering and death.* When Mary and Martha sent a message to tell Jesus of Lazarus' illness, they were convinced that He would come immediately. They knew Jesus loved them. They knew too He was able to heal the sick. And so they sent a message to Him saying, "Lord, behold, he whom You love is sick" (John 11:3).

Can you imagine what it must have been like to wait for His arrival? I wonder how many times they went to the door to look for the One who could alleviate their pain and distress. Watching Lazarus' weakened condition as he fought for life, they wondered if the Lord would come in time.

Years ago I sat with my mother at the bedside of my father in the intensive care unit of the Venice Hospital, waiting for God to heal my father. He had undergone five major surgeries in 12 days. Before they amputated his leg, I looked at his almost-black foot and prayed, "O Father, I know, if You want to, You can speak a word and bring back the circulation to my father's leg." I knew God could—I didn't lack faith—but God didn't choose to heal my father's leg or the rest of his body.

On April 22, 1980, the days God had ordained for my father came to an end. My precious, precious daddy died. And in the process, God allowed him—and us—to suffer. Did God love him or us any less? Was God any less who He is for allowing this heartache?

No! Love has been and always will be one of the attributes of God. Love allows suffering and death.

22 When love delays, when God does not answer your prayers the way you think He should, you can know, precious child of God, He is in the process of building your faith. And in the building of your faith, others will be reached and ministered to. This brings us to the second truth that will loosen death's grave clothes which would incapacitate you and keep you from serving God. This freeing truth is: *For the Christian, suffering and death are platforms for faith.*

Faith is not faith until it is tested, and what could test it more than suffering or death? The way you and I respond in suffering can either contradict the words of our profession or it can bring glory to God.

In John 11:4, we hear Jesus say, "This sickness is not unto death, but for the glory of God, that the Son of God may be glorified by it." To which you may reply, "Yes, God was glorified because Lazarus was raised from the dead, but my loved one died! Can that glorify God?" It can, Beloved, if you will walk in the promise and assurance of who Jesus is, if you will hold fast in faith to the truth that He is "the resurrection and the life." For the one who believes in Him "shall live even if he dies" (John 11:25). God will be glorified if you will not allow yourself to grieve as those "who have no hope" (1 Thessalonians 4:13).

Jesus said to Martha, "Everyone who lives and believes in Me shall never die"; and then He asked her, "Do you believe this?" (John 11:26). He will ask you the same thing when you face death, either your own or that of a loved one. How you answer that question, how you respond to death, will display your faith.

O Beloved, may you and I learn it well: In every trial, every testing, every temptation, we can live out the sufficiency of His grace and the reality of our faith. Everyone wants a story with a happy ending. We hope for a future, not disaster. We long for success, not defeat. We love to hear of those who overcome.

And this, child of God, is our inheritance in Christ Jesus. Every occasion of suffering and death can have a happy ending if we will cling in faith to the blessed hope of the resurrection and the life, where God "shall wipe away every tear from their eyes; and there shall no longer be any death; there shall no longer be any mourning, or crying, or pain," for "the first things" will "have passed away" (Revelation 21:4).

According to John 11:15, Lazarus was allowed to die that others might believe. May you and I see that whatever God permits has a purpose. May we not miss His purpose, but see it as a platform for faith.

23 The fear of death is an incredibly powerful weapon that Satan wields through human agency, and evil men have always sought to intimidate and rule others through this fear. Yet to the Christian, death should be but a rubber sword. When Jesus decided to go back to Judea, to Mary and Martha in Bethany, "The disciples said to Him, 'Rabbi, the Jews were just now seeking to stone You, and are You going there again?' Jesus answered, 'Are there not twelve hours in the day? If anyone walks in the day, he does not stumble, because he sees the light of this world. But if anyone walks in the night, he stumbles, because the light is not in him' " (John 11:8-10).

The Son of Man did not fear death but rested in the sovereignty of God. The Jews could not kill Him until God was ready. When they did crucify Him, it served God's purpose.

Deuteronomy 32:39 assures us that God kills and makes alive. None is greater than God, and none can take our lives without His permission. Satan ruled man through fear of death. The devil at one time had the power of death because of man's sin. At Calvary, Jesus paid the wages of sin—which was death—so that Satan no longer rules over us through sin. "Since then the children share in flesh and blood, He Himself likewise also partook of the same, that through death He might render powerless him who had the power of death, that is, the devil; and might deliver those who through fear of death were subject to slavery all their lives" (Hebrews 2:14,15).

Because we are freed from sin, "death no longer is master" over us (Romans 6:9). Hallelujah! Jesus holds "the keys of death and of Hades" (Revelation 1:18).

24 We come now to the third truth that will loosen death's fear-binding grave clothes: *Following the Light of the world will keep you from stumbling over the fear of death.*

Let me ask you mothers and fathers a question: Would you keep your children home from some mission field of service for fear they might lose their lives? Or for fear that you might not see them again before you die?

To let the fear of death rule you is to walk in darkness rather than in the light. When you walk in darkness, you stumble. To digress from God's purpose, through fear of death or for any other reason, is to walk in darkness. God forbid that you or I should stumble through life, or that we should cause our loved ones to stumble, because we do not believe our God and walk in obedience to His Word. If Jesus had listened to well-meaning people, you and I would not have a Savior.

You need to take a few minutes, Beloved, and meditate upon these truths. Ask God to show you if fear is ruling your life. Wait before Him and write out anything He shows you. Then in faith, put it away. Remember, your times are in His hands—hands pierced by love. Thank Him that His perfect love casts out fear (1 John 4:18).

25 To the Christian, death is not final. A believer simply falls asleep in Jesus and wakes up instantly in the presence of God. If anything ought to loosen death's grave clothes, it is this fourth truth: *For the Christian, death is but falling asleep in Jesus.*

Jesus said to the disciples, "'Our friend Lazarus has fallen asleep; but I go, that I may awaken him out of sleep.' The disciples therefore said to Him, 'Lord, if he has fallen asleep, he will recover.' Now Jesus had spoken of his death;

but they thought that He was speaking of literal sleep. Then Jesus . . . said to them plainly, 'Lazarus is dead'" (John 11:11-14).

As you study what the Scriptures say regarding death and the Christian, it is obvious that death is drastically different for the lost and the saved. For the lost, death is never to experience life. It is to lose any opportunity to ever believe on the Lord Jesus Christ, for "there is salvation in no one else; for there is no other name under heaven that has been given among men, by which we must be saved" (Acts 4:12). Therefore, those who do not believe on the Lord Jesus Christ in this life will perish, for "it is appointed for men to die once and after this comes judgment" (Hebrews 9:27).

Those who die without the Lord Jesus Christ are referred to as "the dead." Someday the dead will stand before the Great White Throne of God and be judged according to the things which were written in the books, according to their deeds. They will then be cast into the lake of fire. "This is the second death, the lake of fire. And if anyone's name was not found written in the book of life, he was thrown into the lake of fire" (Revelation 20:14,15).

What a contrast with those who have received the Lord Jesus Christ! Job wrote: "And as for me, I know that my Redeemer lives, and at the last He will take His stand on the earth. Even after my skin is destroyed, yet from my flesh I shall see God; whom I myself shall behold, and whom my eyes shall see and not another" (Job 19:25-27).

Some say that when Christians die, they sleep in the grave until Jesus returns and raises the dead. However, Paul said, "To live is Christ, and to die is gain" (Philippians 1:21). To sleep in the grave would not be gain! Paul knew that physical death would allow him to "depart and be with Christ," which, he said, "is very much better" (Philippians 1:23).

When Paul talks about putting off our earthly tent, he says to be "absent from the body" is "to be at home with the Lord" (2 Corinthians 5:1-9). In 1 Thessalonians 4:13-18, he refers to those who have died in Christ as having "fallen asleep in Jesus" because this is what death is to the believer—

falling asleep and waking up in the presence of our Lord. Rejoice, O child of God!

26 The very minute you believe on the Lord Jesus Christ you pass from death to life. You will never experience death as the unbeliever does. Your spirit simply leaves your earthly body and goes immediately into the presence of God the Father, the Son, and the Holy Spirit. And at the moment of your entrance into heaven, you will join your loved ones who have preceded you. You will recognize them, even as Moses and Elijah were recognized at the transfiguration of Jesus.

Thus, we come to the fifth truth from John 11 which will loosen death's grave clothes: *Because Jesus is the Resurrection and the Life, the Christian will not see death.* This truth caused Jesus to proclaim, "I am the resurrection and the life; he who believes in Me shall live even if he dies, and everyone who lives and believes in Me shall never die" (11:25,26).

When Jesus says those who believe in Him will never die, it is obvious that He does not mean we will never leave this body through what we call physical death. Rather, I believe He is saying we will never experience death as an unbeliever does.

Why? Because in His death, burial, and resurrection, Jesus "abolished death, and brought life and immortality to light through the gospel" (2 Timothy 1:10). And since our Lord Jesus Christ resides within each believer (Colossians 1:27), we have eternal life within. "God has given us eternal life, and this life is in His Son. He who has the Son has the life; he who does not have the Son of God does not have the life" (1 John 5:11,12). How can one who has His life within ever die?

When my friends Bill and Ramona lost their 17-year-old Bryan in an automobile accident seven years ago, they had never experienced such heart-wrenching pain. Yet Ramona writes:

Our Bryan met Jesus face to face in all His glory. What a glorious day for Bryan. But what a difficult day for our family. For Bryan, it was what he had been preparing for. God looked at Bryan and said, "Well done. Come on in. I have a place prepared just for you." I had read John 11:25,26 many times: "I am the resurrection and the life . . . everyone who . . . believes in Me shall never die. . . ." But the last four words in verse 26 hit me like a ton of bricks: "Do you believe this?"! I knew I had to answer that question. And once I said to the Lord, "Yes, I do believe," God began to show me His other promises. On the day Bryan died, I could either reject God or cling to Him. The choice was mine. Bill and I chose to cling to God. Our hurt was healed by believing His Word.

O Beloved, when you confront death, remember you will not see death. You'll see Jesus face-to-face!

27 "Jesus wept." It is the shortest verse in the Bible and yet one of the most poignant. Although Jesus knew He was going to raise Lazarus from the dead, and that their sorrow would then be turned to joy, He still wept. He knows our pain and understands our sorrow, and He weeps because we weep.

With this, Beloved, we come to the sixth truth: *Because of God's sovereignty over death, the believer weeps but does not wail.* We can weep because the separation of death brings hurt; but we are not to wail, because we have hope. In 1 Thessalonians 4:13, Paul writes, "But we do not want you to be uninformed, brethren, about those who are asleep, that you may not grieve, as do the rest who have no hope." We grieve because death causes separation, loss, and loneliness; but we do not grieve as those who have no hope.

Someday the separation will be over, loss will be gain, and loneliness will be great rejoicing, for we shall all be with the Lord and with one another forever and ever (1 Thessalonians 4:16,17). All of this is ours, Beloved, because God is sovereign—He rules even over death. He is the Alpha and the Omega, the Beginning and the End (Revelation 22:13). From Him, through Him, and to Him are all things; and because we belong to Him, all things are ours as heirs of God and joint-heirs with Christ (Romans 11:36; 8:17).

So weep—Jesus wept. But do not wail. Wailing shows despair, and in Jesus, there is hope.

28 Ramona and Bill had hope because they had seen the change in Bryan's life and because they believed God's Word. Bill shared:

> On Sunday night before his accident on the following Saturday, Bryan was asked by our Minister of Youth to share his testimony. Bryan loved the Lord very much and was a loving and caring young man. He never gave his mother and me any trouble during his 17 years with us. Bryan made a comment to our church that Sunday night: "I am excited about what the Lord is doing, and I feel that He is about to do something very special in my life." Bryan then read Philippians 1:6: "For I am confident of this very thing, that He who began a good work in you will perfect it until the day of Christ Jesus."
>
> On Saturday March 29, Bryan was killed instantly in a car accident on his way to the beach the last day of spring break. He was going only 15 to 20 MPH but hit a slick oil spot. My first reaction was one of disbelief. The next few days and weeks were filled with many feelings and emotions. I was mad at God for letting our son be killed. Then I came to realize that God never makes a mistake; and even though I did not like or understand what had happened, I knew God still loved us and that Bryan was being cared for in heaven.

Bill and Ramona wept, but they did not wail. They rested in God's sovereignty.

29 Death was not God's desire. It came because of sin. Therefore, death has always been an enemy. When

Jesus came face-to-face with death at the tomb of Lazarus, His indignation was so great that He was deeply moved in spirit (John 11:33) and snorted like a horse. This is what the term "deeply moved in spirit" means.[1] At that moment, Jesus, who came to conquer sin and death, confronted an enemy. We come now to our seventh truth: *Death is not an impossible, impassable barrier but a call to battle.*

Death came because of man's sin. God intended fellowship with man, not separation by death. I believe this is why Jesus wept at the tomb of Lazarus. There are three accounts in the Gospels of Jesus weeping, and all of them relate in one way or another to death. Let's look at them.

> And when He [Jesus] approached, He saw the city and wept over it, saying, "If you had known in this day, even you, the things which make for peace! But now they have been hidden from your eyes. For the days shall come upon you when your enemies . . . will level you to the ground and your children within you . . . because you did not recognize the time of your visitation" (Luke 19:41-44).

Jesus wept over Jerusalem because they had rejected Him, their Messiah. Sin had deceived them. Jerusalem would be destroyed because the Jews would not repent, believe that Jesus was the Christ, and be saved. What the Jews longed for—the Messiah and His kingdom, heaven, and eternal life—they would miss. And the One who could have saved them and given them all this wept audibly.

The second account of Jesus weeping is at the tomb of Lazarus.

The third time Jesus weeps is when He faces the awful hell of death when He will be separated from the Father. In Hebrews 5, we get a glimpse not given in other accounts of the agony of our Lord in the Garden of Gethsemane: "In the days of His flesh, He offered up both prayers and supplications with loud crying and tears to the One able to save Him from death, and He was heard because of His piety" (5:7).

Jesus wept in the face of death's separation, for He was to be made sin for us and, in becoming sin, He would "taste death for everyone" (Hebrews 2:9; 2 Corinthians 5:21). For the first time in all of eternity, Jesus would be separated from the Father. The Life and Light of the world would wage war against death and darkness—and He would win!

Death was not an unconquerable enemy. It was not an impossible, impassable barrier for the Son of Man and of God who came to take away sin. Death will have to release its captives at the sound of His voice—even as when He cried, "Lazarus, come forth" (John 11:43). "For an hour is coming, in which all who are in the tombs shall hear His voice, and shall come forth . . ." (John 5:28,29).

30 Can you imagine watching Jesus Christ command a dead man to come forth from the grave and then seeing him appear upon command, and still refusing to believe that Jesus was sent from God? When Jesus said, "Lazarus, come forth," Lazarus was actually propelled to the door of the tomb. It was as if a giant magnet of life pulled him out of death's magnetic field!

Lazarus had been "bound hand and foot with wrappings; and his face was wrapped around with a cloth" (John 11:44). He could neither move nor see in the darkness of that tomb how to get out of it. His eyes were covered with grave clothes, as were his arms and legs. Until someone loosed him and let him go, he could not move. There was no way even a live man bound in grave clothes could have come forth from the tomb.

Jews believed that the soul of a dead person hovered about the body until the third day, when corruption began and the soul took flight. I believe Jesus purposely waited until four days had passed before He came to raise Lazarus from the dead. I think He wanted to prove conclusively that He was the Resurrection and the Life. Here was the miracle of miracles, the sign of signs that would show Him to be the

Christ, the Son of God. Only one sign would remain, and that would be His own resurrection from the dead.

And yet many seeing Lazarus' resurrection still would not believe. In John 11:45,46, we read: "Many therefore of the Jews, who had come to Mary and beheld what He had done, believed in Him. But some of them went away to the Pharisees, and told them the things which Jesus had done."

This brings us to our final truth: *Death exposes unbelief.* When a person comes face-to-face with the certainty of imminent death, then he knows whether he has believed or not.

O, how I have longed to share more at funerals! I believe that every funeral ought to be a time of confronting family and friends with the gospel of Jesus Christ. Is this not what our Lord did at Lazarus' wake? Of course, for it was then that He asked Martha if she really believed that He was the Christ, God incarnate, the Resurrection and the Life.

Have you told your family what you want done at your funeral? Have you ever thought of how, indirectly, you might have one last opportunity, even in your death, to share the glorious gospel of Jesus Christ?

Death, Beloved, exposes unbelief. Make your death count. Let it expose any unbelief in those attending your funeral. Don't miss the opportunity for life to spring out of your death. Write it in your will: "If no gospel is preached, then no inheritance will be given!"

May

Love Wears a Towel to the Throne

1 If you intend to serve Jesus Christ in a way that you aren't ashamed of when you see Him face-to-face, then, Beloved, now is the time. For once again, as at Calvary, the world's "apparent" hour is coming—a night of darkness. "For you yourselves know full well that the day of the Lord will come just like a thief in the night. While they are saying, 'Peace and safety!' then destruction will come upon them suddenly like birth pangs upon a woman with child . . ." (1 Thessalonians 5:2,3).

With all that is going on in Christendom in the United States of America, it is blatantly obvious that judgment is beginning "with the household of God; and if it begins with us first, what will be the outcome for those who do not obey the gospel of God? AND IF IT IS WITH DIFFICULTY THAT THE RIGHTEOUS IS SAVED, WHAT WILL BECOME OF THE GODLESS MAN AND THE SINNER? Therefore, let those also who suffer according to the will of God entrust their souls to a faithful Creator in doing what is right" (1 Peter 4:17-19).

God is in the process of exposing what is "not right" among those who name His name. We can forget that we are called to holiness and righteousness, not to popularity, fame, wealth, success, or ease. This is not the hour for these things. The King has not yet come!

Now is the hour to be identified with our Lord Jesus Christ in His humiliation and His rejection by the world.

The world will treat those who abide in Jesus just as they treated Him. We are not greater than our Master (John 15:18-20).

It seems that many have a lapse of memory regarding their identification with our Lord. And some have not been confronted with the fact that Jesus calls us to the cross, not the crown. The crown will come in time, but only for those who bear His cross.

We see professing Christians who seem to be bidding on what the devil offered but Jesus refused—the kingdoms of this world. They want to live in the luxuries as King's kids before He is crowned King of kings. They want a crown without a cross. They want the Christian homefronts but not Christ's battlefield. They want the lilting, hand-clapping choruses, but not "Onward, Christian Soldiers."

The world has encouraged us to take off the armor of God and to sit down at the tables of detente. So, instead of fighting the good fight, we have negotiated for arms control.

We are called to proclaim God's Word to a lost world. But many are guilty of putting the sword of His Word back into its sheath instead of proclaiming it in a way that will convict the world of sin, righteousness, and judgment. Their focus is more on their well-being than on "being poured out as a drink offering upon the sacrifice and service" of others' faith (Philippians 2:17). The hour has come to be poured out for Him! Are you willing?

2 With His first miracle—turning water into wine at the wedding in Cana—Jesus said that His hour had not yet come. But now as He prepared to celebrate the Feast of the Passover, He declared to His disciples, "The hour has come for the Son of Man to be glorified" (John 12:23).

The hour was testified to by the Law and prophets, and awaited since the Garden of Eden. The hour was promised by God Himself when Adam and Eve partook of the forbidden fruit and, in their act of disobedience, instantly imprisoned all mankind in sin. That long-awaited hour had arrived!

The hour for God to be glorified in the Son of Man was upon them. The hour had come for the grain of wheat to fall into the ground and die so that it would not remain alone.

Mary sensed that if she were going to pour out all she had on Jesus, now was the time. She might not have another opportunity! Six days before the Passover when Jesus came to Bethany, Mary, Martha, and their brother, Lazarus, went to have supper at the house of Simon the leper. She knew what she had to do. Love compelled her. "Mary therefore took a pound of very costly perfume of pure nard, and anointed the feet of Jesus, and wiped His feet with her hair; and the house was filled with the fragrance of the perfume" (John 2:3).

Was Mary oblivious to others in the room with them? We don't know. We do know, though, that once she poured out all she had on her Lord, her consecration became the subject of rebuke and ridicule. "Judas Iscariot, one of His disciples, who was intending to betray Him [Jesus], said, 'Why was this perfume not sold for three hundred denarii, and given to poor people?' " (John 12:4,5).

The others did not understand that Judas' expression resulted "not because he was concerned about the poor, but because he was a thief." Only Jesus knew that since Judas "had the money box, he used to pilfer what was put into it" (John 12:6).

Thus Judas' assessment seemed astute. "Why pour out your all on Jesus! Three hundred denarii!" That was about ten months' wages—probably all of Mary's savings.

It was not uncommon to invest in ointment since it could be sold little by little for a profit. But it was uncommon to make such an investment and then simply lavish it all on one person's feet. "Uncommon and a waste!"

The 11 agreed. And you, Beloved—what do you say?

3 Have you ever been criticized for the depth of your commitment to Jesus Christ? Ever been accused of being a fanatic? Or have you found yourself judging others in this way? Have you felt that they carried their Christianity to an extreme? "After all, he does need time for his own interests. Why does he eat and sleep Christianity? There are other things in this life! And besides, that is really all he ever wants to talk about. I'm a Christian, too! But there is no need to go so far!"

According to those who were having supper at Simon's, Mary went too far. They were quick to give their opinion: "The disciples were indignant when they saw this, and said, 'Why this waste? For this perfume might have been sold for a high price and the money given to the poor' " (Matthew 26:8,9). "And they were scolding her" (Mark 14:5).

Have you ever been scolded because of your consecration? Then you know how Mary must have felt. When family members don't understand, you don't know what to say. You know that even though you are consecrated to your Lord, you aren't neglecting them. Although they have their share of your energies and affection, there are times when they don't like that so much of you is poured out on Him.

If their commitment isn't the same as yours, that isn't your business. You know only one thing—that you have to pour your all out on Him. So when the scolding comes because of your lavish love, what do you say?

When the disciples began to criticize Mary's extravagant love, Jesus said, "Let her alone; why do you bother her? She has done a good deed to Me. For the poor you always have with you, and whenever you wish, you can do them good; but you do not always have Me. She has done what she could; she has anointed My body beforehand for the burial. And truly I say to you, wherever the gospel is preached in the whole world, that also which this woman has done shall be spoken of in memory of her" (Mark 14:6-9).

Others did not understand but Jesus did. Therefore, what did their criticism and evaluation matter about where Mary should put her treasures? She had her Lord's approval! She, like you and I, was created for *His* pleasure (Revelation 4:11). If her sacrifice brought Him pleasure, wasn't that all that really mattered?

4 Has there ever been a time in your life when you felt compelled to do a work for the Lord and others tried to convince you that you were wrong? Maybe they wanted to spare you. Possibly they felt it was too demanding. Maybe they were concerned for your health.

That has happened to me several times. Once in 1976 I felt a strong burden to get people into an inductive study of God's Word. I believed that if they could just see truth personally for themselves, their relationship with the Lord would take on a new level of intimacy. I came to a point of strong conviction that people were perishing for a lack of spiritual food.

Christians were being told repeatedly that they needed to get into the Word for themselves, but they weren't being shown how. Numerous fill-in-the-blank Bible studies were being published, but then there were people like me who weren't challenged by filling in blanks. I've always felt that fill-in-the-blank questions are designed to help you see the author's answer, but do not force you to grapple with the text.

God had taught me how to dig into His Word by observing, interpreting, and applying the text apart from commentaries, and it was such an absolute joy that I could hardly contain it! What confidence it gave me as a teacher of God's Word to see truth for myself.

When I went to the commentaries, I was better able to discern what they were saying, why they said it, and if I did or did not agree. Were the authors simply passing on what they heard or read from others? Or had they discerned truth for themselves? If you do not know what the Scriptures say and mean, then it is easy to accept a wrong interpretation and convincingly pass it on to others who do not know how to handle the Word accurately.

I saw that it wasn't necessary to have a theological degree in order to understand God's Word in a deep way. The Word of God was written for children of God, and they have a resident Teacher whose ministry it is to guide them into all truth. Our Teacher is the Holy Spirit. And if we simply follow the basic principles of observation, interpretation, and application, we can understand the Word of God.

I believed that God wanted me to teach the Word of God "precept upon precept" (Isaiah 28:10 KJV). But it was going to require great discipline and commitment on my part, and some were concerned for my health.

5 Work for our Lord is demanding and requires a degree of "self-sacrifice." Those who warned me against writing *Precept Upon Precept* inductive Bible study courses were genuinely concerned, because they thought I was taking on too much. And although I could appreciate their love and concern, I knew that I had to write *Precept* no matter the cost.

I even remember the place where I stood while two people who love me dearly tried to talk me out of what I wanted to do. I burst into tears, crying, "Even if I die, I have to do what God has called me to do." Because they loved God and wanted to be true to His calling, they never again tried to stop me. Better to lose yourself in the will of God than to save yourself and miss His purpose for your life.

Jesus understands. Remember when our Lord was facing Calvary—the ultimate in self-sacrifice—He said, "What shall I say, 'Father, save Me from this hour'? But for this purpose I came to this hour" (John 12:27).

I know that *Precept* is one of God's purposes for my life—it is a good work which God has before ordained for me to walk in. To write *Precept* and the other studies, to have a television and radio program, to travel and teach internationally all require discipline and sacrifice. And yet, to me this is what Christianity is all about.

Self-sacrifice is not the order of our day, because self is a priority. Our rights and *our* welfare are foremost in our minds. We are not thinking of sacrifice when achievement is determined by who is number one, or who has the most followers. Not when our chief concern is our self-image.

O Beloved, we need to be careful to place our values on the eternal, not on the temporal. We need to look for God's approval, not man's, and we should encourage our leaders and teachers to do the same—no matter what the cost. We should say, "Tell us what we need to hear—not what we want to hear."

It is interesting that Mary was criticized by Judas Iscariot who would soon defect. It was more expedient for him to sell Jesus than follow Him to Calvary.

Apparently, Judas followed Jesus for what he could get. No wonder it upset him so to see all that costly ointment poured out on Jesus' feet! It could have been sold and put into the disciples' coffers where Judas could dip into it.

Judas *seemed* concerned for the welfare for others—but not to the exclusion of his own welfare. Mary's consecration was inconceivable to him.

Have you held back from what He asks because of another's question? Or have you been critical of another because you've not understood their calling? Talk to your God.

6 Have you ever had Jesus come to your defense? You poured yourself out. You sacrificed your time, energies, talents, or some material thing, and it seemed wasted. Yet later, it was proven to have spiritual worth. Then Jesus came to your defense, just as surely as He came to Mary's. Even though others did not audibly hear your Lord's words of defense, still He eventually vindicated your sacrifice by its fruit.

Oh, how sweet it is to know that your Lord understands, that He is there to defend you in His own way and in His own time!

Jesus had come to Mary's defense on another occasion when her consecration was misunderstood.

"Now as they were traveling along, He entered a certain village; and a woman named Martha welcomed Him into her home. And she had a sister called Mary, who moreover was listening to the Lord's word, seated at His feet. But

Martha was distracted with all her preparations; and she came up to Him, and said, 'Lord, do You not care that my sister has left me to do all the serving alone? Then tell her to help me.' But the Lord answered and said to her, 'Martha, Martha, you are worried and bothered about so many things; but only a few things are necessary, really only one, for Mary has chosen the good part, which shall not be taken away from her' " (Luke 10:38-42).

As I read this passage, I cannot help but feel that Jesus' visit was unexpected, the beginning of a close and special relationship with this family.

While Martha was in a dither of excitement, Mary simply sat at the feet of the Lord. What a contrast! Martha was in a flurry, getting everything prepared. Can't you just see her flying around that kitchen? Flour on her fingers, pushing the hair off her face with the back of her wrist, catching the drops of perspiration, and wiping the back of her hand on her apron. All the time wondering where Mary was and why she wasn't in there helping her. After all, when had they had a more important guest!

It was finally more than she could take. Martha had to talk to Jesus about Mary. And when Martha questioned Mary's motivation, Jesus took up her defense.

7 Have you ever felt that what you were doing for the Lord was keeping you from Him? Martha was experiencing this dilemma, and it affected her relationship with her sister. In Luke 10:40, we read: "Martha was distracted with all her preparations. "All her preparations" literally means her "much service." The Greek word for *distracted* means "to draw away." Isn't it interesting that Martha's service for her Lord drew her away from Him instead of to Him?

Martha was obviously oblivious to what was happening. Our Lord pointed it out to her by coming to Mary's defense. Mary had chosen the one thing which was needful. She sat at Jesus' feet. I believe here we find the reason for Mary's consecration, the reason she poured out all she had on Jesus. She sat at His feet because she wanted to know Him intimately.

Sitting at His feet and listening to His Word put the world in proper perspective. It also made Mary sensitive to the times. Therefore, six days before the Passover, she poured out her all for Him. Because of the time she had spent with Him she understood He was God's Passover Lamb. There would not be another opportunity, so Mary did "what she could" when she could (Mark 14:8).

That kind of sensitivity, Beloved, only comes from sitting at His feet and listening to His Word. Sitting at the Lord's feet is a matter of choice. We all have the same number of hours in a day. Some work longer hours than others and some require more sleep. Yet each of us has time when we are not working or sleeping. What we do with those hours makes the difference between being a "Mary" or a "Martha."

"But, Kay," you may say, "I have so much to do for the Lord that I cannot sit at His feet." I understand how you feel, but we must go back to the Word. Jesus says there is one thing which is needful—only one—and then He points to Mary as His example.

That one needful thing is *active sitting*. When you sit actively, you listen, hear, and know what the Lord is saying. The result of active sitting is more effective service, because it is born of the Word and worship, not of duty, obligation, or self-effort.

What you gain from sitting at His feet and listening to His Word will not be taken away from you. It is yours forever, Beloved. If this is what you want, then you must make a choice. And when the "Marthas" do not understand, when they become critical, remember that Jesus understands, and that He will come to your defense.

8 What happens when a Christian is drawn away from the Lord by "much service"? Are there warning signs to alert us of the dangers? I believe there are. Let's look at five things which were true of Martha. Should you see some of these attitudes or behavior patterns in your life, you can take heed and return to Jesus' feet.

Martha's much service made her *critical.* It was hard on Martha when Mary sat while she served. You could, in this case, almost call her "Martyr Martha."

Let me also say that I believe that actively sitting at the Lord's feet and listening to His Word will result in a life that effectively serves His kingdom. True listening brings obedience.

Martha *accused the Lord of not caring.* Listen to her words again: "Lord, do You not care . . . ?" (Luke 10:40). O Beloved, if you do not give the Lord time to talk with you through His Word and prayer, it will be so easy to find yourself doubting His love and His sovereign care. And when things do not go your way, you will find yourself accusing the Lord.

You also will find yourself *anxious, with no peace.* Jesus said, "Martha, Martha, you are worried . . ." (Luke 10:41). But then isn't that logical in light of the fact that Jesus is the Prince of Peace and she was not making time for Him? God tells us that He will keep us in perfect peace if our minds are stayed on Him (Isaiah 26:3).

Martha was troubled because of her circumstances. You cannot live above them without sitting at His feet and getting His perspective. He is the God of the circumstances.

The fourth characteristic of serving apart from sitting is only logical: You find yourself *telling the Lord what to do!* Listen to Martha: "Lord . . . then tell her to help me" (Luke 10:40). If you don't take time to listen, you'll find yourself having a one-sided relationship. You'll do all the talking, rushing into prayer, spilling out your requests, jumping up, running out, and getting busy serving.

Where will it all end? You will find yourself *bothered about so many things.* Temporal things will preoccupy you, because you have not had time to focus on the eternal.

When Mary poured out her earthly treasure on Jesus, it was because earthly things didn't matter anymore. Only

Jesus mattered. Isn't that what you want, Beloved? Choose the one thing which is needful. Then you won't find yourself critical of others, accusing the Lord, anxious and without peace, telling the Lord what to do, and bothered and occupied with things.

9 As I travel and talk with people who don't know the Lord Jesus Christ, I notice that many are without any goals outside of themselves. They want personal happiness, and they desire to find deep satisfaction and contentment. Yet without exception, they have no concrete means of achieving their goals. Most fear dying without ever having reached "success" or happiness. They have no idea what death holds beyond annihilation. They are seeking life; yet they do not know or understand that *life comes out of death!*

It is this point that Jesus made as He spoke of "a grain of wheat" (John 12:24). Our Lord began His statement with "truly, truly." As I've stated before, every time Jesus said "truly, truly," He meant "surely, surely—absolutely." He was stating a fact. And the fact is: "Truly, truly, I say to you, unless a grain of wheat falls into the earth and dies, it remains by itself alone; but if it dies, it bears much fruit." The principle is clear: Life comes from death.

Jesus was referring to His death, for His hour had come to die as the Lamb of God who would take away "the sin of the world" (John 1:29). It was through His death that those who were condemned to death could have eternal life. As He spoke of His own death which would bring forth life, Jesus taught the same principle for their lives when He said: "He who loves his life loses it; and he who hates his life in this world shall keep it to life eternal. If anyone serves Me, let him follow Me; and where I am, there shall My servant also be; if anyone serves Me, the Father will honor him" (John 12:25,26).

Those who would receive eternal life must die to their own supposed right to life. Christians can have only one life, only one Lord. Therefore, when one becomes a true

Christian, you will see a turning from self or, to put it another way, a dying to self.

Let me give you one Scripture to look up and meditate on, and then we'll discuss it more tomorrow. Read Mark 8:34-38 and ask the Lord for understanding.

10 Oh, the blessedness of being poured out for others! The deep joy of losing your life for the sake of the gospel. O Beloved, never are you more like your Lord than when you lay down your rights, your privileges, your expectations, your possessions, your very self for another. This concept is not understood in our society. Many would love to be in the ministry—not to give but to get and to have their own needs met. And in the process, they are missing the blessedness of being poured out for the Lord.

Note that I said "poured out for the Lord," not for others. If you pour yourself out only for others, eventually you can wear out. Your service must be for *Him*—born of Him, directed by Him. If you are responding to His direction, He will sustain you and He will provide. If your service then goes unappreciated or is challenged, you can rest in knowing that human response or results don't matter. You have done it "as unto Jesus."

And how do you pour out yourself for Jesus? Lay all that you have at His feet and give all to Him unconditionally. Wait to learn from Him how to distribute it to others. Then as you move out in obedience to the will of God—ministering according to your God-given gifts, talents, and calling—you will find yourself occupied with others.

Jesus tells of a day when He will return as King of kings to judge the nations. To His sheep, He will say, "Truly I say to you, to the extent that you did it to one of these brothers of Mine, even the least of them, you did it to Me" (Matthew 25:40).

Because Jesus is not physically present on earth right now, you and I cannot anoint His feet as Mary did. But we can do it *to* Him when we do it *for* Him to others.

How will we do it? Each in his or her own way. I will do it through my teaching, my writing, my listening and responding, my hugging and patting, etc. Others will do it through their cooking, cleaning, helping others physically in a quiet way. Then there will be those who will do it through prayer alone because they are housebound, blind, sick, or feeble.

The principle of how it is done is seen in Jesus' words about Mary: "She has done what she could" (Mark 14:8). O Beloved, this is what it means to be poured out for your Lord—the principle of life out of death. The alabaster vial of ointment had to be broken so that the ointment might be poured out on Jesus. The grain of wheat had to fall into the ground and die so that it might bring forth life.

You have to lay down your life, deny yourself, and take up your cross. Then you receive His life. And if you are going to serve Him, you must follow Him.

Jesus did what He could. You are to do the same. No more, but no less! Then you will know fulfillment and life abundant.

11 Jesus was heralded as a King; yet before He could reign, He had to become a grain of wheat. His hour of glorification was not to be seen in wearing a king's crown but in being adorned with a crown of thorns. "King of the Jews" was to be nailed to the instrument of His crucifixion. However, before all this could happen, there was a Scripture from Zechariah 9:9 to be fulfilled: "FEAR NOT, DAUGHTER OF ZION; BEHOLD, YOUR KING IS COMING, SEATED ON A DONKEY'S COLT" (John 12:15).

Old Testament judges and kings rode donkeys when they came on errands of peace. And if there ever was an errand of peace, this was it! Jesus would ride into Jerusalem for the express purpose of laying down His life for sinners, so that they, alienated from God, might be reconciled to Him.

When the multitudes saw Jesus coming into Jerusalem on the donkey, they began to wave palm branches and cry out, "Hosanna! BLESSED IS HE WHO COMES IN THE NAME OF THE LORD, even the King of Israel" (John 12:13). *Hosanna* means "save now." If our Lord had refused the cross and sought only the crown, if He had been unwilling to be our grain of wheat, He might have been heralded as King. But He would not have been able to "save now."

Jesus came up the Mount of Olives on a donkey's colt in order to die. Yet, there is a future time when Jesus will come to the Mount of Olives. Then He will ride not a donkey but a white horse. He will descend from heaven, not to die but to conquer. Then He will reign as King not just of the Jews, but of all the world. It will be as John saw: "And I saw heaven opened; and behold, a white horse, and He who sat upon it is called Faithful and True; and in righteousness He judges and wages war. . . . And He is clothed with a robe dipped in blood; and His name is called The Word of God. . . . And on His robe and on His thigh He has a name written, 'KING OF KINGS, AND LORD OF LORDS' " (Revelation 19:11,13,16).

A king on a white horse, a conqueror . . . This is what Zechariah foretold: "Then the LORD will go forth and fight against those nations, as when He fights on a day of battle. And in that day His feet will stand on the Mount of Olives. . . . And the LORD will be king over all the earth" (14:3,4,9).

That day is coming soon, Beloved. Everyone who did not recognize Him as the only One who could "save now" will bow down to Him as Lord and Savior then. At the name of Jesus *every knee will bow,* of those who are in heaven, and on earth, and under the earth, and every tongue will confess that Jesus Christ is Lord (Philippians 2:10,11).

Have you bowed and cried "Hosanna"? That second hour is almost here.

12 The approaching hour of our Lord's glorification at Calvary troubled His soul. The agony of it caused Him such torment that He literally sweat drops of blood. In the Garden of Gethsemane, He wrestled in prayer with the will of God (Matthew 26:38-44; Hebrews 5:7,8). Yet through tears He uttered, "Not as I will, but as Thou wilt" (Matthew 26:39).

Jesus was born to die! Therefore, He said, "Now My soul has become troubled; and what shall I say, 'Father, save Me from this hour'? But for this purpose I came to this hour. Father, glorify Thy name" (John 12:27,28).

It was through the cross that God would be glorified and His character manifested. On that cross Jesus would honor God by His obedience to the Father's will. Whereas the first Adam disobeyed, the last Adam would obey. Not only would God be glorified, but judgment would come upon the world. The ruler of this world would be cast out. All would be drawn to Jesus.

He prayed, " 'Father, glorify Thy name.' There came therefore a voice out of heaven: 'I have both glorified it, and will glorify it again.' The multitude therefore, who stood by and heard it, were saying that it had thundered; others were saying, 'An angel has spoken to Him.' Jesus answered and said, 'This voice has not come for My sake, but for your sakes. Now judgment is upon this world; now the ruler of this world shall be cast out. And I, if I be lifted up from the earth, will draw all men to Myself' " (John 12:28-32).

The cross of our Lord was the only way God could deal with the world's sin. Only Jesus could provide the cure for the otherwise incurable sin of man. The world was judged when God had to give His only begotten Son to take care of man's sin. And it was there at Calvary that Satan, the ruler of this world, was cast out from his rulership over man. The cross defeated Satan, rendering him powerless, because at Calvary man's sin was atoned for eternally (Hebrews 2:14).

It was the love of Jesus in dying as our substitute on Calvary which would draw all men to Him. We could come no other way to Him, except through what He wrought for us at Calvary.

These are rich truths. Think upon them. Ponder them in your heart.

13 Jesus performed many signs that only the Son of God could do. Jesus gave the people the Father's words and showed them the power of God. But they still would not believe that Jesus was the Son of Man. The Light of the world was there in all His brilliance, and yet they would not walk in Jesus' light.

Although they professed to be followers of God, they had missed Him. When they refused to believe that Jesus was who He said He was, when they refused to receive His sayings, they were cutting themselves off from God and, thus, from eternal life.

Jesus was the only sacrifice who could ever take away sin. He was the only Christ who would ever come. He was the only Light who could ever propel them out of darkness. He was the glory of God, the express image and radiance of the Father.

If they beheld Jesus, they were beholding the Father. If they believed in Jesus, they were believing in the Father (John 12:44,45). To miss all this was an eternal disaster, for Jesus said, "I have come as light into the world, that everyone who believes in Me may not remain in darkness. And if anyone hears My sayings, and does not keep them, I do not judge him; for I did not come to judge the world, but to save the world. He who rejects Me, and does not receive My sayings, has one who judges him; the word I spoke is what will judge him at the last day. For I did not speak on My own initiative, but the Father Himself who sent Me has given Me commandment, what to say, and what to speak. And I know that His commandment is eternal life; therefore the thing I speak, I speak just as the Father has told Me" (John 12:46-50).

There it is—pure, unadulterated truth from the very mouth of God incarnate, but as Isaiah wrote: "LORD, WHO HAS BELIEVED OUR REPORT? AND TO WHOM HAS THE ARM OF THE LORD BEEN REVEALED?" (John 12:38; see Isaiah 53:1).

O Beloved, do you see that every person who willfully refuses Jesus Christ will live forever in black darkness, cut off forever from the Light of the world? There is absolutely no other way to God, but through Jesus Christ.

If you believe this, what are you doing about it? You are a watchman on the wall. Will you have bloody hands? Read Ezekiel 3:16-21 and Acts 20:24-27, and then walk in the light of what God says.

14 Jesus came to explain the Father, to show us the way to the Father, and to restore to us what Adam lost—fellowship with the Father. To accomplish this task, the Son of God had to become the Son of Man.

Now the hour has come for the Son of Man to be glorified. And as Jesus anticipates what will happen when He, the Shepherd, is smitten and the sheep are scattered, His disciples are very much on His mind. He wants to prepare them for what lies ahead. Except for His death, burial, and resurrection, His ministry to the world is finished. Yet He has much more to share with His own. The last hours of His life as the Passover Lamb will be spent with them. With this purpose in mind, Jesus "sent Peter and John, saying, 'Go and prepare the Passover for us, that we may eat it.' And they said to Him, 'Where do You want us to prepare it?' And He said to them, 'Behold, when you have entered the city, a man will meet you carrying a pitcher of water; follow him into the house that he enters. And you shall say to the owner of the house, "The Teacher says to you, 'Where is the guest room in which I may eat the Passover with My disciples?' " And he will show you a large, furnished, upper room; prepare it there.' And they departed and found everything just as He had told them; and they prepared the Passover. And when the hour had come He reclined at the table, and the apostles with Him. And He said to them, 'I have earnestly desired to eat this Passover with you before I suffer; for I say to you, I shall never again eat it until it is fulfilled in the kingdom of God' " (Luke 22:8-16).

They will spend time in that Upper Room. Then they will journey with their Shepherd across Jerusalem over the

Kidron Valley to the Garden of Gethsemane. Jesus is going to explain to the faithful 11 what following Him as a true disciple entails. Remember, they have just witnessed Judas' defection. It is only natural that Judas' betrayal was disconcerting and demoralizing. Don't you imagine they wondered what if they, too, could not stand the pressure? What if they defected? What He will relay will be most enlightening!

As Jesus lays out to His own what following Him entails, He will also show them how it is possible. He will tell them of the Holy Spirit's indwelling and of abiding in the Vine. They will come to understand why Judas betrayed their Lord. They will see clearly why they will not.

As they begin their time together in the Upper Room, Jesus demonstrates true love. He girds Himself with a towel and washes their feet (John 13:4,5). He is about to return to the Father, to His throne. He demonstrates in these moments that love wears a towel to the throne.

Think on that, Beloved. Tomorrow before we get into John 13, I want us to see what following Jesus entails as we look at some key verses in John 12–16. Read these chapters before tomorrow.

15 The world's hour was coming. It was an hour that would bring testing and tribulation to the true followers of Jesus Christ. Knowing this, Jesus gave His disciples the truths of John 13–16 "that when their hour comes, you may remember that I told you of them" (John 16:4). Jesus concludes His teaching with these words: "These things I have spoken to you, that in Me you may have peace. In the world you have tribulation, but take courage; I have overcome the world" (John 16:33). How essential it was then that those who followed the Lord understood all that was involved in this life of commitment. Let's look at what following Jesus includes—as explained by Him in John 12–16.

As we saw previously, if you are going to walk with Jesus as His disciple, *you cannot live your own life*. This is made very clear in John 12:25: "He who loves his life loses it; and he who hates his life in this world shall keep it to life eternal."

No Christian can live a double life—his own and his Lord's. No man can serve two masters. Jesus said, "If anyone serves Me, let him follow Me; and where I am, there shall My servant also be; if anyone serves Me, the Father will honor him" (John 12:26).

Our identification with Jesus Christ in His death and resurrection teaches us that we died with Him in order that we might be raised with Him to walk in newness of life. That newness of life belongs to those who are willing to lose their lives in exchange for His eternal life. Thus, Paul makes a statement which is true for all Christians: "I have been crucified with Christ; and it is no longer I who live, but Christ lives in me; and the life which I now live in the flesh I live by faith in the Son of God, who loved me, and delivered Himself up for me" (Galatians 2:20).

Following Jesus Christ also entails *serving others*. This is to be the lifestyle of those who serve Him, of those who live His life rather than their own.

When Jesus finished washing the feet of His disciples, He said, "You call Me Teacher and Lord; and you are right, for so I am. If I then, the Lord and the Teacher, washed your feet, you also ought to wash one another's feet. For I gave you an example that you also should do as I did to you. Truly, truly, I say to you, a slave is not greater than his master; neither is one who is sent greater than the one who sent him" (John 13:13-16).

Well, Beloved, as we must always do when we read God's Word, we need to examine ourselves. How do we measure up to the Word of God in our affections, our beliefs, our behavior?

16 "I love you" has become a trite phrase to many, and it is especially hypocritical when we say, "I love You" to our Lord Jesus but do not keep His Word. Or when we are so busy that we do not even take time to find out what the Word of God has to say. It is in the Word of God that we discover the will of God.

We now come to the third thing that is involved in following our Lord: *You will keep His Word because you love Him*. Jesus knew that in the time of testing and tribulation the flesh is tempted to take the easiest way out. And often the easiest way out is to compromise.

Compromise falls short of love. Listen to what Jesus said to the 11: "If anyone loves Me, he will keep My word; and My Father will love him, and We will come to him, and make Our abode with him. He who does not love Me does not keep My words; and the word which you hear is not Mine, but the Father's who sent Me" (John 14:23,24).

How can we genuinely tell God we love Him and refuse to do what He says? If we say we love Him and choose not to obey Him, we are not fooling Him, but kidding ourselves.

Let's look at the fourth characteristic of a disciple of Jesus Christ. *True disciples abide in Jesus so as to produce fruit.* Jesus said, "By this is My Father glorified, that you bear much fruit, and so prove to be My disciples" (John 15:8).

It is impossible for a branch to bear fruit unless the life of the vine is flowing through it. If a branch produces no fruit, this is evidence that the branch isn't attached to the vine. Therefore, fruit is the inevitable evidence of abiding in Jesus, the Vine. The fruit will be Christlikeness to one degree or another.

Christlikeness brings with it the fifth result of following Jesus Christ: *The world will hate you!* Are you prepared for that? Jesus wanted to be certain the disciples understood that being hated by the world was a part of following Him. He didn't want them to be shaken like a reed in the pelting rainstorm of the hatred of others.

Bruchko is one of my favorite biographies. It is the story of Bruce Olson who was saved as a teenager. Bruce wanted to be the athletic type, but he wasn't. He loved languages, especially Greek, but Greek books were hard to find. So while he was studying Koine Greek, he dug into a Greek New Testament.

When God saved Bruce, his parents rejected him. Bruce would go to church and return to his home to find that his parents had locked him out of his house in the bitter cold of Minnesota nights. God was "toughening" His disciple for the incredible work He had in store for him as a lad of merely 19.

Following Jesus would bring not only hatred but also tribulation in the world (John 16:33). But, oh, the peace within!

17 Enduring love—a love that loves you to the end, a love that sees you through, beyond your frailties, beyond your mistakes, beyond all your unlovableness, until you become the product of its endurance—this is the love God has for His own. And this is the love that our Lord demonstrated to His disciples in the Upper Room. On the night in which our Lord was betrayed, His disciples were foremost on His heart and mind.

Listen to the words of John, one of the men who witnessed this kind of enduring love: "Now before the Feast of the Passover, Jesus knowing that His hour had come that He should depart out of this world to the Father, having loved His own who were in the world, He loved them to the end" (John 13:1). The words *to the end* are *eis telos* in the Greek and mean "to completion."

Jesus demonstrated to His disciples the enduring love of God. A love that looks on the needs of others and desires another's highest good. A love that lays down its life. Even when Jesus faced the agony of Calvary, in His hour of personal pain, the needs of the disciples took precedence over His own needs. He loved them to the uttermost.

Later in the evening, Jesus would say, "Greater love has no one than this, that one lay down his life for his friends" (John 15:13). By this time, they had witnessed His love demonstrated by girding Himself with a towel and washing their feet—even those of Judas, the betrayer. And

He would demonstrate that love again at Calvary as the Lamb took away their sins.

The secret of enduring love is love of the Father. The Son loved the Father and, therefore, He loved us to the uttermost out of love for Him.

In *Bruchko,* we see that same love in a 19-year-old man. Convinced that God was calling him to the Motilone tribe, Bruce Olson went to South America. No mission board would take him, and, of course, his parents objected. But God had said, "Go." So out of supreme love for the Father, Bruce left for South America with an airline ticket and $70 in his pocket.

Little did Bruce realize, nor would he have cared, that by the age of 30 he would have spoken to the United Nations, lunched with the vice president of the United States, and become a personal friend of the four presidents of Colombia, South America. Bruce would also speak 15 languages, have papers published in linguistic journals, and pioneer in computer translation of tribal languages.

In the world's eyes, Bruce attained some sort of "throne." But how did he get there? Like his Lord Jesus, he wore a towel.

Love wears a towel to God's throne. Love serves. Love endures. One day God will reward it.

18 Bruce's inquiries on how to reach the Motilone tribe all met the same response: "Don't go near them. They'll kill you." Bruce's feverish body, covered with red welts and weak from hunger, stumbled along beside his mule. His red, swollen, bitten hands which now resembled raw meat clutched the mule's rope. Barely in control of himself, he finally saw a village across the deep valley. "Thank God, I have found the Motilones."

When Bruce arrived in the village, only his relief and joy at arriving gave him the strength to endure the curious poking and examination by wrinkled, toothless, filthy people. Bruce could not speak a word of their language. Yet it seemed that in their own way they had accepted him. Finally at 3:30 in the morning, they led him to a hut. When the sun rose, Bruce resumed his attempts at communication:

> Fascinated, I soon forgot everything else. I was beginning to be able to separate some of the sounds, and it was just a question of time, I thought, before I began to get the meaning of some of the words.
>
> Then suddenly, without warning, a blow . . . knocked me onto my face. I lay stunned. A man was standing over me, yelling and wailing at a terrific pitch, slashing at me with whips which he held in each hand. White froth dripped from his lips. I tried to roll away from his blows, but several young men appeared and poked me back toward him with long, sharp arrows which they held in their hands.
>
> Then, at the man's direction, I was picked up by two of the warriors and thrown into the hut in which I had spent the night. No one came in after me. I lay on the floor, panting, almost terrified.
>
> An arrow slashed through one grass wall of the hut and hit the wall on the other side. Other arrows followed. The men had surrounded the hut and were shooting at me through it. The arrows didn't have enough force to break my skin by the time they came through the walls, but they were heavy and made ugly bruises and blood blisters where they hit. After fifteen minutes of this, I collapsed on the floor, my hands over my eyes. . . .
>
> At the moment of my greatest terror, it occurred to me that I needed to pray.
>
> "God," I said, "how long is this going to go on? Do I have to go through this?" I could imagine a future filled with torture, inability to communicate, and death.
>
> Then a strange thing happened. It was as though I were struck down. I seemed to see Jesus on the cross. I started to cry.
>
> "Oh, Jesus," I said, astonished and fearful. "That's what You faced. We must have seemed filthy to *You*, like these Indians seem to me. Oh, how senseless our hate must have been.

> "God, I will give You what I can. I give You my strength, my life. I'll put up with anything, any trouble. I'll even die, if You will let me communicate about Your Son to the Motilones."[1]

Like his Savior, Bruce would love the Motilones to completion in Christ Jesus.

19 Love serves. It wears a towel. And if you are going to follow Jesus, you must remember: "A slave is not greater than his master; neither is one who is sent greater than the one who sent him. If you know these things, you are blessed if you do them" (John 13:16,17). How well John 13 relates to us the truth of Mark 10:42-45: "And calling them to Himself, Jesus said to them, 'You know that those who are recognized as rulers of the Gentiles lord it over them; and their great men exercise authority over them. But it is not so among you, but whoever wishes to become great among you shall be your servant; and whoever wishes to be first among you shall be slave of all. For even the Son of Man did not come to be served, but to serve, and to give His life a ransom for many.' "

Jesus knew that He was going to the Father, that He would return to the glory that was His before His incarnation. Yet that glory was not uppermost on His mind. His supreme concern now was serving His disciples. Yet the owner of the room where they were celebrating the Passover had provided a towel and basin so that a servant could wash the feet of the guests, but there was no servant.

In a dusty land where sandals were worn, foot-washing was a welcome custom. But the washing of feet was left to the very lowest of servants. They would sit at the entrance of the homes, untie the thongs of the sandals of all who entered in, and wash the brown dirt from their feet. Maybe this is what John the Baptist meant when he said he was not worthy to untie the thongs of Jesus' sandals (John 1:27)!

"And during supper, the devil having already put into the heart of Judas Iscariot, the son of Simon, to betray Him, Jesus, knowing that the Father had given all things into His hands, and that He had come forth from God, and was going back to God, rose from supper, and laid aside His garments; and taking a towel, He girded Himself about. Then He poured water into the basin, and began to wash the disciples' feet, and to wipe them with the towel with which He was girded" (John 13:2-5).

And what if you had been in that Upper Room?

20 "Lord, do You wash my feet?" Can you understand Peter's consternation? I can. I've had my feet washed. It was not easy! It was far easier to wash others' feet. When we are in Israel on teaching tours, we often acquire the traditional Upper Room so that we can wash one another's feet.

We simply place several basins and towels in the room and gather in a circle to worship the Lord in song. One by one, someone will leave the circle, go over, take another by the hand, lead them to the chair, take off their shoes, and wash their feet. Tears stream from faces bending down, faces watching a wife, a husband, a friend, or a new acquaintance gently pour the water over their feet and wipe them with a towel. Then shoes back on, they stand, usually embrace, and the other then sits down to have their feet washed.

Jesus washed the feet of the twelve, even the one who He knew would betray Him. But no one washed His feet. I wonder how they felt later, as they stood their distance on Calvary looking at His bloody, bruised, swollen ankles nailed to the cross, remembering that they had not washed His feet. How Mary must have rejoiced that she had poured out her all, anointing His feet with her costly perfume!

When Jesus washed their feet, it was more than Peter could handle: " 'Never shall You wash my feet!' Jesus answered him, 'If I do not wash you, you have no part with Me.' Simon Peter said to Him, 'Lord, not my feet only, but also my hands and my head.' Jesus said to him, 'He who has bathed needs only to wash his feet, but is completely clean; and you are clean, but not all of you.' For He knew the one who was betraying Him; for this reason He said, 'Not all of you are clean' " (John 13:8-11).

Jesus washed Peter's feet. He washed Judas' feet. Peter objected. Judas didn't. Yet Judas would betray Him. Peter would deny the Lord. But because he was clean Peter would come back.

Peter had been made completely clean by faith in Jesus. Judas was different. Although he looked and acted and sounded like a true follower of Jesus Christ, in the end he wasn't.

Did this affect our Lord's attitude or response to Judas? No. Jesus washed Judas' feet with the same love and care He gave to the others. Jesus would love Judas all the way to hell. But then it would be too late.

When Judas hung himself, he locked the gate forever. He never repented or believed. Judas accepted the washing of his feet, but not the cleansing of his soul.

What about you, Beloved? Will you let Jesus wash your feet and your heart?

21 Obedience and perseverance are integral parts of Christianity. If we really believe, we will not turn away. Continuance in the faith is the evidence of our salvation, as is obedience. True faith obeys. Our faith may falter from time to time, but continual disobedience will not be the habit of a true believer (1 John 3:6-10).

Here is the difference between Judas and the 11. Jesus wanted His apostles to understand that He knew Judas would defect. Judas did not turn away because he lost his salvation. He never possessed salvation. Nor did Judas defect because Jesus had failed to keep him. Judas knew and understood Jesus' claims, yet he never made a commitment of faith which produces obedience and perseverance. Look once again at John 13:17,18,20: "If you know these things, you are blessed if you do them." Blessing does not come merely from knowledge but from a knowledge that has "feet to it," a knowledge that acts and obeys, not in order to attain salvation but as a result of salvation. "I do not speak of all of you. I know the ones I have chosen; but it is that the Scripture may be fulfilled, 'HE WHO EATS MY BREAD HAS LIFTED UP HIS HEEL AGAINST ME.' . . . Truly, truly, I say to you, he who receives whomever I send receives Me. . . ."

Jesus knew all along that Judas would not receive Him as his Messiah. And as Jesus reclined at the table, saying all this, "He became troubled in spirit, and testified, and said, 'Truly, truly, I say to you, that one of you will betray Me.' The disciples began looking at one another, at a loss to know of which one He was speaking. There was reclining on Jesus' breast one of His disciples, whom Jesus loved. Simon Peter therefore gestured to him, and said to him, 'Tell us who it is of whom He is speaking.' He, leaning back thus on Jesus' breast, said to Him, 'Lord, who is it?'" (John 13:21-25).

It is interesting, isn't it, that none of them knew who he was! They couldn't spot Judas as the betrayer because on the outside he was so much like them.

Jesus had to identify Judas by dipping a morsel and handing it to Judas. Therefore, when Jesus said, " 'What you do, do quickly' . . . some were supposing, because Judas had the money box, that Jesus was saying to him, 'Buy the things we have need of for the feast'; or else, that he should give something to the poor" (John 13:27,29).

How well Judas portrays 1 John 2:19: "They went out from us, but they were not really of us; for if they had been of us, they would have remained with us; but they went out, in order that it might be shown that they all are not of us."

22

What was the difference between Judas and Peter, since both forsook Jesus in His final hour? Judas would betray Jesus. He walked away from every opportunity that had been his as a disciple, and became an apostate. In fear Peter would deny Jesus. Yet his denial would be temporary. He would return and take advantage of all that had been his as an apostle of his Lord.

In these two men, we can learn lessons for ourselves, and we can perhaps see what goes on in the visible church when someone who seemed so committed to Christ defects from the faith. Let me contrast Judas and Peter and then take a closer look at Judas.

Even though Judas knew that he was going to betray Jesus, he allowed Jesus to wash his feet without the slightest protest. How hard his heart must have been!

What a contrast to the heart of Peter who wouldn't let Jesus wash his feet until Jesus told him that if He didn't, Peter wouldn't have any part in Him. The total tenderness of his heart is seen in his reply: "Lord, not my feet only, but also my hands and my head" (John 13:9). It was obvious from his response that Peter wanted to be a part of Jesus. Separation from Jesus was abhorrent to him. To Judas, separation was convenient, because it looked as if the kingdom they hoped Jesus would establish wasn't going to materialize. The hosannas for Jesus were short-lived. Jesus was now talking about His death, not His reign.

How obvious it would become that Judas followed Jesus for a different reason than Peter. Judas wanted what Jesus offered, but he didn't want identification with Him if that became costly. So Judas plotted Jesus' arrest. He willfully sold Jesus.

Whereas Judas knew he would betray Jesus, it never occurred to Peter that he would deny Jesus. Peter's heart was right, but his flesh was weaker than he thought. He had a heart of iron, but didn't see his feet of clay! Peter had said to Jesus, "I will lay down my life for You" (John 13:37). He would never have thought of selling Jesus. His heart belonged to Jesus and his denial was only temporary. Judas betrayed Jesus in a calculating way, not because he was afraid like Peter.

As we look at Peter and Judas, I have to ask, Why are you following Jesus? What is your heart like?

23 Judas felt the warmth of intimacy with Christ, saw the brilliance of His light, and yet preferred the darkness of this present world.

In his powerful book *The Legacy of Jesus*, John MacArthur writes:

> Judas was an ultimate tragedy—probably the greatest tragedy that ever lived. He was the perfect and prime example of what it means to have opportunity and then lose it. What he became is all the more terrible because of the glorious beginning he had. Judas followed the same Christ as the others. For three years, day in and day out, he occupied himself with Jesus Christ. He saw the same miracles, heard the same words, performed some of the same ministries, was esteemed in the same way the other disciples were esteemed—yet he did not become what the others became. In fact, he became the very opposite. While they were growing into true apostles and saints of God, he was progressively turning into a vile, calculating tool of Satan.
>
> For three years, he moved and walked with Jesus. Initially, he must have shared the same hope of the kingdom that the other disciples had. He likely believed that Jesus was the Messiah. He, too, had left all and followed Jesus. Certainly along the line he became greedy, but it is doubtful that he joined the apostles for what money he could get, because they never really had any. Perhaps his motive at the outset was just to get in on the kingdom that Jesus would bring.
>
> Whatever his character at the beginning he gradually became the treacherous man who betrayed Christ, a man who had no thought for anyone but himself, a man who finally wanted only to get as much money as he could and get out.
>
> Greed, ambition, and worldliness had crept into his heart, and avarice had become his besetting sin. Perhaps he was disappointed because of unfulfilled expectations of an earthly kingdom. Maybe he was tormented by the unbearable rebuke of the presence of Christ. Surely it

> created a great tension in his heart to be constantly in the presence of sinless purity and yet be so infested with vileness. . . . Whatever the reasons, he ended in absolute disaster, the greatest example of lost opportunity the world has ever seen.[2]

O Beloved, have you ever considered the fact that there are many like Judas?

24 Have you ever had a trusted and close friend suddenly turn against you leaving you shattered and in shock? What Judas did to Jesus troubled Him also. Even though Jesus knew Judas would betray Him, and that Judas' betrayal would expedite God's plan, what Judas did was hard. Like Ahithophel of old, Judas lifted up his heel against his close and trusted Friend—One who had loved him to the uttermost. Psalm 41:9 was fulfilled: "Even my close friend, in whom I trusted, who ate my bread, has lifted up his heel against me." The lament of David's heart found its ultimate prophetic rest at the last Passover in the Upper Room.

The expression "lifted up his heel" referred to the brutal and violent act of laying your enemy low and then crushing your heel into his neck. When it is the heel of a close and trusted friend, the anguish of heart is horrendous.

Can you imagine looking up into the face of one whom you considered your trusted friend and watching his heel come down upon your neck? I know of a man who was unjustly sued by his lifelong friend. The betrayal took its toll on him physically, literally putting him to bed with heart problems.

Psalm 41:9 is a reference to Ahithophel, David's counselor, friend, and general who went over to the side of David's son, Absalom. Can you imagine what it was like to not only have your own son turn against you, to plot to take away your kingdom, but then to have your trusted friend turn against you also?

You may relate to the heartbreak because of the schisms in your own family or in the lives of those close to you. O Beloved, if you are forced to taste this bitter cup of betrayal, remember you have a great high priest who can sympathize with your heartache. He has suffered the same, He understands, and He is able to come to your aid (Hebrews 2:17,18; 4:14-16).

25 After His resurrection and Peter's repentance, Jesus told Peter, " 'Truly, truly, I say to you, when you were younger, you used to gird yourself, and walk wherever you wished; but when you grow old, you will stretch out your hands, and someone else will gird you, and bring you where you do not wish to go.' Now this He said, signifying by what kind of death he would glorify God. And when He had spoken this, He said to him, 'Follow Me!' " (John 21:18,19).

Tradition has it that Peter was crucified upside down because he felt unworthy to be crucified in the same manner as his Lord. O Beloved, do you see the contrast between Peter and Judas? Here were two men with the same opportunities, yet only one remained true even unto death.

You know, my friend, it is easy to spot unbelievers, those who do not make any pretense of belonging to Jesus Christ. But it is not easy to spot the hypocrites, those who will apostatize. They can live for years undetected in the church. Usually it is only great trial, a call to some great cost, or an alluring offer from the world which exposes them.

Apostates are people who have exposure to all the gospel offers and who seemingly have believed. Yet eventually they turn away. Hebrews 6:4-9 describes such people perfectly: "For in the case of those who have once been enlightened and have tasted of the heavenly gift and have been made partakers of the Holy Spirit, and have tasted the good word of God and the powers of the age to come, and then have fallen away, it is impossible to renew them again to repentance, since they again crucify to themselves the Son of God, and put Him to open shame. For ground that drinks the rain which often falls upon it and brings forth vegetation useful to those for whose sake it is also tilled, receives a blessing from God; but if it yields thorns and thistles, it is worthless and close to being cursed, and it ends up being burned. But, beloved, we are convinced of better things concerning you, and things that accompany salvation, though we are speaking in this way."

True salvation brings forth an acceptable harvest to God. But the word sown in the apostate's heart yields thorns and thistles. Although they have known the benefits of God's touch upon their lives, in their rejection they are doomed to the fire of eternal judgment. This was Judas.

26 I believe the greatest danger to the church of Jesus Christ is hypocrisy and apostasy from within. We are not being threatened by the fires of persecution from the world. If we were, the church would be purified and become a mighty force in the world. Persecution always separates the false from the true and leaves the church purged, holy, and powerful.

Our problem is corruption from within. Many are sitting apathetically in the pews with no fire in their hearts. They are consumed with their own lusts, and their focus has become their own well-being. A church in this condition becomes a hothouse for breeding false teachers and apostates who feed off the fleshly weaknesses of others. Therefore, among the wheat, you find the tares. They may be hard to recognize—until fruit-bearing time. Jesus, in His parable about sowing and reaping (see Matthew 13:24-42) explains: "The one who sows the good seed is the Son of Man, and the field is the world; and as for the good seed, these are the sons of the kingdom; and the tares are the sons of the evil one; and the enemy who sowed them is the devil, and the harvest is the end of the age. . . . The Son of Man will send forth His angels, and they will gather out of His kingdom all stumbling blocks, and those who commit lawlessness, and will cast them into the furnace of fire."

Only God can deal with the tares. But we need to be aware of their existence. Read 2 Peter 2.

27 False teachers, apostates, hypocrites all have one thing in common: pride. Pride can be defined as "the glorification and gratification of self rather than God." As Philippians 3:18,19 says, "They are enemies of the cross of Christ"; their "god is their appetite"; they "set their minds on earthly things." According to 2 Peter 2, they deny their Master who bought them. Greed is their driving force, and they despise authority unless it is theirs! Second Timothy 3 tells us they hold to "a form of godliness, although they have denied its power" (3:5). And they creep into households "and captivate weak women weighed down with sins, led on by various impulses, always learning and never able to come to the knowledge of the truth" (3:6,7). They oppose the truth through their wrong teachings.

What a contrast to our precious Lord and the lifestyle He lived before us! Even on the eve of His death teaching and equipping His disciples so they could stand in the face of persecution was utmost on His mind. Thus, on the night in which He was betrayed, He stripped Himself of His garments, wrapped Himself in a towel, and washed the disciples' feet—even those of Judas, the tare! By example, Jesus taught us one of the greatest of all truths: Humility is to be the lifestyle of His disciples.

Jesus' example was followed by Paul who became an imitator of Christ (1 Corinthians 11:1). And then Paul called Timothy to the same lifestyle when he wrote: "In speech, conduct, love, faith and purity, show yourself an example of those who believe. . . . Give attention to the public reading of Scripture, to exhortation and teaching. . . . Take pains with these things; be absorbed in them, so that your progress may be evident to all. Pay close attention to yourself and to your teaching; persevere in these things; for as you do this you will insure salvation both for yourself and for those who hear you" (1 Timothy 4:12,13,15,16).

O Beloved, what is your lifestyle? What are your goals? To what do you devote yourself?

Take a few minutes and list in your notebook some words or phrases which describe your way of life. Then see how they compare to the plumb line of God's Word.

28 When our Lord and God put on a towel as the Son of Man and washed His disciples' feet, He girded Himself with humility. Humility is one of the greatest and most-needed of Christian virtues in a world which is chanting, "I'm number one."

God blessed me deeply through a book entitled *Fire in Your Heart*. This "call to personal holiness" shows what happens when genuine revival comes. Its author, Sammy Tippit, calls humility "the soil of grace." While ministering in former East Germany, God touched Sammy's heart through a group of young people who closed each of their prayers with the phrase *"egal was es Kostet"*—"no matter the cost."

> One prayed, "Lord Jesus, come into my heart and make me a Christian, *egal was es Kostet*."
>
> Another said, "Father, please set me free from this habit, *egal was es Kostet*."
>
> I had worked with youth throughout America and Western Europe, but I had never heard Western young people pray, "No matter what it costs."
>
> There is a cost to revival. It costs everything! Too many cry for the power of Pentecost but neglect the cost. We want resurrection power, but we refuse the cross. The cross means death. It means death to our ambitions, dreams, and desires. It means losing our lives in order that we might gain His life. Jesus said, "And he who does not take his cross and follow after Me is not worthy of Me. He who has found his life shall lose it, and he who has lost his life for My sake shall find it" (Matthew 10:38-39, NAS).
>
> After we finished that meeting with the youth, we went to Czechoslovakia. Some of the young people there

had been members of the Communist party at their universities prior to their conversions. Afterwards, they stood in communist meetings and gave testimonies of their conversions to Christ. They were now in prison. They had evidently prayed, "No matter what it costs."

Back in East Germany, I asked one of the girls, "How are you doing now that Christ lives in your heart?"

Tears rolled down her face. "I was the top student in my school. I cannot continue my education because I became a Christian and identified with our church."

I wanted to cry. I didn't know what to say to her. Then a big smile came over her face as she said, "But it's worth it! It's worth it!" She understood what it meant to lose her life in order to gain His life. The glory and grace of God grows well in the soil of such a heart.

The primary characteristic must be humility.[3]

29

The young people in East Germany experienced revival and God's glory because of their humility. They had become nothing so that Jesus could become everything.

Many believers today are fearful to discuss humility. Yet we must discuss it if we are to be serious about God sending a spiritual awakening. Augustine encouraged the church to set about getting humility as her chief characteristic. There is no way for the wind of revival to blow across the nations without humility in the hearts of God's people.

Here are four major reasons humility is of such great importance:

First, humility is a natural response to a knowledge of the holiness of God. A young Christian leader in Romania said, "Humility becomes my natural state *only* as I recognize who God really is!"

Isaiah "saw the Lord" and humbled himself. Andrew Murray defined humility as "nothing but the disappearance of self in the vision that God is all. The holiest will be the humblest. . . ."[4] True humility comes only as we allow Jesus to be all and in all.

Second, humility is the most exemplary characteristic of the nature and essence of Jesus. He is the truest expression of humility. Jesus was, is, and always will be God. And yet at one point, He emptied Himself and became a man. He was called "Immanuel," God with us. The King of glory became the servant of men. He humbled Himself to the point of death, even death upon a cross. There is no greater illustration of humility in all of history. We must behold Jesus! As we see Him, we will hunger and thirst to become like Him. And to become like Him means to be humble, meek, and lowly in heart.

Third, humility has historical significance in the life of the church. When the church humbles herself under the mighty hand of God, it results in dynamic growth—both spiritually and numerically.

The watchword of the great Welsh revival from 1902 to 1905 was, "Bend the church and save the people!" On Thursday morning, September 29, 1904, a young Welshman, Evan Roberts, and nineteen friends went to hear an evangelist named Seth Joshua preach in a nearby town. Joshua prayed, "Bend us, O Lord, bend us."

The Holy Spirit did a deep work in young Roberts' heart. "I fell on my knees with my arms over the seat in front of me and tears flowed freely. I cried, 'Bend me! Bend me! Bend us!' "[5]

Evan Roberts was broken by God and then used to shake Wales. O Beloved, would you join me in praying, "O Lord, bend me. O Lord, bend us"?

30 Are you afraid to pray, "O Lord, bend me"? I understand, for in the midst of writing this devotional for you, I stopped and prayed, "O Lord, bend me." However, I did not pray it without fear. Who wants to be humbled under the mighty hand of God? It can be painful to the flesh!

And yet we forget that our flesh is our enemy, for it wars against the Spirit who resides within (Galatians 5:16,17).

And yet those "who belong to Christ Jesus have crucified the flesh with its passions and desires" (Galatians 5:24). Therefore, we are admonished: "Consider the members of your earthly body as dead to immorality, impurity, passion, evil desire, and greed, which amounts to idolatry. For it is on account of these things that the wrath of God will come" (Colossians 3:5,6).

No, Beloved, praying, "O Lord, bend me" is not simple. Yet, what if we are not bent? What will we say when we see Jesus face-to-face? What will be our response when we find we could have been His instrument for righteousness and revival, had we only been willing to humble ourselves under the hand of Almighty God, that He might exalt us in due time (James 4:10)?

As I prayed and the flesh's fear crept into my heart, a Scripture came to my mind: "It is I; do not be afraid" (John 6:20). As I meditated on that, I saw that I didn't need to fear whatever God would do in answer to my prayer. Whatever was needed would come from Him, the One who loved me with an everlasting love. It would be filtered through His fingers of love. I could break the alabaster box of all that I was and had at His feet; I could be "broken and spilled out" for Him.

The hour had come for Him to be glorified in my death to anything and everything that is not of Him—*egal was es Kostet!* No matter the cost! What about you?

31 Humility is the biblical condition for spiritual revival. This is the fourth major reason Sammy Tippit gives in *Fire in Your Heart* to show the great importance of humility. We love to quote 2 Chronicles 7:14: "[If] My people who are called by My name humble themselves and pray, and seek My face and turn from their wicked ways, then I will hear from heaven, will forgive their sin, and will heal their land." Yet if we would claim this promise from God, we cannot bypass any of that which God says we are to do. The first of the conditions set forth is humble yourself: "Humility dispels darkness because it is the opposite of pride. Pride is the banner of the world. It caused Lucifer to be cast out of heaven. He is the prince of the world, deceiving men and women and building a kingdom of darkness with pride as its foundation. J.C. Ryle stated that the language of the heart will always be that of humility with those who are used to destroy the kingdom of darkness."[6]

Humility is not something you will be conscious of, Beloved. It happens when you humble yourself by walking totally in the Spirit. To humble yourself is to bring yourself low so that Christ might be all in all in every situation of life. It is to choose the Spirit's control. And when you do, the fruit will be "love, joy, peace, patience, kindness, goodness, faithfulness, gentleness (meekness), self-control" (Galatians 5:22,23).

The fruit of the Spirit is the character of Christ! As He was to others, you will be. Their well-being above your own will be your concern, even as it was in the night in which He was betrayed.

Although Jesus knew that after Calvary He would go to the right hand of the Father's throne, still He girded Himself with a towel and washed His disciples' feet, instead of insisting they wash His because of who He was. "For I gave you an example that you also should do as I did to you" (John 13:15). Remember, love wore a towel to the throne.

Someday, Beloved, you and I shall rule and reign with Him, having "AUTHORITY OVER THE NATIONS" (Revelation 2:26). That will be the time of our exaltation. Now is the time of our humiliation in identification with Him.

Don't confuse these times. You cannot reverse the order. First the cross. Then the crown.

Break your alabaster box at His feet while you still have the opportunity. Wear His towel to His throne.

June

When Your Heart Is Troubled . . .

1 Beloved Believer, where do you run during troublesome and dark times? How do you handle the strain of being overwhelmed? Where is your refuge? You must be certain that it is a sure harbor of safety and peace, for these are not ordinary times.

Recent news reports indicate that AIDS is the leading killer of young adults. It has stripped us of friends, family, children, and babies who died before their time. AIDS has declared its death sentence not only on the immoral but also on countless innocent victims. No longer are only adults in danger, but teens are being raped of the future and children doomed to the grave the minute they leave the womb.

If you do not fear the awesome effect of AIDS, does your heart writhe over the rising numbers caught in the claws of pornography? Aren't you frightened that the relentless pursuit of pornography in our nation, largely run by the Mafia, will devastate our society?

Aren't you sickened by crime, graft, corruption? Isn't your heart grieved as you see iniquity abounding on every hand? Don't you want to overthrow the tables of the Temple, in a sense, as you see local and national governments being bought and sold by unrighteous people who flaunt their ungodliness?

When you think of the sin revealed among Christian leaders, are you saddened beyond belief? Don't you want to put the brakes on the commercialism and hype and go back to teaching the Word of God in the house of God and to earnest prayer before a holy God?

Or are you distressed because of family conflicts, personal financial needs, or physical ailments?

Whatever it might be, what do you do when your heart is troubled? Listen to Psalm 61:2-4: "From the end of the earth I call to Thee, when my heart is faint; lead me to the rock that is higher than I. For Thou hast been a refuge for me, a tower of strength against the enemy. Let me dwell in Thy tent forever; let me take refuge in the shelter of Thy wings. Selah."

2 If the one person you felt would be your security for life told you he was going to leave you, could you bear the separation? The pain?

Or what if you forsook everything in life for the sake of a belief, and then nothing turned out the way you thought it would? Could you bear the disillusionment? Would your heart forever be troubled?

For centuries, the Israelites had waited for Messiah's coming. With every period of oppression, the hope of Messiah was renewed as they looked to the time when He would come and conquer every oppressor, ruling them with a rod of iron.

The Israelites awaited the day when the nations would tremble and bow before the Son of Man as He took possession of the kingdoms of this world so that "all the peoples, nations, and men of every language might serve Him" (Daniel 7:14). They awaited the day when "the sovereignty, the dominion, and the greatness of all the kingdoms under the whole heaven" would be given to "the people of the saints of the Highest One" (Daniel 7:27).

Some were now convinced that Messiah had come, after centuries of prophecies and promises. Among His followers were disciples personally chosen by Him, who had left all to follow Jesus of Nazareth, a Man they were convinced was the Christ, the Messiah, the long-awaited King of Israel.

Now alone with His followers in an upper room celebrating the Feast of the Passover, Jesus was telling 12 men He was going away. He was explaining where He was going. He wanted them to grasp the fact that they could not come. To say the very least, His words troubled their hearts. Why, they had left all to follow Him! For almost three years, they had lived together, eaten and traveled together. Jesus had been their Teacher, their Provider, their Guide. Their sole purpose in life had become following Him fully.

He couldn't leave! What would they do? Where would they go? Who would they follow if Jesus weren't with them?

No! He couldn't go away. Their hearts could not bear the loss. The disappointment. The seeming futility of it all! Their Lord's words weighed heavily upon their hearts. Then Jesus made another statement that fell as one more horrific blow to their already-troubled hearts—that bold, brash, fearless Peter, one of the inner circle, would deny Him. It seemed more than they could bear.

A veil of confusion and disillusionment came over them. Jesus knew their hearts were greatly troubled, just as He also knows when yours is. What He said to them, He says to you. Read John 14.

3 This was not the first time Jesus had told His disciples of His forthcoming death and resurrection. However, they really hadn't listened carefully before. Perhaps they didn't want to hear it, didn't want to believe it.

Isn't that the way with us? We hear what we want to hear. We accept what we want to accept!

I find this attitude among many Christians. They pick and choose out of the Word of God what is pleasing to them and ignore the rest. Many want to hear that which will meet an immediate personal need in their lives, or make life easier and more convenient. They ignore those truths that seem unpleasant or demanding.

They want to know of the blessings, but not of obedience. They don't want anyone to rock their comfortable boat which drifts on the sea of pleasant unreality.

"Hope is fine, but don't tie it to holiness. Love is wonderful, but forget judgment. A shining future is great, as long as we don't pass through trials to get there!"

If you relate to this, you need to stop and tell our Father that you want to confront your world in the stability of faith, rather than bury your head in the sand of unreality.

As Jesus told His disciples that He was returning to the Father, He wanted to make sure they were adequately prepared for discipleship. After washing their feet, Jesus explained to them why He must speak to them of such things: "Behold, an hour is coming, and has already come, for you to be scattered, each to his own home, and to leave Me alone; and yet I am not alone, because the Father is with Me. These things I have spoken to you, that in Me you may have peace. In the world you have tribulation, but take courage; I have overcome the world" (John 16:32,33).

As Jesus began His Upper Room discourse with the announcement of His return to the Father and the words "Let not your heart be troubled" (John 14:1), He closed it with the reassurance that even in the midst of tribulation they could have peace. He wanted them to understand that peace does not come from a denial of reality or an absence of trial, but from a right relationship with Him.

4 In his incredibly needful and convicting book *Fire in Your Heart,* Sammy Tippit writes:

> Somehow our view of Jesus has been clouded. In our attempt to make sure we are comfortable and free from pain, we have lost the centrality of the cross of Christ in Christianity. Christianity without the cross is not Christianity at all.
>
> Everything in the life of Jesus pointed to the cross. The cross was ugly and painful. It was the symbol of

death. On the cross Jesus paid the price to make the way for us to come to God. He gave us the contrasting picture of the love of the Father and the sinfulness of man. On the cross Jesus gave His life that we might have eternal life.

But He says to all who would follow Him, "If any man will come after me, let him deny himself, and take up his cross daily, and follow me" (Luke 9:23).

In order to follow Him, we must take up our cross. We shall never see the glory of His resurrection power until we enter into the experience of the cross. And that costs. It costs everything.[1]

When Jesus' disciples finally realized that His hour of glorification was His crucifixion, it was still hard for them to deal with it all. Even at their last supper together, there arose a dispute among the disciples as to which one of them was regarded as the greatest. And the Lord said to them, "The kings of the Gentiles lord it over them; and those who have authority over them are called 'Benefactors.' But not so with you, but let him who is the greatest among you become as the youngest, and the leader as the servant. For who is greater, the one who reclines at the table, or the one who serves? Is it not the one who reclines at the table? But I am among you as the one who serves. And you are those who have stood by Me in My trials; and just as My Father has granted Me a kingdom, I grant you that you may eat and drink at My table in My kingdom, and you will sit on thrones judging the twelve tribes of Israel" (Luke 22:25-30).

It is so thrilling to think of greatness, to accept its glory and anticipate its rewards. But it is troublesome to think you must first carry a cross and face testings. You wonder how you will endure the pain, the loneliness, and rejection, the nagging doubt which stalks your mind because you have not walked the popular route with the multitudes.

Will you, like Judas, betray your Lord? Will you, like Peter, sincerely proclaim in one moment that you will lay down your life for Jesus, and then in the next find yourself denying Him?

The cost of following Jesus when you can't see and feel Him, and the weakness of your flesh are enough to trouble your heart. What can you do?

5 As we study John 14, look at what we can do when our hearts are troubled. There are six steps which will enable us to take our cross and follow our Lord. They are truths which, when embraced, will keep us from denying Him in an hour that calls for the obedience of faith.

Twice in John 14 we read that our Lord commanded His disciples: "Let not your heart be troubled" (John 14:1,27). Peace is to be the state of the Christian. In John 14:27 we read: "Peace I leave with you; My peace I give to you; not as the world gives, do I give to you. Let not your heart be troubled, nor let it be fearful."

The word for *peace* in the Koine Greek is *eirēnē,* which indicates not an absence of outward turmoil but an inward sense of goodness that is unrelated to circumstances. It is an untroubled state of well-being. It is not the peace of the world but the true peace which only God can give to those who will lay hold of it by faith. Thus, we come to the first step we can take in preventing a troubled heart: *Believe in God and in His Word.*

Note that there is a definite object of belief. Merely "believing" in general is not going to take care of a troubled heart. Jesus says, "Let not your heart be troubled; believe in God, believe also in Me"—or it could be translated, "You believe in God; believe also in Me" (John 14:1).

When your heart is troubled, you need to put your trust in God. Trust in who He is and in what He says. Do not rest on what you feel, see, or hear. The key that unlocks the inner sanctum of peace is faith—taking God at His Word.

Some people have a misconception of what it means to have faith in Him and His Word. So that we have a firm grasp of what it means to believe God, tomorrow we'll look at what the word implies in the Greek. But today let me share what Lawrence Richards writes regarding faith and believing: "People today may use 'faith' to indicate what is possible but uncertain. The Bible uses 'faith' in ways that link it with what is assuredly and certainly true. Christians may sometimes speak of 'believing,' as if it were merely a subjective effort, as if our act of faith or strength of faith were the issue. But the Bible shifts our attention from subjective experience and centers it on the object of our faith—God himself.[2]

6 A troubled heart is an agitation of soul and mind, the very psychological core of a person. A troubled heart can throw life into disarray. The first cure for the troubled heart is faith in God.

The words *faith* and *believe* are merely different forms of the same Greek word: *Pistis* is the noun for *faith* and *pisteuō* the verb for *believe*. To believe signifies "reliance upon, not mere credence." In his *Expository Dictionary of Old and New Testament Words*, W.E. Vine says: "The main elements in faith in its relation to the invisible God, as distinct from faith in man, are especially brought out in the use of this noun and the corresponding verb, *pisteuō*; they are (1) a firm conviction, producing a full acknowledgment of God's revelation or truth, e.g., 2 Thess. 2:11, 12; (2) a personal surrender to Him, John 1:12; (3) a conduct inspired by such surrender, 2 Cor. 5:7. Prominence is given to one or the other of these elements according to the context. All this stands in contrast to belief in its purely natural exercise, which consists of an opinion held in good faith without necessary reference to its proof."[3]

It is crucial, Beloved, that you have a biblical understanding of faith, of what it means to believe in God and in Jesus Christ. Many use the word lightly, calling people to a faith that does not have its foundation in the Word of God or in the character of God. Rather, their emphasis is on faith in faith. And a faith that is not biblical or inclusive of the whole counsel of God can leave you bitter and disillusioned with the Word of God or the Person of God Himself when what you have believed does not come to pass.

There is also a counterfeit faith that will delude people into thinking they have eternal life when they do not. This belief "exists as a limited trust in Jesus. Counterfeit belief acknowledges that there is something special about Jesus but refuses to accept Scripture's full testimony about him. Saving faith goes beyond limited belief. It recognizes Jesus as Son of God and trusts completely in him as he is unveiled in God's Word. Saving faith demonstrates belief by acting on the words Jesus has spoken (Jn 8:31-32). . . . The one who does not believe may be impressed with the evidence but will hold back from entrusting himself . . . to Jesus."[4]

O Beloved, apart from saving faith, your heart will never be free from agitation.

7 It is one thing to grab hold of God in faith when your heart is troubled, but it is another not to let go. "Faith is the assurance of things hoped for, the conviction of things not seen" (Hebrews 11:1). Until what you need becomes substance and reality, faith must continue unfaltering. You must keep on believing!

When your heart is troubled, the second step is to *remember that God does not lie.* If there were something amiss in the Word of God, Jesus would have told us so. If we had embraced tales told by the fathers around the Old Testament campfires, if we had been given the reasonings and explanations of human imagination about the creation of the universe and the character and ways of God, then Jesus would have straightened the tale out with truth.

Because He is the Truth, Jesus could not allow us to continue to believe a lie. Either the Old Testament was written by men moved by the Holy Spirit or it was of human origin and, therefore, full of error. Either it could be believed and embraced as our divinely written textbook for life, or it must be sorted through to see what might be from God and, therefore, reliable.

As Jesus called His disciples to faith in Him and His Word as the cure for their troubled hearts, He assured them that although He was about to leave them, the separation would not be permanent. There was a purpose in His going. "In My Father's house are many dwelling places; if it were not so, I would have told you; for I go to prepare a place for you" (John 14:2).

Did you note His words: "If it were not so, I would have told you"? Jesus is the Truth, and the Truth cannot lie. Never forget it, my friend.

When your heart is troubled, you can find yourself vulnerable to the tactics of the enemy. It is Satan, the devil, that serpent of old who wants to remove you from the security of faith. The devil's tactics are the same now as they were in the Garden of Eden. His words spoken there are recorded as a warning to all generations: "Yea, hath God said . . . ?" (Genesis 3:1 KJV). Remember what Jesus said about the devil in John 8:44? "He was a murderer from the beginning, and does not stand in the truth, because there is no truth in him. Wherever he speaks a lie, he speaks from his own nature; for he is a liar, and the father of lies."

O Beloved, do not allow the accuser to torment you. Remind him that he lies. Remind him that God does not.

8 When Jesus' disciples were distressed at the thought of being separated from their Lord, Jesus turned their gaze to the future. When you find yourself distressed and agitated in your soul, *look to God's future for you*. Here we see the third step you can take in guarding your heart. In John 14:3-12 note three things to focus on as you look to God's future for you. Let me spell these out and then we'll cover them one by one.

You need to focus on the eternal, not the temporal (John 14:3-6). Next you need to look to the Father whom you have seen through the Person of His Son (John 14:7-11). Last, you need to look to your calling from the Lord (John 14:12).

Have you ever had to be separated from anyone whom you loved dearly? What sustained you in his or her absence? Wasn't it the thought of seeing the person again? Of course.

And you counted the days until once again you would see each other face-to-face. You lived in the expectation of your reunion.

This, Beloved, was the secret of the power of the early church. They had known the joy of His presence, and they had the promise of His return. They lived in the expectation of again seeing their Jesus face-to-face.

In his first epistle, the apostle John refers to this expectancy as the purifying hope (1 John 3:2,3). When Jesus appeared, the trials and testings of their faith would be over. Faith would become substance. Once again they would behold with their own eyes His hands and His feet. When that day came, all that would matter is that they had been faithful. When their hearts were troubled, they would rehearse His words in their minds: " 'And if I go and prepare a place for you, I will come again, and receive you to Myself; that where I am, there you may be also. And you know the way where I am going.' Thomas said to Him, 'Lord, we do not know where You are going; how do we know the way?' Jesus said to him, 'I am the way, and the truth, and the life; no one comes to the Father, but through Me' " (John 14:3-6).

In Jesus, they had all they needed to handle any trial. Because nothing could separate them from Him, their hearts could be at rest. They were going to be with Him forever and ever. Jesus had said it. That settled it.

Even that dreaded enemy, death, could not trouble their hearts, for all separation was only temporal. He was the life. When their hearts were troubled, they needed to remember that visible things were temporal. The eternal was coming. On that their hearts could rest. And so can yours, Beloved.

9 The next time your heart is troubled, stop and examine why. Was it because of something temporal in nature? Possibly some concern over material needs? If so, believe in God. He said it, and He meant it: "Do not be anxious then, saying, 'What shall we eat?' or 'What shall we drink?' or 'With what shall we clothe ourselves?' For all these things

the Gentiles eagerly seek; for your heavenly Father knows that you need all these things. But seek first His kingdom and His righteousness; and all these things shall be added to you" (Matthew 6:31-33).

As I write this today, our ministry is facing a great financial need. We believe we have God's direction, but we do not yet have the resources. Where will the monies come from? I do not know. All I know is that our God will supply all our needs according to His riches in glory through Christ Jesus our Lord (Philippians 4:19); and while my heart wants to be troubled, I must bring it into subjection to our Lord's command: "Let not your heart be troubled" (John 14:1), and remember that God does not lie.

Keeping all these truths in mind, we must look to the eternal, knowing that this is a trial of our faith and that we must let patience have its perfect work. God is sovereign, and that we must cling to. Christians are not exempt from the testings and trials of faith, no matter how closely we walk with our Lord. (Read 2 Corinthians 4:8-12,16-18.)

O Beloved, do you see how focusing on the eternal—while clinging to your God and His Word in faith—can take you through the temporal storms which would trouble your heart?

10 How often I have watched our sons, Tom, Mark, and David, gather their hurt children in their arms and comfort them. Tears gushing like a torrential rain down the curve of soft, pinkish cheeks are soon dried up as in a sudden summer shower. Because they are in their fathers' arms and secure in their loving care, their troubled hearts are soon put at rest. They are blessed children, for they have fathers who want to be like Jesus.

When Jesus reassured His disciples that they need not be troubled because He was going to the Father and would return to take them with Him, Philip wanted to see the Father then and there. I wonder what it did to Jesus when he made his request. We don't know. Only our Lord's words are recorded, not His feelings. But let's look at His words and see what we can learn: "Have I been so long with you, and yet you have not come to know Me, Philip? He who has seen Me has seen the Father; how do you say, 'Show us the Father'? Do you not believe that I am in the Father, and the Father is in Me? The words that I say to you I do not speak on My own initiative, but the Father abiding in Me does His works. Believe Me that I am in the Father, and the Father in Me; otherwise believe on account of the works themselves" (John 14:9-11).

Jesus had done what He came to do: "No man has seen God at any time; the only begotten God, who is in the bosom of the Father, He has explained Him"(John 1:18). Jesus came to reveal to mankind the Father heart of God—and Philip had missed it!

The Lord Jesus Christ came to explain the Father to you. God has supplied all your needs. Yes, you may have a difficult time relating to God as a Father, because of some experience related to your earthly father; but remember, your heavenly Father wants to reconcile your fears and reluctances. He can! He will! Do not look to the circumstances of life. Look to your Father God. Allow Him to be all you need. Ask Him to manifest His love and care through His Word and through all you can learn about the Son—and then believe.

11 Your earthly father may not have been a good and loving dad, but no circumstance will alter what God will be to you as your loving, protecting Father God. Beloved, your heart need not be troubled. Look to the future, to the time when you will forever be with your heavenly Father. Look to the time when God Himself will wipe away every tear from your eyes. Think of the time when He shall no longer permit any death, mourning, or pain, for the first things shall all have passed away (Revelation 21:4). You will live with God in His very own house—a dwelling place prepared expressly for you by your elder Brother, your Lord and Savior Jesus Christ.

"For you have not received a spirit of slavery leading to fear again, but you have received a spirit of adoption as sons by which we cry out, 'Abba! Father!' " (Romans 8:15). You are an heir of God and a fellow heir with Christ.

So snuggle in God's arms. When you are hurting, when you feel lonely, left out, rejected, let Him cradle you, comfort you, reassure you of His all-sufficient power and love as your El Shaddai. "The sufferings of this present time are not worthy to be compared with the glory that is to be revealed to us" (Romans 8:18).

Look to the eternal; don't fix your eyes on the temporal. If you don't, Beloved, mourning over the temporal will keep you from the full reward of the eternal.

You don't want to be ashamed when you see your Father God face-to-face. You don't want to hear Him say, "But, My child, all day long I stretched out My arms to you to comfort you by My Spirit, to reassure you in My Word, and you would not come to Me. I would have gathered you as a hen does her chicks, but . . ."

Beloved child of God, what more can God do to prove His love to you? "He who did not spare His own Son, but delivered Him up for us all, how will He not also with Him freely give us all things?" (Romans 8:32). You can "overwhelmingly conquer through Him" who loves you (Romans 8:37). "For I am convinced that neither death, nor life, nor angels, nor principalities, nor things present, nor things to come, nor powers, nor height, nor depth, nor any other created thing, shall be able to separate us from the love of God, which is in Christ Jesus our Lord" (Romans 8:38,39).

So, precious child of God, in faith let Him dry your tears with the sure promises of His Word. Don't listen to the lies of the enemy as he whispers that your Father doesn't love you. Look in faith to your future with Him. Jesus has shown you the Father, and it is enough.

12 In the next several days, through a story that has absolutely blessed my heart and encouraged my faith, I want to show you how Jesus explains His Father. It is my prayer that God will captivate you, my friend, with a fresh awareness of His love and power.

As I shared with you earlier, Bruce Olson was called by God as a 19-year-old to take the gospel to the Motilone tribe of Stone Age Indians who live in Colombia, South America. God called Bruce to the cross, as He calls you, as He calls me. Bruce's cross would include capture, disease, terror, loneliness, and torture.

But the sufferings which awaited him were "not worthy to be compared with the glory that is to be revealed to us" (Romans 8:18). Yet Bruce would not have to wait until eternity to see some of the fruit of the harvest he sowed in obedience.

When God finally took Bruce into the Motilone tribe, one of the men assigned by the tribe to care for Bruce was named Bobarishora. However, every time Bruce tried to pronounce his name, it got tangled up on his tongue. So Bobarishora became Bobby. And Bruce Olson became Bruchko to the Motilones.

One day after being on the trail for three days with Bobby and two other Motilones, Bruchko was frozen in his tracks by excruciating cries that pierced the approaching darkness of the warm, green velvet of the jungle. They were hurrying to make it to the village before nightfall. The cries coming from the thicket of the jungle seemed desperate. Never had Bruchko heard such agonizing cries. Arrested by their cries, Bruchko called out to Bobby and the others to stop:

> "What's that shouting?" I asked. "Shouldn't we see if there's anything we can do?"
>
> Bobby looked down at the trail. One of the other men, who was a witchdoctor, shook his head. "There's nothing we can do."

"But what's going on there?"

None of the three said anything. They stared at me with dark, quiet eyes. . . .

"They're sad," I thought. "There's something over there that is too sad for them to bear."[5]

13 I could not help but think of the following verses from Romans 10 as I read what happened on that trail in the Colombian jungle. The cries were, in essence, a reechoing of words recorded in the days of Moses and then again in the days of Paul. They were words of man's feeble efforts to contact God. Read these verses carefully so you will appreciate even more the true account which follows.

"But the righteousness based on faith speaks thus, 'Do not say in your heart, "Who will ascend into heaven?" (that is, to bring Christ down), or "Who will descend into the abyss?" (that is, to bring Christ up from the dead).' But what does it say? 'The word is near you, in your mouth and in your heart'—that is, the word of faith which we are preaching, that if you confess with your mouth Jesus as Lord, and believe in your heart that God raised Him from the dead, you shall be saved" (Romans 10:6-9).

The shouting men were closer than I had thought. And there were only two of them. One I knew well. He was a leader in his communal home, and a fierce warrior. He had killed oil company employees just to get their safety helmets to use in cooking. He wore a necklace of buttons from his victims' clothes, and another necklace of jaguar teeth from a jaguar he had killed with his bow and arrow. Now, standing in front of a hole that he had dug—a hole that was a good six feet deep—he was shouting in a desperate, searching voice, "God, God, come out of the hole."

The other man was in the top of a high tree. He was stuffing leaves into his mouth and trying to chew them, while shouting, "God, God, come from the horizon!"

It was the strangest sight I had ever seen. It could have been laughable, but something kept me from seeing any humor in it.

My three companions came up alongside me, looking sad and embarrassed.

"You knew about this?" I asked Bobby.

He nodded.

"What's the matter?"

He explained that the brother of the man shouting into the hole had died in a region that was not his home. He had been bitten by a poisonous snake and had died before there was time to get him back. According to their traditions, that meant that his language, his spirit, his life, could never go to God beyond the horizon. Now the man was trying to look for God, to get Him to bring his brother's language back to life, to live in his body.

"And what makes him think he can find God by calling into a hole?"

Bobby shrugged. "It's as good a place as any to look." The hopelessness of his expression was transmitted to his words.

This was why God had let me live. I was there to tell them where they could find God. . . .[6]

And you, Beloved, what is your purpose in life?

14 " 'And you will seek Me and find Me, when you search for Me with all your heart. And I will be found by you,' declares the LORD" (Jeremiah 29:13,14).

Perhaps this was an opportunity God had arranged. My body tightened at the thought of having a chance to share Christ after five years of waiting. Yet it seemed too much to expect. Inside I was praying.

The man stopped shouting into the hole, and came over to us. His hair was disheveled, his body covered with dirt. His eyes were holes into black space. "It's no point," he said. "We've been deceived."

"How long have you been here?" I asked quietly.

"Since the sun came up this morning."

"And why do you say that you've been deceived?"

He told me again the story of the false prophet the Motilones had followed, whose false promises had led them away from God. "We no longer know God," he said quietly.

Then the other men tried to explain a Motilone legend that confirmed why this brother's death had such terrifying implications. I didn't understand it all. Motilone legends are as complicated as any theology. But I did understand something new: their great sense of lostness. I had wondered again and again what Christ had to offer them. Their way of getting along with each other was far superior to that of Americans. But there was more to life than that.

I thought of the night Jesus had entered my life. It had been so many years before, such a small point in time. Yet it was the root out of which everything I was had grown. Through it God had brought me peace and real purpose.

And here were the Motilones in a search for God. But how could I explain things like grace, sacrifice, the incarnation? I could tell a simple story, and they would understand. But how could I communicate real spiritual truth?

A lively discussion started. The man who had been in the trees came down and joined us. He reminded us of the legend about the prophet who would come carrying banana stalks and that God would come out of those stalks.

I couldn't quite understand the idea behind the legend.

"Why look for God to come out of a banana stalk?" I asked.

There was puzzled silence. It made sense to them, but they couldn't explain it. Bobby walked over to a banana tree which was growing nearby. He cut off a section and tossed it toward us.

"This is the kind of banana stalk God can come from," he said. It was a cross section from the stalk. It rolled at our feet.[7]

15 One of the Motilones reached down and swatted at it with his machete, accidentally spliting it in half. One half stood up, while the other half split off. Leaves that were still inside the stalk, waiting to develop and come out, started peeling off. As they lay at the base of the stalk, they looked like pages from a book.

Suddenly a word raced though my mind. "Book! Book!"

I grabbed up my pack and took out my Bible. I opened it. Flipping through the pages, I held it toward the men. I pointed to the leaves from the banana stalk, then back to the Bible.

"This is it!" I said. "I have it here! This is God's banana stalk."

One of the Motilones, the one who had been in the tree, grabbed the Bible out of my hand. He started to rip out pages and stuff them in his mouth. He thought if he ate the pages he would have God inside him.

When nothing happened, they began to ask me questions. How could I explain the gospel to them? How could I explain that God, in Jesus, had been like them?

Suddenly I remembered one of their legends about a man who had become an ant. He had been sitting on the trail after a hunt, and had noticed some ants trying to build a home. He'd wanted to help them make a good home, like the Motilone home, so he'd begun digging in the dirt. But because he was so big and so unknown, the ants had been afraid and had run away.

Then, quite miraculously, he had become an ant. He thought like an ant, looked like an ant and spoke the language of an ant. He lived with the ants, and they came to trust him.

He told them one day that he was not really an ant, but a Motilone, and that he had once tried to help them improve their home, but he had scared them.

The ants said their equivalent of "No kidding? That was you?" And they laughed at him, because he didn't look like the huge and fearful thing that had moved the dirt before.

But at that moment he was turned back into a Motilone and began to move the dirt into the shape of a Motilone home. This time the ants recognized him and let him do his work, because they knew he wouldn't harm them. That was why, according to the story, the ants had hills that looked like Motilone homes.

As the story flashed into my mind, I realized its lesson for the first time: If you are big and powerful, you have to become small and weak in order to work with other weak beings. It was a perfect parallel for what God had done in Jesus.[8]

"And the Word became flesh, and dwelt among us, and we beheld His glory, glory as of the only begotten from the Father. . . . The only begotten . . . He has explained Him" (John 1:14,18).

16 Bruchko had found the perfect parallel in the legend of the ant for what God had done in Jesus. But how could he make sure the Motilones would comprehend what he wanted to explain to them?

There were so many unknown factors in the way the Motilones reasoned. How could I be sure that I would convey the right thing?

I couldn't. Yet I felt sure God had given me this time to speak. So I took the word for "becoming like an ant," and used it for incarnation. "God is incarnated into man," I said.

They gasped. There was a tense, hushed silence. The idea that God had become a man stunned them.

"Where did He walk?" the witchdoctor asked in a whisper.

Every Motilone has his own trail. It is his personal point of identity. You walk on someone's trail if you want to find him. God would have a trail, too. If you want to find God, you walk on His trail.

My blood was racing, my heart pounding. "Jesus Christ is God become man," I said. "He can show you God's trail."

A look of astonishment, almost of fear, spread over their faces. The man who had been shouting into the hole looked at me.

"Show us Christ," he said in a coarse whisper.

I fumbled for an answer. "You killed Christ," I said. "You destroyed God."

His eyes got big. "I killed Christ? I did that? How did I do that? And how can God be killed?"

I wanted to tell them that Jesus' death had freed them from meaninglessness, from death and the powers of evil.

"How does evil, death and deception find power over the Motilone people?" I asked.

"Through the ears," Bobby answered, because language is so important to the Motilones. It is the essence of life. If evil language comes through the ears, it means death.

"Do you remember," I said, "how after a hunt for wild boars the leader cuts the skin from the animal and puts it over his head, to cover his ears and keep the evil spirits of the jungle out?"

They nodded, listening closely.

"Jesus Christ was murdered," I said. "But just as you pull the skin over the chieftain's head to hide his ears, so Jesus—when He died—pulled His blood over your deception and hides it from the sight of God."

I stood looking at them, hoping desperately that they would understand. Then I saw on their faces that they did.

I told them that Jesus was buried. A wave of grief swept over them. The man who was searching for his brother's language began to weep. It was the first time I had ever seen a Motilone cry. But the thought that God was dead, that they were lost, brought tears and sobs.[9]

God had spoken by His Spirit through Bruchko—convicting of sin, righteousness, and judgment (John 16:7,8).

17 Jesus said, "The words that I have spoken to you are spirit and are life" (John 6:63).

I picked up my Bible, opened it, and said, "The Bible speaks that Jesus came alive after death, and is alive today."

One of the men grabbed the Bible from my hand and put it to his ear. "I can't hear a thing," he said.

I took it back. "The way the Bible speaks does not change," I said. "It is like the papers of your speech that I have. They say the same word one day to the next. The Bible says that Jesus came to life. It is God's banana stalk."

I showed him the page, and told him that the little black markings had meaning.

"No one has ever come back from the dead in all Motilone history," he said.

"I know," I replied. "But Jesus did. It is proof that He is really God's Son."

They asked many more questions. Some I didn't fully understand. But I was sure that God had spoken through me. That night I prayed, "God, give validity to Your Word. Make it touch these lives." I claimed God's promise that His Word would not return to Him without any response.

Yet there didn't seem to be any response. I continued to walk the trails with Bobby, giving medicine to the witchdoctors and showing them how to do their work more effectively.

One evening, though, Bobby began to ask questions. We were sitting around a fire. The light flickered over him. His face was serious.

"How can I walk on Jesus' trail?" he asked. "No Motilone has ever done it. It's a new thing. There is no other Motilone to tell how to do it."

I remembered the problems I had had as a boy, how it sometimes appeared impossible to keep on believing in Jesus when my family and friends were so opposed to my commitment. That was what Bobby was going through.

"Bobby," I said, "do you remember my first Festival of the Arrows, the first time I had seen all the Motilones gathered to sing their song?" The festival was the most important ceremony in the Motilone culture.

He nodded. The fire flared up momentarily and I could see his eyes, staring intently at me.[10]

Bruchko had walked Jesus' trail; he had taken up his cross and followed Him all the way to Colombia, South America. It had cost him much—death to self. Now after five years he was about to see the fruit of his obedience. The Motilones were to be Bruchko's crown of rejoicing at the appearing of his Lord and Savior (1 Thessalonians 2:19,20).

18 Do you remember that I was afraid to climb in the high hammocks to sing, for fear that the rope would break? And I told you that I would sing only if I could have one foot in the hammock and one foot on the ground?"

"Yes, Bruchko."

"And what did you say to me?"

He laughed. "I told you you had to have both feet in the hammock. 'You have to be suspended,' I said."

"Yes," I said. "You have to be suspended. That is how it is when you follow Jesus, Bobby. No man can tell you how to walk His trail. Only Jesus can. But to find out you have to tie your hammock strings into Him, and be suspended in God."

Bobby said nothing. The fire danced in his eyes. Then he stood up and walked off into the darkness.

The next day he came to me. "Bruchko," he said, "I want to tie my hammock strings into Jesus Christ. But how can I? I can't see Him or touch Him."

"You have talked to spirits, haven't you?"

"Oh," he said. "I see now."

The next day he had a big grin on his face. "Bruchko, I've tied my hammock strings into Jesus. Now I speak a new language."

I didn't understand what he meant. "Have you learned some of the Spanish I speak?"

He laughed, a clean, sweet laugh. "No, Bruchko, I speak a new language."

Then I understood. To a Motilone, language is life. If Bobby had a new life, he had a new way of speaking. His speech would be Christ-oriented.

We put our hands on each other's shoulders. My mind swept back to the first time I had met Jesus, and the life I had felt flow into me. Now my brother Bobby was experiencing Jesus himself, in the same way. He had begun to walk with Jesus.

"Jesus Christ has risen from the dead!" Bobby shouted, so that the sound filtered far off into the jungle. "He has walked our trails! I have met Him!"

From that day our friendship was enhanced by our love for Jesus. We talked constantly about Him, and Bobby asked me many questions. But he never asked the color of Jesus' hair, or whether He had blue eyes. To Bobby, the answers were obvious: Jesus had dark skin, and His eyes were black. He wore a G-string, and hunted with bows and arrows.

Jesus was a Motilone.[11]

Bobby was the fruit of the incarnation. Jesus explained the Father, and now Bobby is part of that great multitude, "which no one could count, from every nation and all tribes and peoples and tongues, standing before . . . the Lamb, clothed in white robes, and palm branches were in their hands; and they cry out with a loud voice, saying, 'Salvation to our God who sits on the throne, and to the Lamb' " (Revelation 7:9,10).

19 I am sure our Lord's words were staggeringly difficult for the disciples to believe. They would do greater works than Jesus! They had seen His works. They knew the multitudes that had followed Him. They had seen His miracles. How could they do works like these—let alone greater ones? How could Jesus talk of going away, of Peter denying Him and the others forsaking Him, and then tell them they were going to do greater works? How? Surely this news must have troubled their hearts even more. Yet it was part of the cure for a troubled heart.

So far this month we have looked at three things we can do to walk in the peace of God when our hearts are troubled. First, we must believe in Jesus as well as in God. Then we must remember God cannot lie; therefore, we must continue to cling to His promises which are yea and amen (2 Corinthians 1:20 KJV). And third, we must look to the future by taking our eyes off the temporal and putting them on the eternal, looking to our Father and to the greater works He has for us to do.

When my heart is troubled, it helps me so much to realize that I am on this earth for one purpose and one purpose alone: to do the will of God who created me for His pleasure.

When the hearts of the disciples were troubled, Jesus reminded them of the importance of believing who He was and what He had accomplished: "Do you not believe that I am in the Father, and the Father is in Me? The words that I say to you I do not speak on My own initiative, but the Father abiding in Me does His works. Believe Me that I am in the Father, and the Father in Me; otherwise believe on account of the works themselves. Truly, truly, I say to you, he who believes in Me, the works that I do shall he do also; and greater works than these shall he do; because I go to the Father" (John 14:10-12).

Two things bore witness to Jesus' incarnation and deity: His words and His works, for His words and His works were the Father's. It is the indwelling of God in you through the Holy Spirit that enables you to do the work of God, even greater works than what Jesus did. Your works can be greater in scope, because His works were brought to an abrupt halt because of His death, resurrection, and ascension to the

Father.

Why don't you take time, Beloved, to ask God to show you the works He has ordained for you to walk in, for you "are His workmanship, created in Christ Jesus for good works" (Ephesians 2:10).

Your life has a purpose. Knowing that purpose is the cure for many a troubled heart.

20 In these past few days, our Father has given me a blessed respite. It has been wonderful to slow my pace and have extended times for prayer and meditation.

As I have sat outside at night watching the sun go down, enjoying the caress of a gentle, warm wind, tears have filled my eyes as I have communed in prayer with our Father. My heart has been overwhelmed with the privilege and responsibility of ministry to which He has called us.

When I think of my past, I am overwhelmed and awed by His grace. I feel as if I have lived two entirely different lives, and in a sense I have. Like Paul and like you, I too am a new creature in Christ Jesus.

Old things have passed away, and all things have become new. I am no longer my own. I have been bought with a price—the incorruptible blood of the Lamb of God who is without spot or blemish. I was bought by love at Calvary. I was set free from my slavery to sin to become His bond-servant forever.

Now my life has purpose, eternal value. What I do will impact the kingdom of heaven and reap an eternal harvest. Many of you are part of that harvest. Even this devotional is in obedience to the leadership of His Holy Spirit and is part of those "greater works" that He ordained.

Extraordinary, isn't it, Beloved, that you and I should carry on the work of the Son! And humbling.

In the days of quiet that He provided, one of the things I reaffirmed is that promotion does not come from the east or from the west—but from the Lord (Psalm 75:6,7). Therefore, He is totally responsible for the breadth of our ministry.

I am simply to be totally available to Him. The words that I speak and teach are to be His words; the works are to be His works. How wonderfully freeing this is. My name does not have to be known—only His! My works do not have to be promoted. If they are His works, they will accomplish His will, and that is all that matters.

It is these—the words and the works—which will prove that He is in us and that we are in Him. Ours is simply to be like our Lord in His relationship to the Father—to always and only do those things which please Him. Nothing else matters.

21 As surely as there is a calling upon my life as a child of God, as a disciple of our Lord Jesus Christ, there is a calling upon your life if you are His. One calling is not greater than another in the kingdom of God. You and I will never be responsible for the scope or impact of our lives. We will be responsible for only one thing: obedience to the will of God.

We are saved by grace. Yet, once we are saved, we are responsible to obey the God who saved us. God is sovereign in our salvation, but we are responsible in our obedience. If it seems a paradox, leave it there, Beloved. Simply know what the Scripture teaches and live accordingly.

Knowing the weakness of our flesh, we wonder how we can ever carry on the work of God. And like Paul we cry, "And who is adequate for these things?" (2 Corinthians 2:16). And yet even as we cry out these words, we know that our adequacy is of Jesus Christ.

When the disciples' hearts were troubled because Jesus was leaving them to return to the Father, He gave them a fourth step to bring peace to their troubled hearts: They were simply to *ask in His name.*

Let's stop for a minute and put ourselves in the sandals of these disciples. For the past three years, Jesus was their constant companion and ever-present Helper. He provided them with all they needed. When tax money was due, He sent them fishing to find the money in the mouth of the fish.

When the storm came, He calmed the sea and brought them safely to the shore. He multiplied the loaves and the fish. Every need was met because Jesus was their constant companion.

Now Jesus was leaving them. How would they survive? His answer to them was twofold: prayer and the gift of the Holy Spirit. One without the other is impossible. Praise God, it is a package benefit!

Why don't you finish our time together by reading John 14 again, asking God to open the eyes of your understanding that you might behold the wondrous promises which are yours.

22 When your heart is troubled, you need to believe. Remembering God cannot lie, look to God's future for you, and ask in the name of your Lord Jesus Christ. When Jesus told His disciples that they were going to do greater works than He had done because He was going to the Father, He immediately followed that statement with this promise: "And whatever you ask in My name, that will I do, that the Father may be glorified in the Son. If you ask Me anything in My name, I will do it" (John 14:13,14).

Although Jesus was leaving them physically, He would not leave them without help. As He supplied what they needed when He was with them, so He would supply what they needed even though He was going to the Father. All they had to do was go to the Father in prayer and ask in His name. Then they could know that it was taken care of—Jesus would do it.

I wonder what would happen in Christendom if God's children actually took Him at His word? To take Him at His word is to live by faith. "Faith cometh by hearing, and hearing by the word of God" (Romans 10:17 KJV).

Genuine faith always has as its foundation or premise the Word of God—not selected verses of God's Word snipped from their context and content, but God's Word in accordance and agreement with the whole counsel of God, in keeping with the person and the work of God. Because many prayers are not in accord with the counsel and character of God, they go unanswered. Possibly they were prayed in accordance with personal desires rather than with the pure Word of God.

The Lord was very careful to tell His disciples that they were to ask in His name. Many prayers can never be answered by God because they are in direct opposition to who God is. This is why John 15:7 is so very important: "If you abide in Me, and My words abide in you, ask whatever you wish, and it shall be done for you."

The promises of God related to prayer cannot be isolated from one another and then be validly presented before "the throne of grace" where we find "help in time of need" (Hebrews 4:16). True prayer finds its foundation in the character of God and the Word of God, which are never contrary to one another. Psalm 138:2 says, "For Thou hast magnified Thy word according to all Thy name." It could be translated: "Thou hast magnified Thy word together with Thy name."

Anything asked in accordance with the Word of God, and in keeping with the name of our Lord, is the will of God. And if it is the will of God, then God will grant it—in His time, in His way. And surely we do not want it otherwise, if our one passion is His will.

23 The tendency of many Christians is to make John 14:13 their servant, rather than seeing it as a means of serving God. If you take this verse in its context, you will see that it is in the setting of serving God, of carrying on the work of the Lord Jesus Christ, the Son of Man.

This is what God intended for man when God created him and gave him dominion over all the earth. Man in the image of God was to walk in complete obedience to and dependence upon God. All was to be done in accord with the will of God.

In John 14 Jesus calls us to that same high calling again. In order to accomplish God's will, in order to serve Him, Jesus will supply all our needs. All we have to do is ask in His name, in accordance with the will of God.

Yet, some people use this promise for their own benefit. They teach it as a blanket promise that guarantees health and wealth to all who will simply believe and ask in faith.

They reason in this way: "God doesn't want His children to be poor, does He? If you were a father and you could make your children healthy and wealthy, wouldn't you do it? Of course! Well, is God any less loving or caring than you are? No. Therefore, if you are not healthy or wealthy, it is a lack of faith on your part."

But, Beloved, is this true? Is it in accord with the whole counsel of the Word of God? Is it supported or testified to by God's dealings with His people down through the ages? Or, is this "a new teaching that those suffering saints didn't know"?

Beloved, God has not hidden truth in the past only to reveal it now. Believers have always been admonished to live by every word that proceeds out of the mouth of God, that they might be thoroughly equipped unto every good work of life (Deuteronomy 8:3; 2 Timothy 3:17).

Sammy Tippit, an evangelist who has worked extensively in Eastern bloc countries, writes:

> This generation parades preachers and teachers promising health, wealth, and wisdom to all who follow Jesus. The only place in the world where that kind of teaching could gain a foothold is in a capitalistic society. One friend in the West told me that if Christians in communist countries trusted God, they would be wealthier and healthier. Third World Christians laugh at such teaching. When they choose Jesus, they choose poverty because of lost job opportunities.
>
> However, they find themselves wealthy in things of eternal value and, in many cases, much more healthy spiritually.

24 I taught a group of university students in East Germany on the doctrine of godly suffering. One of them told me, "You are the first American to come here and teach that it will cost something to follow Jesus." I was embarrassed and ashamed to hear that my fellow countrymen went to such a place with a message of health and wealth.

Now, there is nothing intrinsically wrong with health and wealth. There are many godly people in Scripture and throughout history who were wealthy. But their wealth and health were not equated with their spirituality.[12]

And yet, Beloved, those who teach a "name it in faith and claim it in faith" doctrine really equate a man's physical state with his spirituality; they say that if one does not have health or wealth, it is due to a lack of faith. But can we make John 14:13 and other such verses the basis for such a judgment? Is John 14:13 a blank check which I simply fill in—in faith—in order to get what I want? No!

To ask in the name of Jesus Christ is to ask for that which is consistent with His character. In biblical times, a person's name revealed his character. God's names reveal who He is. To ask in His name is to ask in accordance with His will.

If we are to live as our Master did, if we as His slaves are not to be greater than He was (John 15:20), how can we expect that all Christians are to be wealthy, prominent, successful, and loved? Jesus was "despised and forsaken of men, a man of sorrows, and acquainted with grief" (Isaiah 53:3), accused of having a demon (John 7:20), having "nowhere to lay His head" (Matthew 8:20).

Christ Jesus did not ride in the finest chariots; He walked. He did not live in kings' palaces; His kingdom was not of this world. During His public ministry, He healed some but not all. If healing had been His will for everyone, He would have healed them all. But He didn't.

In his excellent book *The Legacy of Jesus,* John MacArthur comments on John 14:13,14: "What it really means is that when we pray, we should pray as if Jesus Christ Himself were doing the asking. We approach the throne of the Father in full identification with the Son, seeking only what He would seek. When we pray with that perspective, we begin to pray for the things that really matter and eliminate selfish requests."[13]

Prayer like this, Beloved, will bring peace to a troubled heart.

25 Many times when our hearts are troubled, it is because we feel all alone; we have no one who fully understands our situation or who can genuinely come to our aid. We now come to the fifth step we must take when our hearts are troubled: *Never forget you are not alone.* You are not an orphan abandoned by your heavenly Father or your Lord. You have the Holy Spirit. Be at peace; let not your heart be troubled.

In these remaining days of June, I want us to see what we can learn from John 14 regarding the Holy Spirit. In John 14:15-18 we read: "If you love Me, you will keep My commandments. And I will ask the Father, and He will give you another Helper, that He may be with you forever; that is the Spirit of truth, whom the world cannot receive, because it does not behold Him or know Him, but you know Him because He abides with you, and will be in you. I will not leave you as orphans; I will come to you."

The distress of the disciples was natural. It seemed to them that with Jesus' departure they would be totally alone, separated from God as they were before. How could they ever adjust to that once they had shared what they had with their Lord? No wonder their hearts were greatly troubled.

And yet Jesus promised them a continuing intimacy with Him even though He would no longer be present with them physically. Jesus was going to send another Helper. The Greek word for *helper* is *paraklētos,* which means, "to call hither, toward." The Greek writers used the word for "a legal advisor, pleader, proxy, or advocate."[14] The Helper Jesus would send would be to them as He had been.

The Greek word in John 14:16 for *another* is *allos,* not *heteros. Heteros* means "another but not the same as." *Allos* means "another . . . of the same kind, the same quality."[15]

How wonderful this prospect must have been to the disciples! After having Jesus as their Helper, who would want a helper of a different kind? No, if Jesus had to go away, give them someone like Him.

And Jesus said this Helper would be with them forever. What peace this must have brought to their troubled hearts! May it bring great peace to yours also, Beloved friend.

26 This was a new concept! The Holy Spirit indwelling men, abiding with them forever, never leaving them. Never in all of history had this been possible. The permanent indwelling of the Spirit of God would make believers unique among all the people on the earth. Their physical bodies would become temples of the living God in the Person of His Spirit.

Because the world did not see and know Jesus as He was—the Son of God and of Man—the world would not receive Him. Only those who believed that Jesus was the Christ, the Son of God, would have within them "the Spirit of truth" (John 14:17).

Those who refused to believe the truth about Jesus Christ would forever be cut off from the truth. Instead they would believe the god of this world, the devil himself, and would indulge the desires of their flesh and their mind in his lie (Ephesians 2:1-3). Forever they would be cut off, for "the god of this world has blinded the minds of the unbelieving, that they might not see the light of the gospel of the glory of Christ, who is the image of God" (2 Corinthians 4:4).

Never would they know the wisdom of God—"the wisdom which none of the rulers of this age has understood; for if they had understood it, they would not have crucified the Lord of glory" (1 Corinthians 2:8). "But as it is written, 'Eye hath not seen, nor ear heard, neither have entered into the heart of man, the things which God hath prepared for them that love him' " (1 Corinthians 2:9 KJV).

Unbelievers are forever cut off from knowing the things of God and the eternal joys He intended and planned for those He created. Only those who had the Spirit of truth indwelling them would know the truth. "For to us God revealed them through the Spirit; for the Spirit searches all things, even the depths of God" (1 Corinthians 2:10).

Without the Spirit of God within, people would never understand the things of God; for "God is spirit, and those who worship Him must worship in spirit and truth" (John 4:24; see also 1 Corinthians 2:11,12,14,16).

O Beloved, whatever may come to trouble your heart, turn it aside. You have the Helper, and He will guide you into all truth because He is the Truth. What a promise!

27 Do you at times despair of being an effective servant of our Lord? Do you feel woefully inadequate? Do not despair. You have the Helper. He is with you! He is in you! He is adequate for any situation of life into which He sovereignly places you.

Whatever the task to which He calls you, He must supply the means, the gifts, talents, ability. Whatever wisdom you need, He has given you by His Spirit. You have the mind of Christ. Your responsibility is to be obedient, to walk in faith.

How I love to read the biographies of great Christians, those whose lives have been proven to be of God because they fought the good fight, kept the faith, and finished their course. I have been challenged and blessed by *Mother of an Army,* the story of Catherine Booth.

Catherine and her husband, William Booth, were founders of The Salvation Army. Catherine had a severe spinal disease, tuberculosis, and had to drop out of school because of her illness. Her father, who had once professed Christ and become part of the temperance movement, became an alcoholic. As a young single woman, she was kicked out of her church because of her determination to stand for the truth.

She was not married until 26. She waited four years to marry William Booth because he had difficulty in finding a church which would understand his gift of evangelism and his burden for the poor.

Even though her health was poor, after they married, Catherine bore eight children. William Booth had two physical breakdowns. They often did not know where money would come from to provide the bare necessities of life.

Yet, even in this circumstance, Catherine knew God was preparing them to do His will. She felt their poverty would make them more understanding, and it did. They became God's Salvation Army to the poor and the outcast—those whom Jesus came to save.

28 Let Catherine Booth tell you of the adequacy of the Helper, in an incident that occurred when she was the mother of three and before the Salvation Army became a reality:

> "One Sabbath I was passing down a narrow, thickly populated street on my way to chapel, anticipating an evening's enjoyment for myself, and hoping to see some anxious ones brought into the Kingdom, when I chanced to look up at the thick rows of small windows above me where numbers of women were sitting, peering at the passersby, or listlessly gossiping with each other."
>
> While viewing this scene, a new idea flashed into her mind: " 'Would you not be doing God more service, and acting more like your Redeemer, by turning into some of these houses, speaking to these careless sinners, and inviting them to service, than by going [to chapel] to enjoy yourself?' I was startled; it was a new thought; and while I was reasoning about it the same inaudible interrogator demanded, 'What effort do Christians put forth

answerable to the command, "Compel them to come in that my house may be filled"?' (Luke 14:23).

"This was accompanied with a light and unction which I knew to be divine. I felt greatly agitated. I felt guilty. I knew that I had never thus labored to bring lost sinners to Christ. . . ." Convicted, she "stood still for a moment, looked up to heaven, and said, 'Lord, if thou wilt help me, I will try.' "

Noticing a group of women on a doorstep, she forced herself to stop and speak to them; and to her amazement discovered that all fear had left her, and that the women responded eagerly. Encouraged, she approached another group. Again, the results were positive.

As she proceeded down the street, Catherine experienced an intense joy she had never known before. "With a heart full of gratitude and eyes full of tears, I was thinking about where I should go next when I observed a woman standing on an adjoining doorstep with a jug in her hand."

The woman was taking the jug of whiskey to her alcoholic husband. Persuading the fearful woman to take her to her husband, Catherine recalls:

"I read to him the parable of the Prodigal Son while the tears ran down his face like rain. I then prayed with him as the Spirit gave me utterance, and left, promising to call the next day with a temperance-pledge book, which he agreed to sign."

He signed. And within a few weeks so did ten other drunkards:

"In the long run . . . the work told on my health. . . . But my whole soul was in it, and I became deeply attached to the drunkards whom I had been the means of rescuing."[16]

O Beloved, have you made yourself totally available to the Spirit of God in order to do the works of God?

29 When my heart is troubled, when I have been criticized or misunderstood, when the pressures of ministry get heavy and I want to quit, at least for a while, there is one thing that always helps. I stop and remember that I am called to a life of obedience, and I remember that it is my obedience which says to my Father and my Lord, "I love You."

"Love never fails" (1 Corinthians 13:8). It "bears all things, believes all things, hopes all things, endures all things" (1 Corinthians 13:7). And as I tell God of my love and deep gratitude to Him for choosing me to be His child, I reaffirm the fact of my commitment to obedience to His call.

And with that—and all the other things I have shared with you—my troubled heart is quieted, and I am at rest again. Thus, Beloved, we come to our sixth and final step to take in dealing with a troubled heart: *Love Him and obey Him.*

We cannot have love without obedience for they are inextricably linked. The word *love* is used ten times in John 14, and it is the cure for a troubled heart. Remember John 14:1 says, "Let not your heart be troubled," and the same phrase is repeated in verse 27.

The affirmation of love brings a peace to the heart like nothing else. This is why it is good for you to worship your God. Listen to music which stirs your soul and fans the embers of love until it sparks a fire of love in your heart that burns passionately for God and His kingdom.

The church needs a good taste of that heroic type of love that will lay down its life at the stake if necessary. I fear our Christianity has become weakened by the peace and luxury we enjoy. It may be that our Christianity has cost us so little that we do not value it as we should. Like the church at Ephesus, we may have left our first love.

In the middle of telling His disciples that they can ask what they want in His name and telling them of the coming of the Spirit, Jesus makes this statement: "If you love Me, you will keep My commandments" (John 14:15). I think He wants us to understand that true love of God produces obedience, and that it is senseless to ask things from God if we do not love Him and have no intention of obeying Him.

Also I think He wants us to see, as He confirms in John 14:21-24, that there is no indwelling of the Spirit or of the Godhead in those who do not want to love and obey God. Think about John 14:19-23, and then we will talk about it more tomorrow.

30 Jesus does not disclose Himself to those who have no intention or desire to love Him or His Father. The indwelling of the blessed Holy Spirit, the abiding of the Father and the Son within, is reserved for those who will accept Jesus Christ as the Son of God, God incarnate, God's Lamb who takes away the sin of the world (John 1:29). To recognize Jesus as God means that we are willing to turn from our sin of walking our own way in order that we might be married to Christ and bring forth fruit unto righteousness as Romans 7 teaches.

Our desire to turn from sin and to keep His commandments will be evidence of our desire to love God. Of course, this is a witness to the grace of God in our hearts. It is our desire to love and obey Him, which causes us to know that He is in us. Jesus said, " 'In that day you shall know that I am in My Father, and you in Me, and I in you. He who has My commandments and keeps them, he it is who loves Me; and he who loves Me shall be loved by My Father, and I will love him, and will disclose Myself to him.' Judas (not Iscariot) said to Him, 'Lord, what then has happened that You are going to disclose Yourself to us, and not to the world?' Jesus answered and said to him, 'If anyone loves Me, he will keep My word; and My Father will love him, and We will come to him, and make Our abode with him. He who does not love Me does not keep My words' " (John 14:20-24).

Years ago I had the opportunity of meeting Haralan Popov in person. He had come to a local school to speak, and one of the boys invited me to hear him and then meet him for coffee afterward. I was so excited, for I had read *Tortured for His Faith,* his incredible story of suffering for the gospel of Jesus Christ as a prisoner of the Communists for 13 years.

There was one thing I wanted to know. I asked him, "What held you through all those years of torture?" His countenance was puzzled as he replied in broken English, "I am sorry. I don't understand. What do you mean, 'What held me?' "

"I mean, what kept you faithful to God? Was it your knowledge of God's Word? Your . . ."

His pale, white, thin face lit up. "Oh, no," he interrupted. With a voice filled with incredible tenderness, he said, "When you love Someone, you will do anything for Him."

Love Him and obey Him, Beloved, and it will bolster your troubled heart. Hear His words: "Peace I leave with you; My peace I give to you; not as the world gives, do I give to you. Let not your heart be troubled, nor let it be fearful" (John 14:27).

July

"Abiding . . . That You Might Bear Fruit"

1 Harvest was over. It was November and the crisp morning air revived the vine and its branches. Peace settled like the dew. Some leaves released their hold and drifted gently to the ground. They had grown large in order to shelter the cluster of grapes nestled under their umbrella of protection. They had provided shade during the day and collected dew each morning. But now the harvest was in and their work was done.

All was quiet in the vineyard, in a time of restful waiting, an interlude before winter and pruning.

The vinedresser walked through the garden, stopping to fondle the branches and look at the vines. They each had a personality. When it came time for pruning, the vinedresser would have to know exactly what each vine needed to produce a yet greater harvest.

Some of the branches on the vines had been tagged by the vinedresser. These had not borne fruit, and he had to make a decision. Would they ever bear fruit? If not, then they would have to be cut off and burned. And if that happened, then other branches would have to be trained to take their place.

Although the vine and its branches would look naked and unlovely after being pruned, their greatest growth would take place during the barren winter. In winter's cold, the sap would go down into the roots of the vine.

There the vine would become energized, strengthening itself for fruit-bearing.

During the winter there was no need to contend with growth and producing a harvest or even being beautiful. The beauty would come later, springing forth from the wound left by the vinedresser's pruning shears. More beautiful, green leaves to cover the grapes which would take up their shelter beneath them would spring forth.

It is my prayer that our time together this month will bring a beautiful interlude of peace and quietness into your life. May God, your Vinedresser, use this study to prune and dress your life for an even greater harvest.

May I suggest that you read John 15 before tomorrow.

2 The glimmer of the pruning shears brought no fear to the branches abiding in the vine. Pruning was part of being a branch. The blades of the shears were sharp and clean. The vinedresser's hand was deft and he would not leave a ragged wound that would take a long time to heal. His cut would be made quickly. The branches knew this was a season in their life to which they must yield, if they were going to fulfill their purpose.

Carefully the vinedresser inspected the branches, looking for those he had tagged because they had not yet brought forth fruit. The dead wood would have to be removed first, but the decision to remove dead branches was not a hasty one. The vinedresser had worked with the branches, giving them every opportunity to bear fruit, but to no avail. Now, if he didn't remove them, they would bring disease, fungi, or viruses. Or, they might become nesting places for the birds, attracting bugs or insects potentially damaging to the vine.

The pruning of the dead branches would be laborious to the vinedresser and traumatic to the vine. Often there would be a struggle in trying to cut them loose. The rest that the vine would experience after the dead wood was gathered and removed from the vineyard would bring a welcome respite to the other branches. Some of the branches had heard tales of careless vinedressers who did not watch their vineyards carefully and who were lazy about cutting off the dead wood. Oh, the branches showed no apparent sign of being any the worse for it until it came time for the harvest. Then the rot would be detected, but by then it was often too late. A dead branch would eventually affect the root system of the vine, bringing its death. They had even heard of some instances when the vine was so bad that the soil had to be treated before other vines could be planted to replace it. The soil had become contaminated. How important it was to have a wise and careful vinedresser.

Jesus said, "I am the true vine, and My Father is the vinedresser. Every branch in Me that does not bear fruit, He takes away. . . . If anyone does not abide in Me, he is thrown away as a branch, and dries up; and they gather them, and cast them into the fire, and they are burned" (John 15:1,2,6).

3 The branches gave a sigh of relief after the dead wood was removed. They knew that if all the dead wood was not taken away then they might lose their fruit-bearing sprouts. Their little sprouts had the habit of getting tangled up with the dead wood, putting them in danger of being removed in the process of cleansing the vine.

Once the dead wood was removed, the vines and their branches would watch in amazement as the fires burned and burned. The dead wood didn't even burn well. "Son of man, how is the wood of the vine better than any wood of a branch which is among the trees of the forest? Can wood be taken from it to make anything, or can men take a peg from it on which to hang any vessel? If it has been put into the fire for fuel, and the fire has consumed both of its ends, and its middle part has been charred, is it then useful for anything? Behold, while it is intact, it is not made into anything. How much less, when the fire has consumed it and it is charred, can it still be made into anything!" (Ezekiel 15:2-5).

The branches knew they were made by God for one thing alone: to be fruit-bearers. And if they were going to bring forth a rich harvest of fruit, pruning was imperative. Painful, yes, but necessary for fruit.

Having gotten rid of the branches which would not bear fruit, the vinedresser then turned his attention to the fruit-bearing branches. They needed to bear more fruit, and for that, it was necessary to prune them. If he did not prune the branches in the spring, there would be a yellow cast to their leaves instead of a rich green, and the leaves would be smaller. The fruit would have no secure place to nestle out of the heat of the burning sun. And without the moisture which the green leaves held, the grapes would be hard and dry.

If the vinedresser did not prune the branches, they would run wild, crawling all over the ground or over the wires strung for their benefit. Prone to wander, they would expend their sap in all their activity. This would never do, and the branches knew it.

If they were going to fulfill the purpose for which they were created, all their energies had to go into producing fruit, for that was their calling. Therefore, they had to be pruned back close to the vine. It was that closeness of intimacy which would bring forth a great harvest. Pruning would bring intimacy; intimacy would bring fruit.

4 The branch could feel the coolness of the shears. Winter made them cold, but this was the time to prune. The branch would cling to the vine, and the vine would provide the branch with its natural protection, taking care of the vinedresser's incision.

The shears moved quickly. In a moment the excess growth was gone and the cut was clean. The branch had been cut close to the vine, so that it would bear much more fruit.

Silent, crystal-clear tears fell from the branch, dripping on the ground. The vinedresser caught the sap on the tip of his finger and brought it to his mouth. It had a slightly bitter taste to it. But he knew that although weeping would endure for the night, joy would come in the morning.

The next day, as the vinedresser walked through his vineyard, he stopped to look at the wound he had inflicted in love. Ah, it was healing nicely. A film had formed over the cut. In the days to come, the film would become dark and unattractive in color, and would repel the birds, bugs, bees, gnats, or flies which might hurt its wound. Eventually the slimy substance would dry and become hard. Finally, just above the cut, a little bud would emerge and become the continuance of the vine. Pruning was done with only one intent—a greater harvest. To understand more fully spiritual pruning, read John 15:2,4,5,8,9 and Hebrews 12:6,7,10 and 11

O beloved branch, I know not the pruning you are enduring nor the tears you have shed; but I do know the heart of your sovereign Vinedresser. Your pruning is for greater fruitfulness. Abide.

5 Have there been times when you felt so very ordinary that there seemed nothing special about you? Or maybe I should ask if there have been times when you felt very special. That your life had value or significance beyond your day-to-day routine of getting up, doing your job, and then spending the evening relaxing until it was time to go to bed, and in the morning beginning the same routine again.

O Beloved, if you are a believer, there is something very special about you. Your life has significance, for you have been chosen by God, the sovereign Ruler of all creation. Can you imagine that? That God would not only choose you but appoint you—YOU!—to go and bear fruit. And not only appoint you to go and to bear fruit, but guarantee that your fruit will remain. In other words, your life has an eternal impact. Can you imagine affecting people's lives for eternity? That is significance!

But it does not end there, my friend. Jesus also promises that you don't have to do whatever you are called to by yourself. Whatever you need for a life of significance and fruitfulness will be supplied to you through your Lord Jesus Christ. It is as simple as abiding—being at home in God and allowing Him to be at home in you.

A fruitful life is the inevitable result of dwelling in Him and thus allowing His life to flow through you. And everything you need is yours for the asking. "You did not choose Me, but I chose you, and appointed you, that you should go and bear fruit, and that your fruit should remain, that whatever you ask of the Father in My name, He may give to you" (John 15:16).

How do you react to that verse? Think about it, Beloved. Write your answer in your notebook.

If you want a life with eternal significance, this month's devotional was written for you. As we study John 15, I pray that you will learn truths that will impact your life. If you learn what God has to say, and then live in the light of it, your life can have greater significance.

6 Before we can apply John 15 to our lives, we must know exactly what our Lord is teaching His disciples in this chapter. Why did Jesus choose to use the metaphor of the vine and the branches?

Jesus knew that His hour had come. He, our grain of wheat, was going to fall into the ground and die so that we might become part of the harvest of His life: children of the Father (John 12:24).

Through His death a new covenant would be inaugurated—a covenant of grace. And with this covenant would come new life—Christ in you and you in Christ. No longer would the Holy Spirit come and go, resting at times on individuals. With the death, resurrection, and ascension of the Lord Jesus Christ, the Holy Spirit would be sent to indwell all believers, to seal them until the day of the redemption of their bodies (Ephesians 1:13,14). Now the Law engraved upon tablets of stone would be engraved upon hearts of flesh, hearts tender toward God. This new intimacy of the indwelling Christ, of becoming the temple of the Holy Spirit, would be the legacy of every single child of God, not just the 11 to whom our Lord was speaking.

Jesus was preparing them, even as He is preparing you now, to stand fast in faith, even though they seemed to be part of the losing team. Jesus wanted to assure them that no matter what came their way, they would continue to abide in Him. If they didn't, then their lives would not have eternal significance. Apart from His life flowing through them, there would be no life, no fruit. He was their "I AM," Jehovah in the flesh who would provide everything they needed. Theirs was simply to believe and abide.

In John 6:35 we hear Him tell His followers: "I am the bread of life; he who comes to Me shall not hunger, and he who believes in Me shall never thirst." He takes care of our hunger and thirst for life.

In John 8:12 darkness shudders as He says, "I am the light of the world; he who follows Me shall not walk in the darkness, but shall have the light of life." Darkness shudders and death's graves open on the dawn of His light which brings life.

In John 10:9 we see so clearly the way into the Father's house as Jesus says, "I am the door; if anyone enters through Me, he shall be saved, and shall go in and out, and find pasture."

As we enter the sheepfold, we believe His words: "I am the way, and the truth, and the life" (John 14:6), and choose to abide in the One who says, "I am the vine, you are the branches" (John 15:5).

7

Jesus did not begin His teaching on abiding until they left the Upper Room. Judas had separated himself from them, going out into the night to betray the One he had called "Lord." As Jesus and His disciples trudged through Jerusalem to make their way down into the Kidron Valley and across to the Garden of Gethsemane, they would pass the Temple area. It may have been as they caught the moon's glimmer on the vine overlaid with gold, gracing the Temple, that Jesus began His allegory.

The vine was a national symbol of Israel. Centuries earlier, Isaiah the prophet had written: "For the vineyard of the LORD of hosts is the house of Israel, and the men of Judah His delightful plant" (5:7). Like Judas, many of Israel had defected. God had done everything for them: "What more was there to do for My vineyard that I have not done in it? Why, when I expected it to produce good grapes did it produce worthless ones?" (Isaiah 5:4).

Was it the remembrance of Israel's failure that prompted Jesus' allegory or was it Judas' failure? What had caused Judas' defection? That Jesus was not going to set up the kingdom? That Judas wasn't getting what he wanted from the relationship? Was it Judas who prompted Jesus' remarks? In all probability, yes, and possibly also the sight of the vine as Israel's symbol.

Neither Israel nor Judas brought forth the fruit God expected, because they would not abide in their God. They sought to walk independently rather than continuing in the life He had for them. God had tried to tell Israel that abiding was necessary.

Hosea wrote: "O Ephraim, what more have I to do with idols? It is I who answer and look after you. I am like a luxuriant cypress; from Me comes your fruit" (14:8). Branches could not bear fruit unless they were attached to the Source of life.

As they walked across the Kidron Valley, Jesus wanted the 11 to know the importance of abiding. Branches are in the vine for the sole purpose of bearing fruit, but they cannot do it independently. He was the true Vine; they were the branches. It was essential that they abide in Him.

The effectiveness and significance of their lives would be found only in their relationship to the Vine. And, Beloved, what was true for Israel, what was true for the disciples, is true for you. Abide.

8 What is the Christian life all about? It is as simple as abiding. O Beloved, if we could ever capture this truth and hold it in our thoughts so that it becomes the governing principle of our lives, what a rich life of peace we would have! God never intended our walk to be a struggle. You do not see branches trying to hold onto the vine or the tree. No, they simply abide. As the life of the vine or the root and the trunk flows through the branches, it bears its fruit in due season. Life is in the midst of the branch, and the evidence is manifested. And so, Beloved believer, Christ is in the midst of you: "Christ in you, the hope of glory" (Colossians 1:27). Therefore, His life will be manifested. Fruit will come in its due season.

Certain aspects of this allegory are difficult for some people to understand. Before you ever apply any Scripture to your life, it is important to make sure you know what God is saying and what He means.

There is a process to follow which will help you greatly in your understanding of the Word of God and then in its proper application. The process begins with *observation,* finding out what the text is saying. Then comes *interpretation,* discovering what it means. Then having found out what God says and what He means, you make *application* of the truth to your life.

I would like to give you a simple assignment for today and tomorrow which will help you understand how to interpret this passage.

First read John 13–15:8. Every time you come to Judas, write down everything you observe from the text about him in your notebook. Also, note everything you learn about the other 11 disciples, or about what is true of genuine followers of our Lord. Make notes.

Make two columns on a page of your notebook. Then list under the appropriate column what happens to branches that bear fruit and what happens to branches that do not.

9 Continue today in the exercise you began yesterday. Remember, it is imperative that you see truth for yourself, and the work you are doing will result in that seeing. We'll continue tomorrow with our time together.

10 Is fruit the natural, visible, inevitable expression of the abiding Christ? And if people claim to know Christ but do not bear fruit, are they Christians? As people study John 15, some are troubled by John 15:2: "Every branch in Me that does not bear fruit, He takes away" and by John 15:6: "If anyone does not abide in Me, he is thrown away as a branch, and dries up; and they gather them, and cast them into the fire, and they are burned."

Those who believe you can lose your salvation use John 15:6 to support their view, coupling it with Hebrews 6 and 10. Those who believe in the eternal security of a believer are greatly puzzled by this verse. They know other Scriptures which clearly teach that when God begins the good work of salvation in a person, He completes it (Philippians 1:6). They know Paul's words, that those whom God "foreknew, He also predestined to become conformed to the image of His Son. . . . And whom He predestined, these He also called; and whom He called, these He also justified; and whom He justified, these He also glorified" (Romans 8:29,30). In John 6:39 Jesus said, "And this is the will of Him who sent Me, that of all that He has given Me I lose nothing, but raise it up on the last day."

When you read John 6, you will find Jesus repeating this truth. A thoughtful and careful reader of the New Testament will read over and over again of the sovereignty of God in bringing people into the kingdom of God. Yes, our responsibility is stressed as we are admonished to believe on the Lord Jesus Christ; and yet we cannot ignore the mysterious tension of the responsibility of man against the sovereign choosing by God for salvation. In the midst of this seeming doctrinal tension, we find ourselves caught in the confusion of interpreting verses like John 15:6.

I have wrestled with these things for several years. It was the study of the book of Hebrews, along with a clear understanding of the historical and textual context of John 15, that God used to help me come to a point of understanding about what Jesus was saying to His disciples.

I believe there are two categories of people—the saved and the lost. Yet among the lost, I believe there are basically two other categories: those who have no interest in spiritual things at all and would not darken the door of a church and those who participate to some degree in spiritual activities. Yet those in this second category are not really born again; they call Him "Lord," but He isn't in their lives (Matthew 7:20-23). Think on it.

11 Who are the branches in John 15:2 and 6 which are cut off, gathered, and cast into the fire? There are three different views. Let me give you these and then share with you what I believe and why. Then, whether we agree or disagree, we can go on to look at some wonderful and precious truths dealing with the abiding life.

The first view is that the branches which do not bear fruit are Christians who have lost their salvation. Somewhere in their walk with the Lord, they turned away, went back into sin, and therefore lost their salvation. The reason those who hold this view feel that these people were once Christians relates to the use of the phrase "in Me."

The second view is that the branches which are cut off and burned are Christians who have lost their effectiveness for the Lord but are still saved. J. Oswald Sanders, a very godly man, says: "In this paragraph, our Lord did not have salvation in view. His theme was fruitfulness. These verses do not teach that the unfruitful Christian will forfeit his salvation, but that he will lose his reward if his is a wasted life. Such branches are 'cast . . . into the fire, and . . . burned' (15:6). Note that [it] is not God but men who gather the unfruitful branches and burn them. The unfruitful Christian loses his influence for God and his testimony to men. Hence the necessity of abiding in Christ."[1]

Those who hold this view believe that since the wood of the vine is intended for fruit-bearing, then the one who did not bear fruit would continue to be a Christian but have a useless life. This, Beloved, is the view I once held, because of the phrase "men . . . burn," which we will discuss later, and "in Me," which was used in connection with the pruned branches.

Personally, I do not believe that a person who once genuinely becomes a child of God can ever be cut off from God. Because I see in the Word not only the responsibility of man to believe but the sovereignty of God in drawing men to saving faith in Him, I do not believe that we can lose our salvation once God has given it in grace. Yet, I do not see that the doctrine of eternal security gives us license to sin. When people are truly saved by the sovereign grace of God, because of their identification with Jesus Christ in His death, burial, and resurrection, they are freed from slavery to sin (Romans 6). By the Spirit, they have the power to practice righteousness as a habit of life.

This is not to say that a believer will not commit singular acts of sin, but sin will not be the habit of his life because God's "seed abides in him; and he cannot sin [habitually], because he is born of God" (1 John 3:9).

12 The third view regarding the pruned branches is that these people were never saved and yet had a close association with the gospel and Jesus Christ. In other words, they had every opportunity to abide in Him, but chose not to. They, like Judas, are apostates. Through a close association with Jesus and the things which pertain to the kingdom of God, they witnessed the working of the Holy Spirit but did not choose to abide in Him. The definition of *abide* is "to remain, to stay, to continue, to be at home in, to dwell."

After I studied the book of Hebrews inductively, I saw that it was possible for some to have a very close association with Jesus Christ and spiritual things, even to the point that they appeared to be Christians but really weren't. Their exposure as unbelievers usually came under personal duress. They were revealed as unbelievers because they did not continue in the faith.

In the book of Hebrews, we see so clearly that continuance in the faith is the evidence of our salvation. Throughout the New Testament epistles, we find these words repeatedly: "Do not be deceived," and they always connect with true salvation bearing the fruit of righteousness.

Now let me share several verses in Hebrews which show that continuance in the faith is the evidence of our salvation. Note that I said "evidence," not "the means of." Salvation is always pure grace without any human cause or merit; and yet when the grace of God is bestowed upon us for salvation, it produces a changed life. The book of Hebrews was written to a group of Christians under great duress because of their association with Jesus Christ. Throughout the book we will find the author exhorting them to hold fast, to not drift away, to press on, to draw near, to be diligent to enter His rest, to not throw away their confidence. Summarized, all those exhortations could be put in the command of our Lord in John 15:4: "Abide in Me."

In Hebrews 3:6 we read: "But Christ was faithful as a Son over His house whose house we are, if we hold fast our confidence and the boast of our hope firm until the end." And again, so we won't miss the warning, "We have become partakers of Christ, if we hold fast the beginning of our assurance firm until the end" (Hebrews 3:14). It is possible to think you belong to Christ and be deceived. What proves your faith? Fruit!

13 Abiding is the evidence of your salvation, and fruit is the evidence of abiding. Therefore, if a branch does not eventually bear fruit, it is removed from the vine, gathered up, and burned. Although it seemed to belong to the vine, it did not. It was a "Judas branch" because it did not bear fruit. Fruit is not something the branch makes happen; it is something it cannot help happening, if it is in proper relationship to the vine. The principle that our Lord wants us to see is the same one given in Hebrews 6:4-6: "For in the case of those who have once been enlightened and have tasted of the heavenly gift and have been made partakers of the Holy Spirit, and have tasted the good word of God and the powers of the age to come, and then have fallen away, it is impossible to renew them again to repentance, since they again crucify to themselves the Son of God, and put Him to open shame."

The association of these people with Jesus and the Holy Spirit did not produce the true fruit of salvation. There was no continuance in the faith and they fell away.

I believe that this is what Hebrews 6 is saying. This interpretation fits well into the context of Hebrews, and does not violate any other teaching in the Word of God. It parallels 1 John 2:19,27 so well: "They went out from us, but they were not really of us; for if they had been of us, they would have remained with us; but they went out, in order that it might be shown that they all are not of us. . . . And as for you, the anointing which you received from Him abides in you . . . but as His anointing teaches you about all things, and is true and is not a lie, and just as it has taught you, you abide in Him."

Fruit-bearing is the evidence of the abiding life which is the evidence of salvation. Let me take you back to Hebrews 6 where the author gives an illustration about those who have all the opportunities and exposure to benefits of salvation and yet fall away. "For ground that drinks the rain which often falls upon it and brings forth vegetation useful to those for whose sake it is also tilled, receives a blessing from God; but if it yields thorns and thistles, it is worthless and close to being cursed, and it ends up being burned (Hebrews 6:7,8).

Both plots of ground had the same exposure, the same benefits, but they responded differently. Only one brought forth fruit. The other, like the branches which did not bear fruit, was burned. Think on these things, Beloved.

14 We cannot always tell who belongs to Christ and who does not, who is a fruit-bearing branch or who is not. Therefore, it is not our responsibility to cut them off. According to 1 Corinthians 5, if they are not living in righteousness and they claim to belong to Jesus Christ, then they are to be disciplined like a brother but not cut off. That is the Lord's responsibility and not ours. "The firm foundation of God stands, having this seal, 'The Lord knows those who are His' " (2 Timothy 2:19).

In John 15 you noted that the Father is the Vinedresser. He is the One who takes away the branches which do not bear fruit. The branches, the pruning, the cleansing are all the Vinedresser's responsibility. When God prunes and when He takes away the nonbearing branches, then ". . . they gather them, and cast them into the fire. . ." (John 15:6).

Let me take you to Matthew 13. In this chapter of parables, one is given by our Lord on the wheat and the tares: "The one who sows the good seed is the Son of Man, and the field is the world; and as for the good seed, these are the sons of the kingdom; and the tares are the sons of the evil one; and the enemy who sowed them is the devil, and the harvest is the end of the age; and the reapers are angels. Therefore just as the tares are gathered up and burned with fire, so shall it be at the end of the age. The Son of Man will send forth His angels, and they will gather out of His kingdom all stumbling blocks, and those who commit lawlessness, and will cast them into the furnace of fire; in that place there shall be weeping and gnashing of teeth" (13:37-42).

Wheat and tares look alike and are hard to distinguish in the growing season. God tells us that He will separate the wheat from the tares. We are not to, "lest while you are gathering up the tares, you may root up the wheat with them" (Matthew 13:29).

It is interesting that the disciples could not tell who was going to betray our Lord (John 13:21-30). They never recognized Judas as a fruitless branch until the Lord pointed him out as such. When Jesus was washing the disciples' feet, He said, " 'You are clean, but not all of you.' For He knew the one who was betraying Him; for this reason He said, 'Not all of you are clean' " (John 13:10,11). Earlier Jesus had said of Judas: ". . . Did I Myself not choose you, the twelve, and yet one of you is a devil?" (John 6:70). Judas' relationship with the Lord never brought about a new heart. And God looks on the heart.

What, Beloved, does God see in your heart? What does your life produce?

15 Fruit is not something you make happen. It is something you cannot prevent, as long as you are abiding in the vine. The absence of fruit in a person's life is evidence that no life-producing sap is flowing through the branch.

In all probability, Beloved, you are wondering what the fruit of abiding is. Therefore, today I want us to look at some Scriptures that deal with fruit. In James we see that the fruit of faith is works, for he writes: "Even so faith, if it has no works, is dead, being by itself. . . . Faith without works is useless. . . . For just as the body without the spirit is dead, so also faith without works is dead" (2:17,20,26).

In his epistle to the Ephesians, Paul tells us that we are saved by grace through faith, and then goes on to say that "we are His workmanship, created in Christ Jesus for good works, which God prepared beforehand, that we should walk in them" (2:10).

The evidence of Christ within is good works which bear fruit from His life flowing through us. Jesus says, "Apart from Me you can do nothing" (John 15:5). John the Baptist admonished those who followed him, saying, "Therefore bring forth fruits in keeping with repentance, and do not begin to say to yourselves, 'We have Abraham for our father,' for I say to you that God is able from these stones to raise up children to Abraham. And also the axe is already laid at the root of the trees; every tree therefore that does not bear good fruit is cut down and thrown into the fire" (Luke 3:8,9).

Over and over again you see that where the harvest is bad, there is burning: "You will know them by their fruits. Grapes are not gathered from thorn bushes, nor figs from thistles, are they? Even so, every good tree bears good fruit; but the bad tree bears bad fruit. A good tree cannot produce bad fruit, nor can a bad tree produce good fruit. Every tree that does not bear good fruit is cut down and thrown into the fire. So then, you will know them by their fruits" (Matthew 7:16-20).

Isn't this what Jesus was saying to the 11, as they walked toward Gethsemane? Branches that did not bear fruit would be burned. This was the fate of Judas who had every opportunity but did not abide in the true Vine. He was cut off from the Source of eternal life. Therefore, all that awaited him was eternal judgment where the worm dies not and the fire is not quenched.

But you, dear believer, have been "joined to another, to Him who was raised from the dead, that [you] might bear fruit for God" (Romans 7:4). O Beloved, what is the fruit of your life? Does it testify that God is within? Abide.

16 From all that we have seen, it is obvious that fruitfulness is rooted in your personal relationship with the Lord Jesus Christ. The validity of that relationship is seen in your lifestyle, in your day-by-day character. And that, Beloved, is what makes your life so significant. It is not so much what you do as who you are.

Some people feel that they are significant only if they are seen, known, and admired, but this is not true. Our greatness in the kingdom of God is not measured by what we do but by who we are, and by who we are like. And we are to be like Christ. To be like Jesus, to grow more and more into His image, is to impact this world for the gospel.

God, the Vinedresser, is responsible for the breadth of your life. Depth in your life will come from abiding in Him, knowing that He chose you and ordained you that you should go and bear fruit and that your fruit would remain (John 15:16). A life lived in the Spirit and by the Spirit will produce Christlikeness that will impact people.

You know, my friend, we live in sad and discouraging days. Iniquity abounds and the laws of our land shelter it. In countless incidents, the evil are protected and the innocent are left prey to wicked deeds. Evil people bring forth a harvest of fruit unto death, as we see described in Galatians 5:19-21. Compare what you read here with the lurid headlines on those newspapers that greet you in the checkout lanes of grocery stores: "Now the deeds of the flesh are evident, which are: immorality, impurity, sensuality, idolatry, sorcery [the Greek word is *pharmakeia,* which means the use of drugs for magical purposes], enmities, strife, jealousy, outbursts of anger, disputes, dissensions, factions, envying, drunkenness, carousing, and things like these, of which I forewarn you just as I have forewarned you that those who practice such things shall not inherit the kingdom of God."

Our society is being dominated by those who suppress the truth of God in their unrighteousness. And what are we to do in such a society? How can our lives impact or bring a halt to such evil? In only one way, my Beloved, and that is by abiding in the Vine in such intimacy that our lives will be in drastic contrast. Don't you think that one single person filled with "the fruit of the Spirit . . . love, joy, peace, patience, kindness, goodness, faithfulness, gentleness, self-control" (Galatians 5:22,23) is going to have a significant impact? Abide.

17 Are there times when you don't feel very holy? When you know that deep inside you don't measure up to what you profess to believe? When you feel that your life has very little spiritual significance? It's as if you have a lot

of activity but very little impact. When this happens to me, I know that I need to submit to the pruning shears of my Vinedresser.

Have you ever wondered how the pruning is done? Our heavenly Vinedresser has only one instrument. "Every branch that bears fruit, He prunes it, that it may bear more fruit. You are already clean because of the word which I have spoken to you" (John 15:2,3).

The pruning shears of our heavenly Vinedresser is the Word of God. That is why it is absolutely essential that the Christian stay in the Word of God. Those times when I haven't felt holy (set apart unto God), or when I haven't felt that intimacy that I know I should sense in my relationship with God, have happened when I became too busy in my service for my Lord or too slack in maintaining that quality relationship which is so vital. In my busyness I ceased to be in His presence as much as I needed to be.

Being rushed or hurried with God will greatly affect your intimacy level. You see it in marriages, and you can see it in your relationship to your heavenly Bridegroom. Relationships take time, and none is more important than your abiding relationship with the Father, Son, and Holy Spirit.

Some Christians believe that God has to do drastic things to make us effective for the kingdom of God. Although I don't adopt this philosophy, I do believe He uses trials to bring us to the place of pruning: the Word. Where do you run, what do you need in a difficult situation? The Word—its wisdom, its promises, its direction. If you and I will consistently abide in the Word of God in a quality way and in a quality relationship with Jesus Christ, then there will be that consistent, timely, sensitive cleansing by the Spirit of God through the washing of the water of the Word (Ephesians 5:25,26).

O Beloved, are you being made clean through the washing of the water of God's Word? It is His pruning instrument. Yield to it! It will mean more fruit—much fruit.

18 As we are seeking the face of God through an earnest quest to know His Word, we are going to know the will of God for our lives. Our very exposure to the Word of God with a heart that is crying out: "Search me, O God, and know my heart; try me and know my anxious thoughts; and see if there be any hurtful way in me, and lead me in the everlasting way" (Psalm 139:23,24), will bring pruning.

"For the word of God is living and active and sharper than any two-edged sword, and piercing as far as the division of soul and spirit, of both joints and marrow, and able to judge the thoughts and intentions of the heart. And there is no creature hidden from His sight, but all things are open and laid bare to the eyes of Him with whom we have to do" (Hebrews 4:12,13).

When it comes time for the Vinedresser to prune the branches, He needs a sharp instrument, one that will not leave a ragged cut. The Word of God is living, active, and sharper than any two-edged sword. If we will allow it to do its pruning work in our lives, the purging will be quick and effective. The incision will heal rapidly and produce new growth.

To allow the Word of God to do its cleansing work, we must be quick to hear and obey, to actively believe God so that what His Word says we are to do, we will do. And when God's Word tells us to react in a certain way, then we will. This, Beloved, is to be pruned for greater fruitfulness.

The reason so many people have so little fruit instead of the more and much fruit mentioned in John 15 is that they do not expose themselves to the heavenly Vinedresser's shears. And when we stay far from His Word instead of yielding to the inevitable need of pruning, God may use or allow other means for pruning that often leave ragged cuts—because we would not allow God's Word to do His cleansing work His way.

Now, please don't think that consistent exposure to the Word will exempt you from trials or sufferings, for they are sometimes the means of disciplining or "chastening" us when we are not walking as we ought to walk. However, trials and suffering are also merely arenas for the presentation of the gospel or the all-sufficiency of our Christ. In these arenas, death is allowed to work in us so that life can work in others (2 Corinthians 4:7-12). The latter, of course, brings the fruit of souls into the kingdom of God as they behold the fruit of Christlikeness in us. O Beloved, will you not let God's Word prune you for greater fruitfulness?

19 Not only does abiding bring fruit, it also brings answered prayer. Have you ever wondered why some people always seem to get their prayers answered? Have you longed to ask them what their secret is? You were probably embarrassed to ask, for it might make you seem less spiritual than they. Well, you don't need to ask them if you know the Word of God. The secret to answered prayer is intimacy with the Vine through abiding.

In John 15:7,8, we see a connection between abiding, prayer, and fruit. Jesus is very clear: "If you abide in Me, and My words abide in you, ask whatever you wish, and it shall be done for you. By this is My Father glorified, that you bear much fruit, and so prove to be My disciples."

This is also seen in John 15:16: "You did not choose Me, but I chose you, and appointed you, that you should go and bear fruit, and that your fruit should remain, that whatever you ask of the Father in My name, He may give to you."

As you and I deepen our intimacy with our Father by abiding in the Word and allowing it to abide in us, we are going to find ourselves asking God to do, to give, and to move in accordance with what we have seen in His Word. And if we ask according to His Word, then God is going to answer our prayers. And when this happens, then God will be glorified. As we abide in Christ, we abide in His Word, and we learn that the will of God is "good and acceptable and perfect" (Romans 12:2). Knowing this about the will of God, we do not want anything outside His will. Therefore, when we approach His throne of grace in prayer, we will ask according to His Word. Thus, we will have the petitions we have asked of Him.

In John 15:7, the Greek word for *words* is *rhēma,* not *logos. Logos* is used for the person of Jesus Christ in John 1:1 as "the Word." However, *logos* can also be used for a concept or idea, a saying or statement, the word of the Lord, or the Bible as the Word of God; while *rhēma* denotes that which is uttered in speech or writing. *Vine's Complete Expository Dictionary of Old and New Testament Words* states: "The significance of *rhēma* (as distinct from *logos)* is exemplified in the injunction to take "the sword of the Spirit, which is the word of God," Eph. 6:17; here the reference is not to the whole Bible as such, but to the individual scripture which the Spirit brings to our remembrance for use in time of need, a prerequisite being the regular storing of the mind with Scripture."[2]

The secret to answered prayer, Beloved, is His *rhēma* abiding in you.

20 If being able to ask God for things and having Him answer your prayers doesn't show you how special you are to God, I don't know what will. Do you realize the high privilege you have as a child of God? Recourse to the Father in prayer! That is what abiding brings, for when His words abide in you, you are made clean. Sin is pruned from your life. Not only sins of commission, but also sins of omission where you fail to believe God and act in the obedience of faith.

When your life is clean, then you know you have an audience in prayer with your Holy Father. Sin does not alter that relationship, but it does hinder fellowship. Thus, God bids you to stay clean; and if you should sin, then He bids you come immediately, confessing your sins. "If we confess our sins, He is faithful and righteous to forgive us our sins and to cleanse us from all unrighteousness" (1 John 1:9).

Confession is imperative. For "He who conceals his transgressions will not prosper, but he who confesses and forsakes them will find compassion" (Proverbs 28:13). Any time you feel that God is not answering your prayers, you need to examine your heart to make sure that sin has not blocked your communication. "Behold, the LORD's hand is not so short that it cannot save; neither is His ear so dull that it cannot hear. But your iniquities have made a separation between you and your God, and your sins have hidden His face from you, so that He does not hear" (Isaiah 59:1,2).

If there is no known sin unconfessed, then you need to make sure that you know what you are asking is according to His will. "And this is the confidence which we have before Him, that, if we ask anything according to His will, He hears us. And if we know that He hears us in whatever we ask, we know that we have the requests which we have asked from Him" (1 John 5:14,15). To ask in His will parallels asking in His name. Jesus says, "Truly, truly, I say to you, if you shall ask the Father for anything, He will give it to you in My name. . . . Ask, and you will receive, that your joy may be made full" (John 16:23,24).

Answered prayer brings joy, for it affirms our relationship with our Father. It confirms His love and care for us, His own dear children. It strengthens our walk, for we have the confidence that He hears us. It reassures us in the work to which He has called us, for we see His sovereign power.

O Beloved believer, can you see how privileged you are to be chosen by Him? Now abide in Him, and let His words abide in you; then ask that your joy might be full. Your Father loves to have you ask. It demonstrates your faith and total dependence, and it reminds Him of His relationship with His only begotten Son who did nothing apart from the Father.

21

Are there ever times when you doubt the love of God? Maybe you look at yourself and wonder how God could love you. Maybe no one has ever loved you unconditionally, and that makes it difficult to accept or even believe that God would. You are not alone, Beloved. With the destruction of the family, there are many who have been so marred that it is difficult for them to receive and continue in the love of God. And when we cannot believe and receive the love of God for us, it is very difficult to share His love with others.

Here, Beloved, is where faith must come in and override our emotions, so that we can receive the healing power of the Word. How I love Psalm 107:20: "He sent His word and healed them, and delivered them from their destructions." To feel unloved is very destructive. God designed us with a need for love. Thus, Jesus tells His own: "Just as the Father has loved Me, I have also loved you" (John 15:9). Can you imagine, Beloved—you are loved in the same way that the Father loved His only begotten Son! "In this is love, not that we loved God, but that He loved us and sent His Son to be the propitiation for our sins. . . . And we have come to know and have believed the love which God has for us. God is love, and the one who abides in love abides in God, and God abides in him" (1 John 4:10,16).

Have you come to believe the love God has for you? If not, what more can He do than He has already done for you? He chose you out of all mankind to be His own. He crucified His Son for you. He has freely given you all things (Romans 8:32). He has told you: "Neither death, nor life, nor angels, nor principalities, nor things present, nor things to come, nor powers, nor height, nor depth, nor any other created thing, shall be able to separate us from the love of God, which is in Christ Jesus our Lord" (Romans 8:38,39).

Can God lie? Of course not! Can He change so that His Word no longer stands? Of course not! God loves you unconditionally now and always will.

Now abide in His love and love Him back by keeping His commandments. The way you say "I love you" to God is to do whatever He says. Jesus says, "If you keep My commandments, you will abide in My love; just as I have kept My Father's commandments, and abide in His love" (John 15:10). If you want joy, then look carefully at John 15 and believe what is recorded there, for Jesus says, "These things I have spoken to you, that My joy may be in you, and that your joy may be made full" (John 15:11). Don't doubt His love. Rejoice in it!

22 The whole purpose of pruning the branch was to bear fruit for the benefit of others. To live for others is what Christianity is all about. The branches exist for the Vine. The branches are, in essence, co-laborers with the Vine in producing fruit for the nourishment and joy of others. I am sure you are aware of the simple acrostic, JOY: *Jesus first, Others second, You last.*

True joy is never found in a self-centered life. Even a life of service that does not have Jesus as its motivating source will be limited either in the ability of self or in the desirability of the one who is being served. But the life that has Jesus in His proper place of preeminence will minister even unto death, and will serve even the greatest of sinners if this is what the Lord desires.

As our Lord and His 11 disciples walked past the Temple mount and down across the Kidron Valley toward Gethsemane, Jesus knew what awaited Him. His hour had come. And should He say, "Father, save Me from this hour" (John 12:27)? No, it was for this purpose that He had come to this hour.

In the life of Jesus we find our pattern for joy. Jesus lived for the Father's will and good pleasure above all else. Then it was others above Himself. This was the mind of Christ (Philippians 2:5-11). Jesus would abide in the Father, do His will, be obedient unto death, and produce fruit—children for the kingdom of God!

Jesus was trying to help them see that if He spared Himself, if He put His own desires above the will of God, He would continue, but would be alone. That is why He illustrated His death this way: "Unless a grain of wheat falls into the earth and dies, it remains by itself alone; but if it dies, it bears much fruit" (John 12:24). Pruning would bring fruit! And fruit would bring joy. Jesus endured the cross, despising the shame for the joy that was set before Him. It was the joy of pleasing His Father and redeeming mankind (Hebrews 12:2). Jesus would see the travail of His soul and be satisfied (Isaiah 53:11 KJV).

As your Father prunes your life, Beloved, you too will see the travail of your soul—the fruit which shall bring life to others—and be satisfied. Jesus says, "This is My commandment, that you love one another, just as I have loved you" (John 15:12). He loved us enough to lay down His life for us. Do you want joy? Don't listen to the world which tells you joy comes from being number one. That is a lie from the prince of this world. Listen to Jesus.

23 Chosen—not to live for yourself but for God. And if you really live for God, you will live for others. Jesus said He "chose you, and appointed you, that you should go and bear fruit, and that your fruit should remain, that whatever you ask of the Father in [His] name, He may give to you" (John 15:16). You are chosen by the Godhead to go and to bear fruit, but you are not told to do "the best you can." You do not have to produce or provide from your own resources. All the resources of the Vine are yours for the asking. They are there in the name of Jesus. As much as you are to be concerned with the welfare of others, your heavenly Father is far more concerned for the welfare of those whom He has chosen and appointed to go as His ambassadors.

Therefore, Beloved believer, you need to stay in an attitude of prayer, letting your requests be known unto God. And whatever situation you find yourself in, there will be adequate grace to take you through your situation as more than a conqueror.

Helen Roseveare, a doctor chosen and appointed by God to go to Zaire, had this experience. In her book *Living Holiness*, Dr. Roseveare shares numerous incidents that well illustrate and affirm God's provision for the tasks to which He calls us. Over the next few days, I want to share several of her many gripping stories because I believe they will bless you. If you long to be holy, even as He is holy, you will want to read *Living Holiness.* It is a wonderful example of holiness being manifested in day-by-day living.

Today, my friend, let me leave you with words from a hymn by G. Kendrick:

From heaven you came, Helpless Babe,
Entered our world, Your glory veiled;
Not to be served but to serve,
And give Your life that we might live.

Come see His hands and His feet,
The scars that speak of sacrifice,
Hands that flung stars into space
To cruel nails surrendered.

So let us learn how to serve,
And in our lives enthrone Him;
Each other's needs to prefer,
For it is Christ we're serving.[3]

Serve, chosen one, and He will supply.

24 Helen Roseveare tells of an incident in July 1960 when, due to the political unrest, there was a "great evacuation of 'white . . . foreigners,' " leaving her the only European in the village of Nebobongo.

> [That night a] lorry-load of National Army troops had driven through at dusk, chanting ribald songs and threatening, with coarse laughter, to return during the night "to enjoy the white lady's company."
>
> My over-active imagination would not be stilled as I got ready for the night. Fear had come into my home. I lay and tossed on my bed, allowing Fear to grow larger and take possession of my reasoning faculties. . . . An owl threw a shadow across the moon-lit room, and I froze with the thought that I was being watched through the window.

I could stand the tension no longer. In desperation, I crawled out of bed, got down on my knees, and simply asked God to hold me close to Himself. As my heart-beat began to steady down, and quietness regained possession of my vivid imagination, I asked God that, if it were possible, He would produce someone—I had no suggestion as to whom or how or from where—to stay in my home with me until the political crisis was past.

Bang!

I nearly died! My mouth parched, I thought my heart would stop!

"This is it!" my taut mind reasoned. "They've come!"

Again, a quiet knock at the back door, that sounded like a pistol shot in the strained silence of that night.

Somehow I stumbled down the corridor, but it was all I could do to make my voice come out of my frozen lips.

"Who's there?" I struggled to call out.

"It's only us!" whispered back two obviously female voices.

Sagging at the knees, I opened the door in shattered relief and welcomed Taadi, our evangelist's wife, and Damaris, our head midwife.

"Come in, come in," I urged them, shutting the door quickly and firmly behind them and leading them through to the sitting room. I sat down with my head in my hands, trying to recover composure from the wave of shock that had assailed me, and then, dizzily, I asked them why they had come.

"Well," said Taadi, "I woke from sleep, and the Lord said to me very clearly, 'Go to the doctor, she needs you,' so I got up and came."

"That's exactly what happened to me!" exclaimed Damaris. "And, actually, I felt guilty because last evening I had thought about coming to stay with you, but I was afraid that you would think it was cheek, so I did nothing."

. . . We laughed and cried and hugged each other, and then thanked God for His goodness to us.[4]

"You do not have because you do not ask" (James 4:2).

You are chosen, Beloved. God wants you to ask that your joy might be full.

25 One of the evidences of abiding is love toward other believers. Another evidence is hatred from the world. This the disciples must know before Jesus leaves them, for it will help them understand the hatred which will be poured out on Him during His arrest, trial, and crucifixion. It will prepare them for the tribulation which they will experience in the future. "These things I have spoken to you, that you may be kept from stumbling. They will make you outcasts from the synagogue, but an hour is coming for everyone who kills you to think that he is offering service to God. And these things they will do, because they have not known the Father, or Me. But these things I have spoken to you, that when their hour comes, you may remember that I told you of them" (John 16:1-4).

When tribulation and trials come, it is natural for our thoughts to turn inward to our own needs, our own safety or protection. We have a tendency to think, "It's every man for himself," unless, of course, we need the help of others to survive. In times of crisis, natural love goes out the window, and we bail out with it. But the fruit of abiding in Jesus is not natural love but supernatural love. The Greek word for *love* is *agapē*, a love that has the interest and welfare of others on its heart. It is a sacrificial love that lays down its life for another. It expresses itself in unconditional commitment to another. Jesus expressed it this way: "This is My commandment, that you love one another, just as I have loved you. Greater love has no one than this, that one lay down his life for his friends. You are My friends, if you do what I command you" (John 15:12-14).

If we want to be friends of God, then we will love—*agapē*—one another. We will love others the same way Jesus loved us—sacrificially. And that sacrificial love is to begin at home. It is sometimes the hardest place to love, especially if you live with unbelievers. But remember, my friend, God loved us and Christ died for us while we were still sinners, enemies by our own doing, and without hope and totally helpless to save ourselves (Romans 5:6-11). It was in this condition that He moved in love, that He might reconcile us to God and give us the sure hope of eternal life.

I do not know the state of your family, your friends, your neighbors, but I can tell you this: They all need to experience the fruit of His love, His unconditional love-me-right-where-I-am love. They may hate you, despise your Christianity, think you are a detriment to God and His kingdom, but they need to see His love. They are strangers to it, and God wants them to be friends.

26 Love stands with you, even if it means the loss of life. "Greater love has no one than this, that one lay down his life for his friends" (John 15:13).

Helen Roseveare writes:

> During the months of the Simba uprising in 1964, so many stood by me. The savagery of the suffering on all sides made each one of us face up to God's claim on our lives in a new way. Were we ready to die? Could we literally, meaningfully, say with Paul, "To me to live is Christ, and to die is gain"? Was there anything in the way, so to speak, any unresolved conflict in our minds, any unforgiven sin in our practice, any lack of assurance in our spirits? The urgency of the situation made us realists, and we daily sought to have "clean hands and a pure heart." Even if the participants were unconscious of it, this practical search after living Holiness showed itself in simple acts of love.
>
> The first Sunday after the rebel army had invaded us, Basuana preached his heart out on Romans 8:28-39, emphasizing that "all things"—including rebel captivity and unknown atrocities—"do work together for good to those who love God" and that indeed "none of these things" can move us or distress us, because nothing,

absolutely nothing, can separate us from the love of Christ. And I knew, as I listened to him from the back of the church, that he had poured his whole heart into that sermon because of his love for me—to comfort and strengthen me as he sensed the fears in my heart.

A few weeks later, amidst seventeen wild and armed youths, John and Joel climbed into the back of the truck, in which I was being forced to drive these rebels to Wamba. It had been an appalling night, heavy dark clouds blotting out the moon, sweeping rain driven by a blustering gale, the road surface churned into a sea of mud. The vehicle had no lights, no self-starter, no windscreen wipers. Nervously fiddling with the pin of a hand grenade, the diminutive, teenage "lieutenant" of the gang had ordered me to drive into the courtyard of a local palm oil factory, to search for petrol. . . . Ordered out of the truck, I stood a few yards from it, alone in the dark.

That was when I first realised that John and Joel were with me. I sensed them, rather than saw them, one on either side of me.

"Go away from me," I hissed to them. "They will kill me. Don't stand with me!"

They made no move.

I repeated my message. . . .

"Doctor," came their quiet reply, "that is why we are here. You shall not die alone!" . . .

When the rebels had driven off . . . Joel spoke . . . "I felt like one of Daniel's three friends in the . . . fiery furnace. Surely a fourth stood with us whose form was like that of the Son of God!" They had gone through that experience with me purely out of Christlike love. They did not need to be there![5]

27 Persecution for your faith is never easy. Rejection is never pleasant. It is hard to not be accepted, especially when you are doing what is right or when you are seeking to minister to those who are persecuting you. And

when the persecution builds, there is a temptation to forget that to which God has called you.

Jesus knew this. He wanted His disciples to be prepared. Before praying to the Father on their behalf, He said, "Behold, an hour is coming, and has already come, for you to be scattered, each to his own home, and to leave Me alone; and yet I am not alone, because the Father is with Me. These things I have spoken to you, that in Me you may have peace. In the world you have tribulation, but take courage; I have overcome the world" (John 16:32,33).

What may look like the final outcome in our earthly trial is not final. Jesus has overcome the world. You are attached to the Vine, and you have borne fruit. It is your fruit that has brought the tribulation. Tribulation is not a sign of defeat but triumph. Your Christlikeness has been seen and despised.

"This I command you, that you love one another. If the world hates you, you know that it has hated Me before it hated you. If you were of the world, the world would love its own; but because you are not of the world, but I chose you out of the world, therefore the world hates you. Remember the word that I said to you, 'A slave is not greater than his master.' If they persecuted Me, they will also persecute you; if they kept My word, they will keep yours also. But all these things they will do to you for My name's sake, because they do not know the One who sent Me" (John 15:17-21).

O Beloved, when tribulation comes, make sure it is because of your abiding. Then you will have peace.

28 When tribulation comes your way, you can know that it has not only a cause but also a purpose. People may hate you because of your righteous life, and as a result they will persecute you. However, with every such trial, God has a purpose. It will work together for your good, for it will serve to make you more usable for the Master. In *Living Holiness,* Dr. Roseveare shared another incident which is so appropriate to what we are studying.

Mark Anesadze and his wife, Eleanor, lived with their two small children on the same compound with Dr. Roseveare. However, she did not see much of them until the following incident:

> "Nyoka! Nyoka!" rang out over the compound—"Snake! Snake!"
>
> Their four-year-old son, Paul, had been bitten, and despite all we could do, he died the same day. I spent the night in their home, just sitting, holding Eleanor's hand. Others of their tribe from the school squatted round the room and quietly sang hymns through the long hours of darkness, and until the child was buried the next day.
>
> This drew us very close together, and a real friendship sprang up between us.
>
> During their last year in Bible School, they were part of a team of students who came for a ten-day mission to Nebobongo, where I was then working. Through them, God ministered revival to our growing family. Students and pupils, workmen and their wives, children and hospital patients, all came under the gracious movement of the Spirit. Sins were confessed, restitution made; joy became real, and singing replaced grumbling.
>
> Yet, in the midst of all the rejoicing, there was a heavy sorrow in their hearts. Mark and Eleanor asked me to look at their little bright three-year-old, Mary. I felt a terrible load crushing me as I diagnosed a rapidly growing cancerous growth behind her right eye.
>
> The parents were wonderful. . . . After the first awful shock, they rose with quiet dignity to accept the verdict from God's hands.
>
> "We know our loving heavenly Father cannot do ill to us or our children," they said, "and He will not let us suffer beyond what He enables us to bear."
>
> I went with Mary to a Government hospital . . . but the growth was already far too extensive and invasive. I had to watch with the parents during the next two years as it spread to the second eye. Mary never complained. She was . . . being physically disfigured, and yet gaining steadily and surely a rare spiritual beauty.[6]

God was pruning—and it hurt—but it was not without purpose.

"Trust in the LORD with all your heart, and do not lean on your own understanding" (Proverbs 3:5).

29 Whenever God permits affliction, it is for a greater purpose. Remembering this will keep you from bitterness.

A baby brother was born, and Mary delighted to sit and watch little Joseph . . . puzzled that Joseph did not seem to respond to her, and her parents. . . .

It seemed beyond possibility. I was so stunned, I could not even question God's intention. Paul, the first-born, was dead. Mary was dying. And now, Joseph lay there, a helpless living cripple. . . . Little Joseph was never going to sit up, or smile, or talk, or in any wise relate to the family. He was a helpless, yet living, cripple. . . .

Once again, the parents rose to the well-nigh impossible situation, accepting that God had entrusted this helpless infant to their loving care, and they poured their affection on him, resolutely refusing to lose faith in the love of God, as some would surely have been tempted to do.

They completed their Bible School training, and . . . were appointed to an "outchurch," in a small heathen village, full of witchcraft and pagan rites, thirty miles further east. From the outset, the villagers made it abundantly clear that the evangelist and his wife were not welcome, nor was the Gospel message of salvation they had come to share.

It was a very dark period for them. . . . They had to build themselves a home in the midst of that hostile crowd; carve out a food garden from the surrounding forest with none of the usual village camaraderie; testify to the love of God by their actions, for none would listen to their words. They were ostracised. They were lonely. . . . They were "despised and rejected." Like their Saviour?

I planned to spend a weekend with them. . . .

As Mark and Eleanor came out of their home to welcome me, I sensed at once that there was something amiss. . . . The two shared with us an amazing story of the past few days.

They had been looking forward so much to our arrival. . . . Eleanor had freshly laundered the children's clothes and laid them out on the grass roof of their home to dry. In the back yard, they had a chicken, fattening. In their garden, they had ripening pineapples and green vegetables. Mark had just finished building a small chapel, whitewashing its mud walls and placing tree trunks in rows for benches.

"On Thursday morning, Mark set off . . . to fish," and Eleanor and the children went to the garden. "Then everything seemed to happen at once."

"You've never seen such a mess," exploded Eleanor. "The garden was destroyed: just hacked down. Not even stolen. Senseless vandalism. . . . At first, I couldn't think: I couldn't take it in. I felt rising bitterness against whoever could have been so mean."

As Eleanor returned to her home, she smelled the smoke. The chapel was ablaze. Destroyed. Then the chicken was gone and so were the children's clothes. The villagers hated them because of Jesus.[7]

30 "If the world hates you, you know that it has hated Me before it hated you. . . . If they persecuted Me, they will also persecute you . . ." (John 15:18,20).

As Mark sought to put out the fire, it suddenly registered that no one was helping him.

That is so unlike the African. Whatever their differences, when tragedy strikes, everyone moves in to help. One would have expected the whole village to have rushed to their aid. No. On the contrary, sullen and derisive, they had stood in their doorways and watched.

As Mark and Eleanor related the event to Helen, Eleanor chirped, "That's it! . . . Ever since we came here, to bring them the Gospel of love and peace, they have hated us and determined to drive us away."

When they surveyed all the damage inflicted against them, "A great bitterness welled up inside me. I just felt I hated them all," Eleanor confessed. "I almost turned on God, with a deep inner cry: 'Why? Why? Why have You let all this happen to us? Why didn't You stop them? Aren't we serving You? Haven't we given up everything else to be here as Your representatives?' "

[As] Mark and Eleanor had cleared up the mess and debris in silence, with a barrier between them, Mark's big heart of love could reach through the darkness and touch God, and know "that in all things God works for the good of those who *love* Him" (Rom. 8:28), but he could not reach through the barrier to help Eleanor in her bitterness.

In the evening, the children in bed, they had sat together on the verandah. Mark had taken up his Bible to read aloud as usual, but Eleanor shut her heart, she told me, unwilling to hear the words.

"I didn't want to be helped. I was bitter and hurt, and couldn't see why I shouldn't be. I knew if we prayed, I'd have to change, and quite honestly, I didn't want to change. Why shouldn't I be bitter? Hadn't I suffered enough?

"Then I seemed to doze," she continued, "even while Mark was praying. And I saw four large earthen jars—you know, the ordinary kind we all use in our homes. They faded . . . and I jerked myself awake, and wondered vaguely why I had imagined them. They just had no connection with anything else at that particular time."

She went on to say how this had been repeated, just as the first time. She paused, and her eyes filled with tears, and a smile played at the corner of her lips.

"A third time," she whispered, "just the same, only now a Voice spoke, telling me to go near and look closely. And I saw the jars were filled with water. Then as I looked, the level of water began to fall....A trickle snaked across the verandah . . . I stretched out a hand, and touched the jar. . . . The vision faded and I woke."[8]

What God showed Eleanor regarding her trials, I believe He wants us to see also.

31 The vision faded, but suddenly, Eleanor realized what God was saying.

"The jar was *soft,*" she murmured. "Soft . . . unfired . . ."

So the jars were useless to fulfill the job for which they were made. They were made from the right earth, well matured, well rolled, well moulded—but "soft." They had not yet been fired in the kiln.

As they shared this testimony with me, my eyes filled with tears. . . . As we sat and chatted together, they showed me what the Lord was saying to them.

"It isn't really suffering, is it?" Eleanor explained. "God has merely offered us the privilege of being made more like our Saviour, stripped of everything that is unlike Him, or unhelpful to our testimony, or unnecessary for the ministry that He has planned for us. Even when He took Paul home, though it was terribly hard to accept at the time, He told us that He was teaching us to accept His comfort so that we could comfort others in like circumstances."

Mark interjected: "It isn't too bad when the training and discipline only hurts ourselves, but it isn't so easy to see the children suffer too. Sometimes, we haven't had enough food for them, nor money to buy clothes for them, and then it has seemed hard. Yet the Lord has taught us to hold all our possessions lightly.

"We so long to be available to God, so that He can use us to help others," they continued. "And yet there seem so many lessons to learn and we are slow. I think we have seen that the most important thing He is saying to us is to obey Him in everything, and to trust Him to work out the consequences. We don't have to reason it all out . . . we just have to trust and obey."

We knelt together later that evening, and as Mark and Eleanor poured out their hearts to God in childlike confidence in His goodness, I just wanted to whisper: "Dear God, forgive me! I've rebelled at Your ways in my life; I've argued with You and wanted my own way. I've disobeyed so often. Can You forgive me? I want to say, 'Not my will, but Yours, be done,' but I'm afraid. I want to ask You to fire me, in the kiln of Your love, and make me into a vessel capable of fulfilling Your purposes—but I'm scared at what it may cost, how much it may hurt. Please make me willing to be made willing for the discipline of total obedience to Your every known command."

The Master Potter has chosen us, and taken us into His nail-pierced hands, to mould us as clay into the vessels He has planned. He is patiently working on each "lump of clay," ridding it of all impurities, removing every tiny bit of grit that would spoil the beauty of the finished jar. He alone knows how to fire His jar, in what kiln and at what temperature, that it may become "holy, useful to the Master and prepared to do any good work" (2 Tim. 2:21), that He may entrust it to carry about His Treasure: "We have this treasure in jars of clay to show that this all-surpassing power is from God and not from us" (2 Cor. 4:7).[9]

What do you want to say to your Vinedresser, Beloved?

August

Joy in Sorrow . . . Peace in Persecution

1 It's hard to be hated and worse to be persecuted. Our instinct is to seek love. We may not say so, but we want to be accepted. When we're rejected we wonder why. Where did we fail?

To want to belong is natural. And yet, by the very virtue of our association with Jesus Christ, the world is going to hate us. Jesus knew that identification with Him would result in rejection for His followers.

Thus, on the night in which He was betrayed by Judas, He had to make sure that the 11 were prepared for what would happen next. As they walked the dusty streets of Jerusalem in the dimness of approaching darkness, Jesus talked to them of the necessity of love and the inevitability of hatred.

"This I command you, that you love one another. If the world hates you, you know that it has hated Me before it hated you" (John 15:17,18). In His "if," Jesus was saying that hatred from the world was a certainty, not merely a possibility. (The "if" He used here was in the first class condition in the Greek and, thus, indicated certainty.) If the world hated Him, it would hate His disciples. While this hatred might have been hard for the disciples to understand, they had seen the Jews take up stones to kill Him. They knew of the plots to take away the life of the Light of the world.

Jesus went on to explain: "If you were of the world" [this time the "if" was a second class condition which meant "but you are not"], the world would love its own; but because you are not of the world, but I chose you out of the world, therefore the world hates you" (John 15:19).

Once we are born again, we are different. "If any man be in Christ, he is a new creature: old things are passed away; behold, all things are become new" (2 Corinthians 5:17 KJV). It is a natural human tendency to reject those who do not conform to the norm. Those who settle for the status quo do not rock society's boat; of course, they also never set its course to conquer the high seas of new worlds! Followers of Jesus rock the boat, and for this reason the world wants to throw them overboard.

How vital it was that Jesus' followers remember: " 'A slave is not greater than his master.' If [and it is true] they persecuted Me, they will also persecute you; if [and it is true] they kept My word, they will keep yours also" (John 15:20). Some would believe, others would not, but none would remain neutral.

The question to them and to us then becomes: "Are you prepared?" It's vital that you understand the ministry of the Holy Spirit in and through you, so that when the world responds in hatred you won't be caught off guard or draw back from the life of holiness to which the Lord calls all His children. Take time to read John 14–16 in preparation for our study this month.

2 Jesus never left people in neutral. Either they believed or they did not. "But all these things they will do to you for My name's sake, because they do not know the One who sent Me" (John 15:21). It is hard to be hated, unless you remember it is part of being a child of God. Therefore, Beloved, when the world rejects and persecutes you, do not forget that it is because you have been chosen by God to go and to bear fruit. When others see the fruit of your life, when they taste it, it is different than theirs. And it's precisely this difference that brings rejection. The unrighteous will always hate the righteous.

When men revile you, persecute you, and say all manner of evil against you falsely, that is a sure sign of your salvation. The hatred of the world is God's reminder that you have been chosen by God. Paul wrote: "For to you it has been granted for Christ's sake, not only to believe in Him, but also to suffer for His sake" (Philippians 1:29). The suffering has come because the Helper dwells within, and it is He who convicts the world of sin, righteousness, and judgment.

To know these truths, Beloved, is to be kept from stumbling. To understand them will bring confidence from God in the midst of the rejection of the world. To believe that once you are a child of God everyone will love and accept you is to fall into a snare which would keep you from the ministry to which the Lord has called you—being an ambassador of Jesus Christ to carry out the Lord's ministry of reconciliation (2 Corinthians 5:14-21).

To not understand could bring depression, overwhelming sorrow, or turmoil. Jesus was going away; the disciples were going to be left without any visible means of human support. Notice I said "visible." Therefore, it was essential that they understand the world's rejection. Thus, our Lord said: "These things I have spoken to you, that you may be kept from stumbling. They will make you outcasts from the synagogue, but an hour is coming for everyone who kills you to think that he is offering service to God. And these things they will do, because they have not known the Father, or Me. But these things I have spoken to you, that when their hour comes, you may remember that I told you of them. And these things I did not say to you at the beginning, because I was with you. But now I am going to Him who sent Me. . . . Because I have said these things to you, sorrow has filled your heart. But I tell you the truth, it is to your advantage that I go away; for if I do not go away, the Helper shall not come to you; but if I go, I will send Him to you" (John 16:1-7).

The whole purpose of the Upper Room discourse is summarized in John 16:33: "These things I have spoken to you, that in Me you may have peace. In the world you have tribulation, but take courage; I have overcome the world."

And that, dear reader, will be the theme of our devotional study this month: "Joy in Sorrow . . . Peace in Persecution." How I pray God will speak to you in a special way!

3 Jesus had promised His disciples He would not leave them as orphans. Another Helper of the same kind would be sent from the Father. An unseen but indwelling Helper would be with them forever (John 14:16-18). What comfort this was meant to bring, although at the time, it must have seemed merely words and promises. Jesus had begun to bring the good news of salvation to the people. Now that He was leaving, who was to continue the task? They were!

I am sure they felt their total impotence. The thought of being separated from their Lord was overwhelming. Sorrow shrouded His promise of the Helper. Jesus knew this, but He also knew it would be temporary: "Truly, truly, I say to you, that you will weep and lament, but the world will rejoice; you will be sorrowful, but your sorrow will be turned to joy" (John 16:20). The task of the gospel would continue, for when the Holy Spirit would come to indwell them, He would "convict the world concerning sin, and righteousness, and judgment" (John 16:8).

O Beloved, how dwells the Spirit of God in you? Is He allowed to do His work? Or is fear of the world, the rejection of man, or the timidity of your flesh quenching the ministry God wants to accomplish through you?

Have you not realized that suffering and persecution are a gift from God, granted to you with the gift of salvation? Would you have salvation without the suffering? Quite possibly so, but to those who would live like Christ, this is impossible. "Indeed, all who desire to live godly in Christ Jesus will be persecuted" (2 Timothy 3:12). When Paul penned these words, they were not just for Timothy, any more than our Lord's words were just for the faithful 11. In Romans 8:16-18 we read: "The Spirit Himself bears witness with our spirit that we are children of God, and if children, heirs also, heirs of God and fellow heirs with Christ, if indeed we suffer with Him in order that we may also be glorified with Him. For I consider that the sufferings of this present time are not worthy to be compared with the glory that is to be revealed to us."

And would we, Beloved, want to enter heaven on Easy Street when our Lord went the Calvary Road? Of course not! Then it is no wonder that after the apostles were flogged because of the gospel, "they went on their way from the presence of the Council, rejoicing that they had been considered worthy to suffer shame for His name. And . . . they kept right on teaching and preaching Jesus as the Christ" (Acts 5:41,42). Are you experiencing rejection or persecution? You have the Helper. He will give you peace in persecution, joy in sorrow. Hangeth thou in there!

4 O Beloved, are you living your Christian life in your own strength? Your own wisdom? If so, you are discovering your own impotence. It's hard, isn't it, to share your faith? It's so much easier just to live your own Christian life and respect "the privacy of others" when it comes to discussing their relationship with the Lord. Besides, if you are living your life primarily in your own strength and wisdom, in all probability it really isn't having a disturbing impact on your world. Except for overt sin, you are probably in the flow of life, not much different from those around you.

But is this the way it should be? Should your life be ordinary? Without guidance? Without impact or significance? Not disturbing the complacency of the lost—or even the lukewarmness of the many who profess to be Christians? No! This is not to be the experience of those who have the Helper dwelling within.

The word for *helper* in John 14:16 is *paraklētos. Paraklētos* comes from *para* meaning "by the side" and *kaleō* meaning "to call." Therefore the Holy Spirit is the One who is called alongside us as our Helper. *Paraklētos* was used by Greek writers for a legal adviser, a pleader, a proxy, or advocate—one who comes forward in behalf of and as the representative of another. When Jesus said He would send another Helper, the word He used for *another* was *allos*, indicating another of the same kind.

Jesus was going back to the Father, but He would not leave His disciples without help. All that Jesus had been to them during His sojourn on earth, the Spirit would be to them in His absence. Jesus had taught them on earth. Thus He assured them, "When He, the Spirit of truth, comes, He will guide you into all the truth; for He will not speak on His own initiative, but whatever He hears, He will speak; and He will disclose to you what is to come" (John 16:13). The Helper would take that which was of Christ and disclose it to them (John 16:14), for He would be their Teacher (John 14:26).

Jesus was going to leave, but they need not turn then to their own wisdom, nor walk in their own strength. The Helper would be *in* them, "convict[ing] the world concerning sin, and righteousness, and judgment" (John 16:8), guiding them into the truth, leading them step-by-step, and giving them His ninefold fruit of love, joy, peace, patience, kindness, goodness, faithfulness, gentleness (meekness), and self-control (Galatians 5:22,23). You, Beloved, have the same Helper. Lean on Him. Let Him lead, and watch what happens!

5 I have just finished another incredibly wonderful book that has so encouraged and challenged my heart. *Secret Invasion* by Hans Kristian and Dave Hunt is the account of the work of Hans Kristian's ministry to our brothers and sisters who suffered for the sake of the gospel behind the Iron Curtain. It demonstrates well the help and the sufficiency of the Holy Spirit to lead us through all sorts of situations. It will take a week or so, but I feel you would be so immeasurably blessed that I want to share with you one of

many thrilling chapters from the book. At the end of each day, I will give you a Scripture to meditate on:

> Although it was only eight in the evening, the dimly lit streets of Sofia were already semideserted. This was the end of October and the nip of fall was in the air, accented by a biting wind that swirled out of alleys and down the broad avenues in gusts that stung cheeks and eyes and chased leaves and papers along the usually impeccably clean sidewalks. There were a few hardy evening strollers making slow progress as they paused to inspect the sparse displays of merchandise in shop windows; but most of the intermittent pedestrian traffic, collars buttoned, clutching hats and skirts at each new gust of wind, hurried homeward.
>
> Rene and I stood shivering on the sidewalk under a pale, yellow light, trying to read the name of the street and correlate it with the map we carried. The street names were printed in the Greek and Latin characters common to Slavic languages, whereas our map listed only the Latin equivalents. It was a difficult enough problem in daylight for someone speaking Bulgarian, but hopeless for us in the dark. We were carrying substantial funds for two underground pastors and had intended to locate their homes that afternoon, but our plane had been inexplicably delayed [remember this, Beloved, for it will demonstrate the wonderful sovereignty of our Lord], making the difference between afternoon and evening, light and dark, forcing us to abandon any hope of finding either pastor's house that night—and we had to leave for a similar mission in another city early the next morning.
>
> Our one remaining hope was to locate a registered Protestant church in Sofia that had a meeting that very night. Perhaps one of the pastors would be present. A tiny dot on our map marked the location of the church, but how to find our way to it? That was the insurmountable problem occupying us now.[1]

"Commit thy way unto the LORD; trust also in him; and he shall bring it to pass" (Psalm 37:5 KJV).

6 Rene was glancing back and forth from the map to a street name posted high on a building, trying to locate our present position in relation to that tiny dot. I had given up trying to help him, and was praying, which seemed to me the most effective thing I could do. If that failed, I was prepared to abandon the project entirely and get back to our hotel. Already we were attracting too much attention.

I was worried. We had tried to ask directions from several passersby who seemed the least likely to be agents of the secret police, but the only response had been a stiffened back and a quickened pace. Conversations with Westerners must be reported to the authorities, and no one willingly put himself in that position without good reason.

"We're never going to locate that church ourselves," said Rene at last, folding the map and stuffing it back into his pocket with a sigh of resignation. "I know the main street we're on now, but I can't make out the cross streets. I don't even know what direction is north or south. Look, why don't we stop this nonsense and get a cab!"

"I'm as new at this as you are," I replied helplessly. "We have a lot of money with us, and a lot of people to see before we leave Bulgaria, and . . . well, I don't want to announce our arrival to the . . ."

"If this place is as full of informers as we've been told," said Rene skeptically, "the local gendarmes have probably received a dozen reports of two idiots with a map lost in the middle of Sofia. That's not going to cause a red alert, as inept as we must look." He shoved his hands into his pockets and stamped his feet. "I'm freezing."

"May I help you?" asked a soft, feminine voice in German.

We turned to see a girl of about twenty, bundled up in a long coat, a kerchief on her head, standing a few feet away and peering inquisitively at us in the dim light.

The elusive feeling of uneasiness that had been gnawing at me suddenly grew stronger.

"We're looking for Gorky Street," I said, trying to sound relaxed and nonchalant.

"What number on Gorky Street?"

"Oh, no number in particular," I responded quickly, brushing her impertinent curiosity aside. "Just Gorky Street—anywhere on it. Tell us how to get there, and we can find our way after that."

"But you must be seeking a particular address," she insisted. "What number is it? Perhaps we're going in the same direction." A half-amused smile was beginning to form on her face.

That she should walk up to strange men, obviously Westerners, and engage them in conversation was more than enough to arouse my suspicions. But to insistently inquire about our exact destination—now I was sure she must be from the secret police.[2]

"Man's goings are of the LORD; how can a man then understand his own way?" (Proverbs 20:24 KJV).

7 I glanced at Rene, but a shadow hid the expression on his face.

"After all, it's a registered church," I thought to myself. "It would be even more suspicious now if I don't tell her." And then aloud: "We would like to go to number thirty-seven."

"Praise God!" she exclaimed. "I was praying at home and the Lord told me to come and lead two men from the West to our church. This isn't the way I go."

Glancing apprehensively up and down the street, she added quickly in a low voice, "Follow me about twenty paces back and I'll lead you there."

Rene and I looked at one another and went limp. We set off down the street together, following this Bulgarian girl as though she were an angel from heaven.

The church was indistinguishable from other buildings in its neighborhood. When we entered the front door she was waiting for us in a small foyer. The service had already begun.

"Go up to the balcony," she whispered, pointing to a rough, wooden stairway. "I'll see you afterward." She stepped through a door into the sanctuary as we turned to climb the stairs.

The church was crowded. . . .

The balcony ran the entire length of one side of the building. Our place in the front row gave us a good view of the platform and of most of the congregation below. The singing had an indescribable spiritual quality that lifted and captured and made one feel a part of something truly beyond this world. I felt myself caught up in a rising crescendo of glory, and tears rolled down my cheeks as I realized the immediate oneness I felt with these members of Christ's body who seemed to me, from their lives and the persecution I knew they suffered, so much like the early church. It strengthened my confidence in the Scriptures just to be there and to see for myself that same triumphant faith of Bible days still alive and conquering on this earth. Looking around the room at upturned, shining faces, to my joy I suddenly recognized a man on the far side of the church. I knew him from his photograph. One of the pastors we had come to see!

This was the prayer meeting. Everyone knelt on the hard wood floor. I couldn't understand a word they were saying, but I knew they were talking to God. I felt His presence in the room. I had warned people how deceptive and unreliable feelings can be—but still I felt God was there. I felt that they were talking to Him and He was listening, and I knew that I was touching reality, feeling within my spirit a dimension entirely beyond my five senses. . . .

These people were not behind an Iron Curtain as we had thought—they were in heaven.[3]

"Whom have I in heaven but Thee? And besides Thee, I desire nothing on earth" (Psalm 73:25). Read its context; it is so appropriate.

8 The church service had ended. Before I could turn to leave, I felt a hand upon my shoulder. Startled, I looked around to discover who it could be, and found myself face-to-face with the other pastor we had come to see!

"Praise God, Brother Kristian!" he exclaimed in English, embracing me warmly. "We've been expecting you!"

I was stunned. He had never seen me before, couldn't possibly know my name—even my wife hadn't known where Rene and I were going. Our plans had been kept a complete secret, known only to ourselves and God.

Partially recovering from the shock, I replied in a low voice. "I'll see you at your home later tonight." Then I turned away, knowing that the official pastor of this church, whom we had been warned was collaborating with the Communists, would be required to report the names of members of his congregation seen conversing at any length with visitors from the West.

People were greeting us with tears of joy, kissing us on both cheeks, hugging us, pumping our arms up and down with hearty handshakes, making us . . . feel once again that ecstatic love and unity in Christ so real to them.

Making our way slowly downstairs, Rene and I momentarily found ourselves in the crowded hallway next to Sonya, the girl who had met us on the street.

"Tell Pastor Korbut to go home and we'll see him later," I said quickly, naming the other pastor whose face I had recognized among the congregation during the meeting. "And please! We need you to guide us! Can you meet us in about thirty minutes at the Lenin Monument?" She nodded and moved on through the crowd.

The pastor had seen us now. Pushing his way through the departing congregation, he greeted us each with a firm handclasp and welcomed us warmly in German. He told us how happy he was that we were there, what a good thing it was for tourists from the West to be able to see for themselves the freedom of religion in his country, that he hoped we would tell the truth about this when we got home and also bring fraternal greetings from the Christians in Bulgaria to those in Denmark.

I felt sorry for him. He was trying so hard. For another ten minutes he told us of the beauties of the Black Sea, the beaches, the hotels, the restaurants, the warmth and healthful qualities of the sun and water, and urged us by all means to include at least one seaside resort in our trip. . . . With such mundane pleasantries, all delivered in a stiffly formal and labored attempt to seem friendly, he managed to keep us under his eyes and occupied until all the congregation had left.[4]

"The fear of man brings a snare . . ." (Proverbs 29:25) and truly this pastor was caught in fear's snare. He had lost heart by looking at the temporal rather than the eternal (2 Corinthians 4:16-18). He had not been willing to endure hardness as a good soldier; he had not been willing to join others in suffering for the sake of the gospel (2 Timothy 2:3; 1:8). And what about you, Beloved? Is there any way you have compromised the faith because of the fear of man? Have you shied away from the suffering that godliness brings? If so, repent. Nothing temporal is worth eternal pleasure.

9 Sonya was waiting for us, pretending to be engrossed in window-shopping, when we arrived five minutes late for our rendezvous. She noticed us when we were still a block away, and began to walk down the street. We followed, keeping at a safe distance. After we had walked in this manner for about a mile, she slowed down until we caught up with her.

"This is it," said Sonya softly, pausing at last in front of a small, square frame structure with a wide, covered porch. A faint glow around one window indicated that someone was still awake in the house. She pushed carefully on a gate, whispering, "It squeaks!"

We stepped into the front yard. Instead of going up onto the porch, however, she turned onto a narrow stone walk that led to the rear. I assumed that we were entering by a back door, but she continued past the house. After a few yards I saw against the sky the outline of another house behind the first one. Following the narrow walkway, we continued past that one also until we came to a third, smaller than the other two.

"Doesn't Pastor Korbut live in the front house?" I asked softly, worried that she might be taking us to the wrong place. "He used to," she whispered, "but a few months ago the secret police moved into his house and put him back here.

"I'm sure God kept you from finding this street and sent me to guide you, not just to church but here, also. If you had come yourselves, you would have knocked at the front house and asked the secret police for Pastor Korbut!" She clutched her head with both hands. "That would have gone very hard for him! He's just been released from prison. They tortured him—and he broke."

Indeed, Pastor Korbut looked like a broken man. There was a smile on his face when he ushered us excitedly into his humble dwelling, but it was weak and strained, trembling on the surface. He seemed worn and thin, older than his years. A tall, stooping man, he moved about the room dragging two extra chairs from a corner, not just with a limp, but as though every step brought pain, which brought a memory that increased the pain. Having seated us with all the dignity and hospitality of a prince, he sank back into a chair with a sigh.

Something vital was missing in his eyes.

They lacked depth, as though his soul had been torn from his body.

The Korbut family spoke only Bulgarian, so Sonya interpreted everything into German for us, adding bits on the side about this pastor's recent arrest, until we knew the whole pathetic story.[5]

"The LORD's lovingkindnesses indeed never cease, for His compassions never fail. They are new every morning; great is Thy faithfulness. 'The LORD is my portion,' says my soul, 'therefore I have hope in Him'" (Lamentations 3:22-24).

"It is a trustworthy statement. . . . If we are faithless, He remains faithful; for He cannot deny Himself" (2 Timothy 2:11,13).

O Beloved, if you have failed your God, He is still there with outstretched arms. Return to Him. You can because He is merciful.

10 Some months before, a visitor from Sweden had been given a letter . . . to be mailed in Greece in order to avoid the Bulgarian censors. While in Greece, however, he had forgotten to mail the letter. It was discovered in his briefcase . . . by the border guards when he passed through Bulgaria again on his way back to Western Europe. The unsigned letter was addressed to the Bulgarian pastor now living in the West that I had interpreted for when he had visited Denmark. Pastor Korbut was arrested and tortured . . . to make him divulge who had written the letter, although it contained nothing more than Christian greetings.

For years Pastor Korbut had had a circulatory weakness in his legs. Knowing this, the police forced him to stand hour after hour during intensive questioning, until his legs swelled so badly that he could no longer endure the pain. Eventually he had collapsed. In this condition, unable to bear the tortures any longer, he had gasped out the name of the person who had written the letter—another underground pastor. He had been released and the other pastor arrested.

Since that day . . . Pastor Korbut had been tormented by an unremitting sense of shame and remorse. . . .

"Some of Christ's commands are impossible for us to obey under present conditions," said Pastor Korbut. "For instance, the command to 'go into all the world preaching the gospel.' We cannot go to other countries." He shrugged and that weak smile brightened momentarily. "So we must do our best here in our own country. It is difficult." His eyes closed and his face clouded with a look of pain and sorrow. "You cannot know how difficult it is."

Mrs. Korbut reached over and put a tiny, worn hand on one of her husband's.

His expression brightened again and he leaned forward in his chair. "We can pray for those who go into all the world. Someone must pray. This we have learned to do. But we need news from other countries in order to know what to pray for. . . ."

He seemed overwhelmed by our visit, to think that we cared enough to travel many miles to see him, that the church in Bulgaria . . . was . . . not forgotten in the West; that we were actually praying for him, and for the secret congregations he pastored.

Tears rolled down his cheeks when we handed him the money we had brought. A glance around their tiny apartment was enough to assure us that the Korbuts needed it badly. But both he and his wife protested strongly that it was too much. Before finally accepting it, Mrs. Korbut put an arm around her husband and, faces turned upward, weeping, oblivious to our presence for that brief moment, they thanked God together.[6]

"For as high as the heavens are above the earth, so great is His lovingkindness toward those who fear Him. As far as the east is from the west, so far has He removed our transgressions from us. Just as a father has compassion on his children, so the LORD has compassion on those who fear Him. For He Himself knows our frame; He is mindful that we are but dust" (Psalm 103:11-14).

O Beloved, aren't you thankful that your Father knows your frame?

11 It was getting late. We stood to leave. The Korbuts embraced us fervently. They both seemed brighter, as though a burden had been lifted.

Following Sonya back out into the street in the darkness, I had a strong feeling that we had brought more than money. As badly as that was needed, they had a greater need—the reassurance that Christ understood and forgave, that they were not abandoned by their heavenly Father. I was sure that this was the main gift He had sent us to bring them, and my heart was glad.

Reaching the street, Sonya continued on the way by which we had come. At the next corner, however, she turned left for one block, then left again. We were now retracing our steps, but on the next street over, paralleling the one we had taken earlier in the evening. My curiosity about this intriguing maneuver could not be contained.

"Why did you do that?" I asked.

"Because you never go back the same way," she whispered. "There are informers in every block."

"Awake this late at night?" asked Rene incredulously.

"One never knows. Is it worth the chance to save a few steps?"

Neither of us replied. She seemed to sense what we felt.

"There's no way I can explain to a Westerner what this system has done to our country. We never know who the informers are. It could be someone in one's own family. This breaks down the natural affection and trust that there ought to be between human beings. You're suspicious of everyone—sometimes even of other believers. It's terrible."

"I don't think I could live here," said Rene.

"We have no other alternative. If we did . . ."

The unfinished sentence was still hanging in the air when we arrived at Pastor Tisjkob's house fifteen minutes later, where the door opened promptly to our quiet knock.

"All day we've been expecting you!" he exclaimed, giving me a hug. "We've been longing to see you!"

"This I don't understand!" I said, feeling confused. "Nobody knows our traveling route. Even my wife doesn't know I'm here today, so how could you know I was coming?"

"God in heaven knows," he responded simply, and pointed upward. His face was shining with an expression of childish innocence.

"And my name! How did you know that?" I insisted. The question had been burning in my mind ever since he had whispered my name in the church. Surely none of our couriers would have told him! They know better than to let information slip that could become a noose around this pastor's neck during interrogation.

Pastor Tisjkob shrugged and gave me the same enigmatic reply: "God in heaven knows." The expression on his face told me that for him this was explanation enough. It was so simple: what God in heaven knows, He tells to His children on earth when they need to know.[7]

"Who is the man who fears the LORD? He will instruct him in the way he should choose. . . . The secret of the LORD is for those who fear Him, and He will make them know His covenant" (Psalm 25:12,14).

12 "Yes, I realize that God in heaven knows everything," I responded with a helpless laugh."But how did you know?"

He shrugged. "See my daughter over there?" he pointed to a thin, intelligent-looking girl who had been staring at me with a strange fascination ever since I had come into the room.

I nodded.

"She's just nine years old. About a week ago she had a dream. In it she saw two men wearing western clothes, sitting in the balcony of our church. One of them had lots of dark hair like your friend. The other one was quite bald, just like you." He laughed good-naturedly and then continued. "But what impressed her the most was a white handkerchief sticking out of the bald man's suit pocket."

Looking down at my pocket, I saw the white handkerchief. I had intended to change from this obviously western suit to a darker, older one that would be less noticeable on the streets of Sofia, but because our plane was late, I hadn't done it.

"She had never seen anyone wearing a handkerchief like that in her life," continued Pastor Tisjkob. "She talked about it all week."

Rene and I were exchanging glances. This was almost too much.

"But my name," I persisted, struggling to comprehend what he was saying.

"We understood that this dream had special significance, so we prayed for the Lord to give us the interpretation. Last night my wife had the same dream. In it the Lord told her that your name was Kristian, and that you were coming to see us."

I leaned back in my chair and looked over at Rene again. He seemed as nonplussed as I was. We both believed that God uses miracles and visions today, but I could see that he was having the same problem I was accepting a story like this.

It wasn't that I doubted Pastor Tisjkob. I was sure he was telling the truth. But I was staggered by the relationship these people had with God, because it raised a devastating question: If this was Christianity, then what was the game we were playing in the West?[8]

So often Christians fear persecution and suffering, and in the flesh that is natural and to be expected. Fear is a natural reaction, but what would be our reaction if we were to respond in the Spirit rather than in the flesh? I think it would be one of rejoicing. Rejoicing, first, because like those in the early church, we have been counted worthy to suffer for His name's sake. Second, rejoicing because suffering purifies us and makes us unashamed when we see Him, "for I consider that the sufferings of this present time are not worthy to be compared with the glory that is to be revealed to us" (Romans 8:18).

A third reason for rejoicing is that suffering and persecution can draw us into a deeper intimacy with our Lord, if we will draw near to Him in the midst of the trial of our faith (Psalm 119:71). We have a privilege, Beloved, as children of God: access to the mind and heart of God through the ministry of the Holy Spirit. What we need to know God will reveal to us, if we will but be still and know that He is God.

13 Why do Christians suffer persecution? Why does the world hate us? If we are like Christ, shouldn't the world love us? Some people believe that the answer to this last question is yes. They feel that the more we become like Christ, the more the world will love us. But, Beloved, such thinking is not in accordance with the Word of God: "But I tell you the truth, it is to your advantage that I go away; for if I do not go away, the Helper shall not come to you; but if I go, I will send Him to you. And He, when He comes [Comes where? To you!], will convict the world concerning sin, and righteousness, and judgment; concerning sin, because they do not believe in Me; and concerning righteousness, because I go to the Father, and you no longer behold Me; and concerning judgment, because the ruler of this world has been judged" (John 16:7-11).

The Helper comes to live within us so that you and I might become more like our Lord and carry on His work. When this happens, then it is only reasonable to expect the world to respond to us as it responded to Him: "If they persecuted Me, they will also persecute you; if they kept My word, they will keep yours also. But all these things they will do to you for My name's sake, because they do not know the One who sent Me. If I had not come and spoken to them, they would not have sin, but now they have no excuse for their sin. . . . If I had not done among them the works which no one else did, they would not have sin; but now they have both seen and hated Me and My Father as well" (John 15:20-22,24).

It is the Spirit of God within us who brings the conviction of sin, righteousness, and judgment. He is simply carrying on the work of our Lord. Jesus demonstrated what God intends for us—a life lived in faith, believing God by obeying Him; a life of righteousness demonstrated by doing what God says is right; and a life that because of its obedience pronounces judgment upon Satan, who wants to be like God and therefore was judged by God. Thus, as we are restored to the image of God by the Spirit of God, we become the Spirit's instruments of convicting the world of sin, righteousness, and judgment.

As you carefully look at John 16:9-11, you see that the essence of sin is unbelief. Unbelief is demonstrated by a rejection of God's messenger, the Son, or by rejection of His message which is the Word of God. Because you and I have believed in Jesus and accepted the Bible as the Word of God, we have convicted the world of its sin of unbelief. Every time we take the Word of God as the rule or standard of our life, walking in obedience to His precepts, ordering our thinking accordingly, then the Holy Spirit convicts of sin those who do not believe and do not live in accordance with the Word of God.

In the light of this fact, Beloved, can you understand why there is so little conviction of sin in our society? Isn't it because we don't really live as if we believe God?

14 For the majority of those who profess to know Jesus Christ in a personal way, there is little difference between the way they live and the way the world lives. In light of that, don't you think we need to ask ourselves what kind of an impact we are having upon our immediate world?

When the Spirit of God indwells a believer, not only does the Spirit within convict the world of sin, but of righteousness. Righteousness reveals and exposes sin, because our righteous standard of living brings an awareness of the gap between holiness and unrighteousness.

If unsaved people are not going to read the Bible as the inspired, inerrant Word of God, then they need to read us. They "read us" as they view our righteous lifestyle and watch how we order our behavior in the various circumstances of life. They can no longer behold Jesus, but we are here, and they should see our righteousness. When they are convicted of righteousness, we need to tell them of the only One who can make them righteous: the Lord Jesus Christ.

"For with the heart man believes, resulting in righteousness, and with the mouth he confesses, resulting in salvation. For the Scripture says, 'WHOEVER BELIEVES IN HIM WILL NOT BE DISAPPOINTED.' For there is no distinction between Jew and Greek; for the same Lord is Lord of all, abounding in riches for all who call upon Him; for 'WHOEVER WILL CALL UPON THE NAME OF THE LORD WILL BE SAVED' " (Romans 10:10-13).

As I sit here writing, I am remembering a story from the mission field of Africa which illustrates so well how our lives, like a mirror, can expose our unrighteousness, letting us see ourselves as we really are.

A missionary had hung a mirror on the tree outside his hut. That was where he shaved every morning. It had become so much a part of his daily routine that he forgot it until one afternoon when an African chief's wife came to visit him. As they stood outside his home talking, she leaned back as she chatted away and looked up toward the sky.

Suddenly the warmth and delightful beauty of the afternoon was shattered by the horror of her scream. "Who's that ugly person looking at me out of the tree?" The mirror in the tree had caught the reflection of a grotesquely painted face scarred by heathen practices. She had never before seen herself. When the missionary finally convinced her that it was her own face, she begged him to sell her the mirror.

He didn't want to lose his mirror, but because she was the chief's wife, he felt he couldn't say no. The very minute it was in her hands she threw it to the ground, crushing and grinding it with a stone. Because she didn't like what she had seen, she wanted to destroy that which had shown what she was really like. This is often the way people react to pure Christianity.

15 When the Spirit comes to indwell us at salvation, His indwelling presence in us also convicts the world of judgment. Let's read John 16:8 and 11 again: "And He, when He comes, will convict the world concerning sin, and righteousness, and judgment . . . concerning judgment, because the ruler of this world has been judged." These are not easy verses to understand unless you keep them in the context of verses 9 and 10. Therefore, before we look at how the Spirit within convicts the world without of judgment, let me review the other two things the indwelling Spirit accomplishes through us in regard to the world.

First, the Spirit within us convicts people of sin, because they do not believe in Jesus. The very fact that we have believed exposes their unbelief. The essence or root of sin is really unbelief. Second, the indwelling Holy Spirit convicts people concerning righteousness; although they cannot behold the righteous lifestyle of the Son of Man because He has returned to the Father, they can behold our righteous way of life. And seeing our way of life in comparison to their unrighteousness, they are then convicted of their need of righteousness.

They see that righteousness is possible and attainable, because we are living according to what God says is right. Of course, when they comment on the difference in our lives, we must tell them that our righteousness is possible only because of the work of the Lord Jesus Christ at Calvary. It is our Lord who has set us free from sin's penalty and power, and who will someday free us from sin's presence. This is the Good News!

Now let's look at how the Spirit within convicts the world of judgment, comparing John 16:11 with John 12:31. John 16:11 says: ". . . concerning judgment, because the ruler of this world has been judged." In John 12:23-31 Jesus has been telling His disciples that the hour has come for the Son of Man to be glorified. Of course, He is referring to His death by crucifixion.

In His death, Jesus would glorify the Father by His obedience, humbling Himself unto death, even death on a cross (Philippians 2:5-11). It would be through His death that Satan would be deposed of his rule over the souls of men, for Jesus' death would pay for our sins and take away Satan's power.

Since our sins are covered by the blood of Jesus Christ when we in faith trust in His substitutionary death, then Satan no longer has dominion over us. The ruler of the world is judged and thus cast out. John 12:31 says: "Now judgment is upon this world; now the ruler of this world shall be cast out."

The power of death is sin. Because sin was taken care of at Calvary, Satan no longer has power over us (Hebrews 2:14). When the world sees that we are not under Satan's dominion and we do not have to succumb to Satan's power or authority, but have authority over the enemy, it is obvious that anything or anyone having to do with Satan shall be judged.

16 When you look at the lives of unsaved people who seem to live more righteously than others, it is hard to believe they are under the dominion of Satan, pawns in his power. Yet, before *any* man, woman or child ever comes to know the Lord Jesus Christ as Savior and Lord, they live under the dominion of Satan.

In Ephesians 2:1, we read: "And you were dead in your trespasses and sins." In other words because we are all sinners by virtue of our association with Adam, the father of all mankind, we are in a state of spiritual death: "Therefore, just as through one man [Adam] sin entered into the world, and death through sin, and so death spread to all men, because all sinned" (Romans 5:12).

Ephesians 2:2 continues: ". . . in which [referring to your trespasses and sins] you formerly walked according to the course of this world, according to the prince of the power of the air, of the spirit that is now working in the sons of disobedience."

Notice that God refers to unbelievers as sons of disobedience. This is because the root of all sin is unbelief, and unbelief is manifested in disobedience to the Word of God. As

Paul writes this to the children of God at Ephesus, he wants them to remember that they were once part of this great troop of unbelievers. He also wants them to remember that they now are what they are by the mercy and grace of God.

Therefore, he continues: "Among them we too all formerly lived in the lusts of our flesh, indulging the desires of the flesh and of the mind, and were by nature children of wrath, even as the rest" (Ephesians 2:3). All of us were at one time children of wrath, controlled by the lusts of our flesh, indulging the desires of our flesh and our mind. But, praise God, when He saved us the ruler of this world was cast out from his throne of dominion within us! "But God, being rich in mercy, because of His great love with which He loved us, even when we were dead in our transgressions, made us alive together with Christ (by grace you have been saved), and raised us up with Him, and seated us with Him in the heavenly places, in Christ Jesus" (Ephesians 2:4-6).

When God seated us in heavenly places, He placed us far above all rule, power, and authority of the enemy. Hallelujah!

17 Indwelt by the Spirit of God—the One who will never leave us nor forsake us even when we sin! For He is our Helper, the One who comes alongside us when we stray from the path of obedience, convicting us of sin, chastening us as children, giving no peace until we confess and forsake our sins.

How well this was brought home to me several years ago on a park bench in Asia. Jack, Jim and Betsy Bird, and I were in one of Asia's beautiful cities training Asians to do our Precept Bible studies. While the rest of the team went to do the training, I met with a young man who made an appointment after hearing me speak.

It was a very nervous young man who met me in our hotel lobby. Because he wanted to be alone, we walked to a nearby park to talk until dusk became dark. He told me that he was involved in homosexuality. From a broken home, rejected by his family when he left Buddhism, forced by his father to quit school because of his unrelenting commitment to Christ, he was lonely and vulnerable. In the army Sun became friends with another young man close to his age. The unthinkable happened—his friendship took a perverted turn and he found himself "in love" and sexually involved. Knowing what he was doing was wrong, he stopped talking to God. He felt so unclean and therefore unworthy to bow in the presence of his God.

Over the past two years Sun had often contemplated suicide, since death seemed the only escape from the snare of this sin. He had not planned to come to the seminar on spiritual warfare, until God had spoken to him, saying, "Son, I want you to get up and go to the seminar. I love you and I am going to speak to you. There is something I want to say to you."

As Sun told me this, he leaned back against the bench and tilted his face upward as if to keep the tears from spilling out of the pockets of his eyes. "I had to come but I could not sit at the front of the church. My pain . . . my shame was too great. When you told the story of your friend Joel, and of his problem with homosexuality and his wanting to die, that was me. And like Joel, I went home and that night called my friend to tell him that I was hurting God and could no longer continue our relationship. I took everything that had belonged to him, to us, and threw it away like you told us Joel did. But, Kay, it hurts so bad. And my friend is angry with God and says that if this is what Christians are like, he never wants to be a Christian."

As Sun and I talked, he asked me, "Can God ever be pleased with me again? Can I ever know joy again? I cannot bow in His presence because I am so ashamed. Will God help me?"

Yes, through the Helper, God set Sun free and restored to him the joy of his salvation.

18 When a child of God has been ensnared in sin, there must be a thorough cleansing by the washing of the water of the Word. Worldly sorrow leads to regret but not to freedom from the sin itself. Godly sorrow leads to repentance. "For the sorrow that is according to the will of God produces a repentance without regret, leading to salvation; but the sorrow of the world produces death" (2 Corinthians 7:10).

Unless we dealt thoroughly with Sun's sin, there would be no genuine release. Sun had to thoroughly understand the grievousness of his sin to the heart of God. His heart was so grieved over his friend that I was afraid he would be lured right back into the same snare. Sun had to see that God would have to deal with his friend. Even as the Spirit of God had dealt so specifically with Sun, He could do the same with his friend. And so we went through the Word looking at what God said about homosexuality.

Then I took Sun to David's song of confession and contrition, Psalm 51, written after David had committed adultery with Bathsheba and had Uriah, her husband, put on the front lines of battle where he was killed. "Hide Thy face from my sins, and blot out all my iniquities. Create in me a clean heart, O God, and renew a steadfast spirit within me" (51:9,10).

When we finished the psalm, I asked Sun how he thought God felt when he had loved another more than his Lord God. The conviction of the Spirit was so great that Sun broke into sobs. Tears coursed down his face and onto my shoulder as I held this young man who was the same age as our David.

As I looked to heaven, I could not help but thank God for sending me all the way to Asia and for covering our work with the intercessions of several thousands who had covenanted to co-labor with us through prayer. Because Sun could not share his sin with his friends, although they had begged him to tell them why he had lost the joy of his salvation, God sent me. And during the seminar on spiritual warfare, the Spirit of God gave me no rest until I followed His promptings and shared Joel's story of deliverance from homosexuality.

To Sun, my coming was the answer to his cry for deliverance before he destroyed his life through suicide. To me, Sun was another definite answer to our prayer at the seminar that God would speak in such a personal way to each one that they would think God had designed the seminar just for them.

As I sat on the bench listening to Sun talking to his Lord, confessing his love and sharing his grief over how he had failed His heavenly Father, I could not help but remember other countries where very similar instances had taken place. Two women had cried to God to send someone they could talk to who would understand. One needed to confess her sin and know if God could ever use her again. The other needed release from bitterness toward God because He had not stopped her father from sexually molesting her. God heard . . . and the Helper came to their side.

O Beloved, don't ever underestimate the love and forgiveness of God, the work of the Spirit, or the power of prayer.

19 Have you ever stopped, Beloved, to think of the magnificence of all that you have received in the gift of eternal life through the Lord Jesus Christ? Shouldn't this cause all the glitz and glitter of the world to pale to insignificance in the light of the glory of God's "indescribable gift" (2 Corinthians 9:15)?

Maybe things are not the way you would like them to be. Possibly there are disappointments in some earthly relationships. Maybe your financial situation is not what you expected, or perhaps you are all alone.

If you could reach back almost 2000 years, you would find 11 men who could relate to your loneliness. And as their situation brought great concern to the heart of Jesus, so your situation has the same effect on Him today.

Therefore let's turn again to John 16, and see what we can learn that you can apply to your own life, or share with others who are sorrowful.

Sorrow filled the hearts of our Lord's disciples because He was going to leave them. The hour of His glorification, the hour of His ultimate test of obedience, was at hand. What Jesus was about to do was going to win their salvation, but they couldn't understand it. Sorrow had deafened their ears, blurred their understanding. All they could see was *now*.

He was trying to tell them that if He went away, the indwelling Helper would through them continue the work of Christ. The One who would be their Teacher would guide them into all truth and glorify the Father. "A little while, and you will no longer behold Me; and again a little while, and you will see Me....Truly, truly, I say to you, that you will weep and lament, but the world will rejoice; you will be sorrowful, but your sorrow will be turned to joy" (John 16:16,20).

O Beloved, if you will take your eyes off your circumstances, if you will put them upon the love of God, if you will take God at His Word and in faith embrace what He says, your sorrow will be turned into joy. Step out in faith and watch what God does.

20 As you finished yesterday's devotional you may have thought, "But how is God going to meet my needs? How is He going to turn my sorrow into joy, when physical needs have brought my sorrow? How can spiritual words meet physical needs?" Those are valid questions. To answer them we need once again to go back to John 16 with Jesus and His disciples.

About three years before this incident, these men had left everything in order to give themselves without distraction to following Jesus Christ. And in the course of the past three years all their needs had been taken care of by their Lord.

But now that He was going away, what were they going to do? Jesus expected them to carry on the work He had begun. He promised them the Helper. But how would their physical needs be met? Also, He told them they would suffer persecution. How would their needs for love and companionship be met? Those were valid needs. John gives us the answer; over the next few days, we will see how it can apply to our lives.

"Therefore you, too, now have sorrow; but I will see you again, and your heart will rejoice, and no one takes your joy away from you. And in that day you will ask Me no question. Truly, truly, I say to you, if you shall ask the Father for anything, He will give it to you in My name. Until now you have asked for nothing in My name; ask, and you will receive, that your joy may be made full. These things I have spoken to you in figurative language; an hour is coming, when I will speak no more to you in figurative language, but will tell you plainly of the Father. In that day you will ask in My name; and I do not say to you that I will request the Father on your behalf; for the Father Himself loves you, because you have loved Me, and have believed that I came forth from the Father" (John 16:22-27).

Beloved, with every true child of God, sorrow will always give way to joy. This is your birthright because God is your Father, Jesus is your Savior, and the Holy Spirit is your in-residence Helper. In one form or another, sorrow is a very real part of life. And for those who do not know Jesus Christ, eternity will be filled with hell's sorrow.

But this is not your destiny as a child of God. If there is sorrow in your life, it will serve a purpose that will result in your personal good, because it will be used of God to make you more like Jesus. "God causes all things to work together for good to those who love God, to those who are called according to His purpose. For whom He foreknew, He also predestined to become conformed to the image of His Son" (Romans 8:28,29).

21 Do you realize that sorrow can so fill your heart that you cannot receive, let alone hear, anything that is good? Sorrow can so cloud the sun that you forget it is there.

The disciples were filled with sorrow because they were not hearing all that Jesus was telling them concerning His death, burial, and resurrection. They failed to remember the benefits it would bring to them personally. He had told them that when the grain of wheat fell into the ground and died, it would bring forth much fruit. But they could not get past losing the grain of wheat.

Jesus likened the brevity of their sorrow and the joy that would follow to a woman in labor. "Whenever a woman is in travail she has sorrow, because her hour has come; but when she gives birth to the child, she remembers the anguish no more, for joy that a child has been born into the world. Therefore you too now have sorrow; but I will see you again, and your heart will rejoice, and no one takes your joy away from you" (John 16:21,22).

If there is sorrow in your heart in any form, beloved friend, then take a few minutes and write in your notebook what is causing that sorrow. When you finish, ask the Lord to show you what Christlike quality He could work in your life through that particular sorrow.

For instance, maybe you are trying to reach out to one of your children who is not walking with the Lord. Maybe the child is bitter toward you for failing in some way, and there is a wall between you. What could God be working in your life to make you more Christlike? Maybe it is to increase your faith, that whatever your failure in the past God can use it to work together for good in the life of your child. Or maybe God wants to teach you how to love even those who reject you, as God loves those who reject Him. There are all sorts of lessons you could learn. As you go to the Lord, He will lead and speak to you if you will but give Him the opportunity.

"Answer me when I call, O God of my righteousness! Thou hast relieved me in my distress; be gracious to me and hear my prayer" (Psalm 4:1).

22 I am sure one cause of sorrow for the disciples was the fact that they had been leaning on Jesus for the supply of their physical needs. Now He was leaving them. What would they do? How would their needs be provided if they were to continue His work? Would they have to return to their former professions? In all probability these thoughts careened through their minds, screeching at every curve of a new question. What would life be like when Jesus was gone?

For some three years they had watched Jesus talk all things over with the Father. Repeatedly Jesus had said, "I do not ask this for My benefit" or "I do not say this for My benefit." Did the disciples learn by example that believing prayer in accord with the Word of God and in the name of Jesus Christ is the means by which God intends to meet His children's needs? Did they realize that although Jesus was leaving them, they still had the power and privilege of asking in His name? Did it occur to them that God would meet their needs through prayer, even as He had responded to the Son in prayer? Did they remember that Jesus had said: "And whatever you ask in My name, that will I do, that the Father may be glorified in the Son. If you ask Me anything in My name, I will do it" (John 14:13,14)?

Maybe in the sorrow of the moment they forgot. Yet, it was crucial that they remember! Therefore, in those few hours together, Jesus repeated what was theirs through prayer: the supply of all their needs. "Truly, truly, I say to you, if you shall ask the Father for anything, He will give it to you in My name. Until now you have asked for nothing in My name; ask, and you will receive, that your joy may be made full" (John 16:23,24). This same principle was later stated by James: "You do not have because you do not ask. You ask and do not receive, because you ask with wrong motives, so that you may spend it on your pleasures" (4:2,3).

O beloved believer, what Jesus said to His disciples, God says to you. You can know that if your need is legitimate, He will supply it. God has to because He stands by His Word to perform it. How He will do it I do not know. I only know you are to fulfill your part—to ask, in keeping with who Jesus is. Ask in faith, and don't quit until you have your answer.

23 Can you imagine God in all His omnipotence, His omniscience, His omnipresence, confined to the womb of a woman? Can you imagine God being born from a woman He created?

Can you imagine God learning to walk when He transcends time and space? Learning to talk when He is the eternal Word, the Logos, who was in the beginning with God? Can you imagine God growing in wisdom and in stature and in favor with God and man, being subject to human parents, when all authority in heaven and earth belongs to Him?

But God did become man! The concept truly boggles our minds when we stop to consider it. Why would He so humble Himself?

He came in human form so that you would have a merciful and faithful high priest who could be touched with the feelings of your infirmities—who could understand the pull and weakness of the flesh. And He came to die in your place, to set you free from the one who held the power of death, and to deliver you from the fear of death (Hebrews 2:14,15,17). Jesus took the sting of death so that you need not fear it, for if you believe in His substitutionary death at Calvary, you need never experience the second death.

Calvary is the ultimate expression of God's love—His only begotten Son offered up to redeem man. Jesus is God's Gift of gifts. You were born to live. And yet you would die, not only physically but eternally, if God had not had mercy upon you. God's Son was born for the express purpose of dying in your place, to bear your sins and pay their penalty, which is death.

And did He offer you this ultimate expression of His love when you were lovely and lovable? When you decided to get your life in shape, so you would be acceptable to God? Oh no, Beloved!

"But God demonstrates His own love toward us, in that while we were yet sinners, Christ died for us" (Romans 5:8). "In this is love, not that we loved God, but that He loved us and sent His Son to be the propitiation for our sins" (1 John 4:10). God so loved you that He gave His only begotten Son, so that you might not perish but have everlasting life (John 3:16).

"Supply my needs?" You may have echoed that question in your heart yesterday, trying to comprehend it. You may have wondered if He truly would meet them all. But as you think on what we have shared today, you see that He has given you life through His death. If God did not spare His own Son but gave Him up for us, surely He will freely give us all things (Romans 8:32).

Take a few moments and reflect on this incredible provision for your need. You were dead in your trespasses and sins, hopeless and without God in the world, separated from Christ, a stranger to the covenant, and excluded from the commonwealth of Israel (Ephesians 2:2,12). You could never save yourself, for you were under the fear of death and at Satan's mercy. When you were in this awful state, God made a way.

Bare your heart before your God today, remembering that He loved you enough to give His Son. And remember the Son loved you enough to die in your place. How can you not trust that every provision has been made for you? Ask in faith and in accordance with His will, and you will have the requests you make.

24

Yesterday one of the verses we considered together was Romans 8:32: "He who did not spare His own Son, but delivered Him up for us all, how will He not also with Him freely give us all things?"

Today let me suggest something which will cause your heart to be drawn into focus on Jesus and His great provision for you in an even deeper way.

Get *alone,* away from noise and other people. Then think about all that God has given you. Write it out. Then seeing each item as a personal gift from God, thank Him for it. You may want to even write Him a "thank you" letter and then tuck it in your Bible so you can read it from time to time. You'll be surprised what God will do. . . . He loves a grateful heart.

25 Can you imagine the excitement of finding an enormous, exquisitely wrapped package on your kitchen table with your name on it? At a loss to know what is in it, and yet anticipating that it has to be something very special because of its size and wrappings, you can hardly contain your anticipation.

The paper is so costly that you hate to tear it, and immediately you are in a quandary! Should you save the paper and delay seeing what is in the box, or should you quickly tear it off? And what about the beautiful satin ribbon? Should you carefully untie the knot or merely pull it until the stretched threads break?

Whatever you choose, the ultimate prize is in the box! Can you imagine opening the box and finding it totally empty? Not even a piece of tissue paper? No note, no card, no promise of something to come?

You can hear the thud as joy collapses on the floor of your heart, pounding its fists and crying, "But this is not what I expected! It looked so beautiful on the outside, so special, and it's nothing, absolutely nothing!"

If you do not develop your love relationship with God, if you do not spend concentrated time alone with Him on a regular basis, you will face this kind of emptiness and disappointment in your life. Don't focus so on the gifts you desire that you neglect the Giver Himself.

Why don't you spend time today reading John 17–20 and meditating on all that was entailed in sending the Son to earth about 2000 years ago. Ask God to give you a glimpse of the length, breadth, height, and depth of His love in sending Jesus, and then, Beloved, spend time in prayer, thanking Him for His indescribable gift (read Ephesians 3:14-21).

26 "What shall I render to the LORD for all His benefits toward me? I shall lift up the cup of salvation, and call upon the name of the LORD" (Psalm 116:12,13). I have been addressing you as if you were a true child of God. However, there is a possibility that you might think you are a Christian and yet be deceived.

As you read through the Epistles, you will find the authors repeatedly saying to their readers: "Don't be deceived," telling them that if their behavior is like that of the world, if there is no lasting change, then they never have known the Lord Jesus Christ in a personal way. Thus you need to "test yourselves to see if you are in the faith; examine yourselves! Or do you not recognize this about yourselves, that Jesus Christ is in you—unless indeed you fail the test?" (2 Corinthians 13:5).

In the light of this, and the urging of God's Spirit as I write, I must ask: "Are you saved? Do you have a changed life that testifies of the presence of the indwelling Spirit of God? Have you taken the cup of salvation?" Jesus drank the cup of your iniquity, becoming sin for you, taking your rightful death so that you might believe, take the cup of salvation, and become a partaker of His righteousness. Without righteousness no one will see God (Hebrews 12:14). And there is only one way to become righteous, and that is by believing on the Lord Jesus Christ (2 Corinthians 5:21).

To believe means to put your total trust in Jesus. To believe means embracing what the Bible says about Him—that He is God and that He is the only means of salvation. If you really believe in Him, you acknowledge His right to rule over your life. Jesus came to save you from your sins—not just from the penalty of sin, but from the power of sin to dominate your life.

To want to be saved means that you recognize your need to be set free from sin. The essence of sin is turning to your own way, doing your own thing, being your own god (Genesis 3:4,5; Isaiah 53:5,6; 1 Peter 2:24,25). The fruit of walking your own way is seen as sin manifests itself in a variety of ways: lying, cheating, immorality, greed, hypocrisy, pride, etc.

Since Jesus came to save us from our sins, then it is obvious that once a person is truly born again, there must be a change: "Therefore if any man is in Christ, he is a new creature; the old things passed away; behold, new things have come" (2 Corinthians 5:17). When you receive Christ, you literally become a new creation. You are identified with His death, burial, and resurrection. It is in this identification that you die to sin. "Therefore we have been buried with Him through baptism into death, in order that as Christ was raised from the dead through the glory of the Father, so we too might walk in newness of life. For if we have become united with Him in the likeness of His death, certainly we shall be also in the likeness of His resurrection, knowing this, that our old self was crucified with Him, that our body of sin might be done away with, that we should no longer be slaves to sin; for he who has died is freed from sin" (Romans 6:4-7).

Are you a new creature? Would you like to be?

27

Wouldn't it be the greatest of tragedies to celebrate Easter and Christmas year after year and never know the One you are celebrating? So many celebrate these days in a secular way. Yet they have been set aside to remember the birth and resurrection of the Lord Jesus Christ.

Can you imagine blindly going through the motions of Christianity and believing there was nothing more to it? Can you imagine fearing death or believing life ended with the grave? Can you imagine believing you would go to heaven simply because you are a pretty decent person? Can you imagine thinking this way and ending up in a very real hell?

A real hell with no chance of escape? A real hell that would someday surrender its prisoners to stand before God's great White Throne Judgment from where they would all be consigned forever to various degrees of judgment in the lake of fire?

O Beloved, do you have the fruit of a new life that bears witness to the fact that you are a new creation in Christ Jesus, indwelt not only by Christ Himself, but by the Holy Spirit, your resident Helper? Jesus said: "Not everyone who says to Me, 'Lord, Lord,' will enter the kingdom of heaven; but he who does the will of My Father who is in heaven. Many will say to Me on that day, 'Lord, Lord, did we not prophesy in Your name, and in Your name cast out demons, and in Your name perform many miracles?' And then I will declare to them, 'I never knew you; DEPART FROM ME, YOU WHO PRACTICE LAWLESSNESS.' Therefore everyone who hears these words of Mine, and acts upon them, may be compared to a wise man, who built his house upon the rock. And the rain descended, and the floods came, and the winds blew, and burst against that house; and yet it did not fall, for it had been founded upon the rock. And everyone who hears these words of Mine, and does not act upon them, will be like a foolish man, who built his house upon the sand. And the rain descended, and the floods came, and the winds blew, and burst against that house; and it fell, and great was its fall" (Matthew 7:21-27).

O Beloved, where do you stand? On the sand of your own misguided concept of Christianity or on the solid rock of the pure, unadulterated, unchangeable, eternal Word of God?

When you are His child, He roots you in His righteousness, puts His Spirit within you, and causes you to walk in His statutes, so that you are careful to observe His ordinances (Ezekiel 36:27). He will use you to convict the world of sin, of righteousness, and of judgment. And He will prepare you to face sorrow and persecution.

Examine yourself. Are you in the faith? Have you received God's gift—eternal life in Christ Jesus? What is the proof of His indwelling residence? Write out your answer in black and white. It will help.

28 Before you give yourself to the Lord Jesus Christ, it would be good for you to know what you can expect, once you become a child of God. From what you have already read this month, you realize that identification with the Lord Jesus Christ will mean suffering. "For to you it has been granted for Christ's sake, not only to believe in Him, but also to suffer for His sake" (Philippians 1:29). As Jesus said, "Blessed are those who have been persecuted for the sake of righteousness, for theirs is the kingdom of heaven. Blessed are you when men cast insults at you, and persecute you, and say all kinds of evil against you falsely, on account of Me. Rejoice, and be glad, for your reward in heaven is great, for so they persecuted the prophets who were before you" (Matthew 5:10-12).

You may be hated by the world, but you will be loved by God. When your faith is tested, you can exult in the hope of the glory of God, which is to live with Him forever and ever. "We also exult in our tribulations, knowing that tribulation brings about perseverance; and perseverance, proven character [character is not seen for what it really is until it's tested!]; and proven character, hope; and hope does not disappoint, because the love of God has been poured out within our hearts through the Holy Spirit who was given to us" (Romans 5:3-5).

It is the love within that becomes the proof of your salvation. In 1 John we read: "We know that we have passed out of death into life, because we love the brethren. He who does not love abides in death" (3:14). "By this the children of God and the children of the devil are obvious: anyone who does not practice righteousness is not of God, nor the one who does not love his brother" (3:10).

Love is one of the common attributes of those who

belong to God—love of God and love of others: "We love, because He first loved us. If someone says, 'I love God,' and hates his brother, he is a liar; for the one who does not love his brother whom he has seen, cannot love God whom he has not seen. And this commandment we have from Him, that the one who loves God should love his brother also. Whoever believes that Jesus is the Christ is born of God. . . . By this we know that we love the children of God, when we love God and observe His commandments. For this is the love of God, that we keep His commandments; and His commandments are not burdensome" (1 John 4:19–5:3).

If you love God, there will be obedience in your life. This is not to say that you will never displease God; however, disobedience will not be the habit of your life. Obedience to the Word of God confirms that the Holy Spirit has come to dwell in you.

And, because He is in you, you will not find His commandments heavy, stern, cruel, severe—that is what *burdensome* means. His "ordinances are good," they are our "counselors," and they are "exceedingly broad" (Psalm 119:39,24,96).

29

Have you ever been afraid that once you received the Lord Jesus Christ as your Savior you might later turn your back on Him? You may know of others who turned away and fear that you could do the same thing.

May I give you something to consider? I want you to see clearly for yourself that those who are genuinely born into God's family will never turn away. Those who profess Jesus Christ and then turn away from the faith, departing from what they once professed to be true, were never really born again.

It is possible to talk like a Christian, look like a Christian, and even for a while to walk like a Christian. But when the trial of your faith comes in the form of persecution, suffering, or the overwhelming "worries of the world, and the deceitfulness of riches, and the desires for other things"

(Mark 4:19) so that your life reveals its fruitlessness, you will know that you never had salvation.

Reality is not that you had salvation and lost it. The truth is that you thought you had it but never possessed the genuine thing. "They went out from us, but they were not really of us; for if they had been of us, they would have remained with us; but they went out, in order that it might be shown that they all are not of us" (1 John 2:19).

When you become a child of God by grace through faith, you enter into the New Covenant. And the promise of Jeremiah 31:33,34 is fulfilled: "I will put My law within them, and on their heart I will write it; and I will be their God, and they shall be My people. . . . For I will forgive their iniquity, and their sin I will remember no more." This passage is quoted in Hebrews 8:10-12 and 10:16,17, to show us its fulfillment in our lives through the offering of the body of Jesus Christ.

God goes on to promise: "I will make an everlasting covenant with them that I will not turn away from them, to do them good; and I will put the fear of Me in their hearts so that they will not turn away from Me" (Jeremiah 32:40). Isn't that wonderful! You fear for the weakness of your flesh, and you should be careful to walk in the Spirit so that you do not fulfill the lusts of your flesh. And yet you have His promises: "No temptation has overtaken you but such as is common to man; and God is faithful, who will not allow you to be tempted beyond what you are able, but with the temptation will provide the way of escape also, that you may be able to endure it" (1 Corinthians 10:13). "He Himself has said, 'I WILL NEVER DESERT YOU, NOR WILL I EVER FORSAKE YOU,' so that we confidently say, 'THE LORD IS MY HELPER, I WILL NOT BE AFRAID. WHAT SHALL MAN DO TO ME?' " (Hebrews 13:5,6). "My grace is sufficient for you" (2 Corinthians 12:9).

God's family is a forever family. "My sheep hear My voice, and I know them, and they follow Me; and I give eternal life to them, and they shall never perish; and no one shall snatch them out of My hand. My Father, who has given them to Me, is greater than all; and no one is able to snatch them out of the Father's hand" (John 10:27-29). Do you belong to His forever family?

30 Day after day I have left you with questions regarding your relationship with the Lord Jesus Christ. I know that it is not easy to allow the Lord to search your heart.

As I have been writing this for you, God has been dealing with me. Not regarding my salvation but regarding greater sensitivity to people. My heart is grieved because I could have been more sensitive and wise and gentle. There is much transformation that needs to take place . . . and as I look at it, it does not bring joy but sorrow. And yet I know that if I will listen to the Lord, if I will respond to His Fatherly chastening, then my sorrow will turn to joy. I say all of this, my friend, to exhort you to not shy away from allowing the Lord to search your heart.

Now then, how have you answered the questions which I have put before you day by day? Has God spoken to you, showing you truths which you need to take to heart? If so, you need to write out what He has shown you. As you go over what God has shown you, you need to agree with Him.

It is one thing to have something pointed out that needs to be changed, but it is another thing to receive what has been said as being true and therefore worthy of acceptance. To agree with God and to confess will bring forgiveness and total cleansing, even of those sins of which you are not aware. This is His promise in 1 John 1:9: "If we confess our sins, He is faithful and righteous to forgive us our sins and to cleanse us from all unrighteousness."

Because I am such a perfectionist, it is hard for me to deal with failure. I want so badly to go back and live the situation over again, this time doing what is right. But I can't. The opportunity is gone.

Then I have two options about what to do with my failure. I can rehearse it over and over again and be overwhelmed. Or I can confess it, trust God to cleanse me, and go forward, believing God will ultimately use it for good.

Even when we sin and fall short, it is a matter of believing that God forgives, cleanses, and uses it for our good. The Christian life is simply lived by faith, taking God at His word in every situation.

What if God has shown you that you are not yet His child and that you need to be born again of His Spirit? Then you need to tell God that you will repent and allow Him full control of your life.

Tell God that you, in faith, believe that Jesus died as your substitute, paying for your sins in full, and that you believe God honored His death and sacrifice by raising Jesus from the dead, and that you want to receive the living Lord Jesus Christ as your personal Savior. Then thank God in faith for the gift of eternal life.

Welcome to the family! I would love to hear from you if you received Christ this month. If you have known the Lord and are walking with Him, pray for those who have come to Him, asking God to establish them in His Word. Pray also that their personal relationship with Him will grow deeper daily.

31 If you accepted Jesus yesterday, today you begin a new life! If you know Him and are walking with Him, what I have to say today can still be pertinent, if you are willing to take a spiritual inventory.

It is good to always keep before you the reality of Ephesians 5:15,16: "Therefore be careful how you walk, not as unwise men, but as wise, making the most of your time, because the days are evil." You are a steward of your time, accountable to God for what you do with your days. In the light of this, may I suggest that you spend time actively waiting before the Lord for His direction.

Make a list of your spiritual needs—is your need to know God's Word better? Then how about a disciplined Bible study like *Precept Upon Precept, In & Out Bible Studies,* International Inductive Study Series, or *Lord* series. You may want to use the *The International Inductive Study Bible* and begin a systematic study through the whole Bible. For more information on any of these study materials, or to see if there's a class in your area, write: Precept Ministries, P.O. Box 182218, Chattanooga, TN 37422. Be sure to indicate the specific information you want. Also you may find these books in your local Christian bookstore.

Do you need help for your prayer life? There are many good books on the market. If you want to do an effective study that will teach you how to pray, you might want to buy *Lord, Teach Me to Pray in 28 Days* (Harvest House Publishers).

Do you need help with your quiet time? I also have a practical little book on how to have an effective time with your Lord, *A Quiet Time Alone with God.*

Maybe you need a fresh start—a cleansing, a pruning of the dead wood which is keeping you from bearing fruit. Then you might want to get a copy of *Cleansing & Filling*. If all this sounds like a commercial, it's not. I just know that these books have proven effective in helping so many.

What are your goals? List them and take them before the Lord. Are they His goals for you? If so, put an A.U.G.—approved unto God—next to each one that meets His approval.

Once God shows you your spiritual needs, and you have set His approved goals, you need to set some priorities.

Plan your days. When are you going to do your housework or the work by which you earn a living? When are you going to have your quiet time? When are you going to do your Bible study?

Plan your week. Get yourself a calendar and write in your weekly Bible study time and other spiritual activities. Plan all other appointments around these.

Plan your year. Vacations? Christian conferences? Training seminars? Workshops? Retreats? Church activities?

Plan your days. Redeem the time so that you are ready for persecution, prepared to walk through sorrow in a way that will honor and glorify your Savior, your Friend.

September

"Lord, Teach Me to Glorify You"

1 My beloved friend, have you ever found yourself arrested by the truth of our Lord's present ministry on your behalf?

Almost 2000 years ago, Jesus finished everything that was necessary for you individually to have forgiveness of sins and to gain the inheritance of eternal life. Your salvation was made possible through His death, burial, and resurrection on your behalf.

Since Jesus' redemptive work is complete, you may wonder what His work is now. He has one mission, one ministry: He sits at the right hand of the Father interceding on your behalf.

Jesus, the Sovereign Lord of all creation, has you on His heart night and day. He ever lives to make intercession for you—if you are His child. "He is able to save forever those who draw near to God through Him, since He always lives to make intercession for them" (Hebrews 7:25). This reality ought to prostrate us in inexpressible gratitude.

Knowing your Lord's ministry on your behalf, you probably wonder, "What is His prayer for me?" Well, my friend, I think you can know much about His current intercession on your behalf.

Just before our Lord made His final trip to the Garden of Gethsemane on His way to Calvary, He stopped and prayed for you and me in the hearing of His disciples. John recorded that prayer for us in chapter 17 of his Gospel, and it's that chapter that we are going to study this month.

During our time together, you are not only going to see Jesus' heart for you, but I believe you will see the glory of God in a new dimension. Once you understand the glory of God, then you will see how you can glorify Him on earth, by accomplishing the work that God has specifically given you to do. May I suggest that you read John 17 prayerfully, asking the Lord to open the eyes of your understanding. When you finish, write a prayer of response.

2 As we look at our Lord's prayer for His own, my prayer for you, Beloved, is that the glory of the Lord will pass by you in such a way that the passion of your life becomes a deep desire to let others see His glory as you have seen it.

There are three segments to our Lord's prayer in John 17. In verses 1-5 Jesus prays for Himself. In verses 6-19 Jesus prays for the 11 apostles. In verses 20-26 Jesus prays for all believers. Yet, even when Jesus prays for the 11, in verses 6-19, He also prays for all of us: "I do not ask in behalf of these alone, but for those also who believe in Me through their word" (17:20).

When Jesus prays for Himself, He uses two imperatives or commands. The first imperative is "Glorify Thy Son" (17:1). Jesus is asking for glorification of His position as the Son of God and His ministry to the world. Later on, we will talk about the word *glory* and what it means to glorify the Father and the Son. The second imperative in this first segment is "Glorify Thou Me together with Thyself, Father, with the glory which I had with Thee before the world was" (17:5).

The second segment of our Lord's prayer contains two imperatives on behalf of the 11. The first is found in verse 11: "Holy Father, keep them in Thy name." The second is found in verse 17: "Sanctify them in the truth; Thy word is truth."

The final segment contains two requests that our Lord makes on our behalf. First, Jesus prays, "I do not ask in behalf of these alone, but for those also who believe in Me through their word; that they may all be one; even as Thou, Father, art in Me, and I in Thee, that they also may be in Us; that the world may believe that Thou didst send Me" (17:20,21). The second request is given in the form of a desire for you and me: "Father, I desire that they also, whom Thou hast given Me, be with Me where I am, in order that they may behold My glory, which Thou hast given Me" (17:24).

Take a few minutes to meditate upon our Lord's requests and what they mean. We'll go deeper tomorrow.

3 Our Lord's prayer in John 17 centers around two relationships: Jesus' relationship with the Father and the relationship He wants you and me to have with Them. The end purpose of it all is the glory of God and the joy of believers. As you grasp the realities of this prayer, you will find your walk with the Lord taking on a new and deeper sense of abiding joy, even though things around you may be difficult.

Jesus longs for you to fully experience joy. He prayed aloud to the Father in the hearing of the 11, "But now I come to Thee; and these things I speak in the world, that they may have My joy made full in themselves" (17:13).

How wonderful it must have been to hear Jesus pray for them, especially after He had just told them of the tribulation that awaited them! Remember our Lord's prayer follows on the very heels of His Upper Room discourse which began in John 13 and continued as they left that room to walk through Jerusalem and down across the Kidron Valley to the Garden of Gethsemane. That discourse ended somewhere along that route with these words: "Behold, an hour is coming, and has already come, for you to be scattered, each to his own home, and to leave Me alone; and yet I am not alone, because the Father is with Me. These things I have spoken to you, that in Me you may have peace. In the world you have tribulation, but take courage; I have overcome the world" (John 16:32,33).

If anything could give the disciples courage, it would be to remember the things He had just said in the light of this prayer. The image of Jesus lifting up His eyes to heaven and praying in order that their joy might be full would forever be indelibly etched on their minds.

D.A. Carson, in his stirring commentary on Jesus' farewell discourse and prayer, writes: "So we are to understand that this final prayer is the capstone to the instruction that has preceded it. Moreover, Jesus has just talked about his triumph, his victory over the world; and the same triumph is reflected in this prayer. Far from being gloomy and morose, the prayer adopts a long-range view which expects ultimate victory even while presupposing conflict."[1]

Read your Lord's prayer aloud, Beloved, until it is forever etched on the tablet of your heart. To do so will give you joyful assurance.

4

Glory! Do you comprehend the fact that you were created for His glory? When we sing, "Glorify Thy name, glorify Thy name in all the earth," can you conceive how His name would be glorified?

As we read John 17, it is apparent that our Lord's entire prayer was centered around the glory of the Lord. To truly understand our Lord's prayer, we must understand the glory of the Lord. We must also understand how God would glorify the Son so that the Son might glorify the Father.

In order to grasp what glorifying God could entail, let's begin in the Old Testament and move through to the New. Ask your Teacher, the Holy Spirit, to explain to you all things that pertain to life and godliness.

The Old Testament word for glory is *kābōd,* which comes from a root word meaning "heavy or weighty." Therefore, a weighty person was impressive, worthy of respect or honor.

Kābōd means "glory, glorious, honor, honorable" and is centered around a person's feats or achievements. Therefore, to give honor or glory to someone is to say that he or she is worthy of respect, attention, and obedience. When we stop to consider the feats or achievements of God, who is worthy of more honor or respect? Who should be obeyed more than God?

In 1 Corinthians 6:19,20, God reminds us: "Do you not know that your body is a temple of the Holy Spirit who is in you, whom you have from God, and that you are not your own? For you have been bought with a price: therefore glorify God in your body." From what we have seen today, my friend, can you see how you can glorify God in your body? Write your insights in your notebook and then turn them into a prayer of consecration.

5 We first become acquainted with God's glory in the Old Testament, in the unveiling of His person and character. In Exodus 33:18-23 we see the glory of God linked with His self-revelation.

To really appreciate this passage, let's take a few minutes to consider its context. God told Moses to go with the children of Israel into the land of Canaan. God would send His angel before them, but He was not going to go with them: "lest I destroy you on the way," for the Israelites were an obstinate people (33:3).

The children of Israel had not glorified the Lord by trusting and obeying Him. Moses had stayed on Mount Sinai far too long, and they were tired of waiting! They seduced Aaron to make a golden calf for them to worship, and declared that the calf had delivered them from Egypt.

Can you imagine abandoning the omniscient, omnipresent, omnipotent, sovereign God for a speechless, immovable, molten calf made by their own hands? It seems ridiculous, doesn't it? And yet I see people doing this every day. I just received a call telling me that the husband of a special friend has asked her for a divorce. I have seen his problem coming for a long time. This man is so busy making lots of money and seeking to climb the ladder of prestige that he doesn't have time for the God he professes to know. He walked into the snare of riches and fell into a bed of sexual lust. He has forgotten God and turned to a golden calf. But what he is now worshiping will not help him when his day of trouble comes. And it will come.

God told Moses to go on without Him. But God also said that Moses had found favor in His sight. So Moses clung to the word of God with a holy boldness: " 'If I have found favor in Thy sight, let me know Thy ways, that I may know Thee, so that I may find favor in Thy sight. Consider too, that this nation is Thy people.' And He said, 'My presence shall go with you, and I will give you rest.' Then he said to Him, 'If Thy presence does not go with us, do not lead us up from here. For how then can it be known that I have found favor in Thy sight, I and Thy people? Is it not by Thy going with us, so that we, I and Thy people, may be distinguished from all the other people who are upon the face of the earth?' " (Exodus 33:13-16)

Moses knew that without God, it was useless. I wonder if we are as wise. Moses wanted two things: for God to go with them and for God to show him His glory. What do you want from God, my friend? Don't seek it from a golden calf!

6 When Moses said to God, "I pray Thee, show me Thy glory!" God responded, " 'I Myself will make all My goodness pass before you, and will proclaim the name of the LORD before you; and I will be gracious to whom I will be gracious, and will show compassion on whom I will show compassion.' But He said, 'You cannot see My face, for no man can see Me and live!' Then the LORD said, 'Behold, there is a place by Me, and you shall stand there on the rock; and it will come about, while My glory is passing by, that I will put you in the cleft of the rock and cover you with My hand until I have passed by. Then I will take My hand away and

you shall see My back, but My face shall not be seen' " (Exodus 33:18-23).

How clear it is in this passage that the glory of God is the unveiling of His person and His character. Who God is can be seen in His sovereign right to show graciousness and compassion. God desired to reveal Himself to Moses and to have compassion on the children of Israel by going with them. God chose to forgive, to restrain His righteous wrath with His loving compassion. And He chose to show Moses His glory by causing His person to pass by Moses.

In Psalm 24, God is referred to as the King of glory: "Lift up your heads, O gates, and be lifted up, O ancient doors, that the King of glory may come in! Who is the King of glory? The LORD strong and mighty, the LORD mighty in battle. Lift up your heads, O gates, and lift them up, O ancient doors, that the King of glory may come in! Who is this King of glory? The LORD of hosts, He is the King of glory" (Psalm 24:7-10).

Throughout the Old Testament, God's glory is seen also in His works, His ways with mankind. Watch how the Lord deals with you, my friend, and you will see His glory. In Psalm 79:9 we read: "Help us, O God of our salvation, for the glory of Thy name; and deliver us, and forgive our sins, for Thy name's sake." And that is exactly what God did when He glorified the Son, as Jesus asked Him to do in John 17. It was in the glorification of the Son that you received forgiveness of your sins and the gift of eternal life.

"Shout joyfully to God. . . . Sing the glory of His name; make His praise glorious." How? How can you make God's praise glorious? By praising Him for who He is and what He has done. "Say to God, 'How awesome are Thy works!'" (Psalm 66:1-3). Try it, Beloved, and you will find yourself glorifying the Lord.

7

The children of Israel saw the glory of God's presence in a pillar of cloud by day and in a pillar of fire by night. What we call the "Shekinah glory" hovered over the Ark of the Covenant in the tent or tabernacle of meeting. When the tabernacle was completed, God told them that He would meet with them there, thus making it a "tent of meeting."

"And I will meet there with the sons of Israel, and it shall be consecrated by My glory. And I will consecrate the tent of meeting and the altar; I will also consecrate Aaron and his sons to minister as priests to Me. And I will dwell among the sons of Israel and will be their God. And they shall know that I am the LORD their God who brought them out of the land of Egypt, that I might dwell among them; I am the LORD their God" (Exodus 29:43-46).

"Then the cloud covered the tent of meeting, and the glory of the LORD filled the tabernacle. And Moses was not able to enter the tent of meeting because the cloud had settled on it, and the glory of the LORD filled the tabernacle. And throughout all their journeys whenever the cloud was taken up from over the tabernacle, the sons of Israel would set out; but if the cloud was not taken up, then they did not set out until the day when it was taken up. For throughout all their journeys, the cloud of the LORD was on the tabernacle by day, and there was fire in it by night, in the sight of all the house of Israel" (Exodus 40:34-38).

What would it be like to walk out of your home and look up and see the Shekinah glory and know that God was with you? Does it make you long for a pillar of fire by night and a pillar of cloud during the day to show you the way to go, to indicate where to stop and when to leave?

O Beloved, you have something so much better than the revelation of God's glory given to the Israelites! If you have glorified Jesus by believing and receiving God's glorification of His Son, you have the Holy Spirit within.

Jesus came to reveal the fullness of God's glory, to manifest the Father: "And the Word became flesh, and dwelt among us, and we beheld His glory, glory as of the only begotten from the Father, full of grace and truth" (John 1:14). Jesus was "the radiance of His glory" (Hebrews 1:3). His one purpose on earth was to glorify God by finishing the work

God gave Him to do—and that work was seen in the ultimate glorification of God when Jesus became obedient unto death. Think on these things, Beloved.

8 How did Jesus' death glorify the Father? Let's look again at the Greek word for *glory. Doxa* is "an opinion, estimate," and therefore is seen in honor which results from a good opinion.

In John 17, Jesus prayed, "I glorified Thee on the earth, having accomplished the work which Thou hast given Me to do" (17:4). Can you see how obedience is inextricably linked with glorifying God? If you and I are going to give the world a proper opinion or estimate of God, then we must do what He says, no matter the cost. The cost for Jesus was death by crucifixion, becoming our sin-bearer, shedding His blood for the sins of mankind.

In the New Testament we see *doxa* used of the nature and acts of God in self-revelation. In the hour of Jesus' glorification, He glorified the Father by dying on the cross and the Father glorified the Son by accepting that sacrifice and raising Jesus from the dead. Several times in the Gospel of John, Jesus refers to the hour of His death as the hour in which the Son of Man is glorified. In John 12:23,27,28 we read: "And Jesus answered them, saying, 'The hour has come for the Son of Man to be glorified.... Now My soul has become troubled; and what shall I say, "Father, save Me from this hour"? But for this purpose I came to this hour. Father, glorify Thy name.' There came therefore a voice out of heaven: 'I have both glorified it, and will glorify it again.' "

God the Father would be glorified by showing His great love in giving His only begotten Son as a sacrifice for our sins. And when God gave a proper opinion or estimate of the efficacy of Jesus' sacrifice by raising Him from the dead, the Son was glorified.

Every time you think "glory," think "opinion or estimate or honor." You will come to see how you either glorify the Lord or fail to give Him the glory due His name.

Remember, Beloved, how the Father and the Son honored One another.

9 Yesterday we saw that *doxa* was used for the nature and acts of God in self-revelation. *Doxa* is also used in the New Testament for the character and ways of God exhibited through believers. In John 15:8 we read: "By this is My Father glorified, that you bear much fruit, and so prove to be My disciples." The fruit of our lives glorifies God and causes people to have a correct opinion or estimate of who He is.

Recently I wrote to a friend who is going through intense physical suffering. In the trauma she is enduring, there is no bitterness, no anger toward God, no questioning of the truths she knows from the Word of God. Her life is bearing the fruit of Christlikeness. I see her obeying God when it seems beyond difficult. And God is glorified!

What an impact our lives will have if we esteem His grace to be sufficient, His Word to be true, His character. To respond in this way in every situation is truly to glorify Him. It gives those watching a true and perfect opinion of our God and the validity of Christianity.

O Beloved, may you jealously guard His glory.

10 Do you fear death, Beloved? I can understand if you do. It can be an entrance into the realm of the unknown for many, and the unknown brings anxiety. If you've never thought of death as an entrance into the glory of God, then fear is understandable. However, these next several days can be used of God to remove any fear and to give you a sense of joyful anticipation.

All of that brings us to the third way *doxa* is used in the New Testament, to refer to the state of blessedness into which we enter after we leave this earthly body behind.

It is "in glory," my friend, that you will see the Father as He is, and behold the splendor of the Trinity—Father, Son, and Holy Spirit. It is there, in heaven, where God is perfectly honored and worshiped continually. Jesus desired that we would be with Him there: "Father, I desire that they also, whom Thou hast given Me, be with Me where I am, in order that they may behold My glory, which Thou hast given Me" (John 17:24).

Glory was the hope of the early, suffering church. They did not have ready access to written books, so often they memorized doctrinal hymns or statements of faith to remind them of biblical truths. The statement in 1 Timothy 3:16 is believed to be one of these: "And by common confession great is the mystery of godliness: He who was revealed in the flesh, was vindicated in the Spirit, beheld by angels, proclaimed among the nations, believed on in the world, taken up in glory."

Everything that speaks of heaven is associated with glory. When Stephen was being reviled by irate, unbelieving Jews, "he gazed intently into heaven and saw the glory of God, and Jesus standing at the right hand of God" (Acts 7:55). Glory is the destiny of every child of God: "Whom He predestined, these He also called; and whom He called, these He also justified; and whom He justified, these He also glorified. . . . We suffer with Him in order that we may also be glorified with Him. For I consider that the sufferings of this present time are not worthy to be compared with the glory that is to be revealed to us" (Romans 8:30,17,18).

Peter gives us this blessed hope of glory: "And after you have suffered for a little, the God of all grace, who called you to His eternal glory in Christ, will Himself perfect, confirm, strengthen and establish you" (1 Peter 5:10). O Beloved, fear not! It is "glory far beyond all comparison" (2 Corinthians 4:17).

11 As I was writing about glory I thought of my friend Diane, and her precious husband, Howard, and of their children, Michael and Tracie. What a family! If you're like me, you like stories, especially ones that strengthen your faith. You'll need a handkerchief because this story is emotional, but you'll be thrilled with the way the glory of God is revealed.

I want to share from a letter Diane wrote in 1985:

> This letter is far easier for me to write than it will be for you to read. Perhaps to some of you it will seem a strange way to describe my situation, but the fact is, I am going to a very special wedding.
>
> We have all heard of the wedding feast that awaits the Bride of Christ in heaven. Only recently, as a friend introduced me to a contemporary record entitled *For the Bride,* by John Michael Talbot and the London Philharmonic, did I envision so clearly that wonderful entrance of the Bride of Christ into His presence.
>
> Now to what brings me to share this with you. Yesterday I sat in a doctor's office listening to his kindly apologetic description of my chest X rays. As some of you know, I have been experiencing an almost 24-hour-a-day ear and head pain since July, with no one able to agree on the exact cause and with one ailment upon another before that.
>
> However, this doctor concentrated on the fact that my lungs both show tumors which have originated at some other source, perhaps under an also deteriorating eighth rib. The pain in my ear and head may well be another bone area to which the problem has spread. It sounds very gruesome, I know.
>
> After seeing Dr. Kendall on that gloomy, rainy Tuesday, I was suddenly filled with excitement at the realization that I was that Bride about to experience the reality of being ushered into the heavenlies, with Jesus Christ Himself awaiting to embrace me with a love beyond anything I have ever known.

That is glory!

12 I know that you have probably looked to see if I am going to continue Diane's story, and I am, so read on, Beloved!

What I am saying may be hard to grasp for those of you who have not yet had the experience of realizing that Jesus Christ is truly God, come to the earth in human body, that He might move freely about to carry out His Father's perfect plan to give us humans the only way back to God, the Father.

There was a time in my teens when I just could not see why Jesus' death was any more restoring than any other person who died for another. I did not realize Jesus was God, choosing to leave heaven, to suffer, to be tested as any one of us, with one exception: He never gave in to temptation, not once, so His perfect life for my imperfect one paid it all. In 1960 I accepted His costly death to save me, and I repented of running my own life and gave Him lordship over me.

This year as my Bible verse I chose Philippians 3:10, "That I may know Him, and the power of His resurrection and the fellowship of His sufferings, being conformed to His death." Primarily, my desire was to know Him more intimately. I never dreamed the power that raised Him back to heaven would lift me so powerfully so soon. But, honestly, does "no tears, no pain, no sorrow" sound so bad? That is what is awaiting me, and even the best of life here does not compare to that. . . .

I only know right now that I should be shaking with fear, as no one really wants to suffer physical pain, but instead I am planning my wedding day—dress, music, and maybe a rose or two.

I don't know when this celebration will take place, three months or three years, but I hope that you who feel led and are able will join my family for that day. Pray for my children that they will let the loss of the presence of a mother draw them into the gain of a total walking with Jesus and His perfect love and protection.

Perhaps I should also ask your prayers for me that even in this advanced situation I will be open and not closed if it would be the Father's will to heal me.

I hope I have communicated not only the "hard" things that you need to be informed of, but also the sweet grace the Bridegroom has comforted and enthused me with at this possible transitional time.

O Beloved, have you glorified Jesus by receiving Him as your Lord and Savior?

13 As you read Diane's letter, was your fear of death lessened? Didn't her faith cause you to look beyond death's veil to the glory that beckoned her home? It was in His obedience that Jesus took the sting out of death so that Diane, and you and I, need not fear death; for He took our hell for us by paying for our sin.

But what about Howard, Diane's husband, and Michael and Tracie? Would they glorify God? Let me share parts of Howard's letter that came after Diane's home-going. Then you can decide for yourself if God was glorified or not.

> Most of you have received news of Diane going home to be with our Lord. The children and I would like to express our gratitude and thanksgiving for all your gracious acts, your prayers, and your demonstrations of love to Diane and to us. We are thankful and praise our Lord for moving each of you to do so. It would seem appropriate also to tell those of you who don't know the details of Diane's last days and of God's gracious loving care over her.
>
> Actually the final stages of the long but undiagnosed illness (probably 20 years) showed itself at the beginning of last July. Since then it has been a constant series of trips to doctors, specialists, tests, etc. . . . During Thanksgiving week, the tragic news was given. Diane had cancer, and it was terminal. Tests continued and finally the origin was discovered. Diane had cancer in her right kidney, and probably also in the left one as well.
>
> The disease had already attacked the lungs, was into her ribs and spinal column, and in the base of her skull. There were indications that it had spread even far beyond that. There was no point in putting her through any more

> discomfort. When it became obvious that treatments were seemingly ineffective, we decided to bring Diane home. On February 2, I hired a flying ambulance and we went to pick her up. On the entire return flight, we never had a single "bump" of turbulence. Her nurse sat behind me and sang hymns to her while I held her hand. We had an ambulance waiting for our return. It was less than four hours from bed to bed. . . . Diane's last week was uncomfortable for her, but apparently not extremely so. She never had to have any of the high-powered pain medications. . . .

How does one endure watching a loved one suffer? By God's grace. Why should one appropriate God's grace? For God's glory!

14 There is more to Howard's letter, and I want to share it with you because I feel that it might be used to rescue someone from the dark pit of bitterness and raise them to the pinnacle of worship.

> Her last words to me were spoken on Wednesday, February 5, after I did some little thing for her and assured her of my love. Her words, hardly audible as she breathed them out, were that she loved me, too. From then on she rested peacefully and I scarcely left her bedside. At 5:59 A.M., February 9 (Sunday), as I held her in my arms, she departed from her mortal body and went to be with our Lord.
>
> How fitting that a child of the light, a child of the morning, went to be with her Lord in the beginning of morning, and on the morning upon which she worshipped. About three or four minutes later, a bird began to sing—a songbird heralding the beginning of the new life of the day; a fitting tribute to her presence with our Lord.
>
> We had sixteen and one-half years of marriage. . . . While the enemy of our souls was using the constant sickness to rob us of much of the happiness that could have been ours, he was now soundly defeated. Diane had

come to a realization of how much she was loved, and now was beyond all the powers of evil, resting in the glory and peace of our Lord. She was awaiting that great morning when we who are in Jesus Christ shall be assembled together to forever enjoy the faultless presence of each other and be centered in God's eternal and perfect love.

Those of us who loved her will sorely miss her, yet will rejoice in knowing the rich, perfect fulfillment that is hers. I, her husband, count it a privilege and rejoice in whatever I might have done right in our years together to make her life richer, either humanly or spiritually, and the children share the same sentiments.

It is our hope and prayer that you will accept our gratitude for all you have done, and that each of you, as individuals and as families, may also be gathered together with us in that great reunion around and with our Messiah, our Lord and Savior, Jesus Christ.

15 *Glory* is also used in the New Testament to describe brightness or splendor. There is a supernatural glory or splendor as seen in Revelation 18:1: "After these things I saw another angel coming down from heaven, having great authority, and the earth was illumined with his glory." In Revelation 21:23 we read of the brilliance or splendor of God illuminating the New Jerusalem: "And the city has no need of the sun or of the moon to shine upon it, for the glory of God has illumined it, and its lamp is the Lamb."

There is also a natural glory, as of the heavenly bodies: "There is one glory of the sun, and another glory of the moon, and another glory of the stars; for star differs from star in glory" (1 Corinthians 15:41).

And, finally, there is man's glory: his reputation, praise, honor or wealth, human brightness or splendor. We read in Revelation 21 of the glory people bring into the holy city: "And the nations shall walk by its light, and the kings of the earth shall bring their glory into it. And in the daytime (for there shall be no night there) its gates shall never be closed; and they shall bring the glory and the honor of the nations into it" (21:24-26).

As you study the New Testament you will discover that there are basically three expressions of divine glory. The first of these visible expressions is seen in the person of Jesus Christ when He came to earth. Let me clarify that not everyone sees Jesus as a visible expression of the glory of God because this truth is recognized only with the eyes of faith. To some people, Jesus was never more than Joseph the carpenter's son. To others, Jesus is nothing more than a great man who once walked the face of this earth, an ordinary man. Jesus as God's expression of divine glory is recognized only by the eyes of faith.

Take a few minutes and read John 1:14-18 again. By faith you will behold the glory of the Father in the Son.

16 What is the second way in which you and I see an expression of divine glory? By beholding one another. Didn't you see this truth as you read of Diane's death and Howard's response? Like them, you and I are admonished to glorify God in our bodies. Peter tells us we are to be full of glory. When we exercise our spiritual gifts, God is glorified (1 Peter 4:11). Can you imagine the impact we could make on the kingdom of God if we lived in a conscious awareness that we are vessels to contain and reflect the glory of the Lord? "But we all, with unveiled face beholding as in a mirror the glory of the Lord, are being transformed into the same image from glory to glory, just as from the Lord, the Spirit" (2 Corinthians 3:18). Thus, "we have this treasure in earthen vessels, that the surpassing greatness of the power may be of God and not from ourselves" (2 Corinthians 4:7).

O Beloved, never forget that you are a vessel to contain and proclaim His glory. Many people forget what Jesus reminded us to pray: "For Thine is the kingdom, and the power, and the glory, forever. Amen" (Matthew 6:13). The kingdom, the power, and the glory belong to God alone.

We now come to the third expression of divine glory, one that is yet to take place. It is the unveiling of His glory at His appearing: "For after all it is only just for God to repay with affliction those who afflict you, and to give relief to you who are afflicted and to us as well when the Lord Jesus shall be revealed from heaven with His mighty angels in flaming fire, dealing out retribution to those who do not know God and to those who do not obey the gospel of our Lord Jesus. And these will pay the penalty of eternal destruction, away from the presence of the Lord and from the glory of His power, when He comes to be glorified in His saints on that day, and to be marveled at among all who have believed" (2 Thessalonians 1:6-10).

"And then the sign of the Son of Man will appear in the sky, and then all the tribes of the earth will mourn, and they will see the SON OF MAN COMING ON THE CLOUDS OF THE SKY with power and great glory" (Matthew 24:30). "But when the Son of Man comes in His glory, and all the angels with Him, then He will sit on His glorious throne" (Matthew 25:31).

What glory that shall be! Are you ready for it? If so, you are giving Jesus the glory due His name. You are honoring Him as God, esteeming Him above everyone else.

17

The world has exchanged the glory of God for idols, for the deceptions of Satan's kingdom. That is not surprising, for "the god of this world has blinded the minds of the unbelieving, that they might not see the light of the gospel of the glory of Christ, who is the image of God" (2 Corinthians 4:4).

But what about the church? Are we like Demas of Paul's day? Paul wrote to Timothy, his son-in-the-faith, "Make every effort to come to me soon; for Demas, having loved this present world, has deserted me and gone to Thessalonica" (2 Timothy 4:9,10).

Paul was in prison because he lived for God's glory, not his own. If Paul had any desire to live for his own glory, he was given an opportunity to do so in Lystra when he healed a lame man: "And when the multitudes saw what Paul had done, they raised their voice, saying in the Lycaonian language, 'The gods have become like men and have come down to us.' And they began calling Barnabas, Zeus, and Paul, Hermes, because he was the chief speaker. And the priest of Zeus, whose temple was just outside the city, brought oxen and garlands to the gates, and wanted to offer sacrifice with the crowds. But when the apostles, Barnabas and Paul, heard of it, they tore their robes and rushed out into the crowd, crying out and saying, 'Men, why are you doing these things? We are also men of the same nature as you, and preach the gospel to you in order that you should turn from these vain things to a living God, WHO MADE THE HEAVEN AND THE EARTH AND THE SEA, AND ALL THAT IS IN THEM' " (Acts 14:11-15).

Paul knew it well and we need to remember it: God does not share His glory. Earlier in the book of Acts we see what happened when Herod did not remember it: "Herod, having put on his royal apparel, took his seat on the rostrum and began delivering an address to them. And the people kept crying out, 'The voice of a god and not of a man!' And immediately an angel of the Lord struck him because he did not give God the glory, and he was eaten by worms and died" (Acts 12:21-23).

Herod died because he took God's glory for himself. In contrast, Paul loved and served God in an incredibly effective ministry, bringing forth an eternal harvest because he remembered he was but a man. Paul lived in the light of what we must each remember: "I am the LORD, that is My name; I will not give My glory to another, nor My praise to graven images" (Isaiah 42:8).

Whose glory are you serving?

18 O Beloved, if you want to know fulfillment, you must accomplish that for which you were created. To do anything less will leave you with an incredible vacuum. You will always feel that there has to be something more to life than what you have attained, and you will never fill that insatiable void until you bow before God and acknowledge that you were created for His pleasure, His glory, and then live accordingly.

In Revelation 4:11 we read: "Thou art worthy, O Lord, to receive glory and honour and power: for thou hast created all things, and for thy pleasure they are and were created" (KJV). We were created for God's glory (Isaiah 43:7).

This truth was rejected in the Garden of Eden when Adam and Eve chose to be as God and refused to live in obedience to and dependence upon God. But the truth was realized in Jesus Christ who came as the last Adam to show us what God intended for us all along.

The focus of our Lord Jesus Christ's life was the will of the Father, the glory of the Father. It was this goal that took Jesus to the hour of ultimate glory, the cross.

Having learned what we have regarding glory, let's return to John 17 to learn how Jesus glorified His Father, and how we too can live for God's glory.

Jesus was the last Adam. The first Adam chose not to live according to the will and glory of the Father. Every man is either in Adam or in Christ. Man's individual response to the cross of Jesus Christ is the deciding factor. At the cross, embracing Jesus' redemptive act and believing He is who He claimed to be, we pass from death into life, from sin into righteousness.

19 The cross is the supreme glory of God. At Calvary, Jesus glorified God through His total obedience to the will of the Father.

The first Adam disobeyed God in a garden by refusing to do His will. Adam had been told to abstain from eating the fruit of the tree of the knowledge of good and evil. In the face of temptation, Adam and Eve succumbed, choosing to be "like God" rather than to be submissive to Him.

The last Adam also made a choice in a garden—a choice to obey: "Not My will, but Thine be done" (Luke 22:42). The very saying of it glorified God and honored His will.

But before Jesus ever entered the Garden of Gethsemane, He prayed the prayer of John 17. He prayed first for Himself. The remainder of the prayer for the 11 and for those who would believe on Him would have been useless had He not glorified the Father. Therefore, Jesus' prayer begins where it must: "Father, the hour has come; glorify Thy Son, that the Son may glorify Thee, even as Thou gavest Him authority over all mankind, that to all whom Thou hast given Him, He may give eternal life. And this is eternal life, that they may know Thee, the only true God, and Jesus Christ whom Thou hast sent. I glorified Thee on the earth, having accomplished the work which Thou hast given Me to do. And now, glorify Thou Me together with Thyself, Father, with the glory which I had with Thee before the world was" (John 17:1-5).

As Jesus prepared to go to Calvary as the Lamb of God to take away the sins of the world, He knew that His sacrifice would have to be accepted by the Father. If the Father was not propitiated (satisfied), then Jesus could not glorify the Father. Jesus could give eternal life to those whom the Father gave Him only if the Father accepted His sacrifice and raised Him from the dead.

When Jesus asked the Father to glorify Him, He was asking the Father to accept His substitutionary death on behalf of mankind. The cross was the ultimate glorification of God because it demonstrated His righteousness in dealing with sin, and it exemplified the highest act of love through God giving His Son. I believe Calvary was the hour of the supreme glorification of God.

Think on it.

20 As Jesus faced the hell of Calvary, He could not ask the Father to spare Him. It was for this purpose He had become the Son of Man. The author of Hebrews explains it this way: "For it is impossible for the blood of bulls and goats to take away sins. Therefore, when He comes into the world, He says, 'SACRIFICE AND OFFERING THOU HAST NOT DESIRED, BUT A BODY THOU HAST PREPARED FOR ME; IN WHOLE BURNT OFFERINGS AND sacrifices FOR SIN THOU HAST TAKEN NO PLEASURE. THEN I SAID, "BEHOLD, I HAVE COME (IN THE ROLL OF THE BOOK IT IS WRITTEN OF ME) TO DO THY WILL, O GOD" ' " (Hebrews 10:4-7).

Thus Jesus said, " 'What shall I say, "Father, save Me from this hour"? But for this purpose I came to this hour. Father, glorify Thy name.' There came therefore a voice out of heaven: 'I have both glorified it, and will glorify it again' " (John 12:27,28).

After Judas left the Upper Room to betray Jesus: "Jesus said, 'Now is the Son of Man glorified, and God is glorified in Him; if God is glorified in Him, God will also glorify Him in Himself, and will glorify Him immediately' " (John 13:31,32). Jesus was glorified in being the perfect offering for the sin of mankind; the Father was glorified by Jesus' willing obedience. The Father would glorify the Son by offering Him up and by accepting His atoning sacrifice. This acceptance of Jesus' sacrifice would be seen as God raised Jesus from the dead. Romans 4:25 states that Jesus "was delivered up because of our transgressions, and was raised because of our justification." In other words, Jesus' shed blood was sufficient to cover all our sins.

"We have been sanctified through the offering of the body of Jesus Christ once for all. . . . He, having offered one sacrifice for sins for all time, SAT DOWN AT THE RIGHT HAND OF GOD, waiting from that time onward UNTIL HIS ENEMIES BE MADE A FOOTSTOOL FOR HIS FEET. For by one offering He has perfected for all time those who are sanctified" (Hebrews 10:10,12-14).

Hallelujah! The Father glorified the Son! The Son glorified the Father! And the Father bestowed upon the Son the glory which He had with the Father before the world was. You and I have reaped the benefit of this glorification. As children of God, someday we will be with Jesus beholding

His glory, which the Father gave Jesus because He loved Him before the foundation of the world (John 17:24).

Jesus' prayers in John 17 will be fully answered . . . which means, beloved one, you shall be kept by the Father.

21 Jesus said, "I glorified Thee on the earth, having accomplished the work which Thou hast given Me to do" (John 17:4).

Oh, how I want to be able to say the same thing! Do you think this presumptuous, Beloved? I hope not. Jesus is the expression of all that God intended for us before Adam sinned. From Him we learn how we should live. And as God had a specific purpose for His only begotten Son, so He has a purpose for you, the child born into His family, loved before the foundation of the world. Remember Jesus' words: "You did not choose Me, but I chose you, and appointed you, that you should go and bear fruit" (John 15:16). You, Beloved, are "His workmanship, created in Christ Jesus for good works, which God prepared beforehand, that [you] should walk in them" (Ephesians 2:10). Therefore, chosen child of God, let's see what we can learn from the example of our Savior and older Brother.

First, Jesus glorified the Father on earth by accomplishing the works the Father gave Him to do. Are you glorifying the Father by seeking His will for your life? Whether you are a salesman or a doctor, a housewife or a missionary doesn't matter as long as you are there because God directed you. Wherever you find yourself, "You are the light of the world. . . . Let your light shine before men in such a way that they may see your good works, and glorify your Father who is in heaven" (Matthew 5:14,16). If you do not want to be ashamed when you enter glory, Beloved, glorify God now by accomplishing the work He has called you to do.

Second, Jesus also glorified God because He manifested God's name by the life He lived. Jesus' life glorified God. Jesus said, "I manifested Thy name to the men whom

Thou gavest Me out of the world; Thine they were, and Thou gavest them to Me, and they have kept Thy word" (John 17:6). O Beloved, are you glorifying God by giving Him the glory due His name? In Psalm 29:2 we are told: "Ascribe to the LORD the glory due to His name; worship the LORD in holy array." To ascribe the Lord the glory due His name is to live in such a way as to respect who He is, for His name reveals His character. Does your life measure up to who your God is? "Whether, then, you eat or drink or whatever you do, do all to the glory of God" (1 Corinthians 10:31), so that "in His temple everything says, 'Glory!'" (Psalm 29:9).

22 I don't want to leave the last point I made yesterday without showing you the practicality of a life which ascribes to the Lord the glory due His name. I have written a devotional study book on the names of God, *Lord, I Want to Know You*. Letters I have received about that book tell how God has used it to help people see through all sorts of varied circumstances, simply because they knew the meanings of His names. When they found themselves in a particular situation of need, they respected His name by living accordingly. To live this way brings God glory. One precious woman who has truly glorified the Lord wrote the following:

> It is with joy in my heart for the blessing of your ministry that prompts me to write to you. Last year at this time, our ladies' Bible study was committed to a study on the character of God. I purchased your book, *Lord, I Want to Know You*, in order to supplement the group study with more information for myself. That book was such a joy to me—but it soon became evident to me that God had placed it in my hands to supply my future needs.
>
> We received orders to be transferred in July . . . and were staying in the home of some friends in preparation for our departure. . . . We let our eldest son go to spend two days with his best friend prior to our departure. On the evening of the 22nd, both my son and his friend were killed in an automobile accident. I cannot begin to tell you

the devastation of living without my child. But, neither can I begin to tell you the joy that I have for the way I experienced His presence and His provision. And although I cannot imagine anything worse in this lifetime, as we were being told of our son's death, God brought to my remembrance Deuteronomy 32:39. And I was able to agree with God, even in that case, that He is El Elyon—God Most High. It was a further blessing that as I picked up the book to continue where I had left off, on page 159 I found Jehovah-shammah, The Lord Who Is There.

Kay, I do meet God at every turn. I meet Him most often these days with tears in my eyes, and seeking His strength. But I can say as Paul: "I thank Christ Jesus our Lord, who has . . . considered me faithful, putting me into service" (1 Timothy 1:12).

My friend has truly given a proper opinion of the sufficiency of our sovereign God. May you and I, Beloved, determine to do the same, knowing that everything that comes into our lives is filtered through the sovereign fingers of our El Elyon.

23 The third way our Lord glorified the Father on earth was by giving God's Word to those who followed Him. Jesus said to His Father: "Now they have come to know that everything Thou hast given Me is from Thee; for the words which Thou gavest Me I have given to them; and they received them, and truly understood that I came forth from Thee, and they believed that Thou didst send Me. . . . I have given them Thy word; and the world has hated them, because they are not of the world, even as I am not of the world" (John 17:7,8,14).

When Jesus instructed the 12 as they moved with Him from city to city as He proclaimed the gospel of the kingdom, He did not give them His thoughts, His opinions, His knowledge, His wisdom. He gave them God's Word. To which you may reply, "But Jesus was God!" You are right. He was, is, and always has been God. Yet when He came to earth as the Son of Man, He lived in a way that demonstrated to us how God intended us to live. He lived in total dependence upon God the Father. God did not intend that we should know good *and* evil. He intended that we live by every word that proceeded from the mouth of God. To know that would be enough!

Several times in the Gospel of John we see Jesus stressing the fact that He spoke only the words God gave Him. Listen to Jesus' words:

"I have many things to speak and to judge concerning you, but He who sent Me is true; and the things which I heard from Him, these I speak to the world. . . . I speak the things which I have seen with My Father" (8:26,38).

"For I did not speak on My own initiative, but the Father Himself who sent Me has given Me commandment, what to say, and what to speak" (12:49).

"All things that I have heard from My Father I have made known to you" (15:15).

"The words that I say to you I do not speak on My own initiative, but the Father abiding in Me does His works" (14:10).

What then, Beloved, is God's lesson for us? It is written in 1 Peter 4:11: "Whoever speaks, let him speak, as it were, the utterances of God." Why give people human wisdom, philosophy, or psychology, when they are to live by every word that comes from the mouth of God? If your words are going to glorify God, Beloved, they need to be God's Word. Learn the Bible. Share it. We have seen its power over and over again, when it is heard, known, believed, obeyed.

24 Beloved, have you ever wondered if someday the enemy of your soul could so ensnare you that he might snatch you from the protective care of God? Fear not! Jesus has prayed for you . . . and God has heard.

How do I know? After Jesus prayed concerning Himself, He prayed for His disciples and for all those who would believe on His name. When Jesus was here on earth,

He kept His disciples from the evil one. The fourth way Jesus glorified the Father on earth was by His care. And His care continues.

As Jesus prepared to return to the Father, His disciples were on His heart, for He prayed: "I am no more in the world; and yet they themselves are in the world, and I come to Thee. Holy Father, keep them in Thy name, the name which Thou hast given Me, that they may be one, even as We are. While I was with them, I was keeping them in Thy name which Thou hast given Me; and I guarded them, and not one of them perished but the son of perdition, that the Scripture might be fulfilled" (John 17:11,12).

Jesus knew that even though people came to a saving knowledge of Himself, still the conflict with the evil one would continue. Satan would desire to sift believers as wheat; in their own strength or wisdom they could not win the battle. It was necessary for them to be sanctified by the Father through His Word, and kept in the name of Jesus. The almighty, omnipotent, omniscient, sovereign God would see that no trial, testing, or temptation would ever come their way unless they could handle it. Because God is God, there would always be a way of escape for His children (1 Corinthians 10:13).

Jesus did not ask the Father to remove us from the world but to protect us from the prince of this world. He prayed, "I do not ask Thee to take them out of the world, but to keep them from the evil one. They are not of the world, even as I am not of the world. Sanctify them in the truth; Thy word is truth" (John 17:15-17). We are in the world but not of it. We are kept by the power of His name and by the sanctifying power of the Word. The name of the Lord is to us a strong tower, a place to run into for protection. The Word of the Lord, the Bible, is what cleanses us and transforms us (Ephesians 5:26).

How crucial it is then, Beloved, that we know our God and stay in His Word. As we do, and as we share Him and His Word with others, our care of them will glorify God and be used of Him to keep them.

25 Finally, Jesus glorified the Father by coming to the earth for the express purpose of embracing the cross and dying in our stead. His death glorified the Father.

Although we already considered how the death of Jesus Christ glorified the Father, I want us to see the parallel for our own lives. Jesus was called to the cross, and He calls us to the cross also: "If anyone wishes to come after Me, let him deny himself, and take up his cross, and follow Me" (Mark 8:34). The cross is an instrument of death. When we say we want to follow Him, we are proclaiming our willingness to exchange our life for His, our independence for dependence upon Him, our sin for His righteousness.

When Jesus compared His death to a grain of wheat falling into the ground and dying so it wouldn't remain alone, He continued: "He who loves his life loses it; and he who hates his life in this world shall keep it to life eternal. If anyone serves Me, let him follow Me; and where I am, there shall My servant also be; if anyone serves Me, the Father will honor him" (John 12:25,26).

Paul stated it this way: "I have been crucified with Christ; and it is no longer I who live, but Christ lives in me; and the life which I now live in the flesh I live by faith in the Son of God, who loved me, and delivered Himself up for me" (Galatians 2:20).

It was through the cross that resurrection life was made possible for mankind. And it is in embracing the cross that we find newness of life as we "know Him, and the power of His resurrection and the fellowship of His sufferings, being conformed to His death; in order that [we] may attain to the resurrection from the dead" (Philippians 3:10,11).

Some have called this "the exchanged life." It is our life nailed to the cross so that His life might be lived through us in the power of His resurrection. Attaining to the resurrection of the dead as mentioned in Philippians 3, I believe, means that I should seek to so live that I attain to everything that His life provides for me.

O Beloved, may our "death to self," death to our will, death to our desires, glorify our God as we allow His life to be lived through us.

"As Thou didst send Me into the world, I also have sent them into the world. And for their sakes I sanctify Myself, that they themselves also may be sanctified in truth" (John 17:18,19).

26 In Jesus' prayer for His own, we see a great contrast between believers and the world. Jesus lets those listening know that His prayer is not for the world but for those who belong to the Father: "I manifested Thy name to the men whom Thou gavest Me out of the world; Thine they were, and Thou gavest them to Me, and they have kept Thy word. . . . I ask on their behalf; I do not ask on behalf of the world, but of those whom Thou hast given Me; for they are Thine; and all things that are Mine are Thine, and Thine are Mine; and I have been glorified in them" (John 17:6,9,10).

If we allow the Scriptures to mean what they say in their context, we cannot deny the fact that we come to know Jesus Christ because we have been given by the Father to the Son. The Gospel of John so beautifully lays before us our responsibility to believe in the Lord Jesus Christ in order to be saved. Yet, at the same time, we are assured of God's sovereignty in bringing us to the Son: "Jesus said to them, 'I am the bread of life; he who comes to Me shall not hunger, and he who believes in Me shall never thirst. But I said to you, that you have seen Me, and yet do not believe. All that the Father gives Me shall come to Me; and the one who comes to Me I will certainly not cast out. . . . And this is the will of Him who sent Me, that of all that He has given Me I lose nothing, but raise it up on the last day. . . . No one can come to Me, unless the Father who sent Me draws him; and I will raise him up on the last day. It is written in the prophets, "AND THEY SHALL ALL BE TAUGHT OF GOD." Everyone who has heard and learned from the Father, comes to Me. . . . For this reason I have said to you, that no one can come to Me, unless it has been granted him from the Father' " (John 6:35-37,39,44,45,65).

Eternal life is described by Jesus in John 17:3 this way: "And this is eternal life, that they may know Thee, the only true God, and Jesus Christ whom Thou hast sent." Wonder of inexplicable wonders, that God has let us know Him—Father, Son, and Holy Spirit.

27 To some, the doctrine of election is difficult to understand. It seems that if God chooses us first, then we have no choice regarding our salvation and are mere robots. But the Scriptures do not teach that we have no choice. We must be careful not to make the Word of God say more or less than it says. Some try to reason out the doctrines of election, predestination, and the sovereignty of God by taking these doctrines beyond the clear teaching of the Word. In our human reasoning we want to say, "But if this is true and that is true, then the conclusion must be . . ." But we cannot draw conclusions by going to extremes which the Scriptures do not teach.

I am somewhat familiar with the writings of D.A. Carson, and what I have read impresses me. He seems to have a good theological balance in the area of election and the free will of man. In his book on John 14–17 he says: "The disciples have obeyed Jesus' word (17:6). Notwithstanding the predestinatory note just sounded, it must not be thought that the disciples are mere robots or puppets. They believe, they hear, they obey; and the belief is their belief, the hearing their hearing, the obeying their obeying. It is not easy to see how God's unconditioned sovereignty, even in salvation, and man's free agency as a creature in God's universe, can coexist; but coexist they do, according to the Scriptures. In expressing these truths, it is essential to avoid formulations in which God's activity and man's activity become mutually self-limiting. The Scriptures avoid such traps. Of the many stunning examples, perhaps none is clearer than Philippians 2:12,13: 'Therefore, my dear friends, as you have always obeyed . . . continue to work out your salvation with fear and trembling, for it is God who works in you to will and to act according to His good purpose.' Rightly construed, God's sovereignty in these matters serves as an incentive to obedience and a spur to growth, rather than as a stifling, fatalistic disincentive. So here in Jesus' Final Prayer: the text leaps from the Father's predestinatory work to the disciples' obedience with neither impropriety nor embarrassment."[2]

Think on these things, Beloved, and tomorrow we will take another look at the relationship of the disciples to the world.

28 Although the world will hate you, because you are "not of the world even as [Jesus is] not of the world" (John 17:16), still God is not going to take you out of the world (John 17:15). Why doesn't God just save us and then take us home to heaven if the world is not going to accept us or love us?

God doesn't take you home, Beloved, because He has a task for you. He wants to send you out into that hostile world so that others might come to know Him even as you did. Jesus said, "As Thou didst send Me into the world, I also have sent them into the world" (John 17:18).

You and I are to be His ambassadors to the world. God "gave us the ministry of reconciliation, namely, that God was in Christ reconciling the world to Himself, not counting their trespasses against them, and He has committed to us the word of reconciliation" (2 Corinthians 5:18,19). There are other sheep out in the world who have not yet heard the call of their Shepherd. Jesus has given us the Father's Word. His Word becomes ours, and this is what we give to the world. Jesus said, "I have other sheep, which are not of this fold; I must bring them also, and they shall hear My voice; and they shall become one flock with one shepherd" (John 10:16). When those sheep hear His voice through us and come to Him, then they become benefactors of our Lord's prayer in John 17. You can see how Jesus' prayer to the Father was answered in your own life: "I do not ask in behalf of these alone [the 11], but for those also who believe in Me through their word" (17:20).

And what does our Lord want for us who believe through the word of others? Jesus prays, "That they may all be one; even as Thou, Father, art in Me, and I in Thee, that they also may be in Us; that the world may believe that Thou didst send Me. And the glory which Thou hast given Me I have given to them; that they may be one, just as We are one; I in them, and Thou in Me, that they may be perfected in unity, that the world may know that Thou didst send Me, and didst love them, even as Thou didst love Me" (John 17:21-23).

"The 'glory' the Father had given Jesus was the triumphant task of redeeming men to God. As Hebrews states, he was 'crowned with glory and honor' because he suffered death in the process of 'bringing many sons to glory' (Hebrews 2:9,10). By sharing in His calling, they participate in His glory and are united with Him and with one another. God and man are together involved in bringing the new creation into being. The effect of this united testimony is a confirmation of the divine mission of Jesus and of God's love for believers."[3]

O Beloved, are you one with the Father and other believers in this task?

29 It is the love of God that gives you purpose and calling in life. Have you ever seen your calling as an ambassador for Christ in the light of God's love? What a new perspective this gives to your life! You have eternal value once you come to know the Lord Jesus Christ. As an ambassador you are crucially involved in the redemption of souls. You have the privilege of telling people who desperately need to be loved that God loves them and wants to manifest that love to them through the gift of His Son. Jesus came to make

God's name known to men "that the love wherewith Thus didst love Me may be in them, and I in them" (John 17:26).

And the very fact that God has so involved you in this work of redemption testifies to the fact that the Father loves you even as He does His Son. Look carefully at Jesus' words: "I in them, and Thou in Me, that they may be perfected in unity, that the world may know that Thou didst send Me, and didst love them, even as Thou didst love Me" (John 17:23).

Did you notice, Beloved, the connection of being sent with being loved? Notice too the unity that this relationship brings. No longer are we left alone, isolated, vulnerable to be rejected and abandoned. Those who come to Jesus become one with the Father, Son, and Holy Spirit. They become one with other believers. They become one in purpose, in ministry, no longer living in the competitive individuality of unredeemed flesh where "I am number one and I must look out for myself."

In this light, the sharing of the gospel with others takes on a new dimension. It is not just a matter of, "I have to be a witness to please God"; but, "In love, God has given me the privilege of the high calling, the life-calling, of being one with Him and with others in His ministry. I have the honor of bringing people into the kingdom of God, so that they might know the love of God that surpasses all comprehension, and might never be alone again."

Those of you who have heard me give an invitation know that I use the words, "Welcome to the family," when I acknowledge individuals who look at me to indicate that they just invited the Lord Jesus Christ into their life.

Isn't this true worship? To so love and respect the Father that you tell others of His love? What eternal significance this gives to your life! "One generation shall praise Thy works to another, and shall declare Thy mighty acts. On the glorious splendor of Thy majesty, and on Thy wonderful works, I will meditate. And men shall speak of the power of Thine awesome acts; and I will tell of Thy greatness. They shall eagerly utter the memory of Thine abundant goodness, and shall shout joyfully of Thy righteousness" (Psalm 145:4-7).

30 To be where Jesus is. To live with Him forever. To never be separated from Him again. To enjoy His inheritance and the beauty of His home.

To behold with your own eyes the Father, the Son, the Holy Spirit. To see them together. To eat with them. To live in their home. To share their conversation. To share their intimacy as one of the family.

To never again be exposed to the awful, maiming, destructive ravages of sin, but to live in a world of righteousness. To never be torn apart by what your eyes see or your ears hear. To know that all your needs are behind you.

This has to be glory!

Glory it is! And glory you will experience for the Father answers the Son's prayer. Jesus asked, "Father, I desire that they also, whom Thou hast given Me, be with Me where I am, in order that they may behold My glory, which Thou hast given Me; for Thou didst love Me before the foundation of the world" (John 17:24).

You will no longer have to wince, feel sick, or control a righteous anger because of desecrations of our Lord or His name, His Word or His ways. The peoples of the earth will no longer devise a vain thing. The kings of the earth will no longer take their stand nor will the rulers take their counsel against the Lord and against His anointed saying: "Let us tear their fetters apart, and cast away their cords from us!" (Psalm 2:3). You will be in glory, beholding His glory.

My prayer for you and for me, Beloved, is that until we behold our blessed Lord in His glory, everything in our physical temples (bodies) will say, "Glory!" to our Lord (Psalm 29:9) by finishing the work He has given us to do. Amen.

October

"Calvary's Love . . . Poured Out for You"

1 O Beloved, have there ever been times in your life when you doubted the love of God? Maybe it was because you wondered how anyone could love you. Maybe you puzzled in your mind, "How could God know everything about me and still love me?" Doubts troubled you because you felt His love was based on your value to the kingdom of God, and as far as you could see your value was zilch because you had so hopelessly fallen short.

Maybe you felt totally worthless, a remnant off the bolt of humanity, frayed and imperfect. No one could make anything of you!

Or maybe none of the above applies to you. Maybe you have doubted the love of God because of what He has allowed to come into your life. Was it the death of a loved one that made you wonder if God really cared? Have tragedies rolled over you like an incessant tide, knocking you off your feet and catching you in the undertow of doubt—making you wonder why a God who is supposed to be loving didn't come to your rescue?

Or maybe you don't even feel the need to know or experience the love of God. Although you probably wouldn't dare express it, you wonder, "What's the big deal? Others have died before. Some have even laid down their lives for their friends. So Jesus laid down His life." Does the thought leave you unmoved?

Is John 3:16 just another verse in the Bible? Although it seems to be a favorite for people because it is one verse they can say by memory, does it leave you cold? Read it aloud, my friend, and listen to it again: "For God so loved the world, that He gave His only begotten Son, that whoever believes in Him should not perish, but have eternal life."

Jesus said these words only once near the beginning of the Gospel of John. The verse is like a beautiful scarlet rosebud that has not yet opened into full bloom. The magnificence of the unfolded reality remains unseen until the glorious climax of love's expression in the final chapters of John's Gospel.

O Beloved, maybe this is the way it has been with you and the love of God. Maybe you have seen it as a tightly closed bud . . . until now. May God grant to you the awe of watching it unfold so that love's fragrance may permeate every fiber of your being.

2 Saying "I love you" and hearing "I love you" has always been very important to me. They are words I was raised on, and thus they are words I gave back to those who taught me to say them: Mother, Daddy, grandparents, and eventually my friends. Girlfriends, that is! I determined at an early age that I would save those three special words for the man I would marry. I would not scatter them as favors.

Saying "I love you" was not as hard for me as it is for so many, because I was raised on expressions of love. As a little girl growing up with a younger brother, Jack, raised in an atmosphere where love was verbalized, we came up with our own unique way of saying, "I love you." Everyone thought it was cute. I thought it was wonderful because I didn't have to rely on words alone. In my childish ways I found out how to demonstrate the love that overwhelmed my heart.

Jack was into colors, so he loved you in either monochromes or technicolor. There were times when he might just love you red, or blue, or maybe if his love was tested because you hadn't been what you should have been to him, he loved you only in yellow or green. However, more often than not, his little heart would burst with the passion of red, blue, yellow, green, purple, orange, and pink. To Jack, that was real love. But for me, color words were not enough. I needed a physical expression that would convince others of the enormity of my love. Of course, my love could also vary, like Jack's, and I had a way to let others know exactly the current status of that love. How much were they loved by me? They could tell because I would widen my arms accordingly. I might stretch out my arms a little and say, "I love you this much." It depended, as I said, on what they had done. If someone had really toed the line or if my little heart was suddenly overcome with love's emotion, I would burst into the room and throw my skinny, little arms open as wide as I could get them, stretching them way back until my shoulder bones almost touched, and then I'd say in as expressive a way as possible, "I love you *this* much."

Words were not enough for God either. To convince us of His love, God, through Jesus, stretched out His arms on Calvary and said, "I love you *this* much."

But God didn't only say, "I love you." "God demonstrates His own love toward us, *in that while we were yet sinners,* Christ died for us" (Romans 5:8).

3 Those last hours alone with His disciples in the Upper Room had been special to Jesus, "having loved His own who were in the world, He loved them to the end [to the uttermost or eternally]" (John 13:1). But now as they approached the Garden of Gethsemane, walking over the ravine of the Kidron Valley, one thing captured His attention and bound Him as the festival sacrifice with unseen cords to the horns of God's altar: Calvary!

As Jesus had just talked to His disciples of love, of His for them and of theirs for one another, His love was about to be demonstrated in the ultimate expression . . . the laying down of His life. Not just for those whom He loved, but for sinners . . . for enemies, many of whom would never acknowledge His love . . . and also for friends who would forsake Him in His greatest hour of need.

After speaking the words of John 13–16, Jesus "went forth with His disciples over the ravine of the Kidron, where there was a garden, into which He Himself entered, and His disciples" (John 18:1). But John does not tell us of love's wrestlings. For that, we must go to the other Gospels.

Calvary's love is the essence of the balm of Gilead that can heal all of your wounds. Calvary's love is the key that unlocks the bars that keep you imprisoned in the solitary confinement of self. Calvary's love is the power that launches you from the mundaneness of earthly pleasures into the selfless sacrifice of reaching souls for heaven's kingdom. Calvary's love . . .

O Father, may You ignite my feeble and inadequate words with understanding that these precious readers might be convinced of Your everlasting love for them as individuals, just as they are. Convince them that they are special and precious in Your sight and that You willingly gave Yourself out of love for *them.* Free them from ever having to be convinced again of Your great love.

I ask this, Father, for those who are now reading these words, that they might be liberated in the knowledge of Your love. And, Father, I pray that being convinced of Calvary's love, they might forget self and press on to the prize of the high calling in Christ Jesus. That they might receive the prize of the upward call in Christ Jesus and someday, entering into the joy of the Lord, find themselves literally enveloped in the security of His arms.

I ask this, Father, in the faith of the promise that You chose me and ordained that I should bear fruit that would remain and that whatever I asked in Your name You would do it (John 15:16). In faith, I thank You, Father.

4 Although Calvary's love was conceived before the foundation of the world, and was to be demonstrated on a cross, it was decided in Gethsemane's garden. An artist's

rendering of Jesus reclining in peaceful solemnity upon the moonlit rock in Gethsemane is far from the reality of the battle wrought in that garden on the evening of Jesus' betrayal and arrest. When one takes the pieces of Scripture and puts them together, the finished puzzle shows a far different picture.

Let me place the pieces of the puzzle into the framework of all that we have studied in the Gospel of John as it pertains to the life and ministry of our Lord, the Lamb of God, who would take away the sins of the world. In Matthew 26:36-39, we read: "Then Jesus came with them to a place called Gethsemane, and said to His disciples, 'Sit here while I go over there and pray.' And He took with Him Peter and the two sons of Zebedee, and began to be grieved and distressed. Then He said to them, 'My soul is deeply grieved, to the point of death; remain here and keep watch with Me.' And He went a little beyond them, and fell on His face and prayed, saying, 'My Father, if it is possible, let this cup pass from Me; yet not as I will, but as Thou wilt.' "

As we read these words, we might imagine that they were said in a subdued way, simply because Calvary would be part of Christ's experience as the Lamb of God. He had come to die; it was all part of the plan to effect our redemption.

Oh, no, Beloved! This was not the atmosphere in Gethsemane that night. It was electrified, charged with lightning flashes of agony as the storm clouds of Calvary thundered overhead. Jesus did not quietly pray, "Father, if it is possible, take this cup from Me . . . nevertheless . . ." He cried loudly with tears flowing from His eyes as He wept and wrestled with the will of God, with the painful sacrifice of Calvary's love. Oh, how I wish I could tell you this in person . . . that I could add sound and emotion to the words you have just read. And how would I know what emotions to link with these words? The author of Hebrews speaks of "the days of His flesh, [when] He offered up both prayers and supplications with loud crying and tears to the One able to save Him from death" (5:7).

Hebrews was written to believers who had suffered much for their faith. In this book, as in no other, we see Jesus as our great high priest, a priest tempted in all things as we are . . . a priest who can therefore be touched with the feeling of our infirmities. He was a priest who wanted to find out if there was some other sacrifice, some other way, to atone for mankind's sin rather than by drinking the cup of man's iniquity and being separated from the Father. That's why Jesus cried loudly and wept bitterly in Gethsemane.

5 The victory of Calvary was won in the battleground of Gethsemane. The author of Hebrews gives us an insight which we do not pick up in the Gospels: "In the days of His flesh, He offered up both prayers and supplications with loud crying and tears to the One able to save Him from [out of] death, and He was heard because of His piety. Although He was a Son, He learned obedience from the things which He suffered" (5:7,8).

Jesus suffered in Gethsemane. Your salvation is free to you, Beloved, but it cost God greatly. No greater price could have been paid for your salvation. Jesus left heaven, humbled Himself, and became a man, encased in flesh with all of its emotions, temptations, and frailties. It was as man that Jesus, the only begotten Son of God, wrestled with the weakness of flesh in Gethsemane. The welfare, hope, and salvation of all mankind hung in the balance of Calvary's love in that garden, when Jesus as man, God in the flesh, made the choice for love's obedience.

Do not take away from the wrenching agony and the trial of the moment! Do not pass it off lightly, saying, "Oh, Jesus was just going through the motions." Read Matthew 26:38-44 again.

As you read this account, do you think Jesus was just going through the motions? Write your answer in your notebook. What do you learn from this passage about Gethsemane?

6 Three times Jesus went to the Father, asking if it were possible to redeem mankind another way. Was this the only way for God to love the world . . . to give up His only begotten Son so that others would not perish but have the opportunity to become sons of God, adopted children, joint heirs with Jesus Christ?

The cup that Jesus was being asked to drink contained all of the dregs of mankind's sin. It was overflowing with all the sins that ever had been or would be committed. How could Holiness bear such iniquity? Yet that is what Calvary was all about. It was there that the last Adam, Jesus Christ, would literally be made sin for us, so that we might be made the righteousness of God in Him (2 Corinthians 5:21).

Without His righteousness credited to our account, we cannot see God. For all of our righteousnesses are as filthy rags in God's sight. There is none righteous, no not one . . . except the Son of God, born of a virgin, without spot or blemish, tempted in all things as we were but without sin. Although His flesh was weak, He did not yield. He said, and held to it: "Not My will be done, but Thine!"

If it were not possible to redeem man another way, Jesus was willing to take the cup and to drink it to the full. No matter what the cost, Calvary's love was for you, Beloved. As Jesus wrestled with the will of God, your salvation, your well-being was ever on His heart. Also always before Him was His love for the Father and a desire to do the Father's will.

The decision made in the garden was final. Thus, when Peter "having a sword, drew it, and struck the high priest's slave, and cut off his right ear. . . . Jesus therefore said to Peter, 'Put the sword into the sheath; the cup which the Father has given Me, shall I not drink it?' " (John 18:10,11).

This was Calvary's love, Beloved. Because I want you to realize the great personal cost and physical agony of it all, let me share another insight into our Lord's conflict in Gethsemane, from the physician, Dr. Luke. I want you to read it and then meditate on it in light of all that we have discussed today. Then tomorrow we will examine it more closely from a medical point of view.

As Jesus wrestled with the will of God in Gethsemane, "An angel from heaven appeared to Him, strengthening Him. And being in agony He was praying very fervently; and His sweat became like drops of blood, falling down upon the ground" (Luke 22:43,44). Here is a new and greater dimension of the depth of Calvary's love—not only loud crying and tears, but sweat filled with blood falling down upon the ground!

How much, Beloved, do you think God loves you?

7

The human body can endure only so much stress before something has to give. God knew this, and therefore in creating us He provided even a physical "means of escape." When the stress of the moment (either emotional or physical stress) becomes too much, a person normally faints. Thus, as the blood pressure rises, or pain increases, or the stress of the moment seems more than one can bear, the body becomes unconscious to its surroundings. All of this is God's design to keep the brain from hemorrhaging.

However, when a person does not faint and the pressure builds in the blood vessels, the capillaries become engorged with blood and rupture. Thus, blood seeps into the pores of a person's skin, mixing with the sweat so that a person can literally sweat drops of blood.

The agony of Gethsemane was so overwhelming, my friend, that our precious Lord was grieved nearly to the point of death. Under such pressure, Jesus began to hemorrhage and sweat so profusely that His bloody sweat did not merely appear as tiny little beads of water standing on His forehead. Rather, this bloody sweat was rolling off His body and falling continually to the ground. His agony was so intense that the Father had to send an angel to strengthen Him.

And all the while, His disciples slept. So quickly they forgot His words: "Keep watching and praying . . . the spirit is willing, but the flesh is weak." How well their great high priest understood this weakness, for He had agonized almost to the point of death in bringing His flesh in subjection to the will of the Father. And yet, they slept on and were thus unprepared for the test that was just minutes away. They would run; they would deny they knew Him; Peter would weep bitterly. And yet, knowing all of this before it ever happened, Calvary's love held fast on their behalf.

All of this, Beloved, He also endured for you. This is Calvary love poured out for you—one who has lost many a battle with the flesh and yet who is loved unconditionally by God.

8 I don't care how tough you are, or how great your understanding of human weaknesses and inconsistencies. It still hurts to be rejected, or even worse, to be betrayed. And when you have done nothing to deserve it, the hurt is even greater.

Maybe you have thought, "So Jesus was betrayed by Judas. Others have been betrayed, too." Yes, Beloved, others have been betrayed, and you also may have been. Maybe you have even betrayed your God at one time or another. Do you think He still loves you? If you say no, then you do not know or understand the full measure of Calvary's love.

Let's look at two people who betrayed Jesus: Judas and Peter. I think this will help us grasp a new dimension of the love of God that is ours for the believing.

Jesus roused His disciples from their slumber, for the Roman cohort and the one who was betraying Him were nearby.

"And while He was still speaking, behold, Judas, one of the twelve, came up, accompanied by a great multitude with swords and clubs, from the chief priests and elders of the people. . . .

"Judas . . . knew the place; for Jesus had often met there with His disciples. Judas then, having received the Roman cohort, and officers from the chief priests and the Pharisees, came there with lanterns and torches and weapons. Jesus therefore, knowing all the things that were coming upon Him, went forth, and said to them, 'Whom do you seek?' They answered Him, 'Jesus the Nazarene.' He said to them, 'I am He.' And Judas also who was betraying Him, was standing with them. . . .

"And he approached Jesus to kiss Him. But Jesus said to him, 'Judas, are you betraying the Son of Man with a kiss?' " (Matthew 26:47; John 18:2-5; Luke 22:47,48).

Betrayed by a kiss from one Jesus had chosen to be part of a select group . . . one He had discipled for over three years, supplying his every want, seeing to his every need. A man who had heard Him speak the very words of life, assuring of the certainty of heaven for those who would deny themselves, forsake all, take up their cross, and follow Him as a habit of life.

Jesus loved Judas. Even on the night when He was betrayed, Jesus stripped Himself of His garments, girded Himself with a towel, and washed the feet of the one who would betray Him.

Rejecting His love, knowing full well that Jesus knew what was in his heart, Judas received the sop of bread designating him as the betrayer and left to sell his soul to the devil. No words of vindictiveness followed Judas. Calvary's love let him go . . . and still called him "friend" when He received his kiss of betrayal.

9

At first Peter was ready to fight for Jesus. As long as he had his sword and wasn't forbidden to use it, he would stand by Jesus. But stripped of his earthly weapons, he became a coward. Satan would sift Peter as wheat . . . and his faith would temporarily fail. Bitter tears would follow. Can you understand, my friend? Have you ever licked bitter tears from your lips and wondered how God could love you again after you so blatantly denied Him? You and Peter have something in common. Not only the bitter weeping, but also the incredible forgiveness of Calvary's love . . . and the hope of again following Him unto death instead of denial.

Let's look for a few minutes at Peter's denial of our Lord by returning once more to our study in John 18.

"Simon Peter therefore having a sword, drew it, and struck the high priest's slave, and cut off his right ear; and the slave's name was Malchus. Jesus therefore said to Peter, 'Put the sword into the sheath; the cup which the Father has given Me, shall I not drink it?' So the Roman cohort and the commander, and the officers of the Jews, arrested Jesus and bound Him, and led Him to Annas first; for he was father-in-law of Caiaphas, who was high priest that year. . . .

"And Simon Peter was following Jesus, and so was another disciple. Now that disciple was known to the high priest, and entered with Jesus into the court of the high priest, but Peter was standing at the door outside. So the other disciple, who was known to the high priest, went out and spoke to the doorkeeper, and brought in Peter. The slave-girl therefore who kept the door said to Peter, 'You are not also one of this man's disciples, are you?' He said, 'I am not.' Now the slaves and the officers were standing there, having made a charcoal fire, for it was cold and they were warming themselves; and Peter also was with them, standing and warming himself. . . . They said therefore to him, 'You are not also one of His disciples, are you?' He denied it, and said, 'I am not.' One of the slaves of the high priest, being a relative of the one whose ear Peter cut off, said, 'Did I not see you in the garden with Him?' Peter therefore denied it again; and immediately a cock crowed" (John 18:10-13,15-18,25-27).

The crowing of the cock probably shot Peter's face upward, and then the Lord turned and looked at Peter. And Peter remembered his Lord's words when He had told him, "Before a cock crows today, you will deny Me three times" (Luke 22:61). I imagine those words echoed like a thousand haunting voices repeating themselves one on top of another . . . "Peter! Peter! Peter! The cock will not crow . . . the cock will not crow . . . the cock will not crow, until you, you, you deny Me, Me, Me three times, three times, three times. . . ."

10 What kept Peter from totally despairing of the forgiveness of Calvary's love? Why didn't he just figure, "Well, that's it! I've blown it! There is no hope, no future for me. I might as well walk away and hang it up. I can never be God's man again"?

You may have despaired of ever being used of God again because in some way you denied your Lord. Possibly you have known love based only on performance—your performance. A conditional love. An unforgiving love. A love that is temporary. A love that once it is denied walks away never to return again. A love that says, "You had your chance and blew it, so that's that!" If this is true, then you need to know and understand Calvary's love.

Let me take you to Luke 22 where we catch another glimpse into our Lord's time with His disciples in the Upper Room just before they left for the Garden of Gethsemane. Although the Gospel of John records the fact that Jesus told Peter that he would betray Him before the cock crowed three times that day, John does not tell us of Jesus' words to Peter which preceded this awful prophecy—words that temper the news of Peter's denial with the hope of restoration, that assure him even before his failure that Calvary's love is there to keep him from slipping irreparably into a life of failure and uselessness.

Luke tells us that Jesus said, "Simon, Simon, behold, Satan has demanded permission to sift you like wheat; but I have prayed for you, that your faith may not fail; and you, when once you have turned again, strengthen your brothers" (22:31,32). Jesus knew that Peter would succumb to the weakness of his flesh. He would not watch and pray but sleep and fall prey to Satan's sifting. Peter, however, claimed that Jesus was wrong. That would never happen to him! Thus, he responded, "Lord, with You I am ready to go both to prison and to death!" (Luke 22:33). Peter had never quite grasped the reality that the spirit is willing but the flesh is weak. He was absolutely certain that he, of all the disciples, would never be the one to betray his Lord. Thus, in total confidence, Peter replied, "Even though all may fall away because of You, I will never fall away" (Matthew 26:33).

How does one recover after making such a brash statement and then doing just the opposite? By appropriating in faith the Word of his God, "I have prayed for you, that your faith may not fail; and you, when once you have turned again, strengthen your brothers." Calvary's love lets you turn from your sin, receive forgiveness, and go forward to strengthen others by having learned from your mistakes. O Beloved, if you have denied your Lord, Calvary's love is redemptive love. Believe God, cling to His promises, don't miss what His love has provided—forgiveness and restoration!

11 When they bound Jesus and led Him away to the high priest for an illegal trial, it was a cold evening. I imagine His clothes were soaking wet from having agonized and sweat so profusely. Surely the loss of blood had weakened Him even more. They led Him across that Kidron Valley and through one of the gates to the city of Jerusalem (probably the Sheep Gate). On the way to the house of Caiaphas, they passed by the fire where others were warming themselves, and Jesus may have been reminded of the baptism of fire that awaited Him.

The plan was to have Jesus crucified. Oh, the Sanhedrin couldn't put Him to death themselves—Roman law forbade that—but they could let the Romans do their dirty work. The keepers of the Law, in the night in which Jesus was betrayed, broke their own laws. They began a trial at night, and no trial could begin at night. To this infraction they added more, but it mattered not. They would find a way to vindicate themselves. When Jesus was finally bound and in their possession, "The high priest therefore questioned Jesus about His disciples, and about His teaching. Jesus answered him, 'I have spoken openly to the world; I always taught in synagogues, and in the temple, where all the Jews come together; and I spoke nothing in secret. Why do you question Me? Question those who have heard what I spoke to them;

behold, these know what I said.' And when He had said this, one of the officers standing by gave Jesus a blow, saying, 'Is that the way You answer the high priest?' Jesus answered him, 'If I have spoken wrongly, bear witness of the wrong; but if rightly, why do you strike Me?' Annas therefore sent Him bound to Caiaphas the high priest" (John 18:19-24).

Oh, the irony of it all! Slapping Jesus, our great high priest, in the face because of the way He answered an earthly and corrupt priest! It is humiliating to be slapped in the face. What kept Jesus from retaliating? Calvary's love. He had you in mind. So He took the slap . . . and much more.

12 Have you ever been unjustly reviled and ridiculed? Have others ever ganged up on you or made you suffer because they didn't like you? Jesus understands. He has been there. And He endured without flinching or walking away on that night when He was taken bound to the house of Caiaphas.

Annas and his son-in-law, Caiaphas, had a complaint against Jesus for more than one reason. Not only were they threatened by His popularity with the people, but twice in His public ministry Jesus had turned over the tables of the money changers in the Temple mount. It was their concession He had tampered with!

It was quite a night with the scribes and elders gathered together in the house of Caiaphas.

"Now the chief priests and the whole Council [Sanhedrin] kept trying to obtain false testimony against Jesus, in order that they might put Him to death; and they did not find any, even though many false witnesses came forward. But later on two came forward, and said, 'This man stated, "I am able to destroy the temple of God and to rebuild it in three days." ' And the high priest stood up and said to Him, 'Do You make no answer? What is it that these men are testifying against You? . . . I adjure You by the living God, that You tell us whether You are the Christ, the Son of God' " (Matthew 26:59-63).

The minute the high priest said this, he put Jesus under oath. And because Jesus had come to fulfill the Law, He had to answer them. They might break God's Law, but He would have to keep it.

"Jesus said to him, 'You have said it yourself; nevertheless I tell you, hereafter you will see THE SON OF MAN SITTING AT THE RIGHT HAND OF POWER, AND COMING ON THE CLOUDS OF HEAVEN.' Then the high priest tore his robes, saying, 'He has blasphemed! What further need do we have of witnesses? Behold, you have now heard the blasphemy; what do you think?' They answered and said, 'He is deserving of death!' Then they spat in His face and beat Him with their fists; and others slapped Him [or beat Him with rods], and said, 'Prophesy to us, You Christ; who is the one who hit You?' " (Matthew 26:64-68).

Mark tells us: "And some began to spit at Him, and to blindfold Him, and to beat Him with their fists, and to say to Him, 'Prophesy!' And the officers received Him with slaps in the face" (14:65).

Can you imagine slugging God and making a mockery of Him? Can you imagine doing this since He had the power to stop you? He had the power to retaliate by snuffing out your breath and sending you to the hottest hell. But instead He went all the way to Calvary for you and He said, "Father, forgive them for they know not what they do."

That, Beloved, is Calvary's love . . . *love for you!*

13 It must have been quite a night for Jesus—a night of mockery, scorn, abuse, pain, and loneliness. For "the men who were holding Jesus in custody were mocking Him, and beating Him, and they blindfolded Him and were asking Him, saying, 'Prophesy, who is the one who hit You?' And they were saying many other things against Him, blaspheming" (Luke 22:63-65).

There is a place that is thought to be the restored remains of Caiaphas' house in Jerusalem. It is one of my favorite places to go when Jack and I take our teaching tours to Israel. At this site or at the church built over the ruins of the Praetorium, I teach the events that take us from the Garden of Gethsemane to the cross of Calvary.

In the house of Caiaphas is a deep cistern carved out of stone. It is here where Jesus was reportedly put for the remainder of the night, after having been beaten and possibly scourged. Stone steps have been carved in the walls so that visitors can actually descend into this pit to stand, pray, and read Scripture. It has been an incredibly moving experience for those who have toured Israel with us. We stand shoulder to shoulder on the bottom of the pit and up the stairway almost to its entrance. Many tears have been shed in that place as we have sung hymns and offered up prayers of gratitude to our God for the incomprehensible wonder of Calvary's love.

If you stand in the bottom of the pit and look straight up, you see a large hole which, at the time of our Lord and for many years after, was the only means of entering or leaving the pit. The prisoner was lowered or hoisted out by a rope.

If you were to climb the stairs, turn the corner to your left, and walk several feet, you would see the stone-carved room with a window looking into the pit. Under the window is a ledge where the guard of the prisoners could sit and view whoever was in the pit as he extended his lantern into the cold black hole.

I wonder who beheld Omnipotence, the Rock Christ Jesus, confined in a stone pit? I wonder if he knew that Jesus was the only One who could set him free?

14

If the prison guard at the house of Caiaphas turned from peering at his prisoner in the pit, he would look toward another room directly opposite him where other prisoners could be chained to the wall at night with just enough leeway to sit or lie down on the narrow stone slabs. Between the guard and the prisoners was a huge square opening.

On each side of the opening at the top and at the bottom were holes again carved in the stone, where the prisoners were beaten. Oh, the Jews were limited in the number of stripes they could inflict—39 plus 1. No more than 40, lest they kill their victim. That was Rome's prerogative, not the Jews'! Often they would tie ropes around the wrists and ankles of their prisoners, then stand them spread-eagle in the square opening, and proceed to beat them. At the base of the opening, also carved in stone, was a rectangular hole that held the vinegar for the prisoner's wounds.

Did they spread-eagle Jesus there and beat Him with rods, spit on Him, blindfold Him, and then ask Him to prophesy and tell them who it was that had just spit on Him? I don't know. All I can think of is hitting Omnipotence in the face and not having Him react in any way. All I can think of is reviling and spitting on One who is about to die for the very ones subjecting Him to such unjust mockery and abuse. I am awed as I stand in that cell and in that pit and remember the words of an older Peter, "Christ also suffered for you, leaving you an example for you to follow in His steps, WHO COMMITTED NO SIN, NOR WAS ANY DECEIT FOUND IN HIS MOUTH; and while being reviled, He did not revile in return; while suffering, He uttered no threats, but kept entrusting Himself to Him who judges righteously; and He Himself bore our sins in His body on the cross, that we might die to sin and live to righteousness; for by His wounds you were healed" (1 Peter 2:21-24).

It may have been in the house of Caiaphas that the prophecy of Isaiah 50:6 was fulfilled: "I gave My back to those who strike Me, and My cheeks to those who pluck out the beard; I did not cover My face from humiliation and spitting."

Why did He give His back to beating? Why did He not cover His face from spitting? Why did He let them reach up and pull the beard from His face? Why did He suffer and not threaten? So, Beloved of God, that you might know just how loved you are, just the way you are.

15 Can you imagine slapping Veracity in the face because He did not honor a man who was a hypocritical liar? Can you imagine sitting as a priestly sage and stroking the corners of your beard as those who did your bidding plucked the beard of God? Can you imagine putting a rope harness through the arms and across the back of Omnipotence and lowering Him into a pit? Can you imagine confining Omnipresence in a stone cistern, holding Him there in a prison? Can you imagine lowering the Light of the world into pitch darkness as you seek to snuff that Light out because He has thrown light on your sin?

Remember that Jesus was as much flesh and blood as you are, a man with feelings, emotions. One who experienced physical thirst even as you do, who knew physical exhaustion, who ached and cried, even as you have. One who has known the awfulness of loneliness, and has had to deal with rejection and abandonment.

Psalm 88:4-9 may portray Jesus' forsakenness in the blackness of the pit, the night before He died: "I am reckoned among those who go down to the pit; I have become like a man without strength, forsaken among the dead, like the slain who lie in the grave, whom Thou dost remember no more, and they are cut off from Thy hand. Thou hast put me in the lowest pit, in dark places, in the depths. Thy wrath has rested upon me, and Thou hast afflicted me with all Thy waves. Thou hast removed my acquaintances far from me; Thou hast made me an object of loathing to them; I am shut up and cannot go out. My eye has wasted away because of affliction; I have called upon Thee every day, O LORD; I have spread out my hands to Thee."

What, Beloved, would you say to your God? Why not write it out in your notebook?

16 And when it was day, the Council of elders [the Sanhedrin] of the people assembled, both chief priests and scribes, and they led Him away to their council chamber,

saying,"If You are the Christ, tell us." But He said to them, "If I tell you, you will not believe; and if I ask a question, you will not answer. But from now on THE SON OF MAN WILL BE SEATED AT THE RIGHT HAND of the power OF GOD." And they all said, "Are You the Son of God, then?" And He said to them, "Yes, I am." And they said, "What further need do we have of testimony? For we have heard it ourselves from His own mouth" (Luke 22:66-71).

They heard Jesus say with His own lips that He was the Son of God. Everything about His life supported that fact, but they were convinced that Jesus was not the Christ, and therefore had to be put to death. They deemed Him guilty without one shred of evidence. They even went against their own law regarding trials because they were bent on doing away with Jesus.

How incredibly sad! And yet, isn't that often the way with us? We become convinced of something, and we will not allow anything, not even the truth, to change our minds. We become deaf to truth, blind to reality.

God says that He loves us, Beloved, and that nothing "shall be able to separate us from the love of God, which is in Christ Jesus our Lord" (Romans 8:39). Are you going to take Him at His Word? Or are you going to hurl yourself headlong into a lie that will end in destruction rather than in the abundant life God intends for you?

John recorded all of these things in his Gospel that you might believe that Jesus is the Christ, the Son of God, and that believing you might have life. Have you believed? Do you have life?

17

Now when morning had come, all the chief priests and the elders of the people took counsel against Jesus to put Him to death; and they bound Him, and led Him away, and delivered Him up to Pilate the governor. . . .

And they themselves did not enter into the Praetorium in order that they might not be defiled, but might eat the Passover (Matthew 27:1,2; John 18:28).

What hypocrisy! They kept the Law as long as it suited them. I wonder if our Lord's words uttered not many days before pierced their hearts:

"Woe to you, scribes and Pharisees, hypocrites! For you tithe mint and dill and cummin, and have neglected the weightier provisions of the law: justice and mercy and faithfulness; but these are the things you should have done without neglecting the others. You blind guides, who strain out a gnat and swallow a camel! . . . You are like whitewashed tombs which on the outside appear beautiful, but inside they are full of dead men's bones and all uncleanness. Even so you too outwardly appear righteous to men, but inwardly you are full of hypocrisy and lawlessness. Woe to you, scribes and Pharisees, hypocrites! For you build the tombs of the prophets and adorn the monuments of the righteous, and say, 'If we had been living in the days of our fathers, we would not have been partners with them in shedding the blood of the prophets.' Consequently you bear witness against yourselves, that you are sons of those who murdered the prophets. Fill up then the measure of the guilt of your fathers" (Matthew 23:23,24,27-32).

In the name of God, their fathers had murdered God's prophets. Now they, in the name of God, were about to murder God's Son. Were there pricks of conscience, of guilt within? Pilate gave them the opportunity to stop this travesty.

"Pilate therefore went out to them, and said, 'What accusation do you bring against this Man?' They answered and said to him, 'If this Man were not an evildoer, we would not have delivered Him up to you.' Pilate therefore said to them, 'Take Him yourselves, and judge Him according to your law.' The Jews said to him, 'We are not permitted to put anyone to death,' that the word of Jesus might be fulfilled, which He spoke, signifying by what kind of death He was about to die" (John 18:29-32).

If the Jews had put Jesus to death, they would have stoned Him, for this was their way of execution. Crucifixion was the Roman way, reserved for criminals and those who were not Roman citizens. However, much earlier Jesus had indicated the way of His death: " 'And I, if I be lifted up from the earth, will draw all men to Myself.' But He was saying this to indicate the kind of death by which He was to die" (John 12:32,33). Stoning was mild compared to crucifixion. God wanted you to know the extent of His love for you.

18 When Pilate hesitated, the Jews began to accuse Jesus: " 'We found this man misleading our nation and forbidding to pay taxes to Caesar, and saying that He Himself is Christ, a King.' And Pilate asked Him, saying, 'Are You the King of the Jews?' And He answered him and said, 'It is as you say.' And Pilate said to the chief priests and the multitudes, 'I find no guilt in this man' " (Luke 23:2-4).

When Pilate asked if Jesus were a king, Jesus answered, " 'You say correctly that I am a king. For this I have been born, and for this I have come into the world, to bear witness to the truth. Every one who is of the truth hears My voice.' Pilate said to Him, 'What is truth?' " (John 18:37,38).

The One standing before Pilate was the Way, the Truth, and the Life, but Pilate and the Jews were not of the truth. Therefore, they did not recognize who Jesus was.

Beloved, it behooves us to ask ourselves if we really recognize Jesus and the Word of God as Truth. The philosophy of our day claims that there are no absolutes, no final authority. People do not want to be told what is right or wrong. How contrary to the Word of God. Pilate's words—"What is truth?"—are nothing new. People are asking the same question today and walking in the same darkness of unbelief.

Pilate had the greatest of opportunities, and he missed it. He didn't recognize Truth . . . and although his conscience troubled him, he allowed himself to be persuaded to do something he knew was wrong. "He was aware that the chief priests had delivered Him up because of envy" (Mark 15:10). He found no guilt in Jesus, and yet he had Him scourged and put to death. Then he washed his hands, declaring himself "innocent of this Man's blood" (Matthew 27:24). Yet, he was guilty because he had heard Truth and rejected Him. All of this came to pass, but not until Pilate first tried to pass Jesus off on Herod.

O Beloved, would you bear with me for one more question that may or may not be applicable to you? Have you tried to pass off Jesus on someone else, anyone but yourself? You can't. You cannot say, "But I didn't believe or respond to Jesus properly because of what was done to me by someone, or because of the circumstances of my life. Maybe if . . ." "Maybe ifs" won't do it. Truth stands before you. You can find no guilt in Him. What will you do with Him?

19 O Beloved, has there ever been a time when you didn't think you could bear anything more? When you were almost overwhelmed? There is One who understands, One who tasted all the suffering of mankind, so that no one might say to Him as their high priest, "But You don't understand!"

When Pilate heard that Jesus had preached in Galilee, he asked whether Jesus was a Galilean. "And when he learned that He belonged to Herod's jurisdiction, he sent Him to Herod, who himself also was in Jerusalem at that time" (Luke 23:7).

Being sent to Herod was just "one more thing." After the physical, emotional, and even spiritual trauma of the past hours, the walk from the Praetorium to Herod's palace had to be weakening. For a moment, let's reconsider all that Jesus experienced since the preceding evening.

After celebrating the Passover with the twelve and teaching them those things that they would need to know in the light of His death, Jesus walked across Jerusalem, out the city gate, and across the Kidron Valley to the Garden of Gethsemane. It was there that His soul became deeply grieved to the point of death. In His agony, He went into a state of hematidrosis, sweating profusely, even sweat mixed with blood.

From there He was taken to Annas and then to Caiaphas, where he was beaten, humiliated, and where, in all probability, His beard was plucked out. Having been literally slugged by His tormentors, it is obvious that His face was bruised and swollen. How long Jesus had to stand and take this torment, we do not know, but I am sure that His legs must have been weak, aching, and maybe even trembling from the loss of electrolytes that came from His profuse sweating.

After a sleepless night, He was taken from the house of Caiaphas, bound again with ropes, and probably dragged along while others stared and mocked. Walking those cobblestone streets must have been even more weakening and exhausting. Finally arriving at the Praetorium, Jesus once again had to spend His energy answering Pilate and enduring the stress of listening to His unjust accusers. And there was much more to come.

Are you at your wit's end, the limit of your endurance, Beloved? Calvary's love understands and gives you the promise of 1 Corinthians 10:13. Look it up.

20 Now Herod was very glad when he saw Jesus; for he had wanted to see Him for a long time, because he had been hearing about Him and was hoping to see some sign performed by Him. And he questioned Him at some length; but He answered him nothing. And the chief priests and the scribes were standing there, accusing Him vehemently. And Herod with his soldiers, after treating Him with contempt and mocking Him, dressed Him in a gorgeous robe and sent Him back to Pilate. Now Herod and Pilate became friends with one another that very day; for before they had been at enmity with each other (Luke 23:8-12).

"... AS A LAMB BEFORE ITS SHEARER IS SILENT, SO HE DOES NOT OPEN HIS MOUTH" (Acts 8:32). Herod wanted Jesus to entertain him, to amuse him. And because of this, Jesus opened not His mouth. Instead, He stood before them in silence as they mocked and humiliated Him. The King of kings was being mocked by an earthly king who had been given his kingship in the sovereignty of the God who stood before him, adorned in a gorgeous robe. Maybe it was one of Herod's! How ironic that would be, for if Herod had been interested in the person of Christ rather than in His performance, then he might have exchanged the filthy rags of his self-righteousness for the robes of God's righteousness.

Herod is like many whose interest in Jesus extends only as far as what Jesus can do for them. Jesus had done many miracles, signs, and wonders, and Herod knew it. He had taken a great interest in the Jews—his wife was a Jew—and he knew of the promise of a Messiah. But Herod wanted one more miracle, one more proof.

How typical of so many today! They won't believe the record of God's Word. They have to have their own personal, independent proof. So they say, "God, if You will just do thus and so, then I will believe on You." People who name the conditions usually (note I said "usually") do not even believe when the conditions are met.

Herod had enough proof. What he did not know was that one day he would bow the knee and confess that Jesus Christ is Lord, King of kings. Then he would hear from Jesus' lips, "Depart from Me, you worker of iniquity."

21 Once again Jesus was standing before Pilate. "And Pilate summoned the chief priests and the rulers and the people, and said to them, 'You brought this man to me as one who incites the people to rebellion, and behold, having examined Him before you, I have found no guilt in this man regarding the charges which you make against Him. No, nor has Herod, for he sent Him back to us; and behold, nothing deserving death has been done by Him. I will therefore punish Him and release Him. . . . But you have a custom, that I should release someone for you at the Passover;

do you wish then that I release for you the King of the Jews?' (Luke 23:13-16; John 18:39).

"And they were holding at that time a notorious prisoner, called Barabbas. When therefore they were gathered together, Pilate said to them, 'Whom do you want me to release for you? Barabbas, or Jesus who is called Christ?' For he knew that because of envy they had delivered Him up. And while he was sitting on the judgment seat, his wife sent to him, saying, 'Have nothing to do with that righteous Man; for last night I suffered greatly in a dream because of Him.' But the chief priests and the elders persuaded the multitudes to ask for Barabbas, and to put Jesus to death. But the governor answered and said to them, 'Which of the two do you want me to release for you?' And they said, 'Barabbas.' Pilate said to them, 'Then what shall I do with Jesus who is called Christ?' They all said, 'Let Him be crucified!' . . . And when Pilate saw that he was accomplishing nothing, but rather that a riot was starting, he took water and washed his hands in front of the multitude, saying, 'I am innocent of this Man's blood; see to that yourselves.' And all the people answered and said, 'His blood be on us and on our children!'" (Matthew 27:16-22,24,25).

O Beloved, do not let the voice of the world or of the enemy prevail in your life. Listen to God. Heed His warnings. Don't go with the crowd. Listening to them and declaring yourself innocent or washed won't save you. Might is not right. Jesus looked foolish and impotent, but He wasn't. He was demonstrating Calvary's love. "The weakness of God is stronger than men" (1 Corinthians 1:25).

22 "Then Pilate therefore took Jesus, and scourged Him" (John 19:1). It is a simple statement, Beloved, and yet it is filled with the profundity of love's willingness to bear all things and to seek the good of others.

Let me share with you what Roman scourging was like to give you a glimpse of the agony of Jesus' death. The Romans scourged with a short whip called a *flagrum* or *flagellum,* which consisted of various lengths of leather straps or thongs secured to a wooden handle. Attached to these leather thongs were iron balls which would cause deep contusions as the scourge was catapulted onto the victim's back. The blow of these iron balls would produce deep bleeding and pain. However, each leather strap also had barbs or hooks made of sheep bones in order to catch the flesh of the victim and tear it from his body. Oftentimes one hook was on the end of the strap while the second one was secured several inches up.

When the Romans scourged a man, they had no limits on the number of strokes, as did the Jews. The only limitation related to the fact that if a man were to be crucified, he still had to be alive when they nailed him to the wooden cross. The scourging was intended to bring the victim to a state short of death. Often the severity of the scourging depended on the disposition and character of the scourger or lictor.

Crucifixion was a slow death, sometimes taking days unless the victim's legs were broken. If a victim could not push his body up to release the muscular tension from being suspended on two nails, he could not breathe. Once the legs were broken, the victim could not breathe, and death came quickly. A good scourging helped hurry the process of death, especially if the legs of the victim were not to be broken.

The Jews were not involved in the scourging of Jesus. They only viewed the results as He hung naked before them. It is from the works of Josephus, the Jewish historian, and from other historical documents that we learn the details of scourging. The Gospels merely say that Pilate had Him scourged.

In all probability, the scourging took place in the bottom of the Praetorium where the Roman cohorts were gathered, ready to put down any Jewish uprisings during the Passover. I am sure they were restless and glad to have something to do. Romans soldiers were known to be cruel and hard, loving blood and victory. Since the scourging did not take place in the open, they probably did not tie Jesus to a pole. They most likely spread-eagled Him and began the scourging.

As we will see from the Scriptures later in our study, no man would ever suffer as did your God, who died for you. What do you have to say to Him today?

23 As the flagellum struck the back of Jesus, the second hook upward on the strap would grab and probably flail His back in such a way as to allow the end of the strap to coil around His abdomen, anchoring the hook into His side or chest or abdomen. As the straps hit His body, the scourger knew when his tentacles were anchored in our Lord's flesh. Having thrown the whip from the dirty, stone floor over his shoulder with the full thrust of his weight, with a wrench of his wrist he pulled back with all his might, triumph in his eyes, for as the hooks broke through the flesh, his skill as a lictor was evident. Blood began to flow from the Lamb of God.

As the scourging continued, the bone hooks cut deep into the muscles of our Lord's body, tearing loose quivering ribbons of flesh from His body. By the time Jesus had endured 15 lashes, His flesh would have been hanging in bloody strips.

Underneath the back muscles a thin layer of fat covers the arteries. After 16 to 20 stripes there would be no skin left. The little arteries would be spurting blood. Truly, "There is a fountain filled with blood drawn from Immanuel's veins," as hymn writer William Cowper put it, "and sinners, plunged beneath that flood, lose all their guilty stains."

Although Jesus could have called 10,000 angels and immediately put a halt to His suffering, He didn't. Calvary's love restrained Him. The cross was yet to come, for it was there that Christ would redeem us "from the curse of the Law, having become a curse for us—for it is written, 'CURSED IS EVERYONE WHO HANGS ON A TREE'" (Galatians 3:13). Not until Calvary would His blood be spilled out in full.

As the lictor continued his scourging, he attacked his victim from various angles. Scourging was the art of bringing a man to the edge of death without killing him. As he proceeded to lacerate his victim, the back was left in shreds, and often the abdomen was torn open so that the victim's bowels laid exposed.

As was the custom, scourging was not enough. Since they couldn't scourge their victim until He died, why not make sport of this One who was called "King of the Jews"? And so they mocked Jesus, not realizing that the flesh they scourged from His body, that the blood they drew from His wounds, was clothing His deity. They were oblivious to the fact that by the very wounds they had inflicted, they might be healed (1 Peter 2:24).

You're not oblivious to the reason for His wounds, are you?

24 Incarcerated in the Praetorium that day, because of the Feast of the Passover and the potential of a flare-up between the religious Jews and their Roman rulers, the soldiers passed the time by amusing themselves with this Man who had come back from Herod wearing a purple robe.

If you were to visit Jerusalem, you could go to a church on the Via Dolorosa. After walking down several flights of stone steps into what seems to be the basement of the church, you would come into a huge room with very low ceilings where all of a sudden you would find yourself walking on a different type of floor. This pavement becomes part of the Via Dolorosa—the street on which Jesus left the Praetorium to go to Calvary. These stones, over 2000 years old, are part of the ground floor of what used to be the Praetorium. This, Beloved, was where they held Jesus.

On the floor is a dim circle in the stone, where the soldiers played what was called "The King's Game." Apparently they would put their victim in the center of the circle and then make sport of him, using him as a part of their game.

In all probability, this is what we read of in John 19:2,3 and Matthew 27:30,31: "And the soldiers wove a crown of thorns and put it on His head, and arrayed Him in a purple robe; and they began to come up to Him, and say, 'Hail, King of the Jews!' and to give Him blows in the face. . . . And they spat on Him, and took the reed and began to beat Him on the head. And after they had mocked Him, they took His robe off and put His garments on Him, and led Him away to crucify Him."

Can't you hear the soldiers, in their loud, raucous voices shouting, "Kings wear crowns! Where is Your crown, O King of the Jews? If You're going to play in our game, You must have a crown! What shall we have for a crown? Here, I have it. We shall weave Him a crown of thorns!"

Thorns were readily accessible because they were kept in small buckets, to be used as firewood. However, weaving thorns for a crown had to be done carefully, since the thorns were treacherous. About the size of tenpenny nails and as sharp as needles, they could cause severe pain, even to a Roman soldier.

Jesus had refused the crown offered to Him by the devil when he took Jesus up to a high mountain and offered Him all of the kingdoms of this world and their glory if He would only worship him. Now Jesus wore a crown of thorns, so that someday those who believed on and followed Him might rule and reign with Him forever.

O Beloved, whatever the devil offers you, refuse it—despite the temporary pain or mocking.

25 Can you hear the soldiers? "Put on the crown, and we shall bow to this King of the Jews!"

"Hail, King of the Jews! Hail!" they cried, spitting in contempt as they bent their knees. Although the Scriptures do not record the details of the soldiers' mockery of our Lord, we know that a mock scepter was placed in Jesus' hands.

The robe they placed on Jesus acted as a cautery as it grabbed and adhered to His flesh that was seeping serous fluid and blood. But oh, the agony it would bring later when they ripped it from His body!

While all of this was going on, Pilate was still trying to

figure out how to release Jesus. Maybe if the crowds saw Him again, after having been scourged and mocked, it might satisfy their thirst for His blood.

It would be easy to incite a mob against Jesus at this time because it was the Passover, and the walled city of Jerusalem was teeming with people, the population probably doubling from 100,000 to 200,000. Herod had come to Jerusalem bringing his soldiers with him. And Pilate, as procurator of Jerusalem, had the city filled with Roman cohorts should it be necessary to keep the peace.

The scourging had taken place in the Praetorium, which was right next to the Jewish Temple mount. As a matter of fact, when Herod had the Temple rebuilt, the governor's place or Praetorium was constructed so that it shared a common wall with the Temple area. A tower was built on the governor's place so that the Romans could look down on the Temple mount and make sure that no insurrections were being executed from that particular area. Because they were not allowed beyond the Gentiles' court in the Temple area, the Romans could never be quite sure of what might happen within that sacred area. The tower that gave them full view of everything except the Holy Place and the Holy of Holies was crucial. No need to worry about what went on in these holy places, for only the priests were allowed within their confines.

The Jews would not "enter into the Praetorium in order that they might not be defiled, but might eat the Passover" (John 18:28), but from the tower, Pilate could display the scourged Jesus and communicate with the Jews. The Jews would religiously keep the Passover feast, but in their religion they would miss the Passover Lamb.

O Beloved, examine your heart to make sure that yours is not mere religion, but that you have a genuine relationship with the Lamb of God who alone takes away your sin.

26 On the day before the Passover, Pilate said to the Jews, " 'Behold, your King!' They therefore cried out, 'Away

with Him, away with Him, crucify Him!' Pilate said to them, 'Shall I crucify your King?' The chief priests answered, 'We have no king but Caesar.' So he then delivered Him to them to be crucified" (John 19:14-16).

Crucifixion was the Roman form of execution for those who were not Roman citizens. When Titus leveled Jerusalem in A.D. 70, 500 people were crucified daily. Tradition has it that the apostle Peter was crucified upside down, while Paul, a citizen, was beheaded by Rome.

Since crucifixion was common, and since wood was at a premium in Jerusalem, the upright parts of crosses were left standing in place all of the time, anchored in the ground. When we read of a man carrying his cross, it refers to the crossbar of the cross. If a man weighed 170 to 200 pounds, then the upright portion of the cross would be approximately 10 to 16 feet high and would weigh approximately 120 to 200 pounds in order to hold the weight of the man and the weight of the crossbar. The crossbar would then weigh approximately 60 to 75 pounds.

Jesus obviously would have been too weak from all that He had endured to carry His cross. In John 19:17, we are told that Jesus "went out, bearing His own cross," but Luke gives us this perspective: "And when they led Him away, they laid hold of one Simon of Cyrene, coming in from the country, and placed on him the cross to carry behind Jesus. And there were following Him a great multitude of the people, and of women who were mourning and lamenting Him. But Jesus turning to them said, 'Daughters of Jerusalem, stop weeping for Me, but weep for yourselves and for your children. For behold, the days are coming when they will say, "Blessed are the barren, and the wombs that never bore, and the breasts that never nursed." Then they will begin TO SAY TO THE MOUNTAINS, "FALL ON US," AND TO THE HILLS, "COVER US." For if they do these things in the green tree, what will happen in the dry?' " (Luke 23:26-31).

Jesus was led through the jammed streets of that walled city. Those who were preparing to celebrate the Passover would soon be carrying their sacrificial lambs on their shoulders as they made their way to the Temple to slay the paschal lamb and keep the feast.

In all of the ritual connected with the festival, the nation was blind to the fact that the One being led down their streets past the doors of their homes and shops was the true Passover Lamb. From this day on there would never be a legitimate celebration of the Passover, for Christ their Passover was going to be sacrificed on this very fourteenth day of Nisan, at the very hour in which many of them would be sacrificing their lambs. God's Lamb was in their midst, and most of them did not know it!

27 Have you ever stopped to consider what happened to a body suspended by two nails on a cross? That, Beloved, is what I want us to consider for the next few days, to see the "all things" Christ's love endured for you . . . even when you were a sinner, without hope, and an enemy of God.

In John 19:17,18, we read: "They took Jesus therefore, and He went out, bearing His own cross, to the place called the Place of a Skull, which is called in Hebrew, Golgotha. There they crucified Him, and with Him two other men, one on either side, and Jesus in between."

The agonizing hell of crucifixion began as the scourged victim was thrown to the ground, grinding dirt into his back as the soldiers pinned his outstretched arms over the patibulum (the crossbar). They would then place a spike on the victim's wrist, and with a thud of the hammer . . . once, twice, maybe three times . . . solidly anchor him to the wood.

Where exactly was that spike placed? If you will follow your middle finger to the base of the hand where it connects with the wrist, you will feel a hole surrounded by bone. Personally, I believe that when God created man, He designed man's hand to hold a nail . . . for He knew before the foundation of the world that Jesus would be His Lamb, slain by crucifixion.

As the nail pierced the wrist, jolts of excruciating pain shot through the fingers, causing them to contract into the shape of a claw. The nerve running through this portion of the hand pierced by the spike caused the victim to writhe in pain, tossing his body in agony. Can you begin to imagine the searing pain not only of body but also of mind, for there was yet another hand to be nailed to the crossbar? Once that was done, the soldiers would then lift up the crossbar, dragging the impaled Christ through the dirt to the awaiting upright part of the cross. Straining under the weight of that limp, tortured body, it would be a relief for those lifting Jesus to drop the weighty crossbar into the notch at the top of the upright, thus forming a T-shaped cross.

The jolt must have been excruciating as suddenly His whole weight was suspended on the two nails impaling Him to the cross. Oh, Calvary's love! You have engraved us on the palms of Your hands. . . . You cannot forget us! (Isaiah 49:15,16).[1]

28 As the body of the Lord dangled with its full weight suspended from His two pierced hands, it threw His muscles into a pectoral paralysis. The chest and arms went into a contorted twist, making breathing almost impossible.

> The weight of the body, pulling down on the outstretched arms and shoulders, would tend to fix the intercostal muscles in an inhalation state and thereby hinder passive exhalation. Accordingly, exhalation was primarily diaphragmatic, and breathing was shallow. It is likely that this form of respiration would not suffice and that hypercarbia would soon result. The onset of muscle cramps or tetanic contractions, due to fatigue and hypercarbia, would hinder respiration even further.
>
> Adequate exhalation required lifting the body by pushing up on the feet and by flexing the elbows and adducting the shoulders. However, this maneuver would place the entire weight of the body on the tarsals (bones in the feet) and would produce searing pain. Furthermore,

flexion of the elbows would cause rotation of the wrists about the iron nails and cause fiery pain along the damaged median nerves (in the hand). Lifting of the body would also painfully scrape the scourged back against the rough wooden stipes. Muscle cramps and paresthesias of the outstretched and uplifted arms would add to the discomfort. As a result, each respiratory effort would become agonizing and tiring and lead eventually to asphyxia.

The actual cause of death by crucifixion was multifactorial and varied somewhat with each case, but the two most prominent causes probably were hypovolemic shock and exhaustion asphyxia. Other possible contributing factors included dehydration, stress-induced arrhythmias (rapid, irregular heartbeats), and congestive heart failure with the rapid accumulation of pericardial (lining around the heart) and perhaps pleural effusions. Crucifracture (breaking the legs below the knees), if performed, led to an asphyxic death within minutes. Death by crucifixion was, in every sense of the word, excruciating.[2]

Interference with the victim's breathing made it necessary either to place the victim's feet on a small wooden wedge-like platform or to nail them to the cross. With His knees jacked up in a flexed position, the victim had an opportunity to push himself up and thereby relieve the paralysis of the chest so that he could breathe.

Oh, breathe on us, precious Breath of Calvary's love. Fill us with Your life from Your death.

29 From this point on, every breath taken by our Lord would be through the effort of pushing against the nails which pierced His feet. Every push against the bark of the tree would grate against the raw wounds of His already dirt-infected back. And the blood would continue to ooze from His body. The body will do anything it can to get air as breathing literally becomes a fight for life. Jesus, the One who

would breathe into man the breath of life, had to struggle for His every breath in His battle against sin.

Understanding this sheds new light on Psalm 22 which under the inspiration of the Holy Spirit describes what happens physically when a person is crucified: "I am poured out like water, and all my bones are out of joint; my heart is like wax; it is melted within me" (22:14). The heart eventually moves out of its normal position, repositioning itself in the thoracic cavity. Because of the jolting trauma from being dropped onto the upright and suspended by the hands, the bones do go out of joint so that literally one becomes very aware of the bones in his body. Thus, we read: "They pierced my hands and my feet. I can count all my bones" (22:16,17).

As we understand what it took for our Lord to even breathe, I want you to remember that His back was raw, His flesh shreds. The robe put on Him in mockery acted as a cautery to His bloody, oozing, weeping flesh for a while—until it was brutally ripped off His back. Years ago I worked for a while nursing some burn victims. Not knowing what we do now, in those days we dressed their burns with bandages. When it came time to change their bandages and debride their wounds, the pain was excruciating. Thus we would drug our patients with a strong narcotic such as morphine. Yet, everyone still knew when their bandages were being changed because of their screams.

Every breath of our Lord was torment, endured because of Calvary's love.

30 Because every breath was labored, Jesus' words from the cross were few and briefly uttered. Despite all of the pain and abuse He endured as He hung on Calvary's tree, His words were never filled with malice. Comments were hurled at Him by the spectators who had come to view the crucifixion. For Pilate had placed an inscription on the cross that read, "JESUS THE NAZARENE, THE KING OF THE JEWS."

"This inscription many of the Jews read, for the place where Jesus was crucified was near the city; and it was written in Hebrew, Latin, and in Greek. And so the chief priests of the Jews were saying to Pilate, 'Do not write, "The King of the Jews"; but that He said, "I am King of the Jews."' Pilate answered, 'What I have written I have written' (John 19:20-22).

"At that time two robbers were crucified with Him, one on the right and one on the left. And those passing by were hurling abuse at Him, wagging their heads, and saying, 'You who are going to destroy the temple and rebuild it in three days, save Yourself!' " (Matthew 27:38-40).

Little did they realize the import of this comment, for when Jesus had said, " 'Destroy this temple, and in three days I will raise it up' . . . He was speaking of the temple of His body" (John 2:19,21). Later when Jesus was raised from the dead, His disciples would remember that He had said this (John 2:22). However, at the time of His crucifixion even Jesus' disciples could not understand the meaning of His words which His railers were throwing back into His face.

The taunts continued: " 'If You are the Son of God, come down from the cross.' In the same way the chief priests, along with the scribes and elders, were mocking Him, and saying, 'He saved others; He cannot save Himself. He is the King of Israel; let Him now come down from the cross, and we shall believe in Him' " (Matthew 27:40-42).

Here they were wanting another sign! "For indeed Jews ask for signs, and Greeks search for wisdom; but we preach Christ crucified, to Jews a stumbling block, and to Gentiles foolishness, but to those who are the called, both Jews and Greeks, Christ the power of God and the wisdom of God" (1 Corinthians 1:22-24). The only sign that was yet to come for the Jews was the sign of Jonah. When the scribes and Pharisees had said, "Teacher, we want to see a sign from You," Jesus had told them, "An evil and adulterous generation craves for a sign; and yet no sign shall be given to it but the sign of Jonah the prophet; for just as JONAH WAS THREE DAYS AND THREE NIGHTS IN THE BELLY OF THE SEA MONSTER, SO shall the Son of Man be three days and three nights in the heart of the earth" (Matthew 12:38-40).

If Jesus came down off the cross, they would have missed the sign of signs. They would have missed Calvary's love!

31 The soldiers therefore, when they had crucified Jesus, took His outer garments and made four parts, a part to every soldier and also the tunic; now the tunic was seamless, woven in one piece. They said therefore to one another, "Let us not tear it, but cast lots for it, to decide whose it shall be"; that the Scripture might be fulfilled, "THEY DIVIDED MY OUTER GARMENTS AMONG THEM, AND FOR MY CLOTHING THEY CAST LOTS." Therefore the soldiers did these things. But there were standing by the cross of Jesus His mother, and His mother's sister, Mary the wife of Clopas, and Mary Magdalene. When Jesus therefore saw His mother, and the disciple whom He loved standing nearby, He said to His mother, "Woman, behold, your son!" Then He said to the disciple, "Behold, your mother!" And from that hour the disciple took her into his own household.

After this, Jesus, knowing that all things had already been accomplished, in order that the Scripture might be fulfilled, said, "I am thirsty." A jar full of sour wine was standing there; so they put a sponge full of the sour wine upon a branch of hyssop, and brought it up to His mouth. When Jesus therefore had received the sour wine, He said, "It is finished!" And He bowed His head, and gave up His spirit.

"The Jews therefore, because it was the day of preparation, so that the bodies should not remain on the cross on the Sabbath (for that Sabbath was a high day), asked Pilate that their legs might be broken, and that they might be taken away. The soldiers therefore came, and broke the legs of the first man, and of the other man who was crucified with Him; but coming to Jesus, when they saw that He was already dead, they did not break His legs; but one

> of the soldiers pierced His side with a spear, and immediately there came out blood and water. And he who has seen has borne witness, and his witness is true; and he knows that he is telling the truth, so that you also may believe. For these things came to pass, that the Scripture might be fulfilled, "NOT A BONE OF HIM SHALL BE BROKEN." And again another Scripture says, "THEY SHALL LOOK ON HIM WHOM THEY PIERCED" (John 19:23-37).

O Beloved, look on Him whom they pierced. It was finished. Every sin of mankind, including yours, had been atoned for because God so loved the world that He gave His only begotten Son so that whoever would believe on Him would not perish but have everlasting life.

This, Beloved, is Calvary's love. How dare we ever doubt His unconditional love for us! May we hide ourselves in the truth of it all, and then abiding in His unconditional security, love our God with all of our heart, all of our soul, all of our body, all of our strength. Can we do any less? We may, but we shouldn't.

November

"The Resurrection . . . A Matter of Life and Breath"

1 George Whitefield had preached for 33 years, and by the age of 55 he looked as if he were 70. But whatever the toll to his body, it had been worth it all; he had been one of God's principal instruments of the Great Awakening in the colonies.

At the age of 22 after a year of striving to find favor with God, he ceased to struggle and entered into the new birth—something the church in England knew little of in the 1700s. The prayers and sermons of those days were written and proclaimed within the walls of the church by ordained clergy only. Whitefield broke all of these molds. When burdened for the common laborers who never darkened the doors of the church and who were ignorant of the free grace of God through the new birth, he went into the open fields to preach and pray extemporaneously. His actions brought him many enemies in the church, but Whitefield was used of God to build His true church against which the gates of hell could not prevail.

In September 1770, on the day before Whitefield entered the portals of heaven, weak but still burdened to preach the gospel, he stood on a platform in the open air in New Hampshire and announced his text:

> "Examine yourselves whether ye be in the faith." He stood silent. Minutes passed. He said, "I will wait for the gracious assistance of God. For he will, I am certain,

assist me once more to speak in his name." Then he began. The words came hoarse and sluggish at first, the sentences disjointed and rough as if his brain refused to focus. He spoke of men's attempts to win the favour of God by good works and not by faith. George contemplated, as if thinking out loud, the enormity of such effrontery. His mind suddenly kindled . . . and he thundered in tones that reached the edge of the immense crowd: "Works? Works? A man get to heaven by *works?* I would as soon think of climbing to the moon on a rope of sand!"

After that any weakness seemed engulfed in a mighty power that swept him into an unforgettable sermon in which he proclaimed, once again, the glories of Christ. . . .

The first hour passed. Still he preached. . . . It seemed George Whitefield looked right into heaven, viewing the beauty of the Lord Jesus. . . .

Nearly two hours had passed when George cried, "I go! I go to rest prepared. My sun has arisen and by the aid of heaven has given light to many. It is now about to set—*NO!* It is about to rise to the zenith of immortal glory!

"I have outlived many on earth but they cannot outlive me in heaven. O thought divine! I shall soon be in a world where time, age, pain and sorrow are unknown. My body fails, my spirit expands. How willingly would I live for ever to preach Christ! But I die to be *with* him!"[1]

2 How important is the reality of the resurrection of Jesus Christ to you? It is a matter of life and breath!

"A matter of life and breath?" You may be asking, "What do you mean by that?" That, Beloved, is what I want to share with you this month as we look at John 20.

Remember, John's Gospel was written quite a few years later than the other Gospels. In his closing comments John gives us the specific purpose which governed all that he recorded: "Many other signs therefore Jesus also performed in the presence of the disciples, which are not written in this book; but these have been written that you may believe that Jesus is the Christ, the Son of God; and that believing you may have life in His name" (John 20:30,31). The resurrection of Jesus Christ from the dead would be the final sign recorded by John which would prove beyond a shadow of a doubt that Jesus was the Christ, the Son of God, and the only source of eternal life.

Today, I want you to see the masterful way in which John lays out for his readers exactly how the resurrection proves Jesus' deity and demonstrates His right to bestow life on those who believe in His name. I suggest that you read John 20 before you proceed any further.

John 20:1-13 gives us the testimony of the empty tomb. The eyewitnesses, as recorded by John, are Mary Magdalene, Simon Peter, and John himself. Although John does not name himself, he is clearly "the other disciple" who first came to the tomb, and "saw and believed" (John 20:8).

John 20:14-29 records the visible appearances of the resurrected Son of God to Mary, to the disciples, and then to Thomas. His appearance to Thomas occurs in verses 26-29. The tomb was empty, but not because someone had stolen the dead body of Jesus Christ. It was empty because Jesus had risen from the dead! There were witnesses who had seen Him in person, who had been invited to touch the hands and side which had been scarred in His crucifixion. They had not seen Jesus once, but at different times, over many days. It was no illusion, no hallucination. Jesus had risen from the dead!

In John 20:21-23, having shown Jesus as the Son of God, John tells us how life is obtained by believing in His name—life that is only possible because He now lives and can bestow His life upon them.

When Sir Thomas Scott lay dying, he cried, "Until this moment, I thought there was neither God nor hell! Now I know and feel that there are both and I am doomed to perdition by the just judgment of the Almighty."

When Caesar Borgia confronted death, in despair he said, "When I lived, I provided for everything but death; now I must die, and I am unprovided to die."

O Beloved, if Jesus had not been raised, all of us would be unprovided to face the just judgment of the Almighty!

3 How does the resurrection give proof of the deity of Jesus and the life that is ours through faith in Him? These two things, Beloved, are the very tenets of our faith. Take them away and we are without hope. For if these truths are not substantiated by the bodily resurrection of Jesus Christ, then our faith is in vain.

First, I want us to look at how the sign of the resurrection proves that Jesus is the Christ, the Son of God. From the transgression of Adam and Eve in the Garden of Eden, God had promised a Messiah, One who would eventually crush the head of the serpent who had lured them into unbelief. That first promise of the Redeemer is found in Genesis 3:15: "And I will put enmity between you and the woman, and between your seed and her seed; he shall bruise you on the head, and you shall bruise him on the heel."

In this verse we catch a dim but certain view of the resurrection of Jesus Christ. However, while the resurrection might be somewhat veiled, the death of Jesus Christ is not.

Let me diagram Genesis 3:15, and then we will talk about it point by point.

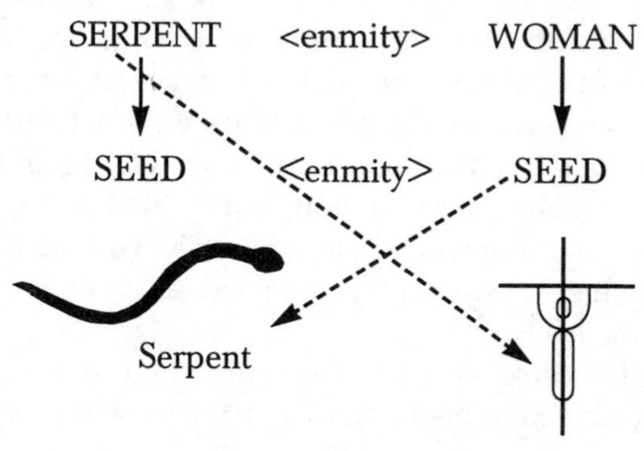

The serpent would wound the heel of the woman's seed. These words are incredibly awesome, since crucifixion is the only death in which the heel is bruised. So here, Beloved, at the beginning of time, we have insight into the substitutionary death of our Lord. Adam and Eve, the parents of all mankind, receive for themselves and for all who will be born of them the promise that one day the woman's seed will triumph over their destroyer, the serpent of old, the devil. Did they understand the promise? I believe that they did.

In Genesis 4:1, we read: "Now the man had relations with his wife Eve, and she conceived and gave birth to Cain, and she said, 'I have gotten a manchild with *the help of* the LORD.'" Now let me explain why I believe Adam and Eve understood the promise of Genesis 3:15. You will notice "the help of" is in italics. This means that it was added by the translators. In the Hebrew Cain means "gotten one." *Manchild* could be translated, "man, the LORD." O Beloved, do you see now, Eve so understood the promise that she thought Cain was the one fulfilling the Lord's promise of the seed who would bruise Satan.

4

What hope God's promise must have brought to the broken hearts of Adam and Eve. There would be triumph over the awful defeat of listening to the serpent's lie!

However, triumph would not come merely because Jesus was delivered up for our sin. Our sin must not only be paid for in full, but death must be conquered. Life must come out of death. In the promise of victory over the serpent, we see not only the death of Jesus Christ, but also the resurrection. Let me quote the verse for you again today so that you can have it before you: "And I will put enmity between you and the woman, and between your seed and her seed; he shall bruise you on the head, and you shall bruise him on the heel."

In this verse we read of two afflictions: the serpent afflicting the Seed of the woman by bruising Him on the heel, and the Seed of the woman afflicting the serpent by crushing his head. The word *bruise* can be translated "crush."

The woman's Seed is the Messiah, the Promised One, the Christ. *Seed* is an interesting term because women don't have seeds. Men do! Thus, couched in this word from the mouth of God is a miraculous prophecy of the virgin birth. The seed will be God's seed placed in the woman, bringing forth deity clothed in humanity.

The woman's Seed will crush the serpent. If there is any question regarding the exact character of the serpent, Revelation 12:9 clears that up: "And the great dragon was thrown down, the serpent of old who is called the devil and Satan, who deceives the whole world; he was thrown down to the earth, and his angels were thrown down with him."

A crushing wound to the head becomes a mortal wound. Since the crushing of the head will be a mortal wound, the crushing of the serpent's head must take place after the serpent bruises the heel of the woman's Seed. It would follow also that there must be the resurrection of the One whose heel has been bruised, since it is He alone who does the crushing.

It is interesting to me that in many churches in Latin America, there are statues of the virgin Mary holding the baby Jesus in her arms; under the sole of one of her feet is the head of the serpent with an apple in his mouth. But it is not Mary who crushed the head of the serpent. Jesus, after being bruised on His heel through crucifixion, was raised to deliver a mortal wound to the devil of old.

Beloved, my goal in writing *My Savior, My Friend* is to disciple you in the Word so that you might know your God and stand firm in your faith. I want you to have grace and peace multiplied to you in the knowledge of God and of Jesus our Lord so that you might know all that has been provided for you for life and godliness.

5 John wanted his readers to know that Jesus is the Christ, the Son of God. The term *the Christ* was the

Greek counterpart to the Hebrew word for *the Messiah.* Both *Christ* and *Messiah* meant "the promised one."

The Promised One, however, would not be of man's seed. Anyone of Adam's seed would be born dead in trespasses and sins. Jesus had to be God's Son. "Through one man sin entered into the world, and death through sin, and so death spread to all men, because all sinned" (Romans 5:12).

Now, Beloved, let us reason together regarding how the resurrection proves that Jesus is the Christ, the Son of God, and not the natural son of Adam. By virtue of being born into the human race of the sperm of a man and the egg of a woman, one is born into sin. We are all sinners by birth for . . . "in sin my mother conceived me" (Psalm 51:5). Thus, if Jesus had been born of the union of Mary's egg and Joseph's sperm rather than of God's seed, He would have had to die and remain dead. He, like all others of the human race, would never have been resurrected. Why? Because by virtue of being in Adam's race, He would have been born into sin, and "the wages of sin is death" (Romans 6:23).

However, because Jesus was born of a virgin upon whom the Spirit of God had come to cause her to conceive Jesus in her womb, He was born a man, but without sin. And because He was without sin, death had no hold upon Him.

O Beloved, before we proceed any further, let me give you several things to ponder today. Be still and let God search your heart. As the psalmist says: "Commune with your own heart upon your bed, and be still" (Psalm 4:4 KJV). How we need to take time for this communion! Our lives are filled with noise that keeps us from hearing the still, small voice of God in the quietness of our hearts.

Have you ever realized that your sin gives Satan a place of occupation in your life? Do you want that? Then stay away from sin. How? It begins with being born anew . . . moving from the family of the first Adam to that of the last Adam, Jesus Christ . . . bearing His image. "The first man is from the earth, earthy; the second man is from heaven. . . . And just as we have borne the image of the earthy, we shall also bear the image of the heavenly" (1 Corinthians 15:47,49).

6 Sin gives death its power over mankind. The root of all sin is walking in one's own way rather than in dependence upon God and in perfect submission to Him by obeying His commandments and doing His will. It was Satan who enticed Eve to break God's commandment and eat of the fruit of the tree of the knowledge of good and evil. He was the one who contradicted the Word of God. He was the one who lied by saying that Adam and Eve would not suffer the consequences of their disobedience. Sin came when Adam and Eve believed a lie instead of the Word of God, which is truth. And with sin came death—just as God had told them.

O Beloved, whom are you going to believe? Whom are you going to obey? As you make your choice, remember that sin always brings forth death in one form or another—death to what could have been, death to a relationship, death to a possible opportunity to serve the Lord, death to hearing God's "well done," or death to receiving a reward when you stand before Him.

Just today I heard of a teenager who went to a party with her date and there succumbed to the pressure of her peers to have a drink. She knew it was wrong. In the first place, she was a minor and it was illegal. In the second place, her parents had forbidden her to drink. And . . . she knew better. She had been raised in the church. She knew that sin was disobedience. Disobedience to God, to parents, to the law of the land. One drink led to another until she was drunk. Her date, tired of trying to persuade her to go home, finally left her at the party. Needing a way home, she accepted a ride with three guys, and on the way home, she lost her virginity. To one . . . to two . . . to three? She cannot remember. She only knows that her disobedience cost her what she could never regain. Never would she be able to give a husband something she had never given anyone else.

What God meant to be beautiful, special, and sacred, she had thrown on the trash heap of sin.

O Beloved, if Jesus had not risen from the dead, what hope would she or any sinner have? If Jesus had not risen from the dead, she might as well have continued to eat, drink, and be merry, for tomorrow she would die and taste death's awful eternal hell. But because of the resurrection, she could hear of the hope of forgiveness of sins and the newness of life which could be hers through the resurrected Lord Jesus Christ.

7 How did the resurrection of Jesus Christ from the dead prove beyond a shadow of a doubt that Jesus was the Christ, the Son of God?

Let me share a word of caution with you. I find a love of doctrine greatly lacking in Christians today. Sad to say, most are more interested in what Christ can do for them to help them solve some particular personal problem than they are in knowing and understanding the essential fundamentals of their faith. They look at doctrine as something sterile and academic, having nothing to do with life. And yet, my friend, doctrine is the foundation which determines how we live.

If you were staring death in the face, knowing that you would die soon, what would be your assurance of life after death if Christ had not been raised from the dead? Had He not been born of a virgin?

However, because Jesus was conceived of God in the virgin Mary's womb, and because He never sinned but always did the will of His Father in heaven, then God could accept Jesus' substitutionary death for the sins of all mankind. He was "delivered up because of our transgressions, and was raised because of our justification" (Romans 4:25). In other words, because the righteousness of God the Father was satisfied when Jesus "who knew no sin [was made] to be sin on our behalf" (2 Corinthians 5:21), God could justly raise Jesus from the dead. In raising Jesus from the dead, God demonstrated that the payment for the sins of all mankind was complete, paid in full. Paid by One who had not sinned: "For if by the transgression of the one, death reigned through the one, much more those who receive the abundance of grace and of the gift of righteousness will reign in life through the One, Jesus Christ. So then as through one transgression there resulted condemnation to all men, even so through one act of righteousness [Jesus' death] there resulted justification of life to all men. For as through the one man's disobedience the many were made sinners, even so through the obedience of the One the many will be made righteous" (Romans 5:17-19).

Life is found only in Jesus Christ. Only those who have received Jesus Christ, either by looking forward in faith to the coming of the Messiah and His substitutionary death or by looking back to His cross in faith, will ever attain to the resurrection of the dead into eternal life. God bore witness concerning His Son by raising Him from the dead. "And the witness is this, that God has given us eternal life, and this life is in His Son. He who has the Son has the life; he who does not have the Son of God does not have the life" (1 John 5:11,12). Do you have life?

8 Now that we have an overview of John 20, as it relates to John's purpose in writing, I want us to move through this chapter, tying its events chronologically with the other Gospel accounts. As we do this, we must remember that the author of each Gospel was selective in what he recorded. Under the inspiration of the Holy Spirit, he chose to include or eliminate that which helped him achieve his purpose.

All four of the Gospels tell us of Joseph of Arimathea. "And after these things Joseph of Arimathea, being a disciple of Jesus, but a secret one, for fear of the Jews, asked Pilate that he might take away the body of Jesus; and Pilate granted permission. He came therefore, and took away His body" (John 19:38).

Mark tells us that Joseph had to gather up his courage before he went to Pilate to ask him for the body of Jesus. Joseph was "a prominent member of the Council," the 70-member body of the Sanhedrin which ruled Jerusalem under the jurisdiction of Rome. Before Pilate would grant Joseph's request, he wanted to make sure that Jesus was dead. This is significant in that it is another proof that Jesus did not merely "swoon" on Calvary as some say, only to be revived in the coolness of a stone tomb. Men usually took longer to die than Jesus had. Thus, "Pilate wondered if He was dead by this time, and summoning the centurion, he questioned him as to whether He was already dead. And ascertaining this from the centurion, he granted the body to Joseph" (Mark 15:43-45).

What was this secret disciple of Jesus like? He was "a good and righteous man" who "had not consented to their [the Sanhedrin's] plan and action" (Luke 23:50,51). He was "waiting for the kingdom of God" (Mark 15:43) and apparently had felt that Jesus was the One who had come to usher in that kingdom.

O Beloved, what kind of a disciple are you of Jesus Christ? Are you a secret disciple? Is your belief in Him hidden for fear of family, friends, or business associates? Do others know that Jesus has impacted your life? What difference has Jesus Christ made in your life? If He has, then summon up your courage and let your commitment be known.

9 Joseph was not alone in his desire to care for the dead One who claimed to be the Christ. "And Nicodemus came also, who had first come to Him by night [John 3:2]; bringing a mixture of myrrh and aloes, about a hundred pounds weight. And so they took the body of Jesus, and bound it in linen wrappings with the spices, as is the burial custom of the Jews. Now in the place where He was crucified there was a garden; and in the garden a new tomb, in which no one had yet been laid. Therefore on account of the

Jewish day of preparation, because the tomb was nearby, they laid Jesus there" (John 19:39-42).

Apparently Nicodemus had pondered long and hard over the conversation he had had with Jesus. He had seen the signs that Jesus had performed and knew in his heart that there was something special about this Man "for no one can do these signs . . . unless God is with him" (John 3:2). Here were two prominent men whose lives had been so affected by Jesus that they had to do what they could . . . even though He was dead.

But they were not alone: "And Joseph bought a linen cloth, took Him down, wrapped Him in the linen cloth, and laid Him in a tomb which had been hewn out in the rock; and he rolled a stone against the entrance of the tomb. And Mary Magdalene and Mary the mother of Joses were looking on to see where He was laid" (Mark 15:46,47).

The Scriptures do not tell us much about Mary Magdalene. When she met Jesus, seven demons inhabited her body. She was among a group of women who had been healed of evil spirits and sicknesses and who had gone with Jesus and the twelve as He went "from one city and village to another, proclaiming and preaching the kingdom of God" (Luke 8:1).

"Mary Magdalene, along with Mary the mother of James and Joseph, and the mother of the sons of Zebedee" had witnessed the crucifixion "looking on from a distance" with other women "who had followed Jesus from Galilee, ministering to Him" (Matthew 27:56,55). The two Marys had helped care for Jesus in life. Now they would not abandon Him in death. After the Sabbath they could return and anoint His body.

As I think about Joseph and Nicodemus and the two Marys, I am impressed that although Jesus' death dashed their expectations against the cold reality of the tomb, still they did not abandon Him. Their love and service didn't stop with their disappointment. As I think about this, my friend, I wonder how set our hearts are on following Him. Would you follow Him even though He disappointed you because things didn't come out the way you expected or thought He told you that they would? I was tested like this when my father died. I thought God had told me that he would live. My faith held. Although I missed what I thought was God's word in that respect, His written Word stood. He is the Resurrection and the Life, and because of that, I will see my father again.

10 "Now after the sabbath, as it began to dawn toward the first day of the week, Mary Magdalene and the other Mary came to look at the grave" (Matthew 28:1). One thing perplexed them, but it didn't stop them. As they made their way in the light of the early-morning sun, "they were saying to one another, 'Who will roll away the stone for us from the entrance of the tomb?'" (Mark 16:3).

"And behold, a severe earthquake had occurred, for an angel of the Lord descended from heaven and came and rolled away the stone and sat upon it. And his appearance was like lightning, and his garment as white as snow; and the guards shook for fear of him, and became like dead men" (Matthew 28:2-4).

"[When the women arrived,] looking up, they saw that the stone had been rolled away, although it was extremely large. And entering the tomb, they saw a young man sitting at the right, wearing a white robe; and they were amazed" (Mark 16:4,5).

"And it happened that while they were perplexed about this, behold, two men suddenly stood near them in dazzling apparel; and as the women were terrified and bowed their faces to the ground, the men said to them, 'Why do you seek the living One among the dead? He is not here, but He has risen. Remember how He spoke to you while He was still in Galilee, saying that the Son of Man must be delivered into the hands of sinful men, and be crucified, and the third day rise again.' And they remembered His words" (Luke 24:4-8).

As I write this, Beloved, I cannot help but feel in my heart that some of you need to release your grief over the death of your loved one to the Father. There is a time to mourn . . . and then there is a time to let go of that mourning. As the angel said to the women: "Why do you seek the living One among the dead?" If your loved one knew the Lord, or if it was your young child, you can know that he or she is not dead, but living in the presence of the Father. As the angels reminded the women of the words of Jesus, so you need to bury your grief under the promises of God and live like those who have hope. You need to let go of the death of your loved one and get on with living among the living. God has left you here because He still has good works for you to walk in.

O Beloved, be about your Father's business. He is coming soon, and He will bring with Him those who have died in Christ; and we will all be caught up together and be with our Lord and with each other. Read 1 Thessalonians 4:13-18.

11 Whatever the disciples believed, one thing at least needed to be investigated: The tomb was empty and they didn't know where Jesus was!

"Peter therefore went forth, and the other disciple, and they were going to the tomb. And the two were running together; and the other disciple ran ahead faster than Peter, and came to the tomb first; and stooping and looking in, he saw the linen wrappings lying there; but he did not go in. Simon Peter therefore also came, following him, and entered the tomb; and he beheld the linen wrappings lying there, and the face-cloth, which had been on His head, not lying with the linen wrappings, but rolled up in a place by itself. So the other disciple who had first come to the tomb entered then also, and he saw and believed. For as yet they did not understand the Scripture, that He must rise again from the dead. So the disciples went away again to their own homes" (John 20:3-10).

Did you notice the statement, "For as yet they did not understand the Scripture, that He must rise again from the dead"? Interesting, isn't it? The Old Testament Scriptures which foretold the death of the Christ had also promised the resurrection of the Messiah; yet, the promises had not been understood.

Although the scribes and Pharisees were students of the Word of God, they had missed the 333 Old Testament prophecies which were fulfilled in the first coming of the Lord Jesus Christ. They were looking for Messiah, awaiting His coming; and yet when He came they refused to believe that it was He, because He didn't fit "their interpretation" of the Word. They had picked up on the prophecies of Messiah as coming King to whom all nations would give homage, but they missed the fact that before He would wear a crown, He would have to bear His cross. Before He could reign as the Lion of Judah, He must suffer as the Lamb of God in order to redeem His people.

The Jews saw themselves as the chosen people of God, of Abraham's seed, but they missed the fact that true children of God would come through the promises "spoken to Abraham and to his seed. He does not say, 'And to seeds,' as referring to many, but rather to one, 'And to your seed,' that is, Christ" (Galatians 3:16). They missed the truth that "if you belong to Christ, then you are Abraham's offspring [seed], heirs according to promise" (Galatians 3:29). The Jews had a zeal for God, but not in accordance with knowledge. If they missed the Scriptures regarding the substitutionary death of Christ, then, of course, they would miss the Scriptures foretelling His resurrection. I wonder how much truth we miss in the Word of God because we don't want anyone to tamper with our doctrine?

Are you teachable, or do you come to the Word of God with your mind already made up?

12 As I left you with those questions yesterday, I thought about the disciples and how they had missed the promise of the resurrection in the Old Testament. Remember, the Old Testament books were the only Scriptures the

Jews possessed in the days of our Lord. They had been accepted as Holy Writ and translated into the Greek language, so that the Hellenistic Jews too could read them.

The New Testament was in the process of being written during the decades of the early church; but until it was complete and divinely superintended, not only in its writing but in its compilation, all that the church had was the Old Testament. Yet, that was enough for them to know about Messiah, the Christ. Two men, walking the seven-mile road from Jerusalem to the village of Emmaus, would see this on the day of Jesus' resurrection, for He would explain His death and resurrection to them from the Scriptures.

Although the prophetic truths were available, because the teachers missed them, the people missed them. The Scriptures were not accessible as they are today. The scrolls were kept in the synagogues where they would be studied, taught, and interpreted to the people.

The Scriptures told of Jesus' resurrection. Peter cited Psalm 16:8-11 in his message on the day of Pentecost. Yet until the resurrection, Peter had not understood or received this teaching.

However, not only did the Scriptures tell of Jesus' resurrection, but Jesus shared the account of Jonah when the scribes and Pharisees asked: " 'Teacher, we want to see a sign from You.' But He answered and said to them, 'An evil and adulterous generation craves for a sign; and yet no sign shall be given to it but the sign of Jonah the prophet; for just as JONAH WAS THREE DAYS AND THREE NIGHTS IN THE BELLY OF THE SEA MONSTER, so shall the Son of Man be three days and three nights in the heart of the earth' " (Matthew 12:38-40).

While in Galilee, Jesus had said to them, "The Son of Man is going to be delivered into the hands of men; and they will kill Him, and He will be raised on the third day" (Matthew 17:22,23).

O Beloved, what a lesson there is in all of this for us. How much do we miss because our teachers missed a certain truth? Or how much do we miss because we do not diligently listen to teachers who are from God? How crucial it is, Beloved, that we be diligent students of God's Word. We need to know His Word for ourselves, and be able to examine what we hear. Are you missing what God is saying?

If you write our offices in Chattanooga, we'll send you information on our Precept Bible studies that will teach you to dig out truth for yourself and to bring your beliefs alongside the plumb line of His infallible Word. It will also help you appreciate a godly pastor who diligently studies and proclaims the Word.

13 When Peter and John left the empty tomb and returned to their own homes, they left Mary behind.

"But Mary was standing outside the tomb weeping; and so, as she wept, she stooped and looked into the tomb; and she beheld two angels in white sitting, one at the head, and one at the feet, where the body of Jesus had been lying. And they said to her, 'Woman, why are you weeping?' She said to them, 'Because they have taken away my Lord, and I do not know where they have laid Him.' When she had said this, she turned around, and beheld Jesus standing there, and did not know that it was Jesus. Jesus said to her, 'Woman, why are you weeping? Whom are you seeking?' Supposing Him to be the gardener, she said to Him, 'Sir, if you have carried Him away, tell me where you have laid Him, and I will take Him away.' Jesus said to her, 'Mary!' She turned and said to Him in Hebrew, 'Rabboni!' (which means, Teacher). Jesus said to her, 'Stop clinging to Me, for I have not yet ascended to the Father; but go to My brethren, and say to them, "I ascend to My Father and your Father, and My God and your God" ' " (John 20:11-17).

Oh, what a message Mary would have the privilege of delivering to them! It was the message of the New Covenant which He had inaugurated in His blood and in His body which had been broken for them. Because Jesus had conquered death, paid for their sin, and satisfied the righteousness of His Father, His God could now be their God,

His Father their Father. The promise of Jeremiah 31:33,34 had come to pass:

" 'But this is the covenant which I will make with the house of Israel after those days,' declares the LORD, 'I will put My law within them, and on their heart I will write it; and I will be their God, and they shall be My people. And they shall not teach again, each man his neighbor and each man his brother, saying, "Know the LORD," for they shall all know Me, from the least of them to the greatest of them,' declares the LORD, 'for I will forgive their iniquity, and their sin I will remember no more.' "

Mary had touched the resurrected Lord and heard His words. And so, "Mary Magdalene came, announcing to the disciples, 'I have seen the Lord,' and that He had said these things to her" (John 20:18). "And when they heard that He was alive, and had been seen by her, they refused to believe it" (Mark 16:11).

O Beloved, you have come to know the resurrected Lord. You have His very words in your possession—the Word of God. Now share the message of the New Covenant, whether others believe or not. He lives!

14 Two of those men who heard Mary's first testimony of the open tomb, along with the testimony of those women who were with her, left the others and set out for the village of Emmaus, about seven miles from Jerusalem.

"And they were conversing with each other about all these things which had taken place. And it came about that while they were conversing and discussing, Jesus Himself approached, and began traveling with them. But their eyes were prevented from recognizing Him. And He said to them, 'What are these words that you are exchanging with one another as you are walking?' And they stood still, looking sad. And one of them, named Cleopas, answered and said to Him, 'Are You the only one visiting Jerusalem and unaware of the things which have happened here in these days?' And He said to them, 'What things?' And they said to Him, 'The things about Jesus the Nazarene, who was a prophet mighty in deed and word in the sight of God and all the people, and how the chief priests and our rulers delivered Him up to the sentence of death, and crucified Him. But we were hoping that it was He who was going to redeem Israel. Indeed, besides all this, it is the third day since these things happened. But also some women among us amazed us. When they were at the tomb early in the morning, and did not find His body, they came, saying that they had also seen a vision of angels, who said that He was alive. And some of those who were with us went to the tomb and found it just exactly as the women also had said; but Him they did not see.' And He said to them, 'O foolish men and slow of heart to believe in all that the prophets have spoken!' " (Luke 24:14-25).

Our Lord's statement was a rebuke to those who have to see in order to believe! God has spoken and others have borne witness. Yet we will not believe unless we see, unless we touch, unless we experience. One of my greatest distresses in regard to the church of Jesus Christ in the United States is the appalling lack of knowledge and discipline when it comes to studying the Word of God. It seems that we have time for everything else, but there is no time to know God intimately. And it shows. The church loves its spiritual junk food, but it has no appetite for the meat and potatoes of the solid food that belongs to those who are mature and who through practice in the Word train their senses to discern good and evil (Hebrews 5:14).

We live in a society where good is evil and evil is good . . . because the church turned from its mission of "equipping of the saints for the work of service, to the building up of the body of Christ; until we all attain to the unity of the faith, and of the knowledge of the Son of God, to a mature man, to the measure of the stature which belongs to the fulness of Christ. As a result, we are . . . children, tossed here and there by waves, and carried about by every wind of doctrine, by the trickery of men, by craftiness in deceitful scheming" (Ephesians 4:12-14).

O Beloved, may we not be fools and slow of heart.

15 How I would have loved to have heard what our Lord shared with the disciples on the road to Emmaus, for "beginning with Moses and with all the prophets, He explained to them the things concerning Himself in all the Scriptures" (Luke 24:27). The Scriptures testified of Jesus, and yet, as He had said to the Jews, "You search the Scriptures, because you think that in them you have eternal life; and it is these that bear witness of Me; and you are unwilling to come to Me, that you may have life" (John 5:39,40).

There is another valuable lesson for us to remember, Beloved—that the veil over the Word of God can be taken away only by Jesus Christ and the ministry of the Holy Spirit in a believer's life. We can be students of the Word of God, even as the scribes, Pharisees, and Jews were, and yet, in all of our study and knowledge, we can miss the truths about the Lord Jesus Christ.

Jesus said to the two disciples, "Was it not necessary for the Christ to suffer these things and to enter into His glory?" (Luke 24:26). And His answer was a resounding, "Yes, it was necessary!" It was necessary because it was all prophesied in the Old Testament. The only problem was that there was a spiritual veil over those prophecies, so that the majority of the nation missed the fact that the Christ must suffer, die, and be raised from the dead before He could ever reign as King of kings and Lord of lords.

Those who read the Old Testament Scriptures and tried to live under the Old Covenant of the Law, read with veiled hearts. "Moses . . . used to put a veil over his face that the sons of Israel might not look intently at the end of what was fading away. But their minds were hardened; for until this very day at the reading of the old covenant the same veil remains unlifted, because it is removed in Christ. But to this day whenever Moses is read, a veil lies over their heart; but whenever a man turns to the Lord, the veil is taken away" (2 Corinthians 3:13-16).

On the road to Emmaus, it was the Lord Himself who took the veil off their hearts as He explained how His death, burial, and resurrection inaugurated the New Covenant of grace. For the Law came by Moses, but grace and truth were realized through Jesus Christ, of whom the Law and the prophets testified.

16 Until that day on the road to Emmaus, there was a veil over the hearts of the disciples which kept them from seeing the truth of the substitutionary death and justifying resurrection of Jesus Christ. The Old Testament had prophesied of these events, and yet the veil kept them from seeing what Jesus had even tried to tell them before He was ever arrested in the Garden of Gethsemane.

That same veil is present today in countless synagogues where orthodox Jews make it a practice to diligently study the Old Testament Scriptures. The veil lies heavily over the hearts of those who live in the land where all of this took place. Israel is an enigma, for although many are looking for their own version of the Messiah, as a nation they do not acknowledge Jesus Christ as the Son of God. Yet, they allow Christians from all over the world to make their pilgrimages to the land of Christ's birth, to the sites of His earthly ministries, and to shrines or places of worship which testify to His death and resurrection.

I will never forget the wonderful adventure the Lord gave us when Jack and I took a group to Israel a number of years ago. As we wandered through the walled city of Jerusalem exploring some new territory, we came across a school of the Talmud. We were told that we could step inside the premises of the school, as long as we stayed in the lobby and did not actually enter the room where the men sat in intense discussion over the weightier matters of the Law and its interpretation.

As we rounded the corner of the entrance, I felt like I was on the movie set of *Yentl.* A wall of glass doors was the only thing that separated us from small clusters of men gathered around ancient books on the tables. Heads topped with yarmulkes bobbed back and forth in animated conversation.

On some, side curls bounced up and down like little black springs, as their hands jabbed the air emphasizing important points. Others sat alone, rocking back and forth in front of the Scriptures, calling upon a God whose Son they did not know, because they had never seen Him in the Scriptures. Then I met Joshua, one of the spiritually blind leaders of the blind. As he explained our surroundings, God seemed to give me openings, and we dialogued about a Messiah Joshua didn't know had already come. I tried so hard to raise the veil, to give him a glimpse of my Lord, but to no avail. Jesus' words echoed in my heart: "O foolish men and slow of heart" (Luke 24:25), and I ached. Today will you pray for those you know who are blind?

17 Even as Jesus opened the understanding of those two men on the road to Emmaus, they still did not realize they were talking to Jesus.

"And they approached the village where they were going, and He acted as though He would go farther. And they urged Him, saying, 'Stay with us, for it is getting toward evening, and the day is now nearly over.' And He went in to stay with them. And it came about that when He had reclined at the table with them, He took the bread and blessed it, and breaking it, He began giving it to them. And their eyes were opened and they recognized Him; and He vanished from their sight. And they said to one another, 'Were not our hearts burning within us while He was speaking to us on the road, while He was explaining the Scriptures to us?' And they arose that very hour and returned to Jerusalem, and found gathered together the eleven and those who were with them, saying, 'The Lord has really risen, and has appeared to Simon.' And they began to relate their experiences on the road and how He was recognized by them in the breaking of the bread" (Luke 24:28-35).

Do you ever think of how wonderful it would have been to have lived then? To have seen, heard, and even touched the resurrected, living Christ! And I am sure our hearts would have burned within us as He opened up our understanding of the Scriptures.

And yet, Beloved, you and I have an even greater advantage. Not only do our hearts burn within us as we read through the Old Testament Scriptures and the Spirit of God opens the eyes of our understanding, but we have in our hands the complete revelation of God. Our hearts can burn even brighter, for we have insight into our Lord's second coming that they did not possess. We have a New Testament, and much of what was hidden in the Old is revealed in the New.

And whereas they were witnesses of the Lord's resurrection, I believe that soon we will be witnesses of the resurrection of those who have died in Christ. "But each in his own order: Christ the first fruits, after that those who are Christ's at His coming, then comes the end, when He delivers up the kingdom to the God and Father, when He has abolished all rule and all authority and power" (1 Corinthians 15:23,24).

The end cannot be too far off, Beloved. Let not your heart be afraid, for He is the Resurrection and the Life! Simply let your heart burn brightly in the light of the fact that death no longer has its sting. It's a fact: Jesus is risen.

18

Although the resurrection of Jesus Christ from the dead was constantly substantiated by His various appearances to the women and to various disciples, it was also always substantiated by the Scriptures. And the One who verified His own resurrection from the dead was the One who continually took His disciples back to the Word of God. Everything, even experience, is valid only as it aligns with or supports the Word of God.

This, Beloved, is why I give myself so diligently to the Word of God. This is why all of us at Precept Ministries have that one urgent call upon our lives: to establish His people in His Word as that which produces a reverence for Him.

Let's return to Luke 24 again and the two disciples who have just recognized Jesus. After He disappeared, they rushed to Jerusalem with the good news.

"And while they were telling these things, He Himself stood in their midst. But they were startled and frightened and thought that they were seeing a spirit. And He said to them, 'Why are you troubled, and why do doubts arise in your hearts? See My hands and My feet, that it is I Myself; touch Me and see, for a spirit does not have flesh and bones as you see that I have.' [And when He had said this, He showed them His hands and His feet.] And while they still could not believe it for joy and were marveling, He said to them, 'Have you anything here to eat?' And they gave Him a piece of a broiled fish; and He took it and ate it before them. Now He said to them, 'These are My words which I spoke to you while I was still with you, that all things which are written about Me in the Law of Moses and the Prophets and the Psalms must be fulfilled.' Then He opened their minds to understand the Scriptures, and He said to them, 'Thus it is written, that the Christ should suffer and rise again from the dead the third day; and that repentance for forgiveness of sins should be proclaimed in His name to all the nations, beginning from Jerusalem. You are witnesses of these things' " (Luke 24:36-48).

O Beloved, isn't it wonderful to know without a shadow of a doubt that you are witnesses of an event that was accurately prophesied in a Book which no man or nation has ever been able to destroy or annihilate, though they have tried? Isn't it awesome to think that you are spiritual witnesses of an event which actually took place and that literally determines the personal and eternal destiny of all of mankind? Oh, my friend, what a responsibility you and I have—a message of life and breath!

19 John gives us an insight into our Lord's appearance to the disciples on the night of His resurrection that the other writers do not. It is an insight that causes me to say that the resurrection of Jesus Christ is a matter of life and breath. I want us to focus in on John 20:19-23 so that we don't miss the crucial point the Spirit of God is making.

"When therefore it was evening, on that day, the first day of the week, and when the doors were shut where the disciples were, for fear of the Jews, Jesus came and stood in their midst, and said to them, 'Peace be with you.' And when He had said this, He showed them both His hands and His side. The disciples therefore rejoiced when they saw the Lord. Jesus therefore said to them again, 'Peace be with you; as the Father has sent Me, I also send you.' And when He had said this, He breathed on them, and said to them, 'Receive the Holy Spirit. If you forgive the sins of any, their sins have been forgiven them; if you retain the sins of any, they have been retained' " (John 20:19-23).

I think the Spirit of God does not want us to miss the fact that Jesus alone is the bestower of life. Remember, John's purpose in writing his Gospel is to prove to us that Jesus is the Christ, the Son of God, and that through believing on Him we might have life in His name. Because Jesus has conquered sin and death, because He has paid the wages of sin, which is death, because God's holiness and righteousness were satisfied in the substitutionary death of His Son for our sins, and because God has raised Jesus from the dead, Jesus is able to bestow life on those who come to the Father by Him.

Thus, not once but twice Jesus proclaims: "Peace be with you" (20:19,21). What is necessary to restore men to peace with God has been done by the Prince of Peace. The prophecy of Isaiah 9:6 has been fulfilled: "For a child will be born to us, a son will be given to us; and the government will rest on His shoulders; and His name will be called Wonderful Counselor, Mighty God, Eternal Father, Prince of Peace."

Jesus is able to proclaim peace, because as the Prince of Peace He has taken care of the enmity between God and man, which came because Adam chose death instead of life. "But God, being rich in mercy, because of His great love with which He loved us, even when we were dead in our transgressions, made us alive together with Christ" (Ephesians 2:4,5).

20 Having removed the enmity between God and man, Jesus proclaims that which is now available to us—peace and purpose. Listen to His words: "Peace be with you; as the Father has sent Me, I also send you" (John 20:21). Once we have been reconciled to the Father through the death and resurrection of the Lamb of God, we are to become ambassadors of reconciliation. "Now all these things are from God, who reconciled us to Himself through Christ, and gave us the ministry of reconciliation, namely, that God was in Christ reconciling the world to Himself, not counting their trespasses against them, and He has committed to us the word of reconciliation" (2 Corinthians 5:18,19).

In the first 17 chapters of his Gospel, John emphasizes that Jesus has been sent by the Father to give life to those who are dead in their trespasses and sins. Now Jesus, the One who has received delegated authority from the Father, is going to dispatch others under His authority. Jesus is not delegating authority to His disciples or to us in the same way that the Father delegated authority to Him. Rather, He is sending them out under His authority. As the bestower of life, and having conquered sin through death and resurrection, Jesus can now give life to others.

I want to show you some verses in John which lead up to John 20:22, when Jesus breathes on them and tells them to receive the Holy Spirit, for it is in this act that Jesus is demonstrating that He is now able to bestow life.

In John 1:4, we saw that life is in Jesus Christ. In John 5:26 we read: "For just as the Father has life in Himself, even so He gave to the Son also to have life in Himself." As the One who has life in Himself, He was sent to bring life to others, for He said, "For I have come down from heaven, not to do My own will, but the will of Him who sent Me. And this is the will of Him who sent Me, that of all that He has given

Me I lose nothing, but raise it up on the last day. For this is the will of My Father, that everyone who beholds the Son and believes in Him, may have eternal life; and I Myself will raise him up on the last day" (John 6:38-40).

O Beloved, do you see that if Jesus had not been raised from the dead, He could not have offered life to others? That is how crucial the resurrection is.

21 Imagine having the authority to tell others that their sins are either forgiven or retained against them! This is the authority with which our Lord sent forth His disciples . . . and believe it or not, it is with this same authority that He sends you forth. Let's look at it by asking questions and seeking their answers from the Word.

First: "How did the disciples have the authority to tell others that their sins had been forgiven or had not been forgiven?" They had that authority because they were sent out under the authority of the resurrected Son of Man. In His vicarious death, Jesus paid the debt for all of mankind's sin. Since this payment satisfied the just and righteous requirements of the Father, He could then raise His Son from the dead. The resurrection was God's means of demonstrating that His righteousness had been propitiated. Therefore, a person's sins could be forgiven through believing on the One who had paid for them in full. Thus, the disciples could tell those who put their faith in the substitutionary atonement of Jesus Christ that their sins were forgiven. To those who refused to believe and accept Christ's death for their sins, they could say that their sins were retained. To reject Jesus is to reject life.

Second: "Why, at this point, does Jesus say to them, 'Receive the Holy Spirit'?" He wants them to understand that He is the bestower of life, and that apart from possessing the Holy Spirit of God, no one can have life. Remission of sins, possession of the Holy Spirit, and having eternal life all go together. To have one is to possess the others. This is all part of the New Covenant.

When people in faith embrace Jesus Christ, God forgives their sins and bestows upon them the Holy Spirit. Having received the Holy Spirit through faith in Jesus Christ, they now have life. Romans 8:9-11 makes it clear that without the indwelling of the Spirit, there is no life.

You can see just how important the resurrection of Jesus Christ is. The same Spirit of God who raised Jesus from the dead will also guarantee the redemption of your physical body from the dead.

22 When the Spirit of God dwells within, we have forgiveness of sin, and we are under authority to tell others how they too can have forgiveness. The resurrection of Jesus Christ from the dead bore testimony to the fact that Jesus had accomplished our justification because He paid sin's debt in full and, thereby, propitiated or satisfied the righteousness of God. This is why Jesus cried, "It is finished" just before He gave up the spirit and died on Calvary's tree (John 19:30). "It is finished" is the translation of the Greek word *tetélestai,* which was a legal term. When one person was indebted to another, a certificate of debt was drawn up stating exactly what was owed and to whom. Once the debt was paid in full, *tetélestai* was written across the debt, showing that it was paid in full. It was finished, for nothing more was owed.

Let's suppose that you and I lived in biblical days and that I incurred a huge debt to you, owing you 10,000 cattle, a great deal of land, and 2,000 talents of silver. (One talent was worth 6,000 days' wages.) You would make out a certificate of debt, listing all that I owed. You would keep that certificate in your possession until I paid you.

Oh, how that debt would weigh upon me! Nothing really could be mine until I had paid off my debt. Therefore, my longing would be to pay off my debt in full. I would work night and day to that end, saving every denarii, adding them up, counting them over and over until finally I could pay back everything that I owed. (A denarius was worth 18 cents.)

Finally, when I was assured that I had all that I needed to pay off my certificate of debt, I wouldn't waste a moment hurrying to your home. No formalities could stay my joy as my words tumbled from my mouth: "Look, look, count it, my friend! It's all here—every last talent, all that I owe you! Bring the certificate!"

Then with great ceremony, you would write across that certificate of debt, *tetélestai*. We would nail it to the door of my house so that all would know my debt was paid in full. O Beloved, God has written *tetélestai* over your debt to Him! But have you activated it by faith?

23 I recently read a true story in *Reader's Digest* which wrenched my heart. A recluse, left alone after his parents' death, was evicted from his home simply because he had not paid the taxes on it. The home had long been paid for by his parents, and the man wanted for nothing except for someone to love and care for him—and to open his mail. He had no friends, and he was ignorant of our tax system. When several notices came to inform him of his overdue taxes, he left them on a table unopened. He had the money to pay his taxes, but he was ignorant of his debt. When some heartless person noticed the small unpaid tax bill, he paid the debt and took possession of the man's home, casting him into the streets without a hope.

O Beloved, can you imagine standing before the entrance to the home of God, glimpsing through its gates of pearl to see the glories of God, only to hear that you cannot enter? "No debtors allowed." Thunderstruck, you start to walk away, shaking your head in unbelief. Then, turning back for one last look, you catch His eyes. Tears! Tears in the eyes of the One with nail prints in His hands! This is not some greedy or heartless person gloating because you cannot have access to His home. No, this is not one who would have you evicted, but One who has called to you over and over. And now when it is too late, you finally listen to Him as you hear Him say, almost in a hoarse whisper choked with emotion, "Your debt could have been paid. If only you had opened and read that which I had written to you. If only you had believed, you could have lived here with Me forever and ever. Now instead you must be cast into a 'furnace of fire; in that place there shall be weeping and gnashing of teeth' (Matthew 13:42).

"Did you not know, did you not believe that 'when you were dead in your transgressions and the uncircumcision of your flesh,' I would have 'made you alive together with [Me], having forgiven [you] all your transgressions, having canceled out the certificate of debt consisting of decrees against [you] and which was hostile to' you, and I would have taken your certificate of debt 'out of the way, having nailed it to the cross' (Colossians 2:13,14)? I am the resurrected Christ, the One who conquered sin and death. Oh, how often I would have gathered you as a hen gathers her chicks, but you would not come to Me. Now the door to heaven is closed.... You closed it in unbelief. Your own neglect of My letters has brought this upon you. I called, but you would not answer. Therefore, because of your own unbelief, your own disobedience, you will remain dead in your transgressions and the uncircumcision of your flesh. Although I came that you might have life and have it abundantly, your sins are not remitted. Weep, for I weep. My home is empty without you."

24 How important is the literal, bodily resurrection of Jesus Christ from the dead? It is a matter of life and breath. Are you beginning, my friend, to understand why I use this phrase? If Jesus Christ was not raised from the dead, then neither will you be. If His was not a literal, bodily resurrection, then yours will not be either. This is the whole point of these crucial verses in John 20:10-20, for in His actions and in His words, Jesus is conveying a very crucial

point. At the risk of being redundant, let me list for you some key truths you must not miss.

First, peace can be yours because the death and resurrection of Jesus Christ has removed the enmity between God and you. "Peace be with you" (John 20:19).

Second, the Father sent the Son so that we might have life in His name. Now the Son sends His disciples forth under His authority to tell others how they can have life through Him. "Peace be with you; as the Father has sent Me, I also send you" (John 20:21).

Third, when Jesus "breathed on them, and said to them, 'Receive the Holy Spirit'" (John 20:22), He was demonstrating the fact that He is the Giver of life. Jesus had conquered death, had been raised from the dead as the Son of Man, and therefore had the authority and power to give life.

In Genesis 2:7 I believe we see the point Jesus is making when He breathes on them. "Then the LORD God formed man of dust from the ground, and breathed into his nostrils the breath of life; and man became a living being." Adam was alive until the day he ate of the fruit of the tree of the knowledge of good and evil. Then he died. God had intended Adam's life to be eternal. Not only did Adam lose his life, but death entered the world through him. Life came through Jesus, the last Adam. This is the truth that Jesus was demonstrating when He breathed on the disciples.

In his Gospel, John continually keeps before us the fact that life is in Christ alone. What the first Adam lost—life—the last Adam restores. I will show you this truth in detail tomorrow as we continue with the third point of John 20:22.

Today, let me close our time with Ephesians 2:14-18. Meditate on it, for you'll really appreciate it in the light of what we have learned: "For He Himself is our peace, who made both groups [Jew and Gentile] into one, and broke down the barrier of the dividing wall, by abolishing in His flesh the enmity, which is the Law of commandments . . . that in Himself He might make the two into one new man, thus establishing peace, and might reconcile them both in one body to God through the cross . . . for through Him we both have our access in one Spirit to the Father."

25 As we continue in John 20:22, we see Jesus breathing on the disciples as He says to them, "Receive the Holy Spirit." What God did in the Garden of Eden, He is doing again in the room where the disciples are hiding for fear of the Jews. He is giving them the life they lost through sin. John has been bringing us to this point, as he has stressed that life is in Christ. Let me share with you, Beloved, the instances where John makes this point. But as I do, please do not skim over them or read them lightly. Remember these are words of life!

"In Him was life . . . that whoever believes may in Him have eternal life. For God so loved the world, that He gave His only begotten Son, that whoever believes in Him should not perish, but have eternal life. . . . Whoever drinks of the water that I shall give him shall never thirst; but the water that I shall give him shall become in him a well of water springing up to eternal life. . . . For just as the Father raises the dead and gives them life, even so the Son also gives life to whom He wishes. . . . For just as the Father has life in Himself, even so He gave to the Son also to have life in Himself. . . . For the bread of God is that which comes down out of heaven, and gives life to the world. . . . He who eats My flesh and drinks My blood has eternal life; and I will raise him up on the last day. . . . The thief comes only to steal, and kill, and destroy; I came that they might have life, and might have it abundantly. . . . For this reason the Father loves Me, because I lay down My life that I may take it again. No one has taken it away from Me, but I lay it down on My own initiative. I have authority to lay it down, and I have authority to take it up again. This commandment I received from My Father. . . . I am the resurrection and the life; he who believes in Me shall live even if he dies, and everyone who lives and believes in Me shall never die. . . . I am the way, and the truth, and the life; no one comes to the

Father, but through Me. . . . Thou gavest Him authority over all mankind, that to all whom Thou hast given Him, He may give eternal life. And this is eternal life, that they may know Thee, the only true God, and Jesus Christ whom Thou hast sent. . . . He breathed on them, and said to them, "Receive the Holy Spirit" (John 1:4; 3:15,16; 4:14; 5:21,26; 6:33, 54; 10:10,17,18; 11:25,26; 14:6; 17:2,3; 20:22).

Thank Him today for life—His life in you!

26 In reporting this singular act of Jesus breathing on the disciples and saying, "Receive the Holy Spirit," John is showing us Jesus' right to give life by giving the Holy Spirit. The full import of this act will be seen by the multitudes on the day of Pentecost when for the first time the Holy Spirit comes to permanently indwell all believers. In the Gospel of John we get a foretaste of the fulfillment of Ezekiel 36:26,27: "Moreover, I will give you a new heart and put a new spirit within you; and I will remove the heart of stone from your flesh and give you a heart of flesh. And I will put My Spirit within you and cause you to walk in My statutes, and you will be careful to observe My ordinances."

The Holy Spirit within would then become the guarantee of the resurrection of our mortal bodies: "Having also believed, you were sealed in Him with the Holy Spirit of promise, who is given as a pledge of our inheritance, with a view to the redemption of God's own possession, to the praise of His glory" (Ephesians 1:13,14).

This is possible only because of the literal bodily resurrection of our Lord. When Paul writes to the church at Corinth, he gives the clearest and most comprehensive explanation and argument for the resurrection in all the Scripture. He also confirms John's *fourth* point, Jesus' words: "If you forgive the sins of any, their sins have been forgiven them; if you retain the sins of any, they have been retained" (20:23). The resurrection of Jesus Christ enables us to testify to others that true faith in Jesus Christ brings forgiveness of sins. "If Christ has not been raised, your faith is worthless; you are still in your sins" (1 Corinthians 15:17).

In raising Jesus Christ from the dead, God was affirming that the righteous requirements of the Law had been met through the atoning, substitutionary death of Jesus Christ. When Paul explains in Romans 4 that Abraham's faith was reckoned to him as righteousness, he wrote a very significant statement in respect to the resurrection of Jesus Christ and our justification: "Now not for his sake only [Abraham's] was it written, that it was reckoned to him, but for our sake also, to whom it will be reckoned, as those who believe in Him who raised Jesus our Lord from the dead. He who was delivered up because of our transgressions, and was raised because of our justification" (Romans 4:23,24).

It is because of this, Beloved, that the disciples, and you and I, have our Lord's authority to tell others that their sins are forgiven or retained, according to what they do with the resurrected Christ.

27

"What if Christ has not been raised?" Do you realize that there are some who claim to know Christ, to be students of the Word, even theologians or ministers, who do not believe in a literal, bodily resurrection of our Lord?

"Now if Christ is preached, that He has been raised from the dead, how do some among you say that there is no resurrection of the dead? But if there is no resurrection of the dead, not even Christ has been raised; and if Christ has not been raised, then our preaching is vain, your faith also is vain. Moreover we are even found to be false witnesses of God, because we witnessed against God that He raised Christ, whom He did not raise, if in fact the dead are not raised. For if the dead are not raised, not even Christ has been raised; and if Christ has not been raised, your faith is worthless; you are still in your sins. Then those also who have fallen asleep in Christ have perished. If we have hoped in Christ in this life only, we are of all men most to be pitied. But now Christ has been raised from the dead, the first fruits of those who are asleep. For since by a man came death, by a man also came the resurrection of the dead. For as in Adam all die, so also in Christ all shall be made alive" (1 Corinthians 15:12-22).

Do you see and understand Paul's reasoning regarding the necessity for the resurrection of Jesus Christ and for the proclamation and belief of it? Either there is a bodily resurrection or there is not. If there isn't, then our faith in Jesus is worthless. If Jesus was not raised from the dead after becoming our sin-bearer, then death still holds Him in its power. If it holds our Lord, it holds us!

Believing in Jesus as our pattern for life without believing in His resurrection isn't going to do it. If we have only the example of Jesus, we are to be pitied. We are like those who worship other gods who died and remain dead because they were not raised from the dead. O Beloved, the tomb of the One we worship is empty. Hallelujah! He is not there. He is risen! We don't have just an example to follow—we have a resurrected Savior who lives within us by His Spirit. The same Spirit "who raised Jesus from the dead dwells in you, He who raised Christ Jesus from the dead will also give life to your mortal bodies through His Spirit who indwells you" (Romans 8:11).

If Christ were not raised, there would be no good news to tell others. Can you give a reason for the hope which dwells in you?

28 From the Garden of Eden, God had warned mankind of the wages of their sin. Yet most still refused to believe in a place called "hell" or "Sheol." They wouldn't take God at His Word then, even as most now will not take God at His Word when He tells them that they will perish without Jesus Christ.

During our Lord's public ministry, He told a story from the other side of death which demonstrates the awful darkness of unbelief. People who refuse to believe God's Word usually will not believe even when they see. They rationalize themselves out of accepting what their eyes see because they don't want to believe it. Now read Luke 16:19-31.

Someone rose from the dead. He again warned of hell, talking of it more than of life. Still, men will not take God at His Word until it is too late. "O Father, we believe. Help, Thou, our unbelief."

29 Let us not doubt, but take God at His Word, recognizing Jesus as our Lord and our God, and thus knowing His blessing for those who believe without seeing.

When Jesus, on the evening of His resurrection, the first day of the week, suddenly stood in the midst of the disciples and breathed on them, Thomas was missing. Later the other disciples said to him, "'We have seen the Lord!' But he said to them, 'Unless I shall see in His hands the imprint of the nails, and put my finger into the place of the nails, and put my hand into His side, I will not believe'" (John 20:25).

Have you ever known people like Thomas? He wanted to walk by sight, not by faith. He wouldn't even take the word of the other disciples who said they saw the resurrected Christ. He would not believe until he had seen and touched Christ himself.

Our Lord was merciful to Thomas. "And after eight days again His disciples were inside, and Thomas with them. Jesus came, the doors having been shut, and stood in their midst, and said, 'Peace be with you.' Then He said to Thomas, 'Reach here your finger, and see My hands; and reach here your hand, and put it into My side; and be not unbelieving, but believing.' Thomas answered and said to Him, 'My Lord and my God!' Jesus said to him, 'Because you have seen Me, have you believed? Blessed are they who did not see, and yet believed'" (John 20:26-29).

In His grace Jesus gave Thomas the opportunity he asked for. And maybe it happened that way for you and for me too. Maybe Jesus wanted to say something to us, to teach us a very crucial lesson of faith and of the blessing from God which accompanies it.

As I write this, I cannot help but wonder if there is not someone who is really wrestling with his or her faith. If it is you, Beloved, take heed to what you have learned and remember: "Without faith it is impossible to please him: for he that cometh to God must believe that he is, and that he is a rewarder of them that diligently seek him" (Hebrews 11:6 KJV).

Or maybe you are having to deal with death—yours which seems imminent, or the death of a loved one. Remember, because Jesus is risen from the dead, death's stinger is gone—it was suffered in His body: "'O DEATH, WHERE IS YOUR VICTORY? O DEATH, WHERE IS YOUR STING?' The sting of death is sin, and the power of sin is the law; but thanks be to God, who gives us the victory through our Lord Jesus Christ" (1 Corinthians 15:55-57).

30 When Jesus appeared to Thomas and the others, suddenly He was present in a room where the doors were shut. How could it be that our Lord could enter a room without entering through the door? John makes this point for us to show that resurrected bodies are different than our bodies. Apparently, in our resurrected bodies we will be able to pass through what we consider solid material. That sounds like fun! Whatever, "it has not appeared as yet what we shall be. We know that, when He appears, we shall be like Him, because we shall see Him just as He is" (1 John 3:2). Therefore, until then, read what the Word of God has to say about our new bodies in 1 Corinthians 15:35-49.

O beloved believer, "If the dead are not raised, LET US EAT AND DRINK, FOR TOMORROW WE DIE." But if they are raised, then let us live as those who shall stand before "Christ Jesus, who is to judge the living and the dead" (1 Corinthians 15:32; 2 Timothy 4:1).

The best is yet to come! A brand-new body—eternal, incorruptible, imperishable...all because God raised Jesus Christ from the dead. Someday you will be like Him—will see Him just as He is. Therefore, "everyone who has this hope fixed on Him purifies himself, just as He is pure" (1 John 3:3).

December

What Do You Do When You've Blown It?

1 What do you do when you've failed God? When your lifestyle or behavior has denied your confession of faith in the Lord Jesus Christ?

If *you* haven't blown it, perhaps people you know have. They are torn up inside about it. How do you minister to them? What do you tell them to do so that the guilt will go away? So they do not have to live in defeat?

Maybe your heart has grown just a little cool toward the Lord and the things of the kingdom of God. How do you regain your first love of Jesus Christ, when the fire has burned down and all that remains are a few smoldering coals?

This, Beloved, will be the subject of our study as we look at the final chapter of John. Tomorrow we'll begin to search out what we can do when we have blown it in our walk with God or when our love for Him seems about to go out.

Today, before you read John 21, why don't you write a prayer to your God. Tell Him all that's on your heart as we move toward the end of our devotional journey together.

2 It almost seems as if John finishes his Gospel and then as an afterthought tacks on chapter 21. It is evident by John 20:30,31 that he has achieved his purpose in writing. He has recorded a more than sufficient number of signs which certainly demonstrate that Jesus is the Christ, the Son of God. He has explained thoroughly what it means to believe in Him. And without a doubt, Jesus has explained the Father. In the Gospel of John we have seen Jesus, and in seeing Him we have come to know the One who sent Him.

In his astute analysis of the Gospel of John, Merrill Unger sets before us various periods in the ministry of Jesus as recorded by John. The Period of Conference was covered in John 12:36b through chapter 17. Then came the Period of Consummation in John 18 to 20, as the Son accomplished the work the Father sent Him to do. The grain of wheat fell into the ground . . . not to lie dormant but to bring forth resurrection life.

Now, I would like to add what I call the Period of Commissioning in chapter 21. John ends his book in the same way the other writers end their accounts—with our Lord's commission to His disciples to go into the world and share what they have heard of the message of life in Him.

However, in John the commission has a slightly different twist because it centers around one person: the apostle Peter. And why Peter in particular? I believe it's because if anyone would feel unworthy or inadequate for such a ministry, it would be Peter. In the midst of the crisis of Calvary, he denied even knowing Jesus—not once but three times. And yet, Jesus privately commissions Peter to feed His sheep and to tend His lambs.

It's hard to believe that Jesus would commission someone who has so desperately failed Him. Although the Word of God doesn't say so, and although the character of God contradicts such reasoning, somehow we think that God can use only perfect people.

And yet, God isn't like us. His thoughts are not our thoughts, and His ways are not our ways (Isaiah 55:8). His ways are so much higher. Remember this truth when you feel low or unworthy to serve Him.

3 What's your motivation, my friend, for serving the Lord? To be popular in Christian circles? Have power? Know success? Receive a reward? Experience self-fulfillment?

There's only one motivation that will anchor you solidly in the Word of God—and in the kingdom of God. It's love. As John brings his Gospel to a close, we see that love must be the motivating force behind caring for His sheep.

In the first 20 chapters of John, we see the love of God demonstrated in a kaleidoscope of ways. Now in one last chapter, there is a call to us through our Lord's commission of Peter to return His love by feeding His sheep and, if necessary, by following Him even to death.

In the first 20 chapters, we view the purpose of Jesus' life: that we might believe that He is the Christ, the Son of God, and that believing we might have life. Now in this final chapter, we see the purpose of our lives: to love Jesus Christ and follow Him.

God calls all of us "in Peter"—in a man who once had the opportunity to lay down his life in love, but who failed, in a man who denied Jesus instead of confessing Him when His life hung in the balance.

In this unique account, we see the mercy, long-suffering, and compassion of our Lord who recognizes the weakness of our flesh—flesh that overrules the willing spirit when we fail to watch and pray. And as we watch our Lord deal with Peter, we can see what our problem could be if we fail to guard our love of God. We also see the cure.

What encouragement and help awaits us! But before we delve into these things, I want you to pause and give the Lord time to search your heart. Where do you stand in respect to His commandment to love and serve Him with all your heart, mind, soul, body, and spirit . . . and to love your neighbor as yourself?

4 Can you remember what it was like when you first came to know the Lord Jesus Christ? When the veil came off of your eyes and you finally saw life from God's perspective? Do you remember the fervency of love and deep gratitude that filled your heart? Do you recall how you wanted to do the will of God, no matter what the cost? You didn't serve your newly discovered Lord out of obligation but out of love. Where are you now?

The book of Revelation records messages given by our Lord to seven churches in Asia. I believe each of those messages has a twofold purpose. First, it was a very personal letter to a church whose situation and needs were known by their omniscient Lord. Second, the letter prophetically described a period in church history, laying out beforehand the state of the church during that time.

The first of these letters was to the church at Ephesus, a church which had left its first love. Read the letter carefully. Then tomorrow we'll discuss it to see what we can learn for our own lives. As you read it, keep in mind what we are studying in our final chapter of the Gospel of John.

"To the angel of the church in Ephesus write: The One who holds the seven stars in His right hand, the One who walks among the seven golden lampstands, says this: 'I know your deeds and your toil and perseverance, and that you cannot endure evil men, and you put to the test those who call themselves apostles, and they are not, and you found them to be false; and you have perseverance and have endured for My name's sake, and have not grown weary. But I have this against you, that you have left your first love. Remember therefore from where you have fallen, and repent and do the deeds you did at first; or else I am coming to you, and will remove your lampstand out of its place—unless you repent. Yet this you do have, that you hate the deeds of the Nicolaitans, which I also hate. He who has an ear, let him hear what the Spirit says to the churches. To him who overcomes, I will grant to eat of the tree of life, which is in the Paradise of God' " (Revelation 2:1-7).

What did Jesus tell the church at Ephesus to do in order to regain their first love?

5 Don't you love the relevancy of Scripture? Maybe you thought you were the first one to ever agonize over a diminishing fervor for the Lord and for things which hold eternal value. And yet this letter to the church at Ephesus certainly dispels that notion.

Sometimes you may feel that you would be more zealous if you only had had the privilege of walking and talking with Jesus or with those who had been with Him. But think of Judas who had every opportunity that the other disciples had. Yet, he sold Jesus for 30 pieces of silver. Seeing Jesus, touching Jesus, hearing Him in the flesh is no guarantee that you'll abide faithfully. The Christian life is a matter of faith! Gut-level faith clings to the Word of God apart from the circumstances or experiences of life.

Listen to what Peter later wrote in his first epistle: "In this you greatly rejoice, even though now for a little while, if necessary, you have been distressed by various trials, that the proof of your faith, being more precious than gold which is perishable, even though tested by fire, may be found to result in praise and glory and honor at the revelation of Jesus Christ; and though you have not seen Him, you love Him, and though you do not see Him now, but believe in Him, you greatly rejoice with joy inexpressible and full of glory" (1 Peter 1:6-8).

Though you have not seen Him . . . you love Him. Think about it.

6 No matter what the proximity to the time of our Lord's sojourn on earth, the Christian life has always been a

choice of believing what the Father, Son, and Spirit said—or of not believing it. Faith is never based on seeing or touching, but depends on taking God at His Word. "Faith is the assurance of things hoped for, the conviction of things not seen. For by it the men of old gained approval. By faith *we understand* that the worlds were prepared by the word of God, so that what is seen was not made out of things which are visible. . . . And without faith it is impossible to please Him, for he who comes to God must believe that He is, and that He is a rewarder of those who seek Him. . . . So faith comes from hearing, and hearing by the word of Christ" (Hebrews 11:1-3,6, emphasis added; Romans 10:17).

We receive salvation because we believe what we hear concerning Christ. However, to hear and to believe is not the end of it. It is the beginning of faith, of a new life, of a new love that is to have preeminence over all other loves. Remember Jesus' call to those who would follow Him? "If anyone comes to Me, and does not hate his own father and mother and wife and children and brothers and sisters, yes, and even his own life, he cannot be My disciple" (Luke 14:26).

Before we were saved, we did not recognize or respect Jesus as God. And true salvation could not come until we were willing to believe in our hearts that God raised Jesus from the dead and to confess Him as Lord (Romans 10:9,10). Until then, it was evident that we did not love Him because we did not keep His commandments. Rather, we walked our own way, did our own thing, and lived as if we were God.

When, Beloved, did you first love God?

7 There's no covering up with God. He knows the motives of our hearts. Although the church at Ephesus was doing all the "right things" externally, God knew that there was a problem with their hearts. Their Christianity was so orthodox that they could spot those who were false apostles. Also, they hated the deeds of the Nicolaitans

because they were not based in Scripture. No prophet could come to them and say, as one had to Jehoshaphat the king of Judah, "Should you help the wicked and love those who hate the LORD and so bring wrath on yourself from the LORD?" (2 Chronicles 19:2).

Doctrinally they were sound. Also, they were involved in good deeds. They toiled for the kingdom of God and persevered. Like their Lord, they did not grow weary in doing good, but endured for His name's sake.

However, with all of this, they had a very serious problem. It was a problem of motivation, of desire, of leaving their "first love." It was a matter of "dead" orthodoxy, of labor without love. How serious was the problem? What does the Lord think of this brand of Christian service? Read Revelation 2:1-7 again and write out your answer.

And what is the cure? We find the answer in Revelation, and also in John 21. The cure is threefold: *First,* remember from where you have fallen. *Second,* repent. *Third,* do the deeds you did at first.

How? We will begin to study that tomorrow as we return to John 21.

8 Peter had returned to fishing. But he was not fishing for men as he was bidden to do when Jesus called him to leave his nets and to follow Him. Ever the leader even in his failures, Peter had decided to return to something that he knew he could succeed at—fishing for fish. Isn't that what we so often do? We try to serve the Lord, fail, give up, and return to our comfort zone.

We hate to fail. I hate to fail. No one in their deepest heart welcomes failure. And yet, if we quit, we will never know success in what we have tried to do. *Perseverance* is a key word in the Christian life—enduring until we accomplish what God has called us to do. If I had quit every time I failed, Precept Ministries would not exist. We would never have reached distant foreign shores with an effective way to study God's Word which will work in any culture.

As I write this, I think of those serving with Precept Ministries in the United States and in other lands. All of them have been tried or tested in one way or another. If they had returned to the security zone of what they did best, instead of floundering in the new waters of faith's obedience, they never would have made it to shore and walked on new frontiers for the Word of God.

O Beloved, don't go back when you fail! Get up! Try again! God is a God of hope, of new beginnings. He does not want us to stagnate in our faith or in our service for Him.

Lamentations was included in the canon of the Old Testament so we could see that failing doesn't mean it's all over. Lamentations was written after the fall of Jerusalem. This fall was the result of failure to obey God and to walk in His statutes. God in His righteousness chastened His children. Read this passage carefully. When you finish, in your notebook jot down a sentence or two that explains what these verses can mean to someone who has failed.

"This I recall to my mind, therefore I have hope. The LORD'S lovingkindnesses indeed never cease, for His compassions never fail. They are new every morning; great is Thy faithfulness. 'The LORD is my portion,' says my soul, 'therefore I have hope in Him.' The LORD is good to those who wait for Him, to the person who seeks Him. It is good that he waits silently for the salvation of the LORD. It is good for a man that he should bear the yoke in his youth. Let him sit alone and be silent since He has laid it on him. Let him put his mouth in the dust, perhaps there is hope. Let him give his cheek to the smiter; let him be filled with reproach. For the Lord will not reject forever, for if He causes grief, then He will have compassion according to His abundant lovingkindness" (Lamentations 3:21-32).

9 It's bad enough to walk away from what you felt God wanted you to do, but it's even worse to return to what you thought you could do and find out that even there you're a failure. It seems a no-win situation. You feel like you're good for nothing.

Remember the words of the hymn: "O Love that wilt not let me go, I rest my weary soul in Thee"? Love would not let Peter go. He went after him—all the way to the Sea of Tiberias.

The disciples had fished all night and caught absolutely nothing, even though they were sweeping the sea with their nets.

Jesus was on the shore, watching the entire fishing expedition and busily preparing to bring Peter back to his place of commitment. Read John 21:5-14 for Peter's response to the Lord's call.

I wonder if Peter's mind ran back to the time when he had been doing the same thing—fishing without catching a thing until Jesus told him where to let down his nets? I don't know. But I do know that Peter couldn't wait to get to shore. The One he had denied was there waiting for him.

He's a God who is always there, my friend. There's no running from Love.

10 When you've denied your Lord, when you've failed Him, when you've blown it, when you've left your first love, you need to remember from where you've fallen.

I believe Jesus was orchestrating the scene for Peter that morning to enable him to return. He was reminding Peter of the place and the time of his commitment to Him.

Now, in your Bible, look up Luke 5:1-11 and see what similarities could have triggered these memories.

Take a minute or two and jot down in your notebook any similarities you see in this situation and John 21.

11 The morning Jesus called Peter to leave all and come after Him followed a night of failure. They had fished all night and had not caught a single fish. After Jesus had taught the multitude, He took the professional fisherman fishing! Jesus told Peter to pull out into the deep water and let down his nets. It seemed a useless request. There were no fish to be found!

I wonder what Peter's tone of voice was when he said, "Master, we worked hard all night [They had done some serious fishing!] and caught nothing, but at Your bidding I will let down the nets" (Luke 5:5).

Obviously, Peter was humoring the Lord; after all, he had just called Him "Master," and so he had to lower the nets. Although he was deferring to Jesus' command, Peter never expected to pull up a net so full that he thought it would surely break.

Have you ever felt that the Lord was telling you to do something that you were pretty sure could never be pulled off? After all, you had already tried something similar, and it hadn't worked. And yet, you knew you had to do what the Lord was saying to do. I have. Sometimes the Lord simply laid it on my heart to speak to someone about Him. It took all the courage I could muster up. I hemmed and hawed and prayed and then did it. Much to my surprise, God worked.

This is the way it was with Peter. When the net came up filled to overflowing with fish, he fell down at Jesus' feet and said, "Depart from me, for I am a sinful man, O Lord!" (Luke 5:8). Peter began to understand that the root of all sin is unbelief. Near the end of Jesus' public ministry, He confirmed this truth as He told the disciples how the Holy Spirit would convict the world of "sin, because they do not believe in Me" (John 16:9).

At that moment Peter not only was smitten with his sin of unbelief but also realized his own impotence. Read

1 Corinthians 1:26-31. Now he was ready to hear the call of Jesus on his life to follow Him and to become a fisher of men. Over 22 years ago I heard Stuart Briscoe say, "God doesn't need your ability. All He needs is your availability." What can you and I add to omnipotence, to total sufficiency? What do we have to offer the great I AM? Nothing. All we can do is say, "I love You, Father," and be available to do His will.

Peter had boasted that although all the others might forsake Jesus, he would not. But because Peter trusted in his own natural abilities to keep himself faithful, he did forsake Jesus. Whenever we trust in ourselves, we'll always reap what the flesh produces. And all the flesh can produce is man's best instead of God's best. What are you trusting in, my friend?

12 Peter had failed. He knew it. Jesus knew it. Although Peter may have been drowning in the despair of failure, the God of all hope would not leave him there. And so our sovereign Lord orchestrated a scene that would remind Peter of the time and the place where he made his commitment to leave all and to follow Him.

The repetition of no fish and then enough fish to break the net had to jog Peter's memory back to the time when he came face-to-face with his sinfulness, his pride of unbelief, his own independence, and God's total sovereignty and sufficiency. When Peter denied Jesus, he had fallen from the place of commitment. And it is that commitment Peter needed to remember when he "left his first love," a love which once had put Jesus in the place of preeminence over all, even above his own safety and security.

It is easy to become so comfortable with your Christianity, so accustomed to it, that the fire of love diminishes to smoldering ashes. The fire is still there, but it is not burning brightly, and I know that you don't want that! You don't want spiritual things to become commonplace, routine. Yes, you have undoubtedly matured in your relationship with your beloved Lord, but maturity deepens love. It does not dim love. It isn't that there has to be that flush of first love like you experienced when you first "fell in love." But there should be that steadfast love of total commitment which keeps the loved one's happiness, needs, concerns, and preferences in the place of preeminence. For me, this is a love that I must be vigilant about.

Oh, my beloved reader, where does your love of Jesus fit into all that I have shared and said? Have you felt the gentle nudgings of the Spirit reminding you of your first love, wooing you back to Him?

What was it like when you were first saved? Take a few minutes to remember. And as you do, record your remembrances in your notebook. Tomorrow I want to share with you some practical things you can do to stir up the embers of your first love.

13 Why do we leave . . . slip away from our first love. How does it happen? The church at Ephesus was doing all the right things. They were persevering, doing good deeds, and checking out false apostles and evil men. Yet they left their first love.

It's obvious from God's word to this church that this had not happened suddenly, as if they had said, "Well, today we won't love Jesus Christ as much as we did before, but we'll keep doing the right things." Leaving a first love is more subtle than that. Why would they continue to do what they were supposed to do and be commended for it if they had willfully decided not to let Jesus be their first love?

Leaving a first love happens gradually. It's kind of like plowing a piece of land to get it ready for planting and then not sowing it right away. You let it lie fallow because you are too busy with other things. Then when you come back to do something with it, you find it lumpy and full of weeds instead of crops. To leave your first love means that you neglect to cultivate that love; when you come back, you find the ground overgrown with weeds.

In the days of Jeremiah, God said that the children of Judah had committed two evils: "They have forsaken Me, the fountain of living waters, to hew for themselves cisterns, broken cisterns, that can hold no water" (Jeremiah 2:13).

First, they had forsaken God. Second, they had turned to other things which could never satisfy their thirst. The words you have just read are in a passage in which God is reminding them of how they once loved Him so much that they would follow Him anywhere. "I remember concerning you the devotion of your youth, the love of your betrothals, your following after Me in the wilderness, through a land not sown. Israel was holy to the LORD, the first of His harvest" (Jeremiah 2:2,3).

They had left their first love, and so God called them to return to Him. He told them, "Break up your fallow ground, and do not sow among thorns. Circumcise yourselves to the LORD and remove the foreskins of your heart" (Jeremiah 4:3,4).

O Beloved, if you have allowed your heart to become unsown and unattended regarding your first love, then it is time to break up the fallow ground.

14 When ground lies fallow, all sorts of weeds and thorns can grow in it. These choke out the good seed. If you are going to return to your first love, you need to get rid of the weeds that grew because your love lay uncultivated. This is where repentance comes in.

> The word that expresses the biblical concept of repentance is *šûb*. This verb is found over a thousand times in the Old Testament, with a wide range of meanings. However, in the 164 uses of this word in a covenant context, it

> indicates turning from evil to God, from evil ways to God's ways, or from God to idols. *Šûb* is that commitment to a faith and way of life that involves turning from a previous way, and this is to "repent."
>
> There is no doubt that at times a change of commitment is preceded by agonizing conviction of sin. But repentance itself, as it is illustrated in the Old Testament, is essentially the "about-face" of a new commitment.
>
> In the New Testament, *metanoeō* and *metanoia* are used in the same way as *šûb* in the Old Testament—to emphasize a change of mind and attitude. To repent is to make a decision that changes the total direction of one's life.[1]

God told the Ephesians to remember from where they had fallen, to repent, and then to do the deeds that they had done at first. He didn't simply say to remember from where they had fallen and to do the deeds they had done at the first. Why? Because there was fallow ground that needed to be broken up and weeded before they could do what they had done at first.

Christianity is not the kind of religion that can lie dormant. Something happens when the Christian is not going forward for Jesus Christ. A lot of weeds and thorns can suddenly crop up because nothing else has been sown in the heart. They have to be dealt with before any new sowing can be done.

Thus we hear God say to Jeremiah: "See, I have appointed you this day over the nations and over the kingdoms, to pluck up and to break down, to destroy and to overthrow, to build and to plant" (Jeremiah 1:10). Before planting could be done, the land had to be cleared. It is the same in our hearts if they have lain fallow in regard to our love of the Lord. Recognizing the weeds and then pulling them out in order to plant is what I liken to repentance.

Take time now, Beloved, to wait before the Lord in prayer and to ask Him to walk through the garden of your heart, exposing the weeds you need to get rid of. In your notebook write down anything that comes to your mind as you wait on Him in prayer.

15 "Break up your fallow ground, for it is time to seek the LORD until He comes to rain righteousness on you" (Hosea 10:12).

For the next several days, I want us to work on breaking up the fallow ground and getting rid of the thorns by asking ourselves a number of questions. If any of these apply to you and you are willing to make a new commitment to the Lord, then put a big "R" next to it and turn it into a prayer of repentance and commitment to love God with all your heart, mind, soul, strength, and body.

____1. Have you given more attention to other loves in your life than to your love of Jesus Christ? What are they? How do they usurp Jesus' rightful place? What do you need to do? Write out your prayer in your notebook.

____2. Have you neglected to have adequate communication with your Lord through His Word and in prayer? Have you taken time to listen to others, to talk with others, but not taken the time with the Lover of your soul who gave His all for you and who said, "Pray without ceasing. . . . Commit your way to the LORD, trust also in Him, and He will do it. . . . Devote yourselves to prayer, keeping alert in it with an attitude of thanksgiving" (1 Thessalonians 5:17; Psalm 37:5; Colossians 4:2). Have you esteemed His Word more precious than your necessary food, or have you tried to live by bread alone rather than by every word which proceeds out of the mouth of God (Deuteronomy 8:3)? Have you been too lazy or undisciplined to study to show yourself approved unto God, a workman that handles accurately the Word of truth (2 Timothy 2:15)? Has your heart become fallow while you watched TV, read newspapers, magazines, or novels? Have you had time to work on your B.S., B.A.,

M.A., Ph.D., but neglected an A.U.G. (approved unto God) degree by studying His Word?

Do you need to repent of anything? What will be your commitment? Write it out in your notebook to the Lord.

____3. Have you so loved the Lord that you have allowed His Spirit to fill you, so that you consistently seek to walk in His Spirit, thereby manifesting His fruit: love, joy, peace, patience, kindness, goodness, faithfulness, gentleness, and self-control (Galatians 5:22,23)? Or have you allowed this plot of ground to go fallow? What is His command? "Be filled [continuously] with the Spirit" (Ephesians 5:18). Do you need to repent? And what will you say to God? Write it out in your notebook.

16 ____4. The sin that separated that serpent of old from God and caused him to be named Satan, or adversary, was pride. He became caught up in his own beauty and splendor until he wanted to exalt himself above the throne of God and be like the Most High. The Bible says that pride goes before a fall. God must resist the proud, but He will draw near to those who are humble (James 4:6-8). O Beloved, have you allowed love and admiration of your Lord to lie fallow while you have worked in the field of self . . . becoming occupied with your self-worth and self-image? Have you become enthralled with self-accomplishments and self-development?

How subtle the serpent's allurements to self! Has he lured you away from the cross where self is crucified and lives no longer? God is a jealous God. He will not share His rightful place with anyone else, not even you. Do you need to repent and give up your love affair with self? Do you need to return to the Lover of your soul? Write out your commitment in your notebook.

____5. God says, "Do not love the world, nor the things in the world. If anyone loves the world, the love of the Father is not in him. For all that is in the world, the lust of the flesh and the lust of the eyes and the boastful pride of life, is not from the Father, but is from the world. And the world is passing away, and also its lusts; but the one who does the will of God abides forever" (1 John 2:15-17). "You adulteresses, do you not know that friendship with the world is hostility toward God? Therefore whoever wishes to be a friend of the world makes himself an enemy of God" (James 4:4).

Have you left unattended the love of God and turned your attention to sowing in the fields of the world? Have you walked by the sight of your eyes, desiring what the world has to offer and not even seeking the Lord to see if this is in His will for you? Have you bought the world's morals, standards, or values about what is important? Have you become caught up in the world's goals or ways of accomplishing things? Have you tried to bring these into your Christianity without first seeking the mind and heart of your God?

What must you tell the Lover of your soul, who left you in the world but prayed to the Father that you would not be part of it? Write it in your notebook.

____6. Have you manifested your love to the Lord by loving those who are His? Or have you neglected Him by neglecting them? "Truly I say to you, to the extent that you did it to one of these brothers of Mine, even the least of them, you did it to Me" (Matthew 25:40). "Whoever loves the Father loves the child born of Him" (1 John 5:1). Have you loved your neighbor as yourself? All the Law and commandments hang on this and the love of God (Matthew 22:37-40; Romans 13:8-10). Love does no wrong to a neighbor. Have you allowed the love of God to become fallow ground because you have not loved your neighbor? What must you say to the Lover of mankind if you are going to repent and return to your first love?

Well, Beloved, there is much more that I could ask, but then this would go on for pages and pages. Ask God to show you any other fallow ground which needs to be broken up, and then do what He says.

17 When Jesus addressed the church at Ephesus and warned them about leaving their first love, He told them to *remember* from where they had fallen and to *repent* and *do* the deeds that they had done at first. Today is going to be spent in beginning to do the deeds you did at first.

I realize that you may not have left your first love, and that is wonderful. However, may I still encourage you to do what I am suggesting. I think you will find it a blessing.

Let's begin by reading what you wrote down on Day 12. This will help you see or remember from where you have fallen, if you have. After you remember from where you have fallen and repent, then you need to do again the deeds you did before. Let me give you some examples.

Remember the song that was in your heart? Put on some worship tapes and sing to Him of your love and adoration. Ephesians 5:18-20 reads: "Be filled with the Spirit, speaking to one another in psalms and hymns and spiritual songs, *singing and making melody with your heart to the Lord;* always giving thanks for all things in the name of our Lord Jesus Christ to God, even the Father."

Remember how hungry you were for the Word of God? Get on your knees and ask Him to show you anything which is diminishing your hunger or desire for the Word. Then act accordingly. As you get into the Word, don't casually read it thinking: "I know all of this." Remember that the Word of God is His love letter to you. Don't read it just for the sake of saying you have read the Word or for information. Read it to know the Lover of your soul in a deeper and more intimate way.

What Do You Do When You've Blown It?

If you feel that you have greatly failed God, don't read it as if God is on your case. Don't read it in unbelief saying, "God couldn't love me as much, as unconditionally as that." Don't call Him a liar in your heart. Remember that His mercies are new every morning, that His compassions fail not. Bask in all that God is . . . in His unconditional, everlasting love. Let God say to you what He wants to say.

Remember how eager you were to talk of Him and the wonder of His love, mercy, grace . . . of the way your relationship with Him transformed your life? Make it a point to talk of Him again. Share Him with others. Joy in His love.

Remember how eager you were to know what He wanted and expected of you? Remember how quick you were to obey? Ask Him again for that same sensitivity. Tell Him you want your eyes to be like "doves' eyes"—which focus on only one thing at a time. Tell Him you want Him to be your primary focus. Say, "I am my beloved's," and I know that "his desire is for me" (Song of Solomon 7:10). Lean on your Beloved.

> Put me like a seal over your heart,
> Like a seal on your arm.
> For love is as strong as death,
> Jealousy is as severe as Sheol;
> Its flashes are flashes of fire,
> The very flame of the LORD.
> Many waters cannot quench love,
> Nor will rivers overflow it;
> If a man were to give all the riches
> of his house for love,
> It would be utterly despised.
> —*Song of Solomon 8:6,7*

Ask God to show you other things that you did when you first loved Him . . . and then do them.

18 Although Jesus manifested Himself to all the disciples at the Sea of Tiberias, John focuses only on what happened between the Lord and Peter. I believe the Lord, through Peter, is giving us a valuable lesson in what we are to do when we have failed Him. In John 21:1-7, we find the Lord telling the disciples, as He once before told Peter, where to cast their nets. This would have triggered Peter's memory of that day when Jesus told Peter to leave his nets and follow Him.

I wonder what emotions were stirred by the charcoal fire? I wonder if Peter's mind went back to that charcoal fire the slaves and officers had made near the door to the courtyard of Caiaphas' house? Would he have been reluctant to put out his hands and warm them over the fire Jesus had made because of the fire where he had warmed himself not too many days before? It was there where people said to him, "You are not also one of His disciples, are you?" (John 18:25). And he vehemently denied it. It was at that fire where Peter had not one but three opportunities to confess Jesus, but denied Him every time. Jesus had seen Peter standing at the fire. Surely Peter could not forget that, for as the cock crowed, "the Lord turned and looked at Peter. And Peter remembered the word of the Lord, how He had told him, 'Before a cock crows today, you will deny Me three times.' And he went out and wept bitterly" (Luke 22:61,62).

If I had been Peter, I would have found it hard to stand with the disciples around Jesus' charcoal fire, without tears coming to my eyes as I remembered how I had said that I would go to death with Him and then how I had denied Him when it meant saving my neck.

Are there certain objects or events, my friend, which trigger memories that bring tears? You can't help the tears; they just come. There are things I remember about my father that bring tears to my eyes. I love him, and I often wish we could talk together. When I share my testimony and tell of my first husband's suicide, tears still come to my eyes. I know that I am forgiven by God for failing as Tom's helpmeet, and I have fully accepted that forgiveness, yet the tears come. I remember the words the Lord gave me the day I received the news of Tom's death . . . and I cling to them in faith's hope.

This could be what Jesus wanted to do for Peter—to counteract the bitter memories and defeat by giving him the remembrance of another fire and new words spoken there . . . words to assure Peter that he would press on to become what Jesus called him to be.

Oh, precious child of God, there is hope—not because of who you are or what you have done, but because God is God.

19 So when they had finished breakfast, Jesus said to Simon Peter, "Simon, son of John, do you love Me more than these?" He said to Him, "Yes, Lord; You know that I love You." He said to him, "Tend My lambs." He said to him again a second time, "Simon, son of John, do you love Me?" He said to Him, "Yes, Lord; You know that I love You." He said to him, "Shepherd My sheep." He said to him the third time, "Simon, son of John, do you love Me?" Peter was grieved because He said to him the third time, "Do you love Me?" And he said to Him, "'Lord, You know all things; You know that I love You." Jesus said to him, "Tend My sheep" (John 21:15-17).

On the night of Jesus' arrest, Peter was questioned three times regarding his relationship to Jesus Christ. Now, three times, Jesus questions Peter regarding his love for Him. Jesus is restoring one of His disciples who has wept bitter tears of disappointment because he failed Jesus in His time of greatest need. How can Peter possibly tell Jesus that he loves Him when he denied Him as he did? He can't.

When Jesus asks Peter the first time, "Simon, son of John, do you love Me more than these?" the word that Jesus uses for love is *agapē. Agapē* is the highest form of love that exists. This is the love that is born of God. It is an unconditional love that does not consider self but desires another's highest good. It's a sacrificial love.

How could Peter say that he loved Jesus with this kind of love when he put his own security and safety first? Oh, at one time Peter thought he loved Him with that kind of love. In the Upper Room when "Simon Peter said to Him, 'Lord, where are You going?' Jesus answered, 'Where I go, you cannot follow Me now; but you shall follow later.' Peter said to Him, 'Lord, why can I not follow You right now? I will lay down my life for You' " (John 13:36,37). Laying down one's life for another is *agapē* love fleshed out. Even Jesus said, "Greater love [*agapē*] has no one than this, that one lay down his life for his friends" (John 15:13).

Thus, when Jesus asked Peter if he loved (*agapē*) Him, Peter could only respond, "Yes, Lord; You know that I love You." The word which Peter used was not *agapē,* but *phileō;* and there's quite a difference between the two. To love someone with a *phileō* love is to feel a strong affection. It's a love born of mutual interest, a brotherly type of love that finds something attractive, appealing, or pleasant in another. It's a conditional love because it has its source in man rather than in God. After what Peter had done, he could not tell his Lord that he loved Him unconditionally.

If Jesus were to ask you if you love Him unconditionally, what would be your response? Do you love God for what He can do for you? What if God were not "good" to you . . . what if He permitted you to hurt, to suffer? Would you love Him then?

20 If Jesus were to sit beside you in the pew at church and ask you if you love Him more than the majority of those in your church love Him, how would you answer Him, my friend?

If He were suddenly to appear in front of the television set while you were engrossed in your routine of watching favorite programs, be it soap operas or Monday night football, and ask you if you love Him more than these, how would you answer Him?

If He were to sit around the family dinner table with you and ask you if you love Him more than you love all those dear family members sitting there with you, how would you answer Him?

If suddenly He were to sit beside you in the golf cart as you drove to the fourth tee and ask you if you love Him more than golf (or whatever your sport might be), how would you answer Him?

If He were to suddenly appear where you work, and ask you if you love Him more than your profession, more than your career, how would you answer Him?

If suddenly you looked over and there Jesus was on the exercise bike next to you, or you swung up your hands in an aerobic session and you caught Him in the corner of your eye standing next to you, and He asked you if you love Him more than your own body, beautiful and healthy, how would you answer Him?

If you were caught up in the delight and pressures of being active for God in a ministry that you love and He asked you, "Do you love Me more than this ministry?" how would you answer Him?

What if you were sitting in your chair, reading the daily stock reports to see how you were doing, and Jesus walked up, gently pulled down the newspaper, peered over it, and asked: "Do you love Me more than money?" how would you answer Him?

What if you were walking through the construction of your new dream home, looking over the plans, and suddenly

Jesus looked over your shoulder and asked: "Do you love Me more than these?" how would you answer Him?

If you were standing in a place of power, giving others your plans and assigning their duties, mapping out what you wanted to see accomplished, and the Lord were to gently tap you on the elbow and ask if you loved Him more than this, how would you answer Him?

If you were to tiptoe into the nursery to gaze again at the precious treasure snuggled in the crib and suddenly the Lord were to stand at your side and whisper, "Do you love Me more than this one?" how would you answer Him?

If you were standing in your yard delighting over its beauty, or at your easel beaming over your painting, or over your latest accomplishment in your handicraft, or over the skill you had achieved in your hobby, and the Lord looked at it and then at you and asked, "Do you love Me more than the accomplishments of your delights?" how would you answer Him?

The first time that Jesus asked Peter if he loved Him, Jesus didn't stop there. The sentence went on . . . *"more than these?"* More than what? More than the fish that he had just caught? More than the other disciples?

Does it really matter? Isn't it just: "Do you love Me more than anything else?"

21

Jesus did not merely ask Peter if he loved Him with an *agapē* love. There was more to the question than that. He asked, "Do you love Me *more than these*?" What love has preeminence in your life?

Jesus will not take second place. For us to put anyone, anything, any accomplishment, any goal, any service in His place is idolatry. It is to leave our first love.

When Jesus asked Peter if he loved Him more than "these," we don't know whether Jesus was referring to Peter's vocation of fishing or to loving Him more than the other disciples loved Him. Peter, who had been called to be a fisher of men, had apparently returned to his fishing—something he knew he could succeed at, something he was comfortable with.

The only pain connected with fishing was not catching fish. That was a lot easier than being involved in ministry with his Lord.

Can you relate, my friend? I can. Leadership, at least as Jack and I have found it, is never without problems, challenges, and pressures. Because of what God has called me to do, there is never a time when I do not have some sort of deadline.

Sometimes when the flak comes because of ministry, I think, "Who needs this?" I am certainly not in ministry for my own ego or to fulfill any personal need. I am here out of a sense of obedience. Like Paul who said, "I was appointed a preacher and an apostle and a teacher" (2 Timothy 1:11), I know that God has called me and gifted me for the ministry He has raised up.

When I am tempted even for a moment to walk away and go back to live an ordinary life as a wife, mother, grandmother, homemaker, and throw myself into a multitude of things I would really enjoy for myself—tennis, golf, reading good books, playing bridge, vacationing, taking up real estate or decorating, puttering around in my yard and the garden I have so wanted, having the girls over for lunch, walking through the malls casually, watching historical movies, going for long walks, entertaining our friends in our home, or getting more involved in our church—I remember that God's call on my life rarely permits much of the above. Yet, these things do not bring the pain, pressures, challenges, or discipline that ministry brings.

O Beloved, is there anything keeping you from the ministry to which the Lord has called you? Do you love "that" more than you love Him?

"If anyone wishes to come after Me, let him deny himself, and take up his cross, and follow Me. For whoever wishes to save his life shall lose it; but whoever loses his life for My sake and the gospel's shall save it" (Mark 8:34,35).

22 How prone we are to leave the cross out of our Christianity. Yet it is really to be the identifying mark of a follower of Jesus Christ. It's the cross that causes all other loves to become subservient to our love for our Lord Jesus Christ.

Come with me, Beloved, and once again bathe yourself in the cleansing water of His Word. Listen . . . examine your heart . . . take a good look at your own life. Read Luke 14:25-35.

There's a cost to following Jesus Christ. If anyone tells you differently, don't listen. Jesus is saying that before we decide we want to follow Him, we need to count the cost. Because He is God, He must have preeminence over all other loves, all other affections, all other relationships, over our own lives and personal goals and ambitions. Those who follow Him are taking up an instrument of death . . . death to self. Theirs will be a new path . . . His.

If you are not willing to do this, you are like salt that has lost its savor—you're worthless. Have you been caught up in this insidious teaching of self-worth? If you want to find worth, Beloved, look to the cross, and follow the One who died on that cross because He loves you.

23 It's not easy to love Jesus more than your father, mother, mate, or children, especially if they do not understand the call of God on your life. Nor is it easy in a period of Christendom when so much of the emphasis is on the home—a happy family and happy children. The pain of your heart can be wrenching, the condemnation of the flesh great, the accusatory whispers of the enemy torturing. But the question does not go away: Do you love Me more than these?

Jesus warned us that our commitment would not go unchallenged or untested in the world . . . and even among those dearest to us. Listen to His words: "Do not think that I came to bring peace on the earth; I did not come to bring peace, but a sword. For I came to SET A MAN AGAINST HIS FATHER, AND A DAUGHTER AGAINST HER MOTHER, AND A DAUGHTER-IN-LAW AGAINST HER MOTHER-IN-LAW; and A MAN'S ENEMIES WILL BE THE MEMBERS OF HIS HOUSEHOLD. He who loves father or mother more than Me is not worthy of Me; and he who loves son or daughter more than Me is not worthy of Me. And he who does not take his cross and follow after Me is not worthy of Me. He who has found his life shall lose it, and he who has lost his life for My sake shall find it" (Matthew 10:34-39).

When Jesus asks you if you love Him more than "these" and you answer, "Yes, Lord," and you follow Him to do His will, remember, precious one, it will not always be easy. Obedience to Jesus Christ does not always guarantee peace in the family or harmony and understanding with your loved ones. You need to remember this, so you don't become discouraged and "go fishing." Peter asked Jesus, " 'Behold, we have left everything and followed You.' Jesus said, 'Truly I say to you, there is no one who has left house or brothers or sisters or mother or father or children or farms, for My sake and for the gospel's sake, but that he shall receive a hundred times as much now in the present age, houses and brothers and sisters and mothers and children and farms, along with persecutions; and in the age to come, eternal life' " (Mark 10:28-30).

Don't forget His words: *"along with persecutions."* You may seem like a loser to the world, to society, to your family; but Jesus goes on to say, "But many who are first, will be last; and the last, first" (Mark 10:31).

24

Leader that he was, Peter influenced the others. When he said, "I am going fishing," they said to him, "We will also come with you" (John 21:3).

You know, don't you, that when we "go fishing," we always take others with us. Although we may not be recognized as a leader, without a shadow of a doubt there is someone watching. And they'll follow us, thinking that if we can "go fishing" when Jesus has called us to follow Him, then they can "go fishing" also.

We are so quick to measure ourselves by others rather than by God's particular call. I've been guilty of that, sometimes disparaging my own walk with the Lord because I don't do things that others whom I admire do. For instance, I am not an early riser. Five in the morning is hard for me, especially when I don't get to bed until very late. Thus, sometimes I start to measure my spirituality by the hour some of my friends get up and meet with the Lord.

I would really enjoy being wide awake, thinking sharply, singing, and rejoicing before the little birds begin their morning songs! But try as I may, 5:00 A.M. is not my time. So I can't measure myself by others.

Neither can I excuse myself by others. Many of us can be quick to lessen our standards, our level of commitment, our obedience, when we see others not living totally committed lives. We think: "They are Christians and they do so and so, so why can't I?" O Beloved, others can never be our standard of measurement.

Neither can we be our own standard of measurement. As Paul wrote: "For we are not bold to class or compare ourselves with some of those who commend themselves; but when they measure themselves by themselves, and compare themselves with themselves, they are without understanding" (2 Corinthians 10:12).

We have only one standard of measurement: "Are we becoming what God wants us to be? Are we becoming more like Jesus? Are we doing what He commanded us to do?" The ministry that our Lord has for each of us is not the same. Even as our spiritual gifts differ, so do our ministries. "Now there are varieties of gifts, but the same Spirit. And there are varieties of ministries, and the same Lord. And there are varieties of effects, but the same God who works all things in all persons. But to each one is given the manifestation of the Spirit for the common good" (1 Corinthians 12:4-7).

O Beloved, by what standard have you been measuring yourself?

25 Was Jesus asking Peter if he loved Him more than the other disciples loved Him? Peter was the one who was always out of the boat first, the one whose zeal for Jesus was very visible. Could he have thought that because he was so eager and open about his love of the Lord, that he really did love Jesus more than the others?

This is a very real possibility. And maybe this is why, after failing so miserably, blowing it so openly as he swore with a curse that he did not know Jesus, Peter could only say that he had a *phileō* type of love for Jesus.

Oh, the other disciples had deserted Jesus also. Peter had thought that *they* might, but he never dreamed that *he* would! That night after they left the Upper Room and went out to the Mount of Olives, "Jesus said to them, 'You will all fall away because of Me this night, for it is written, "I WILL STRIKE DOWN THE SHEPHERD, AND THE SHEEP OF THE FLOCK SHALL BE SCATTERED." But after I have been raised, I will go before you to Galilee.' But Peter answered and said to Him, 'Even though all may fall away because of You, I will never fall away.' Jesus said to him, 'Truly I say to you that this very night, before a cock crows, you shall deny Me three times.' Peter said to Him, 'Even if I have to die with You, I will not deny You.' All the disciples said the same thing too" (Matthew 26:31-35).

After Peter made his statement, all the disciples said they were willing to die too. But Peter had been so bold as to go even further: "Even though all may fall away because of You, I will never fall away."

Maybe Peter did think he loved Jesus more than the other disciples did. But if not, he knew that he at least meant what he said: He was willing to die for Jesus rather than deny Him.

The problem was that Peter hadn't reckoned with the truth which Jesus Himself would share in the Garden of Gethsemane, when He tried to awaken them from their sleep with the admonition to watch and pray because the spirit was willing but the flesh was weak (Matthew 26:41).

Until the Gospel of John, we do not know who the brave and brash one was who drew the sword when the soldiers came to arrest Jesus in Gethsemane. Read what dear John tells us—and in doing so showing us the sincerity of Peter's heart—in John 18:1-11.

Maybe Jesus was asking Peter if he really thought he loved Him more than the other disciples. We don't know. But there is a lesson in all of this for us: Don't compare your love of Jesus with others' love for Him. That really doesn't matter. It only matters how much you love Him when it's costly to follow Him.

26 I wonder what it would have been like to stand eye to eye with Jesus and have Him ask you, "Do you love [*agapē*] Me?" when you have just told Him that you have a strong affection, a *phileō* love for Him?

Peter could not answer any other way than he did the first time: "Yes, Lord; You know that I love [*phileō*] You."

But twice was not enough. The One who loved Peter with an unconditional love "said to him the third time, 'Simon, son of John, do you love [*phileō*] Me?' Peter was grieved because He said to him the third time, 'Do you love [*phileō*] Me?' " (John 21:17).

This time Jesus' question changed dramatically. He was not asking Peter if he possessed an unconditional love for Him, but if he had a strong brotherly affection for Him. Was

Jesus even questioning Peter's strong affection for Him? It seemed that way . . . and it hurt.

All Peter could do was throw himself on the omniscience of his Lord: "You know all things; You know that I love You" (John 21:17). Peter was confident that although he could not say he bore an unconditional love for his Lord, he did have a strong affection for Him. After all, when he had recognized that it was Jesus on the shore, he had thrown himself into the sea, eager to see Him even though he had denied Him. Peter's heart for the Lord had not changed. He was still eager to be in His presence. The only thing that had changed was Peter's understanding of the weakness of his own flesh. Peter knew, as never before, that his spirit was willing but his flesh was weak. Maybe that's why he couldn't say that his love was of the *agapē* kind . . . just the *phileō* kind.

But why was the Lord questioning even this kind of love? I believe He was giving Peter not only three opportunities to say, "I love you, Lord," after denying Him three times, but was also showing Peter that someday Peter would be able to prove that he loved Jesus with an *agapē* type of love.

How? That, Beloved, is what we will look at in a few days. But what about you and what you have just read? God knows your heart. He knows the depth of your love. Simply be careful that you are not deceived, by thinking that you love Him more than you do and then becoming stagnant in your relationship to Him. Guard your first love jealously.

27

Love obeys. Love cares about what concerns the one it loves. Thus, with each questioning of Peter's love and with each affirmation came a command—a way to show his love.

The first command was for Peter to tend the Lord's lambs. The verb for "to tend" is a present imperative. The present tense indicates that this was something Peter was to do continuously, as a habit of life. The imperative mood made it a command. This was the Lord's calling for Peter.

The word for *tend* in the Greek is *boskō*, and it means "to nourish, to provide food." The Great Shepherd of the sheep had the sheep forever on His heart.

The second time Jesus asked Peter if he loved Him, Jesus gave Peter a different command: "Shepherd My sheep." The word for *shepherd* is *poimainō* and means "to guide, guard, and lead." Sheep need more than food; they also need watching over. Not just the lambs, but the full-grown sheep. Thus, when Jesus asked Peter a third time if he loved Him, He gave him a third command: "Tend My sheep." Once again the word is *boskō*, meaning "to nourish, to provide food" not just for the lambs but for the sheep also.

Left to themselves, even mature sheep have a hard time surviving. If they aren't tended, they'll eat foliage right down to its roots, destroying the plants and leaving the ground barren. They'll also eat plants that are not good for them, including poisonous weeds. Unless led by a shepherd, they will live in a rut, furrowing the ground by continually walking the same path over and over. They'll walk in their own excrement and contact all sorts of diseases. Unaware of danger, they are open prey not only to the elements but to the wolves who would love to devour them. They're the dumbest of animals, and without a shepherd they have a very difficult time surviving.

Soon Jesus would ascend to the Father, and what would become of His sheep if there were no one to carry on His work? How important it was that Peter be restored and confident that the Lord was not finished with him. Yes, Peter had blown it, but so had the other disciples. The Shepherd was smitten, and the sheep scattered just as Jesus had said. But now He was back among them making sure they knew that there was a crucial work to be done. They could not go fishing. They had eternal things to do!

28 What kind of an earthly shepherd watches over you, Beloved? The answer to this is very important, for it may determine how you are doing spiritually. I am sure that you have heard the statement that everything rises and falls on leadership. How true this is, especially in the leadership of your church.

This is why Paul took such care in writing to Timothy and Titus. He knew that someday his long-awaited dream of being with His beloved Lord would be reality. However, Paul also knew that when the time came, it was crucial that those who followed him be godly men who understood the high calling of spiritual leadership.

Paul knew that wolves were waiting to devour the flock. Satan would not let God's work go unhindered, and one of his main means of devouring sheep was to lead them into false doctrine. In Acts 20:17-38, look at Paul's last words to the elders at Ephesus as he prepared to go to Jerusalem where the Spirit of God had revealed to him that chains and imprisonment awaited. As you read through this passage, why don't you list in your notebook those characteristics and attitudes of Paul which show you by example what your earthly shepherds should be like?

29 "Feed My lambs. Feed My sheep." This was the concern of the Good Shepherd who had just laid down His life for the sheep. It was one thing for them to have eternal life, but it was another thing for them to have abundant life. Without proper nourishing they would not know abundant life. This is why so many children of God are weak and sickly, going about malnourished, riddled with disease, and unable to fend for themselves. They have not been properly nourished.

We need shepherds who are going to feed us the one food we cannot live without—the Word of God. I believe that this is where pastors will find their greatest accountability. God is not interested in the size of their congregations or the opulence of their edifices, but in the spiritual condition of their sheep. God is not impressed with their press releases, their stature within their denominations, their involvement in community or political affairs, but in the condition of their sheep . . . which are really His sheep. If pastors are not giving the time and effort needed to prepare the food and to feed their sheep properly, nothing else will matter. Now some think that shepherding is all they need: "Forget doctrine. Just teach them to love one another." But you cannot shepherd sheep properly without feeding them properly.

As you read Acts 20 yesterday, you saw that Paul did not shrink from declaring to them the *whole* purpose (counsel) of God. He knew that after his departure, savage wolves would come in among them, speaking perverse things in order to draw away disciples after them. His only means of guarding against their being led astray was to make sure that they knew the whole counsel of the Word of God. In his last epistle, Paul admonished Timothy: "Preach the word; be ready in season and out of season; reprove, rebuke, exhort, with great patience and instruction. For the time will come when they will not endure sound doctrine; but wanting to have their ears tickled, they will accumulate for themselves teachers in accordance to their own desires; and will turn away their ears from the truth, and will turn aside to myths" (2 Timothy 4:2-4).

People love to hear new and novel teachings, and they will follow them if they do not have a biblical plumb line by which they can evaluate everything they hear. This is why Precept Ministries is devoted not only to teaching people God's Word but also to showing them how to study it for themselves, inductively, so they won't be led astray. We want to establish God's people in His Word as that which produces reverence for Him, "admonishing every man and teaching every man with all wisdom, that we may present every man complete in Christ" (Colossians 1:28).

If you would like to be able to study God's Word for yourself, it would be our privilege to put you in touch with a Precept class near you, or to tell you how to get one started in your church or neighborhood. Also, we have many excellent and varied studies in our *Lord* series or the International Inductive Study Series. These are wonderful for Sunday school classes, because they involve students in the study of God's Word and usually require less than an hour of study each week. We also offer *The International Inductive Study Bible,* which gives a tangible way to delve into every book of the Bible.

Whatever you do, Beloved, please do not neglect this one thing. Your well-being hinges on it.

30 I wonder if Jesus had Ezekiel 34 in mind as He spoke to Peter. Study Ezekiel 34:1-16.

God's sheep had suffered greatly for the lack of godly shepherds. This was why Ezekiel was writing from captivity in Babylon, after the second siege of Jerusalem. Judah's shepherds had cared more for their own well- being than for the state of their flocks. Their sheep had merely been raised for the personal benefit of shepherds who cared not for the lost, the broken, the scattered. They did not care that their sheep had become prey for the beasts of the fields.

When God could bear it no longer, He said, "I Myself will search for My sheep and seek them out" (34:11).

And there He was, now standing with Peter beside the Sea of Tiberias, commissioning him to care for His sheep until He returned: "As the Father has sent Me, I also send you" (John 20:21). As the Great Shepherd of the sheep commissioned Peter, I believe He commissions you and me to care for His sheep, even if it is only one. Whomever He gives us, we are responsible to care for them. It matters not that you have blown it, as long as you have repented and love your Lord. Take care of your sheep. Maybe you can help them to keep from blowing it. Or, if they do fail, you can tell them there is hope . . . because there is Jesus.

Tell Jesus that you love Him . . . feed and shepherd His sheep.

31 When you have blown it, there is only one thing God wants to know: "Do you love Me?" If you still love Him, then God is not through with you. Oh, He may not use you in the same capacity or place as before, but He will still use you. For you see, Beloved, if you really love Him, then you will repent and renew your commitment to Him, willing to follow Him no matter where the will of God leads you and no matter what the cost. God knows that you are not perfect. He knows what you are made of.

"For their heart was not steadfast toward Him, nor were they faithful in His covenant. But He, being compassionate, forgave their iniquity, and did not destroy them; and often He restrained His anger, and did not arouse all His wrath. Thus He remembered that they were but flesh, a wind that passes and does not return. . . . For as high as the heavens are above the earth, so great is His lovingkindness toward those who fear Him. As far as the east is from the west, so far has He removed our transgressions from us. Just as a father has compassion on his children, so the LORD has compassion on those who fear Him. For He Himself knows our frame; He is mindful that we are but dust" (Psalm 78:37-39; 103:11-14).

Because of this, our Lord is not quick to cast us aside. In fact, I think this is the point John is making by including this incident. In the first 20 chapters of his Gospel, John demonstrates the love of God in giving His Son so that we, lost sinners, might have hope. Now in this last chapter, he calls for our response to that love.

Each of the other Gospels closes with a commission from the Lord. John is no different, except that chapter 21 is God's commission through Peter to those who feel unworthy of ever being commissioned and used of God because of the weakness and frailty of their flesh.

"Do you love Me?" That is all that Jesus wants to know. And how will we prove that we do love Him? We will heed His command: "Follow Me." *Follow* is in the present tense; we are to follow as a habit of life. Although Peter couldn't say it then, he was going to have the opportunity to say to his Lord, "Lord Jesus, I *agapē* You." How? Jesus tells him (John 21:18,19).

Remember our Lord's words in John 15:13: "Greater love has no one than this, that one lay down his life for his friends." Peter was going to have the opportunity to shout, "I *agapē* you, my Lord," as he hung from a cross. And if tradition is correct, he would say it while being crucified upside down.

And from the portals of heaven, Jesus would see what He already knew. The one who in a moment of weakness had denied Him would deny Him no more. He would be willing to follow Him even to death—even to death on a cross!

Peter was willing, but he couldn't resist asking about John. "Peter, turning around, saw the disciple whom Jesus loved following them. . . . Peter therefore seeing him said to Jesus, 'Lord, and what about this man?' " (John 21:20,21)

Was Peter again wanting to compare himself with the others? I don't know. All I know is what Jesus said to him, and what He says to you and to me: "If I want him to remain until I come, what is that to you?" (John 21:22). In other words, "I am your Lord. You are to follow Me, and it does not matter what anyone else does or doesn't do. You are to follow Me." We do not answer for anyone else. We cannot compare ourselves with anyone else. Nor can we excuse ourselves by anyone else. To our own Master we stand or fall.

And He is able to hold us up. We are simply to love Him . . . and in loving Him to follow Him.

O Beloved, don't sit there in your boat saying: "It's no use. I've blown it," and go fishing. Get out of the boat. Run to the arms of your compassionate Lord. Remember your own impotence. Remember His knowledge of your frailties. Remember His call. It has not altered. Repent. Remember who it is who has called you . . . the Redeemer who will cause all things to work together for your good and His glory. Just tell Him that you love Him and you'll care for His sheep. Heed His call to follow Him until your life ends . . . or until He comes.

"There are also many other things which Jesus did, which if they were written in detail, I suppose that even the world itself would not contain the books which were written" (John 21:25). But you need not know any more than what you have between the covers of the Holy Bible. Learn this, and you have enough for every good work of life.

Rehearse your commitment to love your God with all your heart, soul, mind, strength, and body. And renew again those "marriage" vows. If you are His, you will be part of His bride on that glorious day of the marriage of the Lamb. As you rehearse your commitment, talk to God aloud. I believe that it really does help when we literally "confess with our mouth." Or if you prefer, write it out in your notebook or diary, and date it so you can go back and read it again and again.

Notes

January

1. From time to time we will look at the definition of a word in the Greek. Since the New Testament was originally written in Koine Greek, sometimes it is helpful to go back to the Greek to see the original meaning of the word. There are many study tools to help you if you would like to do this type of digging. One excellent book that will help you understand how to do more in-depth study is *How to Study Your Bible* (Harvest House).
2. The word translated "again" is *anothen*, and can also be translated "from above."
3. Present tense in the Greek, thereby denoting habitual or continuous action. This does not preclude singular acts of sin.

February

1. Merrill Tenney, *John: The Gospel of Belief* (Grand Rapids, MI: William B. Eerdmans Publishing Company, 1948), 40-41.
2. Ibid., 103.
3. Marvin R. Vincent, D.D., *Vincent's Word Studies of the New Testament*, vol. 2 (McLean, VA: MacDonald Publishing Company), 158.

March

1. Lawrence O. Richards, *An Expository Dictionary of Bible Words* (Grand Rapids, MI: Zondervan Publishing House, 1985), 313.
2. Ibid., 416.
3. From time to time we will look at the definition of a word in the Hebrew. Since the Old Testament was originally written in Hebrew, sometimes it is helpful to go back to the Hebrew to see the original meaning of the word. There are many study tools to help you if you would like to do this type of digging. One book that will help you understand how to do in-depth study is *How to Study Your Bible* (Harvest House).
4. Herbert Lockyer, D.D., *All the Divine Names and Titles in the Bible* (Grand Rapids, MI: Zondervan Publishing House, 1975), 17.
5. See the New American Standard Bible footnote on this verse.
6. John MacArthur, Jr., *The Legacy of Jesus* (Chicago: Moody Press, 1986), 57.
7. Ibid.
8. W.E. Vine, Merrill F. Unger, William White, Jr., *Vine's Complete Expository Dictionary of Old and New Testament Words* (Nashville: Thomas Nelson Publishers, 1985), 251.
9. Lawrence O. Richards, *An Expository Dictionary of Bible Words* (Grand Rapids, MI: Zondervan Publishing House, 1985), 119.

April

1. Archibald Thomas Robertson, *Word Pictures in the New Testament*, vol. 5 (Nashville: Broadman Press, 1932, renewal 1960), 202.

May

1. Bruce Olson, *Bruchko* (Orlando, FL: Creation House, 1993), 72-73.
2. John MacArthur, Jr., *The Legacy of Jesus* (Chicago: Moody Press, 1986), 20-21.
3. Sammy Tippit, *Fire in Your Heart* (Chicago: Moody Press, 1987), 64-65.
4. Andrew Murray, *Humility, the Beauty of Holiness* (Fort Washington, PA: reprint, Christian Literature Crusade, n.d.), 42.
5. Sammy Tippit, *Fire in Your Heart* (Chicago: Moody Press, 1987), 66-67.
6. Ibid.

June

1. Sammy Tippit, *Fire in Your Heart* (Chicago: Moody Press, 1987), 10.
2. Lawrence O. Richards, *An Expository Dictionary of Bible Words* (Grand Rapids, MI: Zondervan Publishing House, 1985), 113.
3. W.E. Vine, Merrill F. Unger, William White, Jr., *Vine's Complete Expository Dictionary of Old and New Testament Words* (Nashville: Thomas Nelson Publishers, 1985), 222.
4. Richards, 119.

5. Bruce Olson, *Bruchko* (Orlando, FL: Creation House, 1993), 132-33.
6. Ibid., 133-34.
7. Ibid., 134-35.
8. Ibid., 135-36.
9. Ibid., 136-37.
10. Ibid., 137-38.
11. Ibid., 138-39.
12. Sammy Tippit, *Fire in Your Heart* (Chicago: Moody Press, 1987), 96-97.
13. John MacArthur, Jr., *The Legacy of Jesus* (Chicago: Moody Press, 1986), 63-64.
14. Spiros Zodhiates, Th.D., *The Complete Word Study New Testament* (Chattanooga, TN: AMG Publishers, 1991), 944.
15. Ibid., 884.
16. Charles Ludwig, *Mother of an Army* (Minneapolis: Bethany House Publishers, 1987), 143-45.

July

1. J. Oswald Sanders, *Enjoying Intimacy with God* (Chicago: Moody Press, 1980), 70-71.
2. W.E. Vine, Merrill F. Unger, William White, Jr., *Vine's Complete Expository Dictionary of Old and New Testament Words* (Nashville: Thomas Nelson Publishers, 1985), 683.
3. "From Heaven You Came," from Thankyou Music, 1984; in *The Servant King: Sons of Fellowship*, a Kingsway Publication.
4. Helen Roseveare, *Living Holiness* (Minneapolis: Bethany House Publishers, 1986), 84-86.
5. Ibid., 86-87.
6. Ibid., 124-25.
7. Ibid., 125-28.
8. Ibid., 129-30.
9. Ibid., 130-32.

August

1. Hans Kristian and Dave Hunt, *Secret Invasion* (Eugene, OR: Harvest House Publishers, 1987), 77-78.
2. Ibid., 78-79.
3. Ibid., 79.
4. Ibid., 79-81.
5. Ibid., 81-83.
6. Ibid., 83-84.
7. Ibid., 84-86.
8. Ibid., 86-87.

September

1. D.A. Carson, *The Farewell Discourse and Final Prayer of Jesus* (Grand Rapids, MI: Baker Book House, 1980), 175.
2. Ibid., 185.
3. Frank E. Gaebelein, ed., *The Expositor's Bible Commentary* (Grand Rapids, MI: Zondervan Publishing House, 1981), 167.

October

1. I would urge you to get our videotape on the crucifixion from our Lord, Heal My Hurts series. I think it would help if you could hear my explanation of our Lord's sufferings.
2. William D. Edwards, M.D., Wesley J. Gabel, M.Div., Floyd E. Hosmer, M.S., AMI, "On the Physical Death of Jesus," *Journal of American Medical Association*, March 21, 1986, vol. 255, no. 11: 1455-63.

November

1. John Pollock, *George Whitefield and the Great Awakening* (Herts, England: Lion Publishing Company, 1986), 269-70.

December

1. Lawrence O. Richards, *Expository Dictionary of Bible Words* (Grand Rapids, MI: Zondervan Publishing House, 1985), 522.